MASTERS OF CHAOS

MASTERS OF
CHAOS

The Secret History of the Special Forces

LINDA ROBINSON

PublicAffairs

New York

To those who serve

CONTENTS

Cast of Characters

SFC Andy Brittenham
MAJ Jonathan Burns
COL Charles Cleveland
LTC Christopher Conner
SFC Richard Davis
MAJ Warren Foster
MAJ Simon Gardner
MAJ James Gavrilis
CW2 Tony Goble
LTC Christopher Haas
COL Kevin Higgins (Ret.)
MSG Alan Johnson
SGM James Kilcoyne
MG Geoffrey Lambert
MAJ Andy Lohman
MAJ Tony Martin
COL David McCracken (Ret.)
CW3 James Newman
SFC Matthew Nittler
CW2 John Pace
MSG Steve Rainey
SFC Mark Reynolds
SFC Roderick Robinson
MSG Tom Rosenbarger
MAJ Jeffrey Smith
MSG Michael T. Swift
LTC Kenneth Tovo
LTC Robert Waltemeyer
CW3 Randall Wurst
Other anonymous soldiers (who asked to be identified only
by ODA number and duty position)

INTRODUCTION

T HIS IS THE STORY of Special Forces soldiers and the missions
they have carried out over the last fifteen years. Through them the
larger story is told—of the renaissance of a unique military unit that
was nearly disbanded after the Vietnam War but which now is in high
demand. The war in Afghanistan brought the deeds of the Special
Forces onto the front pages of the newspapers, which captured in vivid
photographs and stories the men on horseback who used lasers to direct
precision bombs at Taliban targets. Far less has been written about their
subsequent roles in Operation Iraqi Freedom, where even more Special
Forces soldiers were deployed than in Vietnam. Although the image of
the Special Forces soldier now may be more familiar to the average
American, the reality of who he is and what he does remains largely
shrouded in mystery and misconceptions.

This book seeks to convey the reality of the Army Special Forces by
recounting missions carried out during six conflicts and other previously

unrevealed assignments, such as their roles in uncovering the first Al Qaeda operation on U.S. soil and the millennium plot to bomb the Los Angeles airport. The stories are told through the senior noncommissioned officers and field grade officers who led their units. By the onset of Operation Iraqi Freedom, these soldiers each had spent some two decades in the field, sharpening their instincts and amassing the experience that is an integral part of what makes them "special." The type of individuals selected, the varied skills they are taught, and their largely self-sufficient twelve-man teams constitute a tool designed to deal with variations of insurgents, terrorists, guerrillas, and small-scale wars—the murky unconventional threats that are prevalent in today's world.

What sets the Special Forces apart is that these soldiers are trained to live and work with the fighters of other countries, as their forebears did with the partisans in occupied Europe, as the Vietnam generation did with the hill tribes in their A-camps, and as has been done by them more recently in Asia, Latin America, the Middle East, and Africa. They have also lived and worked among civilian populations in places like Haiti and the Balkans, using cultural knowledge and linguistic skills to help build a lasting peace. Special Forces soldiers may fight alongside their allies, as they did with the Afghans and the Kurds, but very often the preferred means of assistance is advising, training, and assisting a country in solving its own problems. Because the Special Forces are the only unit in the military required to learn foreign languages and gain regional expertise, members also have an unmatched ability to discover and understand what is happening in remote and obscure hotspots.

There remains widespread confusion about the basic terminology. The U.S. Army Special Forces (Airborne) (known by their distinctive headgear, the green beret) are the subject of this book. The Special Forces are the largest component of the elite units known as special operations forces (SOF), which also include Navy SEALs, Army Rangers, the secret Delta Force (formally called Special Forces Operational Detachment-Delta), Air Force Special Operations pilots and combat controllers, the Army's 160th Special Operations Aviation Regiment, and Civil Affairs and Psychological Operations units. Popular usage frequently refers to all of these units as special forces, but the proper term is special operations forces. In this book Special Forces is synonymous with U.S. Army Special Forces.

The Special Forces number fewer than 9,500 men and are organized into five active-duty groups that are each assigned to a given region: 1st Group (Asia), 3rd Group (Africa), 5th Group (Southwest and Central Asia), 7th Group (Latin America), and 10th Group (Europe); and two National Guard groups, the 19th and 20th. These groups learn the languages and cultures of their respective regions but also may be sent to other regions as needed. The groups report to the U.S. Army Special Forces Command, which reports to the U.S. Army Special Operations Command for all army SOF which, in turn, reports to the U.S. Special Operations Command for all the services' SOF. This latter command may either assign units to the geographic combatant command of a particular theater or direct their activities itself.

The U.S. Army Special Forces were founded in 1952. It was envisioned that they would carry on the role played in World War II by the Office of Strategic Services (OSS), whose paramilitary units parachuted behind enemy lines to organize and fight with local resistance groups in occupied Europe and Asia. The OSS was dismantled soon after the war and one of its veterans, Colonel Aaron Bank, was concerned that this left the United States without any capacity for waging this kind of "unconventional war." Bank considered such ability as integral a component of modern warfare as infantry, armor, and artillery. Because Bank successfully lobbied for the formation of the Special Forces and headed its first group, he therefore is considered the "father" of the Special Forces. Colonel Bank passed away in the spring of 2004 at the age of 101.

Bank considered it essential to have a standing force prepared to conduct unconventional war primarily because the various skills, especially knowledge of the language and the country where the units would be deployed, took time to acquire, and the special forces must be deployed early in a conflict for maximum effectiveness. From the early days until the present, the idea of unconventional warfare nonetheless is a concept that has made many Americans and the U.S. military uncomfortable. For soldiers such as Bank, however, it was a simple necessity to have this capacity to fight as so many adversaries fought. In his memoir, *From OSS to Green Berets*, he observed other countries using guerrilla-style warfare in the postwar years.

> Unconventional warfare [UW] was definitely a weapon that con-
> tinued to be employed. It was a tool of dissidents regardless of
> their cause. Its profound influence would continue unabated
> through the years to alter the military, political, and ideological
> posture of numerous small nations and create friction between the
> major powers. This friction in many instances is due to Soviets
> using this medium to spread their doctrines and gain control. But
> beyond that, on reflection, UW had proved itself during WWII as a
> companion of conventional warfare—a necessary supplement
> whenever the employment of conventional forces would not be
> feasible or would be embarrassing. I wondered when it would
> obtain full recognition by the military leaders of the great powers.*

Even after the founding of the Special Forces, the conventional military leadership would remain ambivalent about their use, but John F.
Kennedy believed that a special warfare capability was essential for the
United States. He saw the challenge posed by wars of subversion and
covert aggression and realized that it called for

> an improvement and enlargement of our own development of
> techniques and tactics, communications and logistics to meet this
> threat. The mission of our Armed Forces—and especially the
> Army today—is to master these skills and techniques and to be
> able to help those who have the will to help themselves.

Kennedy realized, furthermore, that the required tactics were not
purely military but "a full spectrum of military, paramilitary and civil

---

* *From OSS to Green Berets*, Col. Aaron Bank, USA (Ret.), NY: Pocket Books, 1987, p. 153.

action" to counter the adversaries' own broad arsenal of "economic and political warfare, propaganda and naked military aggression."*

President Kennedy wrote those words on April 11, 1962, but they accurately describe the warfare not only of the Communist era but also of the present time, when other groups use the same full spectrum of measures. Special Forces were employed in the Vietnam War in the classic unconventional warfare mold. They set up A-camps in the Vietnamese highlands and recruited and led hill tribes in local defense, and also conducted covert raids into North Vietnam and the sanctuaries of Laos and Cambodia. After Vietnam about two-thirds of the Special Forces, which had been rapidly expanded and, in some instances, poorly trained and led, were deactivated. The low point of its existence mirrored the general crisis of confidence within the army after the worst defeat in its history. Some concluded that the United States was incapable of counterinsurgency, while others argued that the unconventional operations were hamstrung by a military that did not embrace or understand their methods. Still others believed that covert and clandestine warfare was simply un-American. How to best confront those who use unconventional methods was a debate destined to continue.

In the 1980s, after Soviet-backed communist movements gained ground in the Third World, the Special Forces experienced another period of expansion and revival. The strategies of containment and detente left Eastern Europe as Soviet satellites, so U.S. President Ronald Reagan sought to roll back communist gains by waging unconventional warfare in Southwest Asia, Africa, and Latin America. Special Forces played a role in those conflicts as well as in hostage-rescue efforts in the Middle East. The Special Forces' signal achievement of this period was in El Salvador, where over the course of a decade Special Forces advisers professionalized the Salvadoran armed forces and helped them conclude

* Facsimile of letter to the United States Army from John F. Kennedy on White House letterhead, dated April 11, 1962. Copy provided by Maj. Gen. Sid Shachnow (Ret.), former commander of the Special Forces. See his memoir, *Hope and Honor* (NY: Forge, Tom Doherty Associates, 2004).

a long insurgency at the cost of only nineteen American lives. Success did not come until 1992, but it proved to be a lasting peace.

The 1990s brought a new host of challenges. With the breakup of the Soviet Union and the eruption of conflicts all over the globe, the newly resurgent Special Forces had no shortage of work. They participated in Operation Just Cause in Panama from 1989 to 1990, in their first combat missions since Vietnam, and fought in Desert Storm in Kuwait in 1991. The post-Vietnam generation of Special Forces soldiers represented in this book began their careers in the late 1980s or early 1990s and have been deployed frequently ever since.

The premise of this book is that these soldiers' extensive and diverse experiences can inform the larger debate over the need for and proper use of the country's special operations forces. The most common type of threat today comes not from standing armies of enemy states but from groups that wage war from the shadows, wearing no uniforms and claiming no state but able to wreak havoc by using the basic precepts of guerrilla warfare. These actors understand that the only way to confront a larger, stronger enemy is to use unconventional tactics that turn their weaknesses into strengths. They understand that the battlefield is a human one and that creating psychological impact is the key to victory. The sheer number of deaths on September 11, 2001, did not materially weaken the United States, but the perception was that America's security, and its sense of invulnerability, had been shattered.

Terrorism may be best understood as a subset of the broader category of unconventional warfare. It is a particular type of unconventional tactic characterized by attacks on civilians. The official U.S. definition of terrorism is "premeditated, politically motivated violence perpetrated against noncombatant targets by subnational groups or clandestine agents."* The motivation of the group is not the defining characteristic; terrorism has been used throughout history by smaller groups seeking

---

* See the "National Strategy for Combating Terrorism," February 2003 at www.whitehouse.gov, and the State Department's annual report, "Patterns of Global Terrorism," at www.state.gov.

to defeat more powerful ones. Their cause may be sectarian, nationalist, or ideological, but they hold in common the use of this form of irregular warfare.

The first World Trade Center attack, the 1998 bombings of U.S. embassies in Africa, the October 2000 attack on the USS *Cole*, the Madrid train bombing of 2004: the continuing trail indicates that the tactics will be studied, copied, and used in the future. The American public can rightly ask what kind of unconventional capability of its own the United States requires to counter such attacks. Are there ways of addressing these threats before they result in attacks? Can the measures be discriminate to avoid causing the same sort of civilian casualties that are the objective of the attackers?

The elusive nature of the latter-day adversaries and the difficulty of detecting attacks in the offing have led some to conclude, since September 11, that even greater use must be made of special operations forces to disrupt and prevent such attacks. The special operations forces, with their unique capabilities, "are the primary Department of Defense tool for fighting the war on terror," according to Thomas O'Connell, the department's senior civilian official responsible for overseeing SOF. "While special operations forces were originally conceived to be used as forces for supporting or leveraging larger conventional forces or for undertaking discrete and limited strategic missions," he said, "the new reality has confirmed them as a prominent, frontline, essential element in the defense of our nation."* Congress not only agreed with the assessment but authorized funding increases in successive years that were even larger than the administration requested.

There is continuing discussion about how best to use these forces. Some uses of Special Forces—fighting in overt wars, assisting standing governments, and gathering information for military operations—are relatively uncontroversial. Raising guerrilla forces to combat a threat or

---

* Speech by Assistant Secretary of Defense for Special Operations/Low-Intensity Conflict Thomas W. O'Connell at the NDIA SO/LIC Symposium, Washington, DC, February 6, 2004.

staging a covert operation to capture or even kill terrorist leaders are far more sensitive propositions, but are not necessarily contrary to U.S. law or interests. The U.S. laws known as Title 10 and Title 50 provide the legal framework for the United States to undertake overt, clandestine, or covert operations of all these types. There is a standing presidential executive order against assassination, although lethal force has been authorized against Osama bin Laden and the senior Al Qaeda leadership. Some suspected terrorists and accused war criminals have also been seized by stealth. While the American tradition is to frown on secrecy and favor accountability, the nation's legislature nevertheless has seen the need for forces that can conduct operations in the interest of national security in a low-visibility, clandestine, or covert manner.

As with so many moral questions, the answers often are found not in absolutes but in a balancing of good and evil. The current debate about how much secrecy and how much latitude are required echoes the earlier debates of the 1960s and 1980s. That is not surprising, as there is an inherent tension between the secrecy required for special operations to be effective and the openness and accountability of a democratic society. Only through debate, moreover, can the competing demands be reconciled. Some argue that the current rules are insufficient, while others argue that they are too restrictive or require adjusting to the needs of the era. It is important to note, however, that established procedures and strictures do exist. According to one camp, they are so zealously interpreted as to result in a relative few tepid, last-ditch operations that, under such conditions, are almost certain to come up short.*

Special Forces operations are carried out under the provisions of Title 10, which requires that they be authorized by a "national command authority," which is the U.S. president, or the secretary of defense with the approval of the president. Operations may be overt or clandestine. Clandestine means that the planning and execution of the operation remains secret but its U.S. authorship is not denied if discovered or upon

---

* See the work of Richard H. Shultz, Jr., including the epilogue in his book *The Secret War Against Hanoi* (NY: HarperCollins, 1999).

execution. Title 50 governs covert operations, in which the U.S. author-ship is denied or designed to be denied. These are generally carried out by the Central Intelligence Agency and the law requires oversight by congress. Under both laws there is extensive legal review and discussion in the interagency National Security Council.

There is also an inherent tension between the special operations community and the Central Intelligence Agency due to their partially overlapping jurisdictions. The CIA has generally conducted covert action, intelligence gathering, and assistance to resistance or guerrilla groups during peacetime, while the military conducts its operations dur-ing or just before war. Some of the distinctions are less clear-cut in prac-tice than in theory, however, for example: Is the United States currently at peace or at war? Due to the small size of the CIA's paramilitary unit, Special Forces soldiers may be assigned to work under its direction just as they may be assigned to Special Mission Units to carry out classified missions under the direction of the Joint Special Operations Command. Each Special Forces Group also designates one unit that can be deployed in emergencies by the regional combatant commander.

The basic question is whether the United States has a vision of war-fare that encompasses the full spectrum of socio-economic, political, and military activities. That does not mean that the country should or will resort to indiscriminate mass attacks, widespread assassination, or any other rogue state policies that would undercut the basic values and ultimate aims that the country seeks to promote. Lethal force against certain targets, however, and more aggressive policies toward terrorist safe havens such as that of Taliban Afghanistan may be warranted. But, as many of the missions recounted in the chapters that follow suggest, many of the best solutions are those which employ minimum force.

A full-spectrum policy relies even more upon understanding and effectively countering the antagonists' methods through creative means. It requires recognizing that war occurs on every plane of a society. Com-munist insurgencies learned long ago, for example, to co-opt teachers' unions and health workers because they reach so much of the popula-tion and provide ideal recruiting tools for fighters and underground auxiliaries. The co-opting of students in Islamic religious schools (known as madrassas) simply is the same method used by another group seeking to impose its vision of political-religious rule. The specific methods, entities, and guidelines adopted require careful deliberation and a response—likely by a combination of spies, warriors, and diplomats—that is tailored to each particular circumstance.

Rather than propose a formula or blanket prescription for the use of force in this era, this book presents the actual experiences of the Special Forces in the field as a means for exploring what methods work best in various circumstances. Development of the individual soldier's capabilities and his accumulation of experience are what make him able to assess and react effectively to the situation with little, if any, guidance from a distant superior officer. For that reason, individual Special Forces soldiers' careers are examined to reveal how those experiences are processed into lessons and applied in other venues. The pyrotechnics of the profession are impressive, increasingly so as more sophisticated weaponry and surveillance and informational tools are placed in the hands of the operator. It is readily apparent, however, when one observes the day-to-day activities of the Special Forces soldier and his twelve-man team that human perception, judgment, and finesse comprise the sensitively calibrated instrument that navigates the knife-edge of success and defeat. Rarely is a piece of hardware the determining factor.

Like all people, Special Forces soldiers are certainly fallible. The accumulated experience, training, and discipline generally serve as checks on individual failings. The twelve-man team is largely self-policing because the senior members usually detect and address breakdowns in a soldier's performance. There is a high level of intolerance among the twelve for performance that falls short of the standards, and there are also the checks of peer competition with other teams and oversight by the hierarchy above.

I was granted access to the U.S. Special Forces by the Department of the Army and the U.S. Army Special Operations Command to conduct extensive interviews with the soldiers. During Operation Iraqi Freedom

I was one of a few journalists granted permission to cover special operations forces as an "embedded" reporter. During the war, I traveled with them from Umm Qasr to Basra, from there to Nasiriya, Kut, and the Iranian border. I subsequently returned to Iraq, visited Afghanistan, and made multiple trips to Fort Bragg, North Carolina, MacDill Air Base, Florida, and Fort Campbell, Kentucky, to conduct interviews. My research on the Special Forces began during a Nieman fellowship at Harvard in 2001, when a Special Forces officer provided extensive reading suggestions and Widener Library provided the books. This Special Forces officer persuaded his commander that the Special Forces should begin to tell their story. With the requisite command approval, I then visited Fort Bragg for briefings, more reading assignments, and field exercises in September 2001 and 2002. In addition to the Middle East trips, I spent time in Colombia and saw the Special Forces at work there. A cover story on that experience helped pave the way for the embedding assignment and the subsequent book project.

The primary source material for the book was extensive and repeat interviews with the soldiers, supplemented by the author's reporting, official documents, and archival material. The extant literature in books, magazines, and newspapers was also consulted for background information. Some restrictions were placed on the interviews and the scope of the book. The command requested that some tactics, techniques, and procedures not be described in detail to avoid rendering them useless for future operations. The command also requested that three dates and the names of three countries not be used. A few soldiers who participated in classified operations during their careers were not permitted to discuss them. These compromises were made in the interest of telling a much fuller story about Special Forces missions than has yet been told for this period between the Vietnam era and the present. The intent of the book is not to provide an exhaustive account of every mission in every conflict but rather the fullest account possible of the careers of Special Forces soldiers as they deployed on successive assignments. The goal is to give the reader a realistic appreciation of the career of a Special Forces soldier during the past twenty years.

The soldiers who are profiled are introduced in Chapter One. The experience of the Q course, in which soldiers attempt to earn the green beret, is recounted in Chapter Two along with the historical background of the Special Forces. Chapters three, four, and five recount the soldiers' missions in El Salvador, Panama, Kuwait, and Somalia from 1989 to 1992. Chapters six and seven recount their exploits in the mid-1990s, including counter-terror and counter-drug operations and the Balkans experience, as well as the all-important continual cycle of training that every soldier undergoes.

Chapters eight through fourteen recount missions in Afghanistan and Iraq. Because Afghanistan has been written about elsewhere, this account is more episodic than comprehensive and focuses primarily on one team's key missions involving "high-value targets," Tora Bora and Operation Anaconda. The opposite approach was taken for Operation Iraqi Freedom, where the extensive role of Special Forces has received very little attention. Large numbers of Special Forces played pivotal roles in the cities of the south, in the western desert, and in the north. Special Forces were the only U.S. ground force in the west and the north for most of the major combat phase of the war. This represented an enormous economy of force for the conventional forces, which were able to concentrate their efforts on the march north into Baghdad.

Chapter Fifteen profiles the individual soldiers upon their return from war, some of them for the last time, and Chapter Sixteen examines the future of the Special Forces. Their experiences over the previous fifteen years suggest some lessons about how they should be employed and what they require to do those jobs. The way in which the United States views the threats it faces today and the degree to which it comes up with thoughtful, sophisticated, and effective responses will determine the future of the Special Forces—and of everyone else.

MASTERS OF CHAOS

CHAPTER 1

LEAVING HOME

Humans are more important than hardware.

—FIRST SOF TRUTH

THE WIND HOWLED up through the limestone caves of western Tennessee to meet the icy blasts coursing through the Cumberland Valley and the Land between the Lakes. Fort Campbell was not a pleasant place in the wintertime. At least Fort Carson in Colorado had mountains right out the back door. Chief Warrant Officer 3 Randall Wurst clapped his hands to warm them, which was impossible because the doors of the vehicle bay stood wide open to the frigid gusts. Raised in the west, Randy would never get used to the dampness of the eastern United States. The rest of the company and battalion officers were in their offices packing up maps and personal equipment. Randy should have been inside with them, but he wanted to see how the rear gun mounts had turned out. He and the sergeants had spent hours tinkering to come up with the best way to rig an M240 machine gun on the back of a Humvee. In Afghanistan they had built a prototype, and an outfit down the road in Nashville was now turning out custom mounts to rig guns on every position of their trucks. The Taliban had called them "the boxes with thorns." The Afghans had learned to fear the "bearded ones" who drove the boxes and fought with such tenacity and ferocity.

One of the privileges of the Special Forces was the freedom to modify the army's standard-issue equipment or buy off-the-shelf products that would help get the job done. They were always seeking to improve their basic kit, whether gloves or guns or sights or vehicles. Randy gave thanks every time he saw a pair of German-made Hanwag boots. Perhaps their best find ever, those boots had carried him through long days of trekking in Afghanistan. Their rough-cut leather uppers had molded instantly to his feet with no painful breaking-in period and, best of all, their rubber soles had stuck like glue to the sheer mountains and scree-strewn crevasses of Tora Bora where the Special Forces had searched for the caves of Al Qaeda and its leader, Osama bin Laden.

Randy climbed into the rear bed of the nearest Humvee and sat down on the bench by the M240 to check out the handiwork. The official army mount had been by the passenger side door, which limited the field of fire. So the team had soldered a new mount and put it on the rear corner. They had stripped the Humvees' rear gates and mounted racks for additional fuel and water cans. The M240 was the critical backup weapon for disengaging from a larger force or a tank. When the big .50-caliber gun in the turret (the one Randy manned) stopped to change ammunition cans, this one kept firing. Randy swung the gun toward him, crouching over it to aim in the same movement, swiveled with it in an arc, then snaked it back. It was much better, but it wasn't perfect—the mount could still stick in the stowed position. On the battlefield, that could make you a dead man. The square can that fed the belt of 7.62-mm rounds into the gun had to be placed at just the right angle or it would not feed properly. They would keep tinkering over in the desert. Humans are more important than hardware, as the special operations saying goes, but the humans need their hardware to fight.

Special Forces teams were heavily armed for their small size: they had either a .50-caliber gun or an Mk 19 grenade launcher in the Humvee turret and an M240 machine gun on the back. They had AT-4 anti-tank weapons strapped to the roof edges, and each man had his M4 rifle, 9-mm pistol, and grenades. At least one team member also had an M203 grenade launcher attached under the barrel of his M4. This was a formidable amount of weaponry for twelve men.

The ritual of preparing for war was a familiar one for Randy, but this time it had a special poignance. This was likely to be the last war he would fight, at least on the frontlines, and he was having a hard time assimilating that fact.

Being a Special Forces soldier was the pinnacle of his life, and it seemed that everything had led him inexorably down this path. The blood of warriors ran in his veins. His grandfather was a Blackfoot, born on a reservation, who had founded an outfitting business in 1921. Randy grew up on a ranch, learning to ride his buckskin pony, Sugarfoot, at the age of three. He became a cowboy, adept at riding and breaking horses, and learned the arts of survival from his family of ranchers, trappers, hunters, and outfitters. His nickname, "Rawhide," would later become his call sign. When he left home, his beloved grandfather gave him his medicine bag containing the talismans of long-ago battles and places sacred to his people.

After some detours Randy joined the military, following his father and brother who had served in wartime. For him it became a career when he earned a coveted place in the Special Forces. Twenty years and five wars later, he knew that he would have to hang up his soldier's spurs soon.

Many of the senior Special Forces soldiers who would play a pivotal role in the war in Iraq had begun their SF careers in Desert Storm or a couple of years earlier in Just Cause in Panama—the first time Special Forces had seen combat since Vietnam, officially anyway. The soldiers now formed a seasoned group whose members had worn their green berets through numerous wars, backwater conflicts, and secret operations. They were not only the backbone and institutional memory of the Special Forces but often were the most experienced of any soldiers on the frontlines.

Randy had lost track of how many countries he'd been deployed to and how many Christmases and birthdays he'd spent away from home, but he did not lose count of the comrades he had lost over those years— their names and faces were etched in his heart. Some of them were remembered in a small grove of trees planted on the east side of their grassy parade ground at Fort Campbell. A plaque listed each man's name and unit.

The earth was still fresh around trees that had been planted for the men who had died in Afghanistan, the largest group of casualties since an entire team crashed in a Black Hawk helicopter during a training exercise in Yuma, Arizona, in 1989. There was a tree for J.D. Davis and those who had died with him. There was one for Nathan Chapman, who had pulled every string to get transferred from Asia to the fight in Afghanistan; Stanley Harriman, a chief warrant officer like himself, who had died trying to save his men; and, in the corner, Bobby Deeks, killed in Somalia in 1993. Randy said a quick prayer for them all as the sun lowered through the leafless branches of the slender trees, and then walked quickly from the bay toward the dun-colored three-story barracks.

He bounded up the cement steps and yanked hard on the barracks' door. Built in 1952, the buildings were as old as the Special Forces. The door vents were rusted through, the cinderblock was crumbling, hinges were rusted, and insulation hung out of the ceilings. The Special Forces' low-rise complex, clustered around the parade ground just off Bastogne Avenue, was the oldest on the entire base. One ground-floor office had a finger-sized crack that went through to the outside. The Special Forces were proud of their make-do philosophy, but they carped just the same about being the unloved stepchild at Fort Campbell, which was wholly and completely dominated by the Screaming Eagles of the 101st Airborne Division. The largest tenant unit of any army base always ruled the roost, and the famous 101st did so with particular zeal. Additionally, its commanders did not like the fact that some of their best and brightest noncommissioned officers tried out for the Special Forces, attracted by the idea of roaming the world in twelve-man teams on secret missions. Special Forces had to become high-altitude parachutists, so soldiers with wings, like those in the 101st, had an advantage.

Cruising down the hallway, Randy saw Master Sergeant Alan Johnson disappear into the company commander's office. Alan was like a brother to him, but these days he also was a reminder of loss. Randy had left the twelve-man team that they together had led through Kosovo and Afghanistan, and Alan knew that Randy was bereft. Randy had served for fourteen years on Operational Detachments Alpha (ODAs), as the twelve-man teams are officially called. That was about as long as anyone had managed to stay in the ground-level units. He had been kicked upstairs to the company staff.

Alan was one of the most popular team sergeants around. He was a force of nature, as audacious and intelligent an operator as ever produced, with an irrepressible sense of humor. A handsome light-skinned African American, he had a thousand-megawatt smile and a deep rumbling laugh. Men loved serving with him. Randy and he had been on the same team, 563, for three years. They greeted their company commander, Jonathan Burns, a major who had just transferred that summer from Fort Bragg. He had the pale skin and red-brown hair of the Irish, a group well represented in Special Forces' ranks, and a subversive wit. He'd stenciled his call sign, Wildman, on the back of his armored Humvee. Alan went off to discuss his mission with the battalion commander, and Randy sat down to review his duties with Burns. Randy feared that he would not even get close to the frontlines now that his job was to oversee intelligence and operations for the whole company, but he vowed not to complain. He suspected Burns was a frustrated gunslinger too—it came with the seniority.

Alan headed to the end of the second building on the southern flank of the complex to see the battalion commander. The unlucky bachelors slept on the third floor of the dilapidated barracks. He was spared that fate. He had a wife, and if all went well, they would have a baby soon. He knocked on the open door and Lt. Col. Conner's aide waved him in. Conner was bent over a canvas duffel spread out on the floor, on top of a small Afghan carpet and a rug embroidered with the Special Forces' crossed-arrow insignia and motto "De Oppresso Liber" (to free the oppressed).

"Have a seat, Al," Conner said. "Let's talk while I get this last stuff stowed."

Alan squeezed his frame onto the small couch. Special Forces soldiers tended to fall into one of two categories: the big and burly or the compact and wiry. The big ones had to have the stamina to make it through the Special Forces' selection process. Willpower, not size, was the common denominator. Alan was a big man, 190 pounds of solid muscle, but his geniality tended to soften his size into a less intimidating package, until he put on his game face.

Lieutenant Colonel Chris Conner was also a big fellow, six feet two and 220 pounds, but his temperament was so placid that his size did not dominate the conversation. Conner had assumed command of the battalion over the summer, though he was no stranger to Fort Campbell. He had spent his early Special Forces career here and had returned from serving in Washington on the Joint Staff, where one of his colleagues called him the finest action officer he'd ever seen. It was a happy homecoming for a low-key, well-liked officer. He knew many of the older sergeants from his previous posting here, and he had known Randy from his first days in the Special Forces tryout. The sergeants tend to stay put in the same battalion, or at least the same group, for the bulk of their careers, which makes them the institutional memory of the organization. This is important for any organization, but it is especially valuable given the mandate of the Special Forces.

Each Special Forces group is organized into three battalions: 1st, 2nd, and 3rd. Each battalion has three companies, called Alpha, Bravo, and Charlie. Each company, in turn, is composed of six teams, the twelve-man Operational Detachments Alpha which are known by number. The group, battalion, and company echelons all have headquarters and support staffs. Some groups only field five teams per company because there are not enough Special Forces to fill all the authorized slots. The deep cuts in army personnel in the mid-1990s made it even more difficult to find qualified personnel.

Alan had gone to talk to Colonel Conner because the battalion commander was intimately familiar with the area in Iraq to which his team had been assigned. To prepare for their mission, Alan and his team had read the after-action reports of the earlier war. "Hey, the old man was here!" one of them exclaimed upon seeing that the report was signed by (then Captain) Chris Conner. Conner had been on a secret reconnaissance mission in exactly the same spot twelve years before, in Operation Desert Storm, when a handful of U.S. and British special operations forces were inserted clandestinely deep within Iraqi territory.

The team plied the "old man" with questions as they planned their operation. Not many Americans had set foot in Iraq, and nothing could prepare them better than the firsthand "ground truth" of one who had. Conner and his team had learned that lesson the hard way.

Conner and his fellow commanders had carefully chosen which teams would be assigned to which missions in Iraq. Many of his senior sergeants were veterans of Desert Storm. One of them, Master Sergeant Steve Rainey, had helped train and fight with the Saudis, working side by side with Conner's team until Conner was tapped for the reconnaissance mission. Rainey was a perfectionist, cynical and hard-bitten. He drove his men hard but drove himself harder. Few could outshoot him, even though he had a few fingers missing on his right hand. The Saudi army had not been much of a fighting machine, but in a few short weeks Rainey's team had managed to drill soldier skills into it.

Rainey had since become the team sergeant of ODA 544; he and two other senior NCOs brought more than a half-century of Special Forces' experience to their team. That experience was the real secret of the Army Special Forces. No other ground-level unit anywhere in the U.S. military could claim such a store of military knowledge and capability. The captains, who command the teams, come straight from the schoolhouse to an eighteen-month stint in charge of the twelve-man operational detachments. After that, the captains move to higher echelons while the ten sergeants and the chief warrant officers continue to serve on teams for years.

Colonel Conner knew what he was doing when he and the company commander, Major Andy Lohman, decided to make ODA 544 the "pilot team" that would enter the critical southern city of Najaf first.

The Special Forces are not a rapid deployment force; the secret of their success is intensive preparation. The men studied the area they were assigned as thoroughly as any Ph.D. student. They sucked up every available open-source and classified assessment of the demographics, tribal clans, local politics, religious leaders and schisms, history, terrain, infrastructure, road maps, power grids, water supplies, crops, and local economy. They planned, debated, and rehearsed both combat and follow-on operations. As part of the Special Forces' hallmark method, they often isolate themselves physically while preparing for missions. At Fort Campbell, the 5th Special Forces Group (Airborne) has an isolation facility built especially for this purpose. Some of the teams moved to the fenced-in building on the western edge of their complex before they left for the Middle East. They would eat, sleep, study, plan operations, exercise, and practice maneuvers there with no contact with outsiders.

Conner chose another experienced team, Operational Detachment Alpha 554, for an important mission. He had known its team sergeant, Michael T. Swift, since Desert Storm. Master Sergeant Swift had been in the military for twenty years, fifteen of them in the Special Forces. He was short and compact, and a perfect foil for his best friend, the team's chief warrant officer, Jimmy Newman. Conner considered them the best team sergeant–chief duo he'd ever seen. "Michael T." played the tough taskmaster while Jimmy could charm the pants off any friend or foe. Jimmy, a garrulous Louisiana Cajun, would "talk to a stick," they joked, if there were no live bodies around. Extroverts were essential commodities for the teams. In the foreign lands where they spent most of their time, they had to make friends quickly to uncover the information they needed, to bond with the foreign forces they were fighting alongside, and sometimes literally to save their own skins. This time they would be sent in early to accomplish a vital secret mission in southern Iraq.

Michael T. had seen some memorable teams and some memorable places. As young sergeants, he and Alan Johnson had been among the first ones into Somalia in 1992 along with their team sergeant, a bear of a man universally known as Killer thanks to his surname. James Kilcoyne was now the senior NCO in their company. His slow and deliberate way of speaking cloaked a steely will that had kept many a sergeant's nose to the grindstone. His pink cheeks and round face gave him a look most unlike a killer's, but he was in fact a dead shot, and after fifteen years in 5th Group he knew more about every job and mission than anyone. Killer knew the power of a few, well-timed words, and while no one wanted to be called a father figure, he just naturally filled the bill. When the other guys went to "chase bright shiny things," as one team sergeant called their roving operations to unearth targets or intelligence, Killer made sure the jobs got done.

While Conner's men, including Burns, Randy "Rawhide" Wurst, and Jim "Killer" Kilcoyne, would be running around the southern battlefield, the west would be the province of 5th Group's 1st Battalion, led by Lt. Col. Chris Haas, who had also led it into and out of Afghanistan. Haas's men were preparing a technological extravaganza that would make the Scud hunting of Desert Storm look like a wild goose chase by comparison. They would sprint through the desert in closely orchestrated movements aboard heavily armed 2.5-ton trucks, an invention they had built and christened the "war pigs," and would have a dedicated fleet of Air Force jets on call around the clock. The battalion's Charlie Company had been working on this concept for large-scale mounted operations— a novelty for the Special Forces—since the 1990s.

Haas had given Bravo Company commander Major Jim Gavrilis six weeks to duplicate what Charlie Company had spent years constructing. A meticulous man with a laser-like focus, Gavrilis bent to the task. He relied on veteran sergeants like Andy Brittenham, for whom such challenges were mother's milk. The cocky, dark-haired Scot was the intelligence sergeant of ODA 525, a scuba team that calls itself the Sharkmen. Scuba teams, which specialize in underwater infiltration, maintain a highly demanding physical regimen and tend to attract gung-ho characters. Brittenham's brio was grounded in twenty years of military service and extensive electronics expertise. An avid reader and passionate talker, he would introduce newcomers to the literature of special warfare and regional classics like T.E. Lawrence's *Seven Pillars of Wisdom*.

Gavrilis was also counting on a chief warrant officer named John Pace. Like other Special Forces sergeants looking for a way to stay on the teams where the action is, Pace had gone to school to become a chief warrant officer. "Chiefs," as they are called in the Special Forces, serve as second in command of ODAs, after the captain. If there is no captain, or if the team operates as two halves, the chiefs become the commanders. Pace had just become the second in command of ODA 523 and hoped he would live up to the job.

Pace and Mike Swift, who had been his team sergeant, had once dangled off a mountain in Turkmenistan in a near-death experience. Pace, a 200-pound, six-foot man, had clipped a 120-pound Turkmen interpreter to his belt and started to rappel down the face of the mountain at the end of the day. The rest had already begun their way down. The force of their combined descent had ripped the anchoring piton out of the rock. They had narrowly avoided plunging to their deaths; Pace had made it to a ledge while Swift rigged a new line. Now Pace was about to get another baptism by fire, as his team was assigned one of the highest-stakes missions in the western desert.

During December 2002, Fort Campbell slogged through its harshest winter in memory. The Tennessee-Kentucky state line splits the base along the Screaming Eagles Boulevard at main Gate 4. Except on Christmas day, the Kentucky side, where 5th Group was located, was abuzz with activity. The 5th Group had just returned from rehearsals in Jordan and the American west. Since August they had been preparing for 1003—the code name for the plan to invade Iraq and remove Saddam Hussein from power. Ten-oh-three had been on the shelf since Desert Storm, when the U.S. military drove Iraqi troops out of Kuwait. The old hands knew in their guts that it was just a matter of time before they were ordered to execute it. Now they were packing for the Middle East, to take up their assigned positions and await the final order to launch.

Fort Campbell's 5th Group was not the only hub of activity. At Fort Carson, the 10th Group commander Colonel Charlie Cleveland and two of his battalion commanders were preparing their men to perform the classic Special Forces mission of linking up with indigenous fighters, in this case the Kurds of northern Iraq. Cleveland was a no-nonsense officer with a long track record. He had been at the center of Special Forces' operations in Operation Just Cause in Panama thirteen years earlier, and had designed and created a Bolivian anti-drug training mission before that. He had spent the mid-1990s perfecting gray-area peace operations in the thorny Balkans conflict.

It was not unusual for the Special Forces groups to help each other out in their respective areas, if extra manpower or expertise was needed. Fifth Group had loaned its Muslim expertise in the Balkans. Just fifteen months earlier, Randy Wurst, Alan Johnson, and others had been in Kosovo. This would not be 10th Group's first foray into northern Iraq— it had played a leading role there in Operation Provide Comfort a decade before, when Saddam Hussein crushed a Kurdish uprising and sent thousands starving and freezing into the mountains and across the border into Turkey. Cleveland's two battalion commanders, Ken Tovo and Bob Waltemeyer, were veterans of both missions. The three men had worked hand-in-glove for years, and no Special Forces officers had more direct experience in trying to quell vicious ethnic conflicts. Still, Cleveland's skills as field marshal and diplomat would be tested like never before.

Tenth Group had an important godfather in Major General Geoffrey Lambert, who had led it before assuming command of all U.S. Army Special Forces on the eve of September 11, 2001. Lambert would funnel all the resources he could find to Cleveland's Kurdish mission. Cleveland had served under Lambert for years in the Balkans, and they had known each other for twenty years, since their days in 7th Group and Panama. They could not have been more opposite personality types: sandy-haired Charlie Cleveland was a quiet, buttoned-down commander, while

Geoffrey Lambert was a big, rangy redhead with an outgoing personality to match. But they were of one mind on what the Iraq war meant for the Special Forces. Unlike Desert Storm, where Special Forces had been handed bit parts, they were now being given major roles by Tommy Franks, the Central Command four-star general, with active support from the Pentagon. This was the Special Forces' star turn, and they would give it all they had.

More special operations forces would be deployed at one time than ever before, and they would be used in a dizzying variety of ways. The army Special Forces would work alongside two lesser-known members of the special operations community, the 4th Psychological Operations Group and the 96th Civil Affairs Battalion. These two units played far more important roles on the battlefield than commonly realized.

Psyop was the fastest, most bloodless way to win a war. If the potent reality of the U.S. military's overwhelming might were communicated in the right way at the right time to the target audience, the message alone could induce mass surrender. Similarly, the job of active-duty Civil Affairs soldiers was to influence the population as the war was unfolding, to shape that part of the human battlefield and prepare the transition to the postwar phase. The 96th Civil Affairs noncommissioned officers were former Special Forces soldiers, so they could be out in the middle of hostilities and join their Special Forces' partners in combat as needed. Given the extraordinary importance of psyop and Civil Affairs functions, it was mind-boggling that there were only two such active-duty units.

Randy Wurst was delighted to find that an old buddy of his, Warren Foster, would be leading a Civil Affairs team alongside them. History was repeating itself. As sergeants, Randy and Warren had fought side by side over the barricades in Kuwait in a nasty and little-known battle. The bond forged during wartime among teammates is a lifelong tie. The more ghoulish the situation, the more treasured the human beings alongside you are, because they keep you human. When everyone else thought the war in Kuwait was over, Randy and Warren had found themselves fighting a vicious guerrilla-style conflict in city streets amid an inferno of smoke and burning oil. No one wants to be the last casualty in a war, and Randy and Warren had fought together to avoid that most forlorn fate.

After Desert Storm, Warren had gone to officer candidate school and then went through the Special Forces' grueling qualification course a second time to become a Special Forces officer. Then, to continue working in the field rather than behind a desk, he switched to Civil Affairs, which also meant he could keep his family at Fort Bragg. After eight moves in ten years, his wife hoped to have a career at last. As they got ready for Iraq in January 2003, Warren, like Randy, thought this would probably be his last combat deployment.

As he looked ahead to the war, Randy Wurst also looked back. A nostalgic man, he was inclined to see the epic sweep of things. He knew that war was terrible in the way that only veterans can know. Yet it was no contradiction to feel pride as he and his fellow soldiers girded themselves once more for battle and kissed their wives and children goodbye. They were the latest in a long line of warriors, men who answered the call. Randall Wurst had traveled a long and circuitous route to this point. From his present vantage point, he could see the setbacks he had encountered as the equivalent of rough stones that are needed to polish a diamond. Without them a man has no chance to hone his warrior spirit. He had fallen down many times, sometimes spectacularly, but what counted most was that he had gotten up again. He learned that lesson at Fort Bragg, where his great adventure began.

CHAPTER 2

EARNING THE GREEN BERET

One hundred men we'll test today, but only three win the Green Beret.

—THE BALLAD OF THE GREEN BERETS

E VERY ASPIRING Special Forces soldier has a moment of truth during the "Q" course, and he remembers it for the rest of his life. The men use a typically laconic phrase to describe the Special Forces qualification—hence Q—course: they call it a "gut check." The experience will forever color the soldier's memory of Fort Bragg. For some it is a second home to which they will gladly return, for others, it is a waystation to the next post. But for each one it is the place where he had to prove his mettle to gain entrée to the brotherhood.

The would-be Special Forces soldier must spend many a damp chill night in the pine barrens wilderness, face to face with his strengths and weaknesses. The experience is designed to pose the question: How badly do you want this?

Seventy-five miles south of Raleigh, North Carolina, Fort Bragg sprawls in a 130,000-acre oval west of the city of Fayetteville. It is home to the Special Forces headquarters and the largest collection of special operations forces, including two Special Forces Groups and the Joint Special Operations Command where some men disappear to carry out the most highly classified missions. It is home also to the JFK Special Warfare Center and School, which selects and trains the men who become Special Forces soldiers. They will spend their careers roaming the globe, but Bragg is where they begin.

Bragg is full of history, some of it still living. President Kennedy blessed their Green Beret here. Their museum is here. And many old warriors are hereabouts. The Special Forces' first mission, after their founding in 1952, was to prepare for guerrilla warfare if the Soviets overran the rest of Europe. Many of the first recruits were immigrants from countries behind the Iron Curtain. One of them, Joe Lupyak, joined in 1954 in hopes of freeing his parents' homelands, Lithuania and Czechoslovakia. The Special Forces did not go there, but he had an eventful career that included training Cuban exiles for the Bay of Pigs invasion and participating in the Son Tay raid in Vietnam. After he retired as the command sergeant major of 5th Group in 1980, he went to work in 1983 as a civilian instructor and branch chief at the Special Warfare Center where he helped forge thousands of fighters over the past two decades.

Scrubby pine trees dot the rolling sandy hills, which are laced with tar pits and streams that feed the propitiously named Cape Fear river. The men trying out for the Special Forces come to know Fort Bragg's geography intimately. Chris Conner would not forget the calvary of Bones Fork Creek, where men's uniforms are shredded by its thorn-infested banks, and where packs are lost in the attempt to throw them across the creek before soldiers must plunge into its neck-high depths. Men are tested alone and in groups for endurance, stress management, and ingenuity. They go through survival, escape, and prisoner of war training. Later, they learn high-altitude parachuting. A wind tunnel was built in the late 1980s so that men could practice the rigid body posture before leaping out over the unforgiving fields of the Sicily drop zone. Although the details of this purgatory have varied over the years, the basic structure of the Special Forces tryout has remained constant. First there is selection, a month-long weeding-out process. Then follows the qualification course, which trains and tests soldiers in three phases. A soldier may fail (or quit) at any time during the roughly yearlong tryout.

In 1988, at the start of another round of Special Forces tryouts, Sergeant Randall Wurst moved into the four-man bunkrooms at Camp MacKall. They were crude wooden structures covered in tar paper. He put his duffel bag at the end of his bed and hurried down to the mess hall where the roster and schedule was posted. It offered very little information. Reveille at 5:00 a.m., physical training (PT, as soldiers call it) at 5:30, chow at 7:00, and formation at 8:00. Randy called his wife, as he would have little free time once the Q course began until it ended, for better or worse. "Good luck, honey," she said when it was time to hang up. "I know you want this more than anything." She knew that this had been his dream since he heard the Barry Sadler hit song, "The Ballad of the Green Berets," as a ten-year-old boy. He'd missed the draft by one day and, unlike the attitude of many of his generation, this disappointed him. He had watched his brother go off to Vietnam, and when he tried to enlist in the Marines, his parents refused to sign the papers and made him finish college. Ever since then, he had felt guilty that he had not gone to Vietnam to fight.

Aspiring Special Forces candidates did not move their families all the way to North Carolina for the yearlong tryout process because the washout rate was so high. Only a few hundred made the grade each year, which meant that in any given class the attrition rate was around 70 percent.

When Warren Foster went through the Q course in 1984, only 17 of 130 made it through, including two "SF babies" of which he was one. SF babies were brand-new recruits who were permitted to enter the competition. Usually a soldier wishing to try out for the Special Forces had to have served in the army for at least two years.

This effort to expand the force rapidly in the 1980s was one of several cycles of expansion and contraction that the Special Forces had been through since its inception. The first boom came right after its formation, but the manpower and resources dwindled by the end of the 1950s as the focus shifted to conventional forces and nuclear weapons. Then

President Kennedy's enthusiasm for the force as a way to fight communism led to its rapid expansion from 1961 to 1972. Off-the-street recruiting was allowed. The attrition rate in the Q course dropped from nearly 90 percent to 70 percent as the Special Forces ranks were quadrupled. They were sent all over the world but particularly to Southeast Asia, including on missions in Laos, Cambodia, and North Vietnam that remained secret until the 1990s.

The classic Special Forces mission in South Vietnam, portrayed in the 1968 John Wayne movie *The Green Berets*, was led by a twelve-man team in a firebase with a hundred or so Vietnamese tribesmen. They formed 249 of these bases all over Vietnam, in a program called the Civilian Irregular Defense Group. The hill tribes, or Montagnards, populated more than 70 percent of South Vietnam's territory, and many proved valiant fighters capable of defending their villages against the local Viet Cong insurgents. But they were no match for the divisions of North Vietnamese regular army that overran their camps as the war took an increasingly conventional turn. *The Night of the Silver Stars* recounts one of the heroic last stands of Green Berets and tribesmen in a camp called Lang Vei. The Special Forces also conducted covert missions across the borders into North Vietnam, along the Ho Chi Minh Trail and in the sanctuaries of Laos and Cambodia. Although the United States ultimately lost the war, studies such as Charles Simpson's *Inside the Green Berets* document numerous counterinsurgency successes as well as lessons learned from the failures.*

Insurgencies continued to sprout up everywhere, but the Vietnam experience consigned the Special Forces to a period of severe contraction. The focus once again shifted to large-scale war and deterrence scenarios. Many in the conventional army had been antagonistic toward elite units generally and particularly suspicious of unorthodox approaches. In 1979–80 the Special Forces played a role in the failed effort to liberate the American hostages in Iran; they sent men under

---

* See *Inside the Green Berets: The First Thirty Years*, Charles M. Simpson III (Novato, CA: Presidio Press, 1983).

cover into Tehran to gather intelligence and planned to rescue three hostages being held in the defense ministry. The entire mission went up in a giant fireball when helicopters and refueling planes collided in the Iranian desert en route to the rescue.

After Vietnam, the Special Forces were reduced to three active-duty groups (5th, 7th, and 10th) with minimal budgets. It took most of the 1980s to regrow a carefully selected and trained force. Army chief of staff General Edward C. Meyer embraced the resurgence of the Special Forces, as did President Ronald Reagan. At the very same time that the Special Forces were reviving, parallel efforts to build a premier hostage-rescue strike force had begun, resulting in the creation of the Special Forces Operational Detachment-Delta and then the Special Operations Command. Both were necessary and important developments but also gave rise to competition within the bureaucracy for both resources and the small pool of men who could meet the challenging requirements.

Reagan, like Kennedy, saw the Special Forces as a valuable tool to fight communist expansion on the periphery and supported their deployment in the 1980s. First Group, assigned to Asia, expanded and began training a South Korean Special Forces unit. Although the Central Intelligence Agency had the lead, Special Forces were assigned to help raise anti-Communist forces to fight in Afghanistan, Africa, and Nicaragua. The Special Forces' most extensive mission of this period took place in the little Central American country of El Salvador. There, they advised and trained Salvadorans in a ten-year counterinsurgency effort that defeated guerrilla offensives, reformed the military, and led to a historic peace accord in 1992.

The Special Forces also participated in Just Cause in Panama in 1989–90, which marked the formal return of the Special Forces to a combat role. This was a watershed, a publicly visible turning point, but it could not have occurred without the institutional rebuilding that had occurred inside the force. Only after protracted lobbying had the Special Forces been designated as a "major command" in 1983, which meant that it would be led by a two-star major general. Only an officer of that rank could begin to compete for resources, standing, and missions in the army and the Pentagon where key decisions were made.

Similarly, the designation of Special Forces as a military branch in 1987 meant that officers could now devote their entire careers to the Special Forces rather than leaving for other posts to advance in rank. It was now formally coequal to infantry, armor, military intelligence, and the other branches of the army. That meant that senior officers would one day emerge who thoroughly understood the doctrine, theory, and practice of unconventional war to combat the unconventional threats of the world. Those officers would fortuitously arrive in command berths just as the new century dawned.

Randy had donned his army greens relatively late in life: he was thirty when he enlisted. After college, he had traveled around the world and then returned to his hometown of Cody, Wyoming, to work as a cowboy, sheriff, and sharpshooter on the SWAT team. When Randy told a family friend and mentor that he had decided to join the army, she said simply, "I wonder what took you so long."

Randy had signed up to go directly to Special Forces selection, but then the army decided to halt the "SF baby" program, and he was sent instead to the 25th Infantry Division in Hawaii. He was delighted to find that it had a Ranger Indoctrination Program, which paved his way to Ranger school and jump school. Passing those two hurdles made him an attractive candidate for the Special Forces. Earning the Ranger tab—the shoulder patch awarded upon graduation from Ranger school—meant a soldier had already weathered the most grueling treatment the U.S. infantry could devise. Jump school qualified him for static-line jumps with round parachutes; the high-altitude stuff would come later.

Randy tended to have good luck and bad luck in equally improbable doses. He was blessed with the former in that both his battalion commander and captain at the 4th Ranger Battalion had themselves been in the Special Forces. Many Rangers tried out for the Special Forces, often despite opposition from their commanders, who did not want to lose good soldiers. But Randy's commanders saw him as prime SF material; he had the skills and the maturity. They helped him with the paperwork and bureaucratic hurdles required to secure a slot in the course. His sergeant major, however, never forgave his forsaking of the Rangers. The bad luck came just before jump school, when Randy went home to visit his family and had some planter's warts burned off his feet. It was a routine procedure, but the doctor had burned deep into his soles. For the next three weeks of jump school, Randy's boots were full of blood at the end of each day. "I'll kill you if you say anything," he warned the cadets bunking next to him, who were horrified at the condition of his feet. Because injuries were common at a school where men hurtled into the ground with the force of a car crash, instructors kept an eye out for anyone who so much as limped. If they pulled him from jump school, Randy would lose the slot he'd finally won in Special Forces selection. His feet would have to suffer.

The first days of the Special Forces tryout were filled with long runs, rucksack marches, and endless PT. The earliest bonds (and rivalries) in the Special Forces brotherhood were formed in the Q course. Soldiers had weeks and months to take the measure of each other in the brambles and tar pits and creeks. After they were pushed to their limits physically, they would be sent to the classroom to absorb massive amounts of information and be tested on it. The instructors were evaluating their ability to function under stress and fatigue. There were also team tests that required collaboration—loners would fail. Not even Samson could move a ton of equipment alone with four wheels and two poles, which was one of the challenges posed. Officers and enlisted men went through this phase together, which taught an early lesson in the Special Forces ethic: distinctions of rank mattered less than whether you could pull your weight.

Lieutenant Chris Conner was one of the officers in Randy's group. A tall, athletic Texan who had been commissioned out of his Virginia college, he seemed little fazed by the rigors of the Q course so far. Conner had already seen some of the world. His father, in the Army Corps of Engineers, had taken his family to live in Saudi Arabia.

After young Conner received his commission, he went to Fort Carson where he led a tank platoon and then a scout platoon. Then he decided to try out for Special Forces and went off to the officers advanced course and jump school before arriving at Fort Bragg.

The first phase of the Q course ended with the toughest test so far, land navigation. Randy brimmed with confidence: his home base in Hawaii ran one of the most challenging land navigation courses in the U.S. military, and he had breezed through the one at Ranger school. The test began at 4:00 a.m. and at several starting points men were given individual sets of coordinates, which they plotted on their maps with compasses. Each man oriented his map, shot an azimuth to the horizon with his compass to show the correct direction to head, and then took off into the darkness at a trot. There were miles to cover. An instructor waited at each station to verify that the soldiers had found the spot and to give the next set of coordinates. They would have to find a half-dozen points in as many hours. They were not allowed to walk or run on any roads they encountered, and instructors drove the roads looking for violators. At the stations, instructors also sometimes toyed with the increasingly haggard men, hinting that they were falling behind or attempting to throw them off course.

Randy plotted his course, shot his azimuth, then put his compass into his pocket. In the darkness he could see the dog kennels nearby. The unlucky guys to his south would be running through the swamp. If they were smart, they would use the boxing method to skirt it, because the brambles in there would tear the bejeebers out of them. He ran along, ticking off the terrain features he could make out in the dim light against the map in his hand. He found the first point and shot a new azimuth with the new coordinates he plotted, then pocketed the compass and forged on, using the map to verify features as he passed them. He arrived at the next point just as the sun rose. In horror he realized that he had somehow come back to the previous point. Other soldiers hustled by en route to their own stations. Randy threw his rucksack against a tree, kicked it, and cursed; then he pulled himself together, grabbed his pack, and set off running. He had been the second-fastest runner in California during high school, and his wind hadn't left him yet. When he reached the correct point, a waiting instructor told him, "You're not going to make it. You're way behind." Randy yelled back, "I'm not a quitter!" and took off running again.

He made it to the final station before the time expired. About a dozen other soldiers were milling around and there was no sign of the instructor who marked the exact point. They were never right out in the open, but this one simply could not be found. The men searched high and low but, try as they might, they could not find him.

Randy was glum. The candidates were allowed two tries to pass land navigation, but his ego was sorely bruised. In a bit of bravado as they lined up that night, Randy vowed: "Two things will happen tomorrow: the sun's gonna rise and I'm gonna pass this land nav course."

"That's pretty bold talk," another soldier muttered. He, along with three-quarters of the candidates, had failed that day's test. But Randy tried to figure out what he'd done wrong. He had been able to find the right stake among many in the Hawaiian gorges overgrown with foliage. Why had this happened to him here? Having lived all his life outdoors, Randy's instinctive habits were deeply ingrained. He had always relied on the method of orienting the map to the terrain. He realized that this had been his mistake in his first attempt: navigating by sight rather than by compass. Navigation by sight worked just fine for the sharp features of the western United States and Hawaii, but in North Carolina a saddle, a spur, or a draw might be so subtle that orienting solely by sight from the map could lead to error. On the second attempt, after hours of trekking Randy found himself about five miles off course. He had made the same mistake. He ran back, retracing his steps, pushing himself faster.

It began to rain. Randy ran on, his panic growing. He had too much ground to make up. His tears mingled with the raindrops as he begged God for help. A truck went by, heading the other direction. It stopped and turned around.

"Son, you look like you need a ride," the driver said.

"Yes, I do sir. Do you know what this is?" Randy asked him.

"Yeah, I do," the farmer said. "Get in back and lay down."

It sounded like he'd helped some hapless soldiers before. Randy looked at his watch. This was his only chance to get back on course. He had tried so hard to get this far, five years in all, he was not going to turn down this offer. He was contrite, to be sure, but he believed that this must be God's answer to his prayer.

The farmer dropped Randy off where the dirt road met pavement. He checked his plotting and took off running to the next point, reaching the final station with fewer than five minutes to spare. A few other soldiers were searching for the same point, where an instructor should be found. Randy ignored them—they might be off course. He retraced his steps, checked his compass, and came to the same spot as before. No instructor. Then he noticed a large brush pile, an impenetrable thicket with no trace of a path leading into it. He had to be in there. Randy barreled through the branches and found the instructor, sitting inside a tent.

"You only have three minutes left. This isn't the station you want," the instructor said.

Randy let out an agonized wail. "Just shoot me! If you have a bullet, just shoot me."

"Naw, just kidding," the instructor said. "You made it."

When he got back to camp, Randy learned that so many others had failed that the instructors decided to run a third test, which was unheard of. Randy knew that he had only made it to that last point because a farmer had miraculously appeared to give him an illegal lift. He had broken the rules but he hadn't been caught. He was contrite, but not so contrite that he would confess and risk a third test. It did make him think about his approach to soldiering, however. He had to learn to use his head more—barreling through worked some of the time, but not always.

His Ranger unit in Hawaii, the Wolfhounds, had prided itself on being tough. Randy tried to outdo everyone and usually succeeded. He had been one of two soldiers in the entire 25th Infantry Division to win a competition to attend Malaysian jungle school in 1985. The prize had been nine weeks of arduous survival training, with no food, no English speakers, and nothing but a machete.

Randy was, as they said, as hard as woodpecker lips, but that reputation had also been used to beat him. During an ambush exercise in Hawaii, his opponents had anticipated that he would bring his men through a thorny guava patch. In theory it was the least-expected route because it was the path of most resistance, but his fellow soldiers knew him and predicted his tactics. "These gnarly bushes will rip you a new asshole," the opposing leader said. "But that means Sergeant Wurst is going to come through there, sure as I am sitting here." He laid a trap, and when Randy and all his men came through as predicted, he "killed" them all.

Now Randy was vying to join a unit that put a premium on thinking. The solutions in this line of fighting were not the obvious ones. The weak could only outfox the strong by being clever—that was the essence of unconventional warfare.

Of the 350 men who had begun the training program, only one hundred remained at the end of the first phase, even with the third navigation test. Chris Conner had emerged from the briars of Bones Fork Creek wearing little but his shorts but as unruffled as ever. He and the other officers were told to report to survival school, just down the road, in forty-eight hours. For him, the Q course was about to escalate several notches.

The official name of the course is SERE, for Survival, Evasion, Resistance, and Escape. It had been created in 1981 by Nick Rowe, the Special Forces' legendary former prisoner of war. Captured by the Viet Cong in 1963, Rowe had escaped on his fourth attempt after five years of captivity and torture. Rowe and the instructors imparted the methods he had developed for resisting mental stress, continuing to fight, and maintaining a soldier's bearing even while imprisoned. Conner would not have a chance to meet Rowe, however, because he had just been sent to the Philippines as a military adviser and was assassinated there the following year.

After a few days of classroom instruction, the fun began. For several days Conner and a dozen others were chased through the woods and underbrush by tracker dogs and "opposition" soldiers. Hunted like animals, they were forced to forage for food in the streams and hollows while completing assigned survival tasks. Special Forces founder Aaron Bank deemed this a perfect spot for survival training because of the abundant food it offered—frogs and snakes. The men lost an average of thirty pounds by the end of the course.

Finally they were "captured." Then began a brutal program that simulated prisoner-of-war conditions and treatment, and tested their ability to resist. The four days in the Resistance Training Laboratory were described by a SERE commander in an official publication as "quite possibly the most challenging training that the students will ever experience.... Students learn quickly that they must work together as a team in order to survive captivity."

Everything was taken from them. They were dressed in yellow uniforms made of thin cotton marked with the initials PW. When they dared, they relieved the grimness with a few moments of humor, that timeless defense. Conner and the other "prisoners" were forbidden to talk about the specific techniques used during those four days to anyone who had not been through the school. They involved, among other things, sticks, small cages, and a giant, bearded SF veteran who played his sadistic role with relish.

Conner and his cohorts left the SERE school intact and kept their vow of silence. The next hurdle was two months of officer training, which alternated more grueling physical trials with classroom work on Special Forces doctrine and leadership drills. One field exercise involved people chasing them again. At night they camped in the rain, and it was so cold they had to double up in sleeping bags to conserve body heat. Living out in the elements taught them a vital lesson: if they could not cope with the physical conditions and maintain their weapons, the environment would get them before the enemy did. The final outdoor event of this phase was the Troy Trek (named for a town at the edge of the Uwharrie National Forest) in which the men had to cover seventy-five kilometers with a fully loaded, hundred-pound rucksack in three days.

Throughout this phase, the instructors continued to push on the young officers' endurance and navigation skills; they also were testing the ability of the candidates to make sound decisions under stress. Those who passed this course would be leading eleven other men halfway around the world in unknown or hostile territory, thousands of miles from any superior officer. These young men in their twenties had to be able to shoulder such responsibility. This was why the instructors used the psychological ploy of not letting the candidates know how they were doing; they had to be self-directed individuals. Whatever was thrown at him over these long months, Conner reminded himself that the instructors were trying to mess with his mind. He just had to keep his cool.

While Conner and the other officers were going through their courses in phase two, the enlisted candidates chose and were trained in one area of expertise, called a military occupational specialty: weapons (18B), engineering and demolition (18C), field medicine (18D), and communications (18E). The medic and communications specialties required twelve and six months of training respectively, and the other courses were three months long.

After Christmas came the third and final phase, a five-week exercise that had been called Robin Sage for decades. The name was a hybrid derived from the names of the town near the exercise's starting point (Robbins) and the officer who helped develop it, Col. Jerry Sage. Sage had been an OSS comrade of Aaron Bank and commanded 10th Group in the 1960s. The basic design of the exercise had remained the same for years: the soldiers were to conduct unconventional warfare by linking up with a "guerrilla" force and forging an alliance. To pass this test they had to draw upon all the individual and collective skills they'd acquired over the prior year. Robin Sage was designed to find out who had the aptitude and ability to implement the concepts and methods of unconventional warfare, where heads were just as important as bodies. Only those who passed would at last earn the beret.

The men were assigned to teams of twelve for the exercise, just as they would be in actual deployments. Randy found himself on a team with Conner as his commanding officer. For two weeks before the soldiers went out into the bush to meet the "guerrilla" chieftains, Sergeant Major Joe Lupyak coached them on the tradecraft of unconventional warfare. He taught the seven-stage process and the formation of armies, auxiliaries, and undergrounds. He reviewed methods of assessing areas, planning operations, and conducting briefbacks to rehearse the plan for the commander. Finally, the candidates practiced infiltration techniques via parachute and helicopter.

After three weeks they were ready to parachute or helicopter into the fictional country of "Pineland" where they were to find and recruit the "guerrillas" and lead a successful liberation of the country. Pineland was actually hundreds of square miles in the Uwharrie forest and rural farmland west of Bragg, and the guerrillas were Special Forces soldiers. As luck would have it, the February weather was unusually nasty. It rained for four days before the men set off, and the night they arrived in Pineland the mercury dropped and the rain turned to sleet. They holed up in a tarpaper shack that was their temporary headquarters. The next day it snowed. The men did not have parkas for the unusual weather, but the team still had to conduct reconnaissance of the area where they were to meet the "guerrillas."

When darkness fell no one noticed Randy shivering, and, true to his Ranger upbringing, he would not tell his teammates that he was in trouble. When he started slurring his words and stumbling, someone identified the telltale signs of hypothermia, which sets in when the body core temperature falls a few degrees. His teammates built a fire and dried his frozen clothes by the flames.

The next day, Conner and his assistant commander were to call on the "guerrilla" boss. As weapons sergeant, it was Randy's job to set up a countersniper position where he could protect Conner if the encounter went south. As they waited for the rest of the team to fan out in security positions around the perimeter, Conner entertained them with his imitations of Inspector Clouseau. It hardly seemed possible that he was about to undergo his biggest test in the entire exercise. The initial encounter with the rebel chieftain, or any irregular force, was the most delicate moment. There was no way to predict what tack the role-player would take—suspicious, sinister, deranged, or merely aggressive—but it was always as difficult as he could make it. Conner's task was to establish contact and open negotiations with the leader, and explain how an alliance could benefit the rebels. The guerrilla leader would invariably bluff, bully, and threaten the young captain. The "guerrillas" normally tried to extract all the supplies and hardware they could while ceding as little as possible in return. They might be utterly hostile and not want to have anything to do with the Americans. Whatever the ploy, Conner knew that, for him, Robin Sage was going to be one long test of psychological gamesmanship. He would not only have to win over the rebel force but also woo the rebels' underground, the community leaders, and the uncommitted population.

After two days of protracted bargaining, Conner struck a tenuous alliance with the domineering rebel chieftain. Just because they had reached an agreement did not mean that the alliance then ran on autopilot. Guerrilla alliances were tedious, treacherous, and fraught with pitfalls. Once recruited, there were continual struggles over strategy, leadership, salaries, supplies, and discipline. The "guerrillas" alternated between raising the stakes and hurling accusations that the team was double-crossing them. Conner had to win them over and also make sure that he accomplished his objectives. He had to think on his feet and use whatever information he'd been given to come up with a solution. Emotional maturity was essential for everyone; playing the arrogant American and trying to strong-arm the rebels was a sure-fire way to wind up tied to a tree with an AK–47 aimed between one's eyes.

On the third day the snow thawed and the guerrilla base turned to muck. The men slogged around in mud that was as icy and thick as an ankle-deep milkshake. The weather would remain one of the biggest challenges. It had been easy enough in the classroom dry run to think fast and stay flexible, but in the Uwharrie forest everyone was miserable. Unconventional warfare is rarely conducted in physical comfort. It could be in the mountains or the jungle, in burning heat or freezing cold. By definition, guerrillas did not live in easy places. Pineland was proving to be suitably nasty.

In real unconventional warfare, forging the alliance and training the rebels is estimated to take two and a half months; in Robin Sage candidates had to do it in a few days. The team set about improving the military skills of the rebels, who usually have little formal training. The sergeants trained and equipped them, planned and rehearsed operations, resupplied themselves through airdrops, and worked with the local population to gain their support and counter the opponents' propaganda. The long-time residents of this area of North Carolina loved to volunteer and played their civilian roles with gusto. After a successful military operation was conducted, Robin Sage ended with the invariably tense process of disarming and demobilizing the "guerrillas" once their country was liberated.

The last time it snowed, near the end of those two long weeks, nobody cared—they were on the home stretch. Sergeant Major Lupyak decided to check on the boys. He was concerned about the harsh weather—he wanted to make sure the harsh weather had not caused the role-playing instructors to ease up on the candidates. They had to be able to perform their mission no matter what the physical conditions. These two weeks were as close to the real thing as they would get. The essential scenario of Robin Sage had remained unchanged for one reason: it accurately represented what the Special Forces could expect to encounter in the field. Year after year, soldiers returned from deployments marveling at how much the reality in the field had mimicked their Robin Sage experience.

Joe Lupyak knew firsthand the value of the army truism "train like you fight and fight like you train." He had taken part in one of the most rehearsed missions in the Special Forces' entire history, the Son Tay raid.* It was still considered a model for how to train and prepare for missions, so Lupyak always told the story in his classes and directed the men across the street to see the scale model that was the centerpiece of the little Special Forces museum. Outside the museum, in JFK Plaza, a lunging bronze statue depicts the raid's leader, the legendary Colonel Arthur "Bull" Simons. It is an accurate likeness down to the massive hands that nearly swallowed his revolver.

In 1970 Simons was tapped to lead a mission to rescue American prisoners of war from the Son Tay prison in North Vietnam, twenty-three miles outside of Hanoi. The veteran Special Forces officer, who had led successful counterinsurgency efforts in Southeast Asia and Latin America in the 1960s, left nothing to chance. He hand-picked his men and put them through no fewer than 170 full-dress rehearsals. They built an exact replica of the prison camp at Duke airfield in Florida and dismantled it every day before the Soviet satellites passed overhead. They planned for dozens of contingencies and went to great lengths to maintain total secrecy of the operation. Without the element of surprise, they would never get into the heart of enemy territory, or get out alive. Finally, Simons gave the men one day off. They were bused to Fort Walton Beach and given cokes and hot dogs. It rained. "We might as well have kept working. It was miserable," Lupyak said. He remembered Simons as tough but fair. "He looked mean but he had the biggest heart. He'd chew you out if you weren't doing your job but he'd never scream or holler." And, the sergeant major recalled: "Simons always had a cigar in his mouth. Never saw him without one."

Three platoons of fifty-six Green Berets staged a breathtakingly bold raid into the heart of enemy territory in November of 1970. Lupyak was in the platoon code-named "Red Wine." Its helicopters touched down just outside the prison camp. The men piled out, quickly set explosive charges to breach the wall, and stormed the guard houses. Simons'

* See *The Raid: The Son Tay Prison Rescue Mission*, Benjamin F. Schemmer (NY: Harper & Row, 1976).

"Blue Boy" platoon landed in the middle of a nearby compound, which intelligence had identified as a school but which turned out to be filled with dozens of armed Chinese. A fierce firefight ensued. "Green Leaf" platoon's helicopter deliberately crash-landed inside the compound—a tactic the raiders had dreamed up to achieve maximum surprise and speed. Green Leaf's role was to free the prisoners and usher them through the hole that Lupyak and his men had blown in the wall.

All three elements of the raid were executed simultaneously, on schedule, and without any loss of life. They were airborne again in twenty-seven minutes. In all these respects, it was a model execution of the most difficult of commando missions, hostage rescues. Most often, they never get off the ground, are aborted, or end in massive loss of life. In this case, the men of Red Wine, Blue Boy, and Green Leaf performed exactly as intended, but when they entered the camp they found guards but no prisoners. It turned out that the prisoners had been moved four months earlier. Worse yet, U.S. intelligence had picked up indications that high flood waters had led to their removal, but this information was never shared with the raiders.

When news of the raid broke, the immediate reaction in both Washington and the press was that the operation had been a disaster, a failure, and a scandalous provocation. Simons told the secretary of defense that his men had executed their plan and risked their lives to try to save fellow Americans. Simons' attitude was that they had done their best and they had been prepared for failure. It was a great shame, but it was not their fault, that they were not given the latest intelligence. The Son Tay raiders were devastated because they had failed to bring their comrades out. As they flew back home, many men wept.

The national perception of the event began to change three years later when Ross Perot staged a ticker tape parade and threw a lavish reception at the Fremont Hotel in California for the Son Tay raiders and the newly released POWs. John Wayne, Clint Eastwood, Red Skelton, and the Supremes were among the celebrities on hand to greet them. Perot planted a new $100 bill on each man's plate. The best recompense for the SF veterans of Son Tay, however, was to hear the POWs tell how it had lifted their spirits to hear that someone had tried to come for them. The audacity of the raid also had rattled the North Vietnamese, who had no idea what the Americans might do next. It led to an immediate improvement in POW conditions. The Vietnamese moved the prisoners from primitive camps into the large prison nicknamed the "Hanoi Hilton," and gave them better care and feeding. Increased contact with their fellow Americans gave many renewed strength to hold out.

Son Tay was emblematic of the Special Forces' role in Vietnam. Much was accomplished that was bold, brave, and innovative, yet the perception at home was that the entire war was a disaster. Only when hostage-taking became rampant a decade later did the experts turn back to Son Tay as a textbook for rescue missions. Meticulous attention to detail, including exact replicas of terrain and structures in which to practice the maneuvers; rehearsals with the aircraft and crew that would be used; factoring in of weather and ground conditions; diversions (which had been staged simultaneously in other parts of North Vietnam); and surprise tactics like the crash-landing all became standard procedure for the hostage-rescue units that were created at the end of the 1970s and in the 1980s. Intelligence sharing remained a thorny and complex issue; riven by bureaucratic tension, it would only improve gradually.

Simons' career was over, however. The military did recognize his valor by awarding him its second-highest honor, the Distinguished Service Cross, but he was passed over for promotion to general and retired the next year, in 1971. The Son Tay raiders received Silver Stars, the military's third-highest award, but only after an attempt was made to downgrade them to lesser medals. Simons' skills were called upon again, in 1979, by Ross Perot who asked him to help rescue two employees who had been jailed in Tehran as Islamic revolution was engulfing the country. Simons accepted immediately—for free. He put together a team of Perot employees with military experience, trained them quickly, and spirited the captives out of Iran's chaos.

To Lupyak, turning out the newest Special Forces soldiers was no less momentous than the preparation for Son Tay. He had to make sure they were ready to hit the ground running, because this class was likely to wind up in a war zone very soon after receiving their green berets. The only question in his mind was which of the many trouble spots they would be sent to. Latin America had been roiling for most of the 1980s, so it seemed the most likely destination. Lupyak had long served in 7th Special Forces Group, and so he still kept an eye on the region. El Salvador's Marxist guerrillas had been fighting for years and were rumored to be gearing up for a final offensive. The Special Forces' biggest and longest counterinsurgency effort since Vietnam was unfolding there. A Special Forces soldier had been killed when the base he lived on was overrun by the Salvadoran guerrillas, and others had recently helped fend off an all-night attack on another base.

Panama (where one-third of 7th Group was based) and the United States were on a collision course. An entire group had once been based in Panama and led by Bull Simons, but it had been deactivated after Vietnam. By 1989, it looked like Panama's leader, a one-time ally named Manuel Noriega, had lost his mind. He had forced a president to resign at gunpoint, stolen elections, and ordered the candidates beaten up. He had been indicted for drug trafficking and had started harassing U.S. soldiers. The U.S. stake in Panama's canal and its treaty obligations meant that this problem could not be ignored.

Another possible deployment for the newly qualified SF soldiers was the perennial powder keg of the Middle East. Lupyak had served as command sergeant major of 5th Group, which covered a vast swath that ran from Afghanistan through the Arab world to the Horn of Africa. He had been among the last Special Forces who trained the Shah's troops in Iran and had walked through the American embassy compound a few weeks before it was taken over in the hostage crisis in 1979. When the rescue of the hostages was attempted the following year, shades of Son Tay had come back to haunt him. He had watched in dismay as Operation Eagle Claw was forced to abort after its aircraft collided in the desert. A decade later, the spotlight was shifting to Iraq, which had emerged from a long and bloody war with Iran with the fourth-largest army in the world and an appetite for aggression.

For a brief moment, the first Special Forces class to graduate in 1989 did not have to think about that. They could rejoice in their substantial victory of winning a green beret. Some fell out in the final cut, but Randy and Conner made it. Their lives as Special Forces soldiers began when they received their green berets. The current generation did not like to call themselves Green Berets: they preferred to say they *earned* the green beret and *wore* the green beret. The new class received their historic headgear at a dinner and ceremony at Fort Bragg, where the 86-year-old founder of the Special Forces, retired Colonel Aaron Bank, welcomed the newcomers with a speech. Then Randy, Conner, and the other newest members of the brotherhood donned the green wool felt hats. The flash, or badge, was worn just over the left eye. Each regional group had a different flash. Randy and Conner wore the same black flash trimmed in white thread, because they had both been assigned to 5th Group.

They were now officially Special Forces soldiers, but that did not mean their training was done. They still had to attend language school and learn one of the dominant tongues of their assigned region: 5th Group studied Arabic and Farsi; 7th Group studied Spanish and Portuguese; 10th Group primarily learned German and Russian; and 3rd Group learned French or an African tongue. First Group had the toughest assignment with its array of dissimilar Asian tongues: Chinese, Japanese, Thai, and Tagalog. To help master them the group sent its best linguists to Asian universities. A score of 3+/3+ denoted complete fluency. The Special Forces are the only unit in the U.S. military with a language requirement, so even achieving basic competency added a critical skill to their arsenal. Native or fluent speakers were valued team members who carried their teammates and helped devise ways to raise their functional level. Each group has a language lab where the soldiers studied, tested their proficiency, and learned additional languages. Many played foreign-language CDs as they drove to and from work. Being deployed "downrange," however, was the quickest way to learn.

Randy was on cloud nine after winning his beret, but Arabic was going to be a mighty challenge for him. He had been identified as dyslexic late in grammar school, and reading required painstaking effort that he often got around by using memorization. But this Arabic was going to be a bear. Conner, on the other hand, would manage to tuck away Arabic, Russian, and Spanish over the course of his career. Occasionally the right word from the wrong language would pop up in his sentences, as when he used the Russian word for fourteen when talking to an Arab sheikh. After months of dogged effort, Randy had mastered enough Arabic to hold a simple conversation and make himself understood if he was giving basic orders. Many soldiers achieved only basic mastery of their language; it was a time-consuming process and they had a great many other demands. Although the Special Forces might cross-train in various skills, their natural talents would inevitably make each soldier better at some things than others. On teams, the men learned to play to each other's strengths and carry each other when needed.

Randy's forte was apparent to those who had watched him on the range during the Q course. He was probably the best marksman any of them had ever seen. With a scoped rifle he could repeatedly hit inside a two-inch radius from 300 meters away. Such tight shot groups were rarely bested. "He's a guy I'd want by my side in a dark alley," Conner said. When it came time for each enlisted man to choose his individual military occupational specialty, no one doubted that "Rawhide" would choose to be an 18 Bravo, a weapons sergeant. All his life he'd been around guns; he'd hunted with guns, used them as a sheriff, and even had a firing range on his ranch. He had been trained as a sniper on the SWAT team and knew room-clearing techniques. As a weapons sergeant his job was to know everything about all the small arms and crew-served weapons in use around the world: Soviet-made systems, black-market weapons, customized weapons. He had to know how to use them, train on them, fix them, clean them, dismantle them, and disable them. Part of the final exam for his course was the "pile test," which required assembling a massive jumble of weapons parts into nine guns. Randy could do it in forty-five minutes.

Randy's expertise with guns was not his only strength. By coming into the military at the relatively mature age of thirty, he brought more real-world experience with him than most other soldiers. He was also a man who led with his heart, which sometimes got him in trouble, but he was as loyal as a Saint Bernard. "Heart of gold, great sense of humor, and loyal to a fault," was how Chris Conner described him.

As the first class of 1989 neared the end of its time at Fort Bragg, army recruiters arrived on post to take pictures for their newest recruiting literature. They took many photos of many soldiers. They found what they were looking for in the face of newly promoted Staff Sergeant Randall Wurst. Predictably, his newly minted SF brothers all razzed him for being a Special Forces poster boy. "What Makes Special Forces So Special?" they asked, mocking that year's recruiting slogan. But they were secretly pleased that their friend had been selected to represent them. Standing at attention, Sgt. Wurst stared from the cover of the promotional pamphlet in his green dress uniform and perfectly cocked green beret. His solemn brown eyes looked out over a straight nose and high cheekbones that hinted at his Blackfoot ancestry. Black hair flecked with early gray peeked out from the beret with the 5th Group flash. The symbols affixed to his uniform pay homage to Indian field-craft: the crossed arrows on the lapel are the Special Forces insignia and a reference to the Indian scouts who led the way for American troops in the 1800s. The Army Special Operations patch worn on the left shoulder is a sky-blue arrowhead bearing the trademark dagger crossed by three lightning bolts that symbolize infiltration by land, sea, and air. The photo was of a man who had assumed his place in the long lineage of warriors to which he belonged. Rawhide was his call sign, and the look in his eyes promised: I won't let you down.

CHAPTER 3

JUST CAUSE
1989

War is not an independent phenomenon but the
continuation of politics by other means.

—KARL VON CLAUSEWITZ

T HE HUMID SUMMER was settling around Fort Bragg when the
newly minted Special Forces soldiers packed up to go to their new
post at Fort Campbell, Kentucky in June 1989. Chris Conner, now promoted to captain, assumed command of his first Special Forces team,
ODA 532. Each ODA was commanded by a captain, with an assistant
commander who was a chief warrant officer. The other ten members
were sergeants of varying rank. Randy was thrilled to be assigned to
ODA 574, one of the so-called HALO teams, which specialize in high-
altitude low-opening (HALO) parachuting. Everyone in Special Forces
had to know how to do this military free-fall parachuting, which they
had developed as a silent means of infiltration, but only certain teams
had to maintain permanent readiness. It was difficult and dangerous,
and keeping one's qualification required frequent practice jumps.
They jumped at night, with rucksacks and equipment weighing 170
pounds or more, from altitudes of 30,000 feet or higher, using oxygen

on their descent. They plunged earthward at 120 miles an hour, then opened their square steerable chutes and piloted themselves to their destination.

Randy and Chris were just settling into their respective team rooms in the cinderblock barracks when they got word of their first assignment. They were ordered to learn Spanish. Randy thought he had died and gone to hell when told to master another language. A half-dozen ODAs of 5th Group were told to prepare to help 7th Group handle its burgeoning load in Latin America. There was no hotter region in the 1980s than Latin America, which was awash in violent groups from the Maoist Shining Path in Peru, to a welter of insurgencies in Colombia, to the chaotic brew of Central America with its Sandinista Marxists, anti-communist contras and Salvadoran guerrillas, and armies of drug traffickers around the Andes. There was no shortage of work for Special Forces. They were training troops and officers from many of these countries at the U.S.-run School of the Americas, located on one of the U.S. military bases in Panama, and sending mobile training teams to some of the countries.

The Special Forces' biggest mission of the 1980s was in El Salvador. The government was on the verge of toppling under the onslaught of the Farabundo Marti National Liberation Front (FMLN), whose 12,000 fighters nearly outnumbered the army and controlled about one-third of the country by the early 1980s. In that decade, there was no assignment anywhere in the world more on the frontlines than working with the Salvadoran army's Third and Fourth Brigades in the rebel-held north. A Special Forces officer and an NCO would live out there for a year, amid the ubiquitous wood-smoke smell of cooking fires that suffuses rural El Salvador. One of the most densely populated countries in the Western world, it was also home to some of the most proficient and dedicated guerrilla fighters. The brigades at El Paraiso and San Miguel were the most dangerous, so they were postings most sought-after by the Special Forces. Both brigade camps had been attacked and overrun numerous times. El Paraiso was hit in 1983, 1986, 1987, and 1988.

One Special Forces soldier who served there was Kevin Higgins. He first went to Latin America in 1977–79 and fell in love with the gregarious people and lush landscape. He came back in 1983 as an adviser in El Salvador and spent the rest of his career in the region—even after a bout of tropical disease that left him little more than skin and bones at barely 105 pounds. The 1980s were a dramatic time in El Salvador's history. The country's future hung in the balance: the guerrillas were very close to winning, with help from the revolutionary government that had taken power in next-door Nicaragua in 1979. They had a fully developed support network and underground movement at home, and received arms and training from Soviet-bloc countries.

Higgins, a West Pointer, was the archetype of the thoughtful man of action. He had reddish brown hair and green eyes, stood at six foot one and carried only 160 pounds. He was slender but tough as cat gut, and fighting certainly ran in his blood: he had been West Point's champion welterweight boxer and a Golden Gloves finalist. Yet out of the ring and off the battlefield, he projected an easy calm and almost professorial manner, belied by the wry grin and crooked nose that gave away his feisty side. One of his subordinates believed that Higgins would have been a priest if he hadn't become a soldier.

Higgins was promoted to major and lobbied hard for another assignment to El Salvador. He won it, and spent 1986–88 in San Miguel during some of the war's fiercest days. The guerrillas had resorted increasingly to mines, bombs, and booby traps, and civilian casualties were soaring. San Miguel, a principal city in the war zone, was the scene of frequent attacks. One night in 1988 the FMLN raked the brigade (in the middle of the city) with machine-gun fire to keep Army helicopters grounded while FMLN members blew up the power station. Although the Special Forces were there to advise, not fight, the rules of engagement permitted self-defense. Higgins did not need to fire his weapon in that glancing attack, but it was a different story a few months later in a neighboring province.

A Special Forces major named James Parker was asleep in his shorts when a massive assault began on El Paraiso firebase on September 12,

1988.* Parker and a Special Forces sergeant dashed to a bunker where they had stowed a supply of arms and ammunition. Their foresight paid off because the guerrillas' well-planned attack destroyed much of the camp's ammunition depot. The guerrillas advanced into the camp and seized the artillery guns on the high ground, then turned them on the men in the bunkers. The guerrillas then overran the mortar pits in the middle of the base. Finally, a Salvadoran airforce AC–47 gunship arrived and fired on the guerrillas, holding them at bay until the gunship ran out of flares to illuminate its gunfire and left. The Special Forces advisers fought throughout the night alongside the Salvadoran soldiers. At sunup the guerrillas disappeared, leaving a dozen of their own dead. They had killed thirty-one Salvadoran soldiers and wounded another nineteen in this single attack. The two Special Forces soldiers survived, unlike the previous year's attack in which Sgt. Greg Fronius had died defending the very same firebase. El Paraiso was attacked twice more while Parker was there, as the FMLN built up to their "final offensive" in November 1989.

At the same time that the Salvadoran guerrillas launched their offensive, the two-year-old crisis in Panama was finally coming to a head. The failure of economic sanctions and diplomatic negotiations to produce results, combined with Noriega's growing aggressiveness, made it more and more likely that the United States would act to remove him from power to protect its bases and the canal.

Based permanently in Panama, 7th Group's 3rd Battalion constantly rotated teams in and out of Salvador and Honduras on training missions, as well as down south in Bolivia. But from mid-1988 3rd Battalion was also planning for the possibility of war in Panama itself. It knew the country, the players, and the bases. Its operations officer, Captain Charles Cleveland, knew Panama better than most, as he had gone to high school there when his father was posted to one of the U.S. bases

---

* This account is based on a transcript of then-Lt. Col. Parker's interview with U.S. Army Special Operation Command historian Dr. Richard Stewart on February 16, 1993 (courtesy of USASOC archives). All other accounts in this book are based upon firsthand interviews with the author.

bordering the canal. Blond-haired and blue eyed, no one would ever mistake Cleveland for a Panamanian, but he spoke Spanish well and understood the culture.

The 3rd Battalion commander had already spotted the young officer's gift for strategic thinking when he appointed Cleveland to his previous job as a company commander, despite the fact that he was only a captain and company command was a job for majors. Cleveland not only juggled his teams' assignments in El Salvador but dreamed up and launched a program to train an anti-drug police force in Bolivia. He went to Bolivia to oversee the construction of the Chimore training camp in the middle of the drug region, and was there when it was attacked by drug traffickers and armed coca growers. The fledgling Bolivian force, the Green Berets, and their DEA cohorts held the fort.

When Cleveland became the operations officer for the battalion, his friend Higgins, who had just returned from Salvador, took over the company command. Higgins brought with him a Salvadoran bride who had no trouble sleeping through gunfire after living through war in San Miguel. He kept busy trying to handle everything that Cleveland had set into motion: the missions in Salvador and Bolivia and getting ready for the possible showdown with Panamanian strongman Manuel Noriega.

As of mid-1988, the use of force in Panama still seemed like a remote prospect, and few units in the U.S. military had given it any thought, but Cleveland believed they needed to have a plan. He identified which places Noriega most likely would flee to and which of his units were most likely to stand and fight. Cleveland had previously served in the military intelligence branch before he joined the Special Forces, so he knew exactly what kind of information should be collected. With the help of Higgins and his men they meticulously gathered intelligence on twenty-nine different locations and units and prepared "target folders" with the information. Cleveland then mapped out how the operations themselves should be conducted and met with the Special Forces' five-helicopter detachment to discuss the logistics.

The possibility of intervention grew in 1989, and Cleveland started arranging for the transfer home of U.S. civilians and dependents based in

Panama. Rehearsals began for twenty-nine target missions. The entire military began planning for war in earnest, and the jockeying for pieces of the action followed. The Special Forces' official capacities included direct action and reconnaissance missions, and the SF had done plenty of both in Vietnam and had trained for such missions every year since. The secret Delta force and SEAL commandos landed the jobs of capturing Noriega and rescuing a CIA asset from jail. But 7th Group, with its intimate knowledge of Panama born of its Latin expertise and year-round presence, had a grasp of the "ground truth" that no one else could match. Panama was a critical test for the Special Forces. This was the Special Forces' chance to show that they had fully recovered from the post-Vietnam lows. If they did not prove that in Panama, the largest major military action since Vietnam, then they might not be given any roles in subsequent wars, and if opponents and competitors could argue that the Special Forces were irrelevant and their day was done, the SF funding and prestige almost certainly would dwindle.

In early December 1989, Cleveland's plan was approved and the Special Forces had their missions and the schedule for executing them. Task Force Black, the Special Forces' command structure for the war, was formed by melding the staffs of 3rd Battalion and the Special Operations Command South. Cleveland, even though he was the most junior officer, was the officer with the most detailed grasp of all the moving parts that were about to be set in motion.

Task Force Black still lacked a command post. The logistics officer found a vacant hangar on Albrook Air Station, one of the military bases lining the Panama Canal. The hangar's second-floor conference area was divided into a planning area and operations center. Two small tables sat in the middle, a few feet from the banks of radios that blared a cacophony of transmissions from the field. The off-duty officers slept under the tables, where they could be quickly roused. Downstairs the ODAs took over and marked out their territory with equipment and cots, while the final countdown to war began. War was not inevitable, but President George H.W. Bush was very close to making the decision.

Even as the preparations for war were being made, the Special Forces continued with their other assigned missions. At midnight on December 18, Higgins went to Howard air base on the canal for a trip he was scheduled to make to Bolivia to check on the Special Forces there. The senior official he was supposed to accompany did not show up and, finally, at 3 a.m., Higgins called headquarters. "Don't you know what's happening?" the officer said. "Go to Albrook right away."

When Higgins arrived, the hangar was abuzz. The president had given the order to launch Operation Just Cause. His decision had been triggered by the killing of a U.S. soldier by Panamanian troops, but it would not be made public until the action was under way. Higgins' ODAs, which had trained for the special reconnaissance missions planned by Cleveland, had gone to relieve the teams in El Salvador and Bolivia. The teams returning from El Salvador had just landed at Albrook. Higgins called them while their plane was still on the tarmac, and said: "Don't go to your barracks, and don't go home. Drive your pallets of gear over here right away."

Higgins went to see what kinds of last-minute adjustments were being made to Cleveland's plans. One of the truisms of war is that no plan survives first contact. It is impossible to envision every scenario, so a plan is merely the blueprint which must then be tailored to reality as events unfold. The plan had been to put one of Higgins' reconnaissance teams at the Pacora Bridge, which sat midway between Tocumen Airport and the Cimarron Cuartel, where some of Noriega's best and most loyal fighters were quartered. The reconnaissance team was supposed to watch the fighters' movements and report if or when they came to Noriega's aid.

As the clock ticked toward H-Hour on December 19, the task force decided that a more sizable force was needed to be able to stop Noriega's forces at the bridge, a natural chokepoint, if they came out to fight. Two Ranger battalions were to jump in to secure the other two major concentrations of Noriega's crack forces, one at Rio Hato, where a unit of well-trained Panamanian commandos was based, the other at Tocumen, the main military and civilian airport. Higgins would later wonder why the 3rd Ranger Battalion did not jump into Cimarron, as it held the third major concentration of troops most likely to fight. The Rangers, the U.S. military's premier light infantry force, were specifically designed to seize large targets like airfields and bases. The kind of direct actions that the Special Forces are suited for are quick in-and-out strikes where their smaller units can prevail.

There was no time to wonder about this on December 19. Higgins had to cobble together as sizeable a force as possible, and hold the bridge as best he could. He picked three captains and a total of twenty-four men, with himself as mission leader. If Noriega's men came out of Cimarron, Higgins and his men might face as many as 800 opponents.

Operation Just Cause was scheduled to begin at 1 A.M. At 12:30 A.M. Higgins and his men headed to the helipad for the twenty-five-minute flight to Pacora when, suddenly, all hell broke loose. From the highway next to Albrook Air Station, a busload of armed Panamanians opened fire at soldiers and the Task Force Black hangar. Word of the invasion had obviously leaked.

Rounds ricocheted through the aluminum hangar and off the cement floor. The Special Forces had already removed the grates from the drainage ditches outside the hangar so they could use them as trenches. The men ran from the hangar, jumped into the ditches, and started shooting back—with a barrage so intense it set a nearby warehouse on fire.

The intelligence officer ran up to Higgins on the helipad. "We just got reports that a convoy, a ten-vehicle convoy, is leaving Cimarron Cuartel for Panama City," he said. "H-hour has been moved up fifteen minutes." Higgins told his three captains and they scrambled into the waiting UH–60 Black Hawk helicopters. He put on the headset to hear the pilot tell him that he'd have to set down on the west side of the bridge, not the east as they had intended. The original landing zone was not big enough for three Black Hawks to set down at once. It turned out to be a fortuitous change of plans. The pilots flew to Pacora directly over Panama City and not, as originally planned, circling around it. From the air, Higgins saw the Panamanian convoy's headlights approaching the east end of the bridge. It was a race to see who would get there first.

Battle at Pacora Bridge

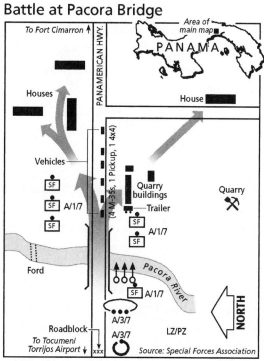

A/3/7 = Alpha Company, 3rd Battalion, 7th Special Forces Group

It was a tie. The Black Hawks swooped down and the men tumbled out just as the first trucks in the convoy hit the east side of the bridge. The men had to scramble up a thirty-foot-high bank from their landing spot to reach the bridge. Higgins's radio operator grabbed one of their AT-4 light antitank weapons and jumped up onto the bridge to fire it. The missile sliced under the truck and bounced off the bridge like a skipping stone. In the dark they could not see if it hit anything, but the explosion caused the first truck in the convoy to slam to a halt. One of the captains, John McNamara, fired off a second AT-4.

Higgins had ordered his men to take turns stepping out onto the bridge to fire their eight antitank missiles. He had seen a Salvadoran guerrilla commander's head blown off by the backblast of a rocket-propelled grenade. Even such a veteran in the heat of battle could forget just how deep and wide the danger zone is—which varies depending on the type of weapon. A rocket-propelled grenade has a backblast extending about thirty meters back in a triangular cone that is fifteen meters wide at the farthest extremity. Higgins had no idea what the backblast of the new AT-4 would be, because antitank backblasts ranged from five to forty meters and some had front blast ranges as well. So he took no chances and kept all but one man off the bridge. Fratricide, death by "friendly fire," was the unheralded killer lurking on every battlefield.

A third man scrambled to the bridge to take his turn once McNamara was clear. The AT-4 had only been issued to them a few hours earlier. They had been quickly instructed in how to expand its telescoping tubes, aim it, and fire it. With its 84-mm charge, the lightweight, recoilless, one-shot weapon could penetrate most armor from up to 300 meters away. It would become their standard antitank weapon because it was so portable—weighing only fifteen pounds—and easy to use. By the time the third missile was fired, the Panamanians were either dead inside the vehicles or had fled from the trucks and begun a flanking movement to the sides. In the darkness Higgins could not see all the vehicles, but the rumbling engine of one sounded like an armored personnel carrier. He braced for its heavy caliber guns to be turned on them as his three units, each led by a captain, took up their designated positions. One faced east to the bridge, the second element was in the middle with Higgins, and the third unit faced west to defend the flanks and against any forces arriving from Panama City.

A U.S. AC–130 Spectre gunship appeared overhead almost immediately. The SF had not known whether they would get any air cover. The war commanders had cut the gunship loose from Tocumen, where the Rangers were parachuting onto the tarmac. The air force combat controller attached to Higgins's unit made contact with it right away. "I've got commo," he shouted to Higgins. "He can't fire unless you approve danger close." As the ground commander, Higgins would direct the fire, and in this case he would have to authorize the overriding of safety regulations. Normally the AC–130s were barred from firing their guns if friendly forces were 175 meters or less away: this was "danger close." Higgins's men were only 100 meters away from the Panamanians. But twenty-four men were not going to be able to hold off the larger force on their own. "Bring it on," Higgins said, and then told his men to get down.

The AC–130 let loose its awesome firepower. Its 25-mm guns and 40-mm cannons rained down on the convoy. The pilot then began stitching up and down the eastern side of the bridge. With his infrared radar the pilot detected men running toward the river and alerted the SF. The attackers would have a clear shot at the Americans dug in on the side of the embankment. Higgins kept them at bay by periodically raking the elephant grass with gunfire. At dawn they would find the AC–130's unexploded ordnance all around them—they might have been killed by Higgins's order to bring the gunship's fire in that close, but it was a risk he had to take. But at least they had had a small margin of maneuver. If their helicopters had landed as planned on the east side of the bridge, they would have been right in the middle of the Panamanian force. The gunship would not have been able to fire on the Panamanians without also hitting them. They would have had to fight the entire battle on their own.

The battle continued for the next several hours. Traffic began coming from Panama City and Tocumen. Higgins had his men fire off to one side to see whether the vehicles would stop; instead they turned and fled. Then a military convoy came rolling down the highway from the west—and kept coming. Things started to look bad for the two dozen men, who were on foot, exposed, and sandwiched in between two units: the troops from Cimarron to their east and now this new force. Higgins's air force controller called for help and a second AC–130 arrived to orbit over the convoy, which then turned back. A little while later four Panamanian soldiers came over the bridge from the east, wearing gas masks and carrying a mortar tube. Higgins wondered if Noriega had obtained some kind of chemical weapons from Qaddafi. His men had no protective masks of their own. Two sergeants, Dana Bowman and Jose Roman, leaped onto the bridge and fired at the four men. Two fell dead and the others jumped over the side of the bridge.

Later, the Special Forces soldiers heard rustling sounds underneath the bridge. Were Panamanians under there preparing to counterattack? Bowman threw a hand grenade under the bridge and Roman fired. The noise ceased. When the sun came up, they could hear a man groaning under the bridge. Sgt. Roman, a medic, went down to patch him up. Roman had shot him in one leg, and the other had been broken in his fall from the bridge.

The Panamanian had a paycheck in his pocket, and asked Roman to take it for safekeeping. Roman delivered it to him about a week later at the POW clinic where he was recuperating. For years afterward, his comrades would rib Roman about shooting and then patching up the same man—who was grateful enough for the latter that he forgave the former. The Special Forces combat medics have the same role as any other soldier during hostilities. If their own men are wounded, they stop fighting and administer first aid, and once the fighting is over they will treat the opposing side's wounded. The medics' year-long training includes stints both in trauma rooms and performing emergency surgery.

Roman's experience epitomized the many contradictions of the war in Panama. Until 1987 the two countries had been very close allies. Indeed, Panama had been something of a U.S. protectorate created for the construction of the canal, and the United States military had built and trained the Panamanian force. The ties were deep, historical, and even familial. Quite a few U.S. servicemen, including Special Forces, had married Panamanian women, some of whose brothers were serving in the Panamanian Defense Force (PDF).

Higgins's men were hunkered down around the bridge about 4 A.M. when a PDF soldier came peddling across the bridge on a bike. He refused orders to halt, so the men shot the tires out. The Panamanian had seen the PDF trucks and thought they were on nighttime maneuvers; he had no idea a war had started. Another SF company came to reinforce Higgins at dawn, and they carried out a sweep of the opposite side of the bridge. Cleveland landed in their helicopter and relieved the soldiers of the prisoners they had taken so far. When the Americans searched the other side of the river, they found seventeen soldiers who had stripped off their uniforms and hid in surrounding homes. Cars streaming out of the city held fleeing civilians, but others were full of young men who had stashed automatic rifles in the trunks.

That afternoon, the 82nd Airborne came rolling up in its Sheridan tanks. The Special Forces radioed to them that the area was secure, but the tank drivers had to maneuver according to their battle script and roll on to Cimarron, which by then was empty. At about 5 P.M., Higgins's men and the rest of their prisoners were flown back to Albrook.

The PDF quickly disintegrated as an organized fighting force, but no one knew whether Noriega loyalists would continue to fight from the shadows. Noriega had gone underground. To prevent Noriega or his loyalists from broadcasting appeals for violent resistance, a commando raid had been launched at the invasion's start to disable the television transmitter on Cerro Azul. Panama's official Radio Nacional was still on the air the following day, broadcasting from the Contraloria building along the Panama City waterfront. The mission for halting its transmission went to Higgins's fellow company, Charlie Company of 3rd Battalion, which specialized in raids and close-quarter battle. Its commander, Major David McCracken, an enthusiastic dynamo with ice-blue eyes and a perpetually hoarse voice, led the quickly planned assault with thirty-three men at 6 P.M. on H-day, December 20. One team landed in front to provide security while McCracken and his men fast-roped onto the building's flat roof. As the helicopters flew away, the men realized there was no door or hatch leading from the roof into the building.

While Panamanians in neighboring high-rise buildings stared at a scene that could have come from a movie, McCracken and his black-suited men rappelled off the edge of the roof to an undercut terrace on the floor below, then ran across the terrace, through an empty cafeteria, and into the stairwell. They descended and turned corners in an orchestrated flow, covering each other's blind spots as they went. Captain Robert Louis led the demolition team down to the seventh floor where the radio station was located and found it vacant. They taped explosive charges to every transmitter node they could find and detonated them. As they raced downstairs to leave, it was reported that AM transmissions had stopped but FM transmissions continued.

Louis and his team went back up the stairwell and found that an electrical fire had started. They located two fire extinguishers, but neither worked. They shot at the circuit board to disable the equipment, but the growing fire and smoke forced them out. Finally, they radioed for the helicopters and raced to the landing zone near the U.S. embassy, a white Mediterranean-style building on Balboa Avenue. Panama City was the Casablanca of Latin America, but it had not seen such a show for a long time.

Out in the countryside, Noriega's second-in-command, Colonel Luis del Cid, was publicly threatening to mount a guerrilla war from his base in the second-largest city of David. Task Force Black mulled over its next steps. Cleveland leafed through intelligence reports and back-channel messages that indicated Noriega's lieutenants might actually be ready to give up the fight, although some attempts to elicit surrender had been met with gunfire. "Why don't we just call them on the phone?" Cleveland suggested. The Special Forces had the phone numbers of all the barracks, most of which Cleveland had visited in the past two years. The Americans could call the Panamanian commander at each one and give him an ultimatum to surrender peacefully. An intell officer warmed to the idea, saying, "Why don't we call it the Ma Bell operation?" It was decided that Higgins's company would go to David to test the scheme on Col. Del Cid. Cleveland recalled that there was a pay phone at a school outside the base that he had once used to call his wife.

Over the next twenty-four hours, every time Higgins passed someone in the Albrook hangar he was given a quarter. They all knew the story of the 1983 Grenada invasion, in which a pinned-down unit had no radio and no coins, so they couldn't even use the pay phone to call for help. Higgins let them fill his pocket with quarters, but he realized that only Cleveland knew exactly where the telephone was. The scheme required them to be very close to the base when they called, so they could move in quickly if the Panamanian commander decided to bolt. Why take a chance of not finding the phone when they had Charlie right there? Cleveland was delighted to have another chance to get out from behind the planning board and into the field.

On Christmas Day they flew to David, refueling en route. One Black Hawk put Higgins and Cleveland down near the schoolhouse. The plan was to give Del Cid one hour to turn over the cuartel and the airfield. If the barrels of the anti-aircraft ZSU guns at the airfield were still pointed skyward by the time the Rangers arrived one hour later, they would assault both compounds. Higgins dropped a quarter into the phone's coin slot. No dial tone. Another quarter. No luck. After a few more quarters, he began punching the phone, bloodying his knuckles but getting no other result.

An old man in a straw hat sat reading on a bench nearby, seemingly unperturbed by the helicopters hovering overhead. Finally he looked up. "Do you need a phone? There's one in the school." The men raced to the schoolhouse door and prepared to break it down. "Hold on," the man called, shuffling after them. "I have the keys. I'm the janitor." Once in, Higgins and Cleveland called Del Cid from the principal's office. "What day would you like to come?" the Panamanian asked. He was told that he had one hour to surrender before the Rangers arrived. Del Cid agreed and he asked for time to clear the airfield.

When Higgins, Cleveland, and the other Special Forces soldiers arrived, hundreds of Panamanians were cheering and waving small flags. They surrounded the group of thirty Special Forces soldiers as they entered the cuartel. Colonel Del Cid, one of Noriega's most notorious sidekicks, blithely agreed that there might be some changes ahead in the Panamanian government. He continued in this surreal vein, saying that he did not want his men to give up their guns. Higgins told him that there was a meeting in Panama to discuss these future matters, and Del Cid said he would like to attend. Because Higgins was so cordial, the Noriega loyalist got on the helicopter, apparently believing that he would be treated as one of the brokers of the country's future, even though he was named in the same indictment for drug trafficking as Noriega. The next day at Howard air base, Del Cid was hustled onto a plane bound for Miami, protesting all the way that he had been double-crossed.

While Higgins and Cleveland were sweet-talking Del Cid, the other Special Forces were rushing to clear the airfield before the Rangers arrived. The men raced around, pushing all the ZSU–23 barrels toward the ground before the hour was up. They lined up every Panamanian commando, soldier, and airfield employee so there would be no chance of mistaking stray movements for hostilities. The Special Forces took very seriously the Ranger commander's vow to assault.

The 3rd Battalion of the 75th Ranger Regiment was disappointed at the loss of its only assault opportunity in Just Cause. The "Ma Bell take-downs" nevertheless proved to be a great success at cuartels around Panama. Higgins and his men spent the following days taking down the provincial posts outside David, including a border post manned by an anti-Noriega guerrilla squad. Rangers or 7th Infantry troops and an AC–130 were nearby to back them up if needed.

The Ma Bell takedowns became one of the most famous innovations of Just Cause. It was a dramatic demonstration of what the Special Forces meant by calling themselves an "economy of force" organization. Small teams could accomplish the work of entire battalions and, as often as not, they would find some ingenious way to do it with no shots fired. That meant fewer casualties, fewer widows, fewer grievances, fewer insurgents. It was a simple equation. Just because they carried guns did not mean they were compelled to use them. In fact, merely carrying the guns could be enough.

The entire Panamanian military eventually was demobilized and written out of the constitution, and a new police force installed. In the first weeks after the intervention, however, the Special Forces used the available force to keep a modicum of order. Those senior PDF officers who had been charged or suspected of crimes, like Del Cid, were detained, but most often the Special Forces just instructed the foot sol-diers on the new rules of the game and had them resume their duties. As a result, the countryside remained peaceful and there was none of the looting that plagued Panama City. Granting that Panama was a tiny country with a long association with the United States, the postwar tran-sition was remarkably rapid and peaceful.

In January 1990, Just Cause rolled into Operation Promote Liberty, the name given to the formal postwar stabilization mission that largely was performed by the Special Forces. As operations officer for 7th Group, Major Geoffrey Lambert had warned that the military was not ready to implement the postwar plan to fill the vacuum on day two, when everything from the police to customs to the Noriega-controlled taxi union fell apart. Putting a country back together is part of the conflict, in the Special Forces' view. War is not just the period between when the shooting begins and when it ends.

In this phase, Higgins and his company were ordered to work in the environs of Panama City. He was sorry to leave the cool, coffee-growing hills around David, because his men had established strong rapport with the locals and were helping the province back to its feet. But with half the population of the country residing in Panama City, the capital, a few miles from the canal, the area could not be ignored. Former Noriega cronies including an armed paramilitary group were still stirring up trouble. Higgins assigned one of his best captains, John McNamara, to San Miguelito, which was the largest poor suburb of Panama City and a hotbed of crime and unrest. If anyone could handle it, his silver-tongued fellow Irishman could. McNamara had a perpetually upbeat personality; had Higgins sent him to the gates of hell, he would have gone whistling. For his part, Higgins, with his easy charm and fluent Spanish, captured the hearts of the Chorrera residents, who declared him their mayor.

Special Forces teams fanned out all over Panama to provide security, governance, and administration in the months ahead. One of the young sergeants, Tom Rosenbarger, was on his first tour and fell hard for Latin America and the SF way of life. It would not be the first time an American southerner recognized the warmth and congeniality common to both cultures. "Rosie" was an interesting package; he had a blond brush cut, pink cheeks, and a gleaming smile of big white teeth. He inherited a Sicilian toughness from his mother's side, but it was sheathed in a velvety southern charm. When his authority was questioned or his territory was infringed, he could put the hammer down hard. Rosie and his teammates worked in Rio Serrano and the northern towns around David to demobilize the old PDF, stand up a new police force, and oversee infrastructure projects. Rosie's team lived not on a base but in a house they rented and, to his great delight, their daily diet was Pana-manian food instead of military rations. The more Panamanians the teams came into contact with, the better sense they had of the popular sentiment and how well the reconstruction effort was proceeding. The conventional military pulled out quickly, but they stayed behind to fol-low through.

Also helping out in Panama's Atlantic provinces was the 7th Infantry Division. One of its lieutenants was Tony Martin, a former SF sergeant who had become an officer despite breaking his back, and who was return-ing to the Special Forces as soon as he completed his obligatory conven-tional tour. He was a tough customer, with jet black hair and a piercing intellect. Two days after Just Cause ended, Martin's commander went down in a helicopter during a storm just east of David. The raging tropical weather and the shock of losing their leader disoriented some around him, but Martin took charge. He made a call and got a rescue crew flying from Florida. He then led a twelve-hour search mission into the jungle and found his commander's body on a hillside. Mindful of his young troops' grief, he put the captain in a body bag before he and the company com-mander carried him down to the helicopter. Martin was admonished for taking the initiative but he didn't care. He knew he'd done the right thing.

Although Just Cause succeeded, relatively few medals were awarded to soldiers. The army had been criticized for lavishing medals in other conflicts, so commanders were determined that the victory in Panama not be tarnished by such allegations. Better to have the mission quietly accomplished than have it noisily criticized. Nonetheless, Sergeants Bowman and Roman and another sergeant received Bronze Star medals with the valor device for their actions at Pacora Bridge. It was not until the year 2000 that McCracken won for his men the right to wear the bronze arrowhead for their combat assault on Radio Nacional in Panama City. In his typically tireless fashion, he kept prodding the bureaucracy as he rose in rank to become commander of 3rd Group. In the case of El Salvador, Congress did not approve any combat awards until 1998, six years after the war had ended. A Silver Star was awarded to a soldier who had staved off one of the San Miguel brigade attacks.

In Special Forces circles, legends count as much as medals, and the Pacora bridge battle became an oft-told tale of improvisation against a numerically superior force, especially because it was the first combat mission since Vietnam. Twenty-four men backed up by gunships had accomplished the job of a Ranger battalion. Higgins became known as a leader who looked out for his men and who did not seek the spotlight for himself. One of those commanders who men will follow anywhere, he possessed the mix of cultural finesse and warrior skills prized by the Special Forces. For his role in Salvador, Panama, and the fights to come, he became the role model for a whole generation of young Green Berets.

Just Cause was a watershed for the Special Forces, because they played significant roles in both combat and the critical postwar stabilizing missions. The Special Forces were the logical choice for key roles in both phases because they knew Panama so well. They had been posted there for twenty-five years, first under Bull Simons' command.

Unlike Just Cause, El Salvador would never be widely recognized as the success story it was. The United States had fought a successful counterinsurgency but only the men on the ground knew it. They had done it largely by helping their allied country, not by fighting themselves. After the FMLN's "final offensive" failed in 1989, the guerrillas began seriously negotiating and a peace accord was reached in 1992.

The Special Forces' world is a small club, closed to outsiders but a hothouse atmosphere within. They are a tribe, bound by shared experiences in remote places, and equally strong antipathies. While some Special Forces' soldiers stayed in the same region, others would take the experiences from one group to fertilize those of another. Higgins, McNamara, Martin, and others would stay in 7th Group, while Cleveland and Rosenbarger would wind up in different groups but together again years later in Iraq. From Panama, Cleveland went to staff college and then to 10th Group, where he became its commander and spent long years directing missions in the Balkans. Colonel Geoffrey Lambert, who helped plan Just Cause and Promote Liberty, would also leave 7th Group for 10th Group, which he commanded during the Balkans war before ascending to the command of all Special Forces. Martin would return to 7th Group, complete a Ph.D., teach at West Point, and later serve as General Lambert's intelligence officer during the war in Iraq. In the small community that is Special Forces, their career paths would often crisscross over the years, or they would hear through the SF grapevine of each others' doings at opposite ends of the world.

Those who stayed in one region, like Higgins, were anchors. The Higginses provided a formidable store of institutional knowledge that fed the groups' regional expertise. They developed a breadth and depth of understanding rivaled by few officials in the government, because they worked out in the field and not behind embassy walls or in air-conditioned cars. In El Salvador, the Special Forces studied the local health, economic, legal, educational, and security needs in the province where they were assigned. A counterinsurgency effort cannot succeed unless it addresses every facet of peoples' lives. To extend the Clausewitzian metaphor, politics and social work and land reform is war by other means, when it is recognized that the battlefield is human, not territorial. The ability to understand a situation and work using the local population was a priceless skill. In the no man's land between Peru and Ecuador, where Higgins went to help the two countries disengage from a deep-seated rivalry that had broken out into war, he became so beloved that one border village actually renamed itself Higginsville. He used local indigenous customs to get the two warring countries to look at themselves in a new way. Hollywood could have its Colonel Kurz; the Special Forces had Kevin Higgins. There was something about long, tall Kevin—with his crooked smile and boxer-bashed nose—that Latins just found irresistible.

As 1990 unfolded, it turned out that the men of 5th Group who were cramming their Spanish-language textbooks did not get a chance to use them down south. The rumblings in the Middle East suddenly overwhelmed the demand for their services. Iraq, which had been hectoring and threatening Kuwait throughout the first seven months of 1990, overran its small southern neighbor in less than forty-eight hours on August 2. Randy, Chris, Warren, and other soldiers of 5th Group were off to a war of their own.

CHAPTER 4

DESERT STORM

Invincibility depends on oneself; the enemy's vulnerability on him.

—SUN TZU

RANDY TOOK his grandfather's medicine bag out of his dresser drawer. He untied the doeskin pouch and slid its contents into his hand—a piece of the oldest tree in America, an Indian tear quartz, a heart stone. They were his icons too. He wondered what war would be like. He'd worn the army uniform for seven years and been through the highest-caliber training programs it offered. Now he would be tested, for the first time, in a real-world operation. Would he measure up to the warrior tradition when the bullets were fired to kill? Would he keep his head in the chaos of war? He stacked his rucksack and canvas duffel by the door of his Tennessee home and spent the last couple of hours with his wife. He held her close, his heart sorry to leave, but his mind was already racing across the ocean to Saudi Arabia.

The Saudi desert in August is one of the hottest places on the planet. Temperatures reach 120 degrees daily. The Special Forces landed at King

Fahd air base and then went to King Khalid Military City. Some stayed there and others went north to the border with Kuwait and Iraq. First Battalion was ordered to link up with Saudi troops to defend any thrust that Saddam Hussein might make into Saudi territory; Conner and a young sergeant named Steve Rainey drew that duty. Second Battalion would advise and train Arab coalition armies; Killer was first assigned to the Syrians and later to the Egyptians. Third Battalion was assigned to work with the Kuwaitis. Randy and Warren drew this mission. They were sent to a secret camp out in the desert to prepare the Kuwaiti special forces and accompany them on a raid into Iraqi-occupied Kuwait City. The American military machine would deliver the bulk of the fighting power, but the plan was for Arab forces to play visible, frontline roles in the liberation of Kuwait.

Randy and ODA 574 arrived at their isolated camp, a few canvas tents surrounded by nothing but sand as far as the eye could see. They set up a training schedule, not knowing how long they would have to accomplish their mission. The war preparations alone might convince Saddam Hussein to pull out of Kuwait. The team began drilling the Kuwaitis in the new weapons and tactics being provided.

One day, not long after training started, the intelligence sergeant lifted the flap and ducked into the team's tent. Randy was sitting on his cot with a dejected expression, so the sergeant asked him what was wrong. "They hate me," Randy said. "I'm a total failure." The sergeant peeled off his sweat-soaked T-shirt and sat down on the opposite cot. Randy and several other sergeants on the team were on their first overseas deployment and had never dealt with foreign troops before. The intelligence sergeant had come straight into the Special Forces as one of the "SF babies," so he'd been dealing with foreigners since his career began. It often required unbending the ramrod-straight stick-to-the-book standard army attitude—especially in Arab countries where physical labor was scorned.

"You're killin' 'em, man. You've got that hooah Ranger attitude," the sergeant suggested.

"They don't like working, that's for sure," Randy said.

"Just loosen up and try having a little fun," his teammate urged.

The Kuwaitis had certainly been friendly to the Americans. As a welcome gesture, they had found a toilet seat somewhere and nailed it to the slats of the latrine floor. They knew that Americans didn't use the squat-style toilets common in the Middle East, so they thought Americans might like to sit on the ground if they gave them a seat. The team thought it was hilarious and took pictures to send home.

It wasn't just his Ranger background that made Randy so relentless. His first team sergeant when he got to ODA 574 was without a doubt the hardest-driving individual he had ever come up against. For the past year he'd had them behave as if they were in a war zone. It didn't matter if they were walking down the road, he had them doing it as if they were stalking or evading. After their HALO jumps, they would never just roll up their chutes and walk off the drop zone. They went into a battle drill and covered each other, moving in formation. They did PT in full combat gear. Because Randy was the weapons sergeant, the team sergeant would have him load up all the claymores, grenades, and belts of ammunition that he would take into battle and run with it. If they saw a telephone pole lying on the ground, he would make them pick it up and run with it for miles.

That year, quite a few men left the team. The team sergeant took a special interest in grooming Randy. He picked him up every day and drove him to work; he also loaned him field manuals from his own collection. Randy knew that the team sergeant's methods were extreme, but he also understood what he was trying to achieve. Constant drilling would etch soldiering skills into the men until the skills became reflexes. Randy only had one quibble with his team sergeant: he would not ease up even when men were injured. Not allowing the body time to recuperate could inhibit recovery or cause a more serious or permanent problem.

Randy had learned his team sergeant's lessons and survived them, but the current situation called for something other than toughing it out. He was dealing with foreigners, so he recalled the Q course lessons on unconventional warfare—working through and with foreign allies. There it was, it had been drummed into them: rapport-building. He needed to make friends first.

The next day Randy tied a bandanna around his head. It was the beginning of the Rawhide act: he was going to win the Kuwaitis over with a little razzle-dazzle. He gave them a machine-gun demonstration that Buffalo Bill would have wanted in his Wild West extravaganza.

"This is what you can do with practice," he said. Standing fifty meters from the mark, he hoisted a Soviet RPK machine gun to his shoulder and let off a controlled burst, showing them how to home in on a target with the gun on automatic mode. They were teaching the Kuwaiti commandos on all-new Soviet-made equipment.

He moved back fifty meters, then fifty more; each time showing them how the gun could be controlled in steady streams. This technique was used for suppressive fire, to keep the other side's heads down. The brass casings piled up around his ankles as he systematically mowed down the targets. The Kuwaitis clapped and whistled in appreciation.

"Now, it's your turn."

Randy then divided the group into competing squads and staged the rest of the day as a round-robin tournament. First they had to learn how to hit the target with the gun on semi-automatic single-shot mode. He stapled new paper targets to the plywood planks.

The transformation in his image and his audience was complete by day's end. The Kuwaitis hooted and hollered for their teammates, and they didn't even stop working at the usual midday mark. Soon other platoons were dropping by, asking when they would get to come onto the range. Randy was delighted with his newfound popularity.

Enough Kuwaitis spoke English that they usually had all the interpretation help that they needed. But Warren Foster, Randy's teammate and one of 5th Group's best Arabic speakers, had also made up mnemonic cards for their classes. Similar to flash cards, they were combinations of pictures and English words that would remind them of the correct pronunciation of key Arabic words. All Randy and the others had to do was remember connecting phrases like "and then do this." Then they would physically demonstrate how to perform the action on the named piece of equipment, for example, how to take the barrel apart, align the mortar, or clear a jammed ammunition cartridge.

On Christmas day, the Special Forces trained the Kuwaitis as if it were any other day. As the day ended, one of the Kuwaitis heard the Americans talk about Christmas and was amazed that the Americans had worked on one of their holiest days. A little later, some of the Kuwaitis piled into one of the trucks and drove off. The desert grew chill with the setting sun. ODA 574 built its usual fire of camel dung and sat around to chat. The dried camel dung made Randy think of his Blackfoot ancestors who had used buffalo chips for fuel because there were no trees on the American great plains.

"If you could have any present you wanted, what would you pick?" someone asked. They went around the circle. Nobody would have admitted it, but they were homesick. They had no mail delivery up there on the border, so there were no letters and certainly no presents. "Big Rich," the team's medic, got up and went into the tent. He came back and handed each man a small box.

"Merry Christmas, brothers," he said.

Some time ago, back in King Khalid, he had ordered everyone locking jackknives, ingenious and sturdy little tools. Maybe he'd foreseen that they'd be out there, waiting for war to start, four months later. It was a thoughtful gesture of friendship just when the men needed it, out in that lonely desert among foreign troops.

A little while later the Kuwaitis drove up and invited the soldiers to their campground a couple hundred yards away. They had roasted a goat in honor of the Americans' holiday. The crispy brown meat was surrounded by vegetables and sprinkled with deliciously aromatic spices. Randy was grateful for their generosity and, particularly, the form it took. He had been struggling with the boiled meat, rice, and vegetables they'd been given so far. He never wanted to eat another boiled piece of food again. These two small acts made it a Christmas he would remember for years. Not having much made one appreciate what there was, not a bad lesson for the corners of the world where he would be spending his life from now on.

In early January, the secret mission of ODA 574 and the Kuwaiti special forces was cancelled. The war planners had decided that it was not feasible. The team and the Kuwaiti commandos were to have flown into the heart of Kuwait City in the stealthy special-operations helicopters and then seized their target. But the planners feared that the SF and Kuwaitis would not be able to hold it against a concerted counterattack by Iraqi tanks until American forces arrived to reinforce them. Randy and his teammates were crestfallen. War looked increasingly imminent, as Saddam Hussein had shown no sign of leaving Kuwait and the United Nations' deadline was only weeks away. Their team had no mission. They felt like thoroughbreds who'd been led to the gate only to be told they couldn't race. It was an early lesson in the nature of the commando business: for every operation that gets a green light, many more never get off the ground. The crisis may pass, the intelligence may not be adequate, the risks may be deemed too high, or some other unit could get the mission—and sometimes they never learn the reason why.

After a week or so, ODA 574 was sent to a camp outside Dhahran and ordered to train a newly formed group called the Badr Brigade. It was a collection of politically connected Kuwaiti civilians that the emir had assembled and insisted be given a prominent and early role in the fight. He had grown concerned that the Kuwaiti military might see the war as a chance to take power, or at least that was the rumor. The Badr Brigade contained everything from businessmen to twelve-year-old boys to a seventy-year-old shepherd from an important tribe—but no regular soldiers. What could be done with them in a few short weeks? The Special Forces have all kinds of sayings like "Give me a penknife and a two-by-four and I'll build you a house." If they could turn this motley crew into a militia in three weeks they would have a Robin Sage story that might even impress old Joe Lupyak.

Captain Chris Conner's mission had also changed. His team, ODA 532, had been training the Saudi's mechanized 10th Battalion near the Saudi-Kuwaiti border, but in early January it was recalled to King Fahd for a top-secret assignment. The Red Dragon alerts started, signaling inbound

Scud missiles. Saddam was not turning tail. Conner was to take half of his team on a special reconnaissance (SR) mission. SR was a specialty of the teams whose numbers end in two (just as HALO teams ended in four and scuba teams in five). Their mission was to spot any signs of a counterattack against the big left hook that the U.S. Army was about to punch into southern Iraq.

Conner was perfect for reconnaissance missions. Unflappable as they come, he could sit in a hide site for four days without losing his mind. His teammates' personalities were also important; he needed to select two trios of the most compatible men for extreme close-quarter living. They were going to dig a hole in the desert and crawl into it, and once inside they would not leave until their mission was accomplished. They would crap in baggies and pee in bottles and breathe each other's bad breath. Both of the communications sergeants had to go along, one in each trio, because the point of the mission was to send back information. Conner chose one of the engineers to complete his group and told his team sergeant to lead the other one.

The next step was to rehearse rapid hide site construction. There were a variety of techniques, so they had to experiment to determine which would work best for this mission. They also had to divide the tasks and practice to see just how fast they could do it. They took turns, two men digging while one stood guard. When the pit was big enough for three men and their gear, they ringed the pit with sandbags. Constructing the top was the tricky part. They set up a frame that looked something like an umbrella, put two pieces of plywood over it, then placed a tarp, burlap, and sand on top of that. They would squeeze into a small opening they had left and then pull a bush over the hole. The goal was to finish an hour or so before first light so that the wind would blow the sand over the structure in natural contours. Any signs of artificiality could give them away.

There were no second chances on reconnaissance missions. A small error could lead to the team being discovered. If compromised, the team, in all probability, would have to flee to another location or pull out entirely, and then there might be no way to conduct surveillance, collect intelligence, and send it back. The chances of having to engage in a firefight were high and getting out, always the most difficult part of a reconnaissance mission, was immeasurably harder.

With stakes that high, none of Conner's men lacked motivation, even though the heat of the Saudi desert was blistering. After a couple weeks' practice, the two three-man teams could build an undetectable hide site in three hours' time. Each trio took turns trying to discover the others' hole. That little tumbleweed bush might mark the exit and air hole, or it might not. When Conner was able to survey the wind-sculpted dunes that stretched in front of him, knowing the men were in there but unable to say where, he knew they were ready.

An U-2 air force spy plane overflew their flight path and landing zones in Iraq and reported that all was clear. The night before the ground war started, Conner and his men boarded the special operations MH–53J Pave Low helicopter, a $40-million 21-ton machine that was crammed with top-secret avionics and armed with 7.62-mm miniguns and .50-caliber machine guns. The two teams would be set down about four kilometers apart, so that if one was compromised the other could continue. The two turbo engines spun to a high scream and they lifted off. They crossed into Iraq flying 150 miles an hour and less than a hundred feet off the ground, skimming over fence tops. Every special operator who flew in these birds was awed by the skill of the Pave Low pilots, who sat in their blacked-out cockpits orchestrating a dozen different navigational systems with the help of two other crew members. The terrain-detecting terrain-avoiding radar and forward-looking infrared radar painted a ghostly electronic tunnel for the pilots as they flew into the pitch dark, watching their screens through the latest generation of night-vision goggles, or nods as they were commonly called.

Two minutes from the landing zone the pilot came on the headset.

"Ok, team leader. We're at the release point." A few seconds later he came back on.

"Camp left."

"Camp right."

"Guns left. Guns left. Camp right. Guns right."

All the way in the pilot called out bedouin camps and emplaced or mounted guns as he spotted them, none of which the U–2 had seen. Conner leaned out the open door into the rushing night air. He had on his nods too and verified everything the pilot was pointing out. So much for the assessment that this was an unpopulated area. Not tonight, anyway.

They reached the landing zone and the pilot said, "OK, team leader. It's your call."

Conner had to decide whether to proceed or cancel the mission. No one would have questioned a decision to cancel, with all the activity they had discovered down there on the ground. But they had practiced for three long weeks and were ready. Conner believed they could sneak around the bedouins.

"We're going."

"Roger that."

The pilot put the Pave Low down in the darkness, and lifted off only moments later.

The trio shouldered their enormous rucksacks. They carried the poles and all the material to construct their hide sites, as well as redundant communications gear and weapons that they would cache for emergency. They had to hurry to their designated site and dig in before daylight, a few hours away.

Conner focused his senses on the dark, the smells, on how close the nearest inhabitants were. He smelled animals, fire, trash, burned trash. He took a few steps and realized what he was walking on. It was not sand but earth, covered with vegetation, which meant roots. He knelt down and examined the ground.

They were in a winter wheat field. This was a far cry from the Saudi desert with its loose sand dunes. It would be impossible to dig seven-foot holes into this in the few hours they had. No U.S. soldier had previously set foot here, so their briefing reports had contained no firsthand intelligence. West of the Euphrates the Iraqi desert is fine dirt and rock-strewn *wadis* or draws, but east of the Euphrates there is enough water for the dirt to become soil that sustains vegetation.

Soldiers use the term "ground truth" as a metaphor for knowing what is really going on in a given country or situation: planning a military operation without the ground truth risked failure or disaster. Here, Conner thought, was a very literal demonstration of the term ground truth and what not having it meant.

The important thing now was to adjust course and find a way to accomplish the surveillance mission without digging a hide site. They had to find a position from which they could observe Highway 8 and construct some kind of cover before daylight revealed their presence to every bedouin in the Qwam al Hamza countryside. His team was hundreds of miles inside Iraq and hundreds of miles from any other U.S. troops. Now that they knew their plans would have to change, Conner told the communications sergeant to send a radio message that they would not be making the hide site at their pre-selected spot by the highway.

The dogs found them first. The pack circled and moved in, barking and howling furiously. Conner fired one shot over their heads to disperse them and prayed it would not rouse the bedouins from their camp. The team then stole away under the cover of night as fast as possible.

They cached their backup radio and other supplies, then crawled into the biggest bushes they could find and sat, back to back, covered with burlap. It was important that they be hidden by "first light," which was far more relevant for soldiers than dawn, when the sun actually appeared over the horizon. First light appeared a good hour before the sun. That day they sat as still as possible while the bedouin herded their sheep all around them. The snake-repellent-soaked burlap and their uniforms and socks, soaked in permethrin and snake repellent, must have acted as sheep repellent too.

Headquarters did not expect the first report from them for twenty-four hours after they arrived, so they had some time to gather information and decide on the best course of action. They could see people coming and going from the bedouin camp and along the highway, conducting their daily business. They saw no military activity so far. In the afternoon they saw a helicopter fly by in the distance. The men instantly thought of the other three-man team. Then they heard gunfire. Conner knew that if the other trio were in a firefight, the team sergeant would go down fighting and take a whole town or a battalion's worth of soldiers with him.

"If they're in a fight up there, I feel sorry for the Iraqis," Conner said to his men. He had no idea at the time how accurate his guess was. For three hours, the other trio held off about 150 armed Iraqis who had arrived after the Americans were discovered by a little girl and an old man they took to be her grandfather. A helicopter came in to extract them, slamming down onto the ground about fifty meters away from the Iraqis.

When the sun went down Conner's communications sergeant tried to get the SATCOM radio up and working, but for some reason he could not. Conner decided it was time to move. He found a location that he thought would do, equidistant from the nearest bedouin camps and with a vantage point to the highway. They had not been farther than 125 meters from armed Iraqis since the moment they hit the ground. Conner took up the shovel, and soon the chorus of bedouin dogs had started up again. After a while the engineer tapped him on the shoulder and said, "We can't stay here."

"Why's that?"

"See those tracers?"

The captain looked up and saw tracer bullets flying overhead. He could not tell if the bedouins were just shooting in the general direction the dogs were barking. No one seemed to be coming after them. Still, the sergeant was right, it was a risk they didn't need to take. They packed up to move on again.

A shallow irrigation ditch about three feet deep and next to a wheat field offered a natural hiding spot. They spotted a low palm tree with thick fronds that arched into the ditch all the way to the ground. They made for the frond tent and pulled their gear underneath it as well.

As day broke once more they could make out two footpaths that ran on either side of the ditch. People came walking down the trails in both directions, passing within feet of the three men. Once a dog poked his

head under the fronds and barked at them. Slowly Conner drew his
9–mm pistol, careful not to disturb their crude nest. The dog backed out
and turned away from the strange sight, then trotted along after his master, who strode by heedless.

In the early afternoon, people began shooting over their heads from
behind. Conner and the two sergeants could pick out the sound of three
or four AK–47s firing at regular intervals. Had they been seen? Had yes-
terday's firefight deterred the Iraqis from approaching them? Fearing the
worst, the engineer set a claymore mine out in front of them, as a last
act of defiance. Although its fearsome ball-bearings were pointed forward toward their presumed attackers, they could not be sure that at
that close range the explosion would not also maim them. But they were
not going to go down without a fight.

Sunset of the second day marked the approach of their next forty-
eight-hour reporting deadline. The communications sergeant, try as he
might, still was unable to get the radio working. They would have to
retrieve the spare radio they had cached the first night. When they
returned to that spot, they found that a bedouin tribe had moved in and
set up camp right on top of it. The sergeant swore that if they made it
out, he was going back to school to become a Special Forces medic, anything but an 18 Echo. "I am not going to be a communicator any more,"
the exasperated sergeant declared.

If the team did not make contact, the command back in Saudi Arabia
would assume that they had gone into escape and recovery mode. That
meant that they were to move to a pre-determined pickup zone where a
special ops helicopter would make a flyover to attempt recovery even if
they'd heard nothing from them. What the men in the Iraqi desert did
not know was that a giant sandstorm had just hit Saudi Arabia. Everything was fogged in and the helicopters were grounded—no helicopter
flew their escape and recovery corridor that night. The men grimly
wondered if the command had not read their plan. As their third dawn
approached, they set off to find a new hiding place.

They found a cluster of bushes and crawled into them. It was near
the highway so that if by some miracle their radio came to life, they

could call in reports. Conner kept careful track anyway. Buses full of Iraqis were being pulled back from the front. If the helicopter did not come tonight, they would attempt to get themselves back to friendly territory.

The men picked out a vehicle, a red pickup truck, that they would steal and drive west toward the Euphrates. It was parked in front of a walled compound holding four buildings, the typical hamlet where an entire clan lived. The men planned to cross over into the desert to a corridor designated for search and rescue flights. They still had to wait until nightfall, so they settled into their bush hideout.

Even after nightfall people continued to mill around. They would have to make their move soon. Three A.M. was the appointed hour, and it still was possible that a helicopter might come, because this was the general area they had planned to be operating in. But if none came, they would have to steal the truck and head for the river. They began packing up their gear.

Conner's temperament had helped them manage the constant stress of the last three days. His deadpan humor kept their spirits up and he never let them think that they were out of options. Conner was not about to show his concern to his sergeants, but he did wonder what had happened to those choppers. After tonight, all the available air support would be covering the ground forces' advance. If they were lucky, there would be no Iraqi forces flowing south, only troops falling back from Kuwait in headlong retreat. The trio had not seen any signs of reinforcements being readied along this north-south axis.

Conner's calculations were interrupted by the whir of helicopter blades. The engineer heard it at the same instant and grabbed the IZLID infrared strobe (a device resembling a flashlight) and dashed out into the field beside their bushes. The lead helicopter was gone but there was a second, and he waved the IZLID in a circle. The infrared beam caught the pilot's attention and he banked sharply to come back around. It was an MH-60 from the 160th "Nightstalkers" regiment. The pilot recognized his fellow special operators and dropped into field. The men had grabbed their gear and were ready to load. They ducked under the beating rotor blades, catapulted into the open side door, and were lifted up and out of Iraq. It had been the pilots' final pass in search of the team.

Conner later found out that the commander in charge of special operations forces for Central Command had told the pilot that the risks of flying that night outweighed the possible gains, and that there was no data to go on. "We haven't heard from these guys in three days. They're either dead or captured," he said. But the pilot had insisted.

The pilots of the army's 160th Special Operations Aviation Regiment were famous for dedication to getting the men in—and getting them out. As they flew out of Iraq, Conner told the pilot, "I will buy you a beer anytime, anywhere, on demand, for the rest of your life." As soon as they set down at King Fahd, Conner and the team were debriefed so that their information could be funneled to the ground commanders racing north and east into Kuwait and Iraq.

Staff Sergeants Steve Rainey and Jim Kilcoyne were both on ODAs that were assigned to accompany the Arab coalition armies into battle, Rainey with the Saudis and "Killer" Kilcoyne with the Egyptians. It was an important political statement that the Arab nations were willing to come together to defend another Arab country. But it was no small task to get them ready for battle and orchestrated to fight as one—with their different radios, tactics, and organizations.

Steve Rainey was a droll, cynical guy who never minced words. The Saudi national guard unit he wound up with was pretty inexperienced, but they were a far sight better than the Saudi infantry battalion his team, ODA 531, had started out with. The latter had actually marched in the wrong direction, toward the enemy lines just a few miles away, on a training maneuver. Rainey, with his caustic wit, found the humor in this potentially disastrous situation. He had to, because a perfectionist like him could go crazy otherwise. As it turned out, Rainey and his ODA took their Saudi partners through all the phases of standard infantry training including its culminating event, a live-fire battalion-size exercise. Live fire meant with real ammunition, not blanks, so they made sure that their allies were shooting in the right direction. The team had vastly improved the Saudi battalion's skills in a few short months, although Sergeant Rainey would never admit it. His tactic was to always ask for more time and more tools.

As the war plans continued to evolve, so did the assignment. After completing the training exercise, ODA 531 was reassigned to accompany a Saudi National Guard unit into the war. Unlike other countries, Saudi Arabia's guard actually was a more professional force than its regular army. It was assigned to protect the royal family and had received training from an American company called Vinnell for many years. Nonetheless, the Saudi culture does not rate the work ethic very highly, so the basic problem remained. Rainey's team began doing what it could in the few weeks that remained.

Just before the ground war was launched, the Iraqis launched a spoiling attack across Kuwait's border and overran the Saudi city of Khafji. The intent was to test the Saudi resolve and to disrupt the U.S. war plan. The Saudi National Guard unit that Rainey's team had been training was ordered to Khafji to repel the attack, but the unit did not move out. Finally, on a direct order from the king, it headed into the city just as the Iraqis were withdrawing.

By this time, Steve Rainey was philosophical. He had come into the army to make his mark in the world, but he understood that things were different in a country with 5,000 royal princes and the largest oil reserves on the planet. These people just weren't going to be the same as a nation of middle class and working folks, and they didn't have to be. He decided to save his fretting for the things he could do something about. The National Guard units that had received the most training from Vinnell had arrived promptly and fought well, so perhaps years of sustained effort could change cultural habits. Rainey and his unit stayed in Khafji while the United Nations deadline for Saddam Hussein to leave Kuwait came and went. The ground war began on February 23, and at the appointed hour Rainey, his team, and their Saudi unit rolled north from Khafji on the main highway and into Kuwait.

At the same time that Rainey's caravan struck out northward, Killer's team breached the western border of Kuwait with the Egyptian armored brigade they had been training. They had been based at Ar Ruqi for months, calling in CAS (close air support) on targets they spotted across the Iraqi border. Once inside Kuwait, the Egyptians' assigned route was to head north, then east, and stop at the hills on Kuwait City's western outskirts. Each time the Egyptians ran into Iraqi tank columns, the communications sergeant on Killer's team would call in the air force to engage the tanks and clear a path.

The primary job of both Killer and Rainey's teams now that the war had begun was to keep headquarters apprised of their coalition partners' exact location and situation. The Special Forces were like little intelligence nodes blinking all over the battlefield.

Because most of these Arab troops had never fought, and certainly never had fought as a coalition, keeping them all on course and out of each other's way was a critical job. Having a Special Forces team embedded with the countries' principal units provided a means of communicating with each of the foreign forces.

Killer's team found their Egyptian partners to be as navigationally challenged as Steve Rainey's first Saudi unit had been. His team, ODA 564, was tucked in behind the headquarters element of the Egyptian brigade, twelve men crammed into two Humvees and a Toyota Land Cruiser. They used their Magellan GPS and the trusty old map and compass to track their column's progress. More than a few times, they had to convince the Egyptian commander that his lead units had veered off course. Some of the Egyptians did not understand how their armored personnel carriers' and tanks' Loran guidance systems worked, and had turned them off once they got a fix on their location. They did not realize that the system had to track the vehicles' progress continually to identify where they were at any given point. The Egyptians would drive on for a while and then turn the system back on, getting an incorrect reading. Killer, an 18C engineer sergeant and naturally handy with machinery, and the team's communications sergeants went forward more than once to reset the Lorans and get the brigade back on course.

In such moments Clausewitz's fabled "fog of war" seems potent and vivid. Those who never have been on the battlefield do not appreciate the difficulty of knowing what is going on beyond one's immediate vicinity, and sometimes even right there. A man in a tank has a restricted field of vision; exploding ordnance can drown out communications; and so on. The chaotic nature of war is only partly mitigated by technology, and friendly-fire and accidental casualties may even become more common, not less so, as weaponry becomes more lethal and automated, especially if the training is inadequate. Soldiers using the long-range weaponry that is increasingly common in conventional war do not see what they are killing.

Killer was one of the more seasoned Special Forces soldiers in his company. He had passed the Q course in 1986, joined 5th Group in 1987, and made the move to Fort Campbell in 1988. He'd served in the 82nd Airborne from 1982 to 1986, and had seen some of the Central American wars from Honduras as a private. Killer was in his thirties but he still had the look of a little boy about him. He had full pink cheeks and big brown eyes, and a short fringe of brown hair that barely covered his sunburned forehead. Jim Kilcoyne, who might as well have been baptized Killer as that is the only name anyone called him, tended to speak in terse one-liners. His inflected drawl could invest a single word or phrase with more meaning than a five-minute discourse from his more loquacious teammates. One of his favorite sayings was "He's a hero," which he turned into a four-letter epithet meaning "You are the biggest fool who ever walked this earth." He was a rock, a man one might not notice walking down the street, but an absolute pillar of common sense, technical proficiency, and keen awareness. He knew how things worked from the team level all the way up to battalion.

Conventional military commanders who did not know much about the Special Forces were often surprised to find so much expertise and experience in the ODA. A senior noncommissioned officer would not be found in a squad-sized unit in the regular army, and ten experienced noncommissioned officers in a squad-sized unit was incomprehensible.

In the conventional force, these men would be used to lead much larger units of privates and corporals or be in staff positions running enlisted affairs. Some conventional officers saw this an extravagant waste of non-commissioned officers, who are the lifeblood of a professional force. It would be a waste if the ODA was employed like an infantry squad, part of a larger formation and under the constant direction of higher echelons. The ODA was designed to function without any of that overarching structure, and to do many things, but not light infantry work.

Killer's superiors were considering making him a team sergeant after Desert Storm—normally one first would be promoted to the rank of master sergeant in order to hold the position of team sergeant leading nine staff sergeants and sergeants first class. Killer would be one of the group's youngest master sergeants when he was promoted, and would go on from there to become a sergeant major.

As Killer's team and the Egyptians made their way toward Kuwait City, they encountered Iraqi soldiers surrendering first by the hundreds, then by the thousands. They could not do anything with the prisoners except line them up in company formations and have them wait until the cattle trucks came from Saudi Arabia to take them back down to a stadium being used for prisoners of war. The team and the Egyptians reached their designated spot on the outskirts of Kuwait City. They received orders to stay put—there were plenty of troops heading into the city and they did not need to join the fray. Killer sat back in the Humvee and drained his canteen. He could see this war was about over, at least his part of it.

ODA 574 had started out slightly after Killer and Rainey's teams. "We look like a gypsy caravan," Warren Foster, the communications sergeant, said as they inched their way forward in the vast snake uncoiling into Kuwait. He had never seen such an awesome mass of military hardware in his life. Their own little caravan was far less martial. The Badr Brigade was loaded aboard brightly painted buses, with colored water cans, wash basins, and duffel bags of gear tied onto the sides and top rack.

When they went to check the Badr barracks before pulling out, Warren and Randy found half of the brand-new equipment that the CIA had provided lying around on the floor. Their charges, businessmen and other civilians not used to heavy packs, had not wanted to carry it all. The team had only two military vehicles, Humvees specially modified for use in the desert. They had larger radiators and fan belts, and deeper-treaded tires that could grab the sand better. The team also had two Toyota Land Cruisers, part of a fleet that Japan had donated to the war effort. They had mounted a .50-caliber machine gun on the back of each. Their merry band was completed by two brand new Ford F150s adorned with red crescents and pictures of the emir of Kuwait—these were the medical vans.

Randy Wurst was the gunner in one of the Humvees, which were spliced in between the Badr Brigade buses. The chaplain gathered the teams to say a prayer, and then the battalion commander and sergeant major dispensed their final advice.

"You have your radios to call for support from air or artillery," the commander reminded them. "The army's job is to get you into the city." He added, "Sergeant Wurst, we are expecting high casualties. Use your radio. We do not want you guys killed, so do not get yourself forward."

Randy replied, "Thank you, sir, but you don't lead these guys from the rear. They will do whatever you tell them but you have to lead them." Then they loaded up and headed out. Amid the rumble of heavy vehicles snorting to life, Randy caught snatches of Steve Earle's "Copperhead Road" emanating from the team's other Humvee. He cranked up his own boom box with the song he'd chosen as his own inaugural war anthem, and rolled into Kuwait to the strains of Pat Benatar's "Hit Me with Your Best Shot."

Once across the border, massive war wreckage littered the roadside. From their staging area in Saudi Arabia, Randy had felt the ground shake as the B–52s bombed the path they would follow. He had felt sorry for those who were in the way, because there was just no escaping that terrible pounding. Instinctively he spun the gun turret in every direction, alert, but all he saw were surface-laid mines scattered for miles around. Warren eyed the oil-filled trenches, some of which had been set ablaze to impede their advance. In the distance he could see the oil wells and what looked like smoke billowing on the horizon. If those had been set afire, it would be a conflagration the likes of which they had never seen.

Their destination the first day was the equestrian club on the southwest side of Kuwait City. The other U.S. forces paused at the city's outskirts to let the Kuwaitis be the first to reclaim their capital. If they met organized resistance, the calculation was that the Badr Brigade would probably sustain 60 percent casualties. Randy and his team had trained them as hard as they could in three weeks, but they'd had to start from the ground up. Most of the brigade were civilians who had never previously handled a gun. They had had to be drilled on basic safety—like not turning around to talk to someone without lowering the muzzle.

Knowing that the brigade would be fighting inside the city, the team had tried to impart the essential principles of military operations in urban terrain. There is no more challenging environment in which to fight than built-up areas where combatants mingle with noncombatants. Taking such greenhorns into combat was a risky proposition, but that's what the emir wanted, and it was his country. Furthermore, the Kuwaitis knew the city's layout and would be invaluable as guides able to locate targets quickly and minimize destruction. A quick handoff would make the symbolic point that Kuwait had been freed by and for the Kuwaiti people, and would also transfer responsibility for restoring law, order, and services to the reinstated government.

In the city, ODA 574 soon encountered U.S. troops who were receiving sniper fire, so the team pulled up to lend a hand. The Iraqis had prepared for block-by-block fighting—many windows along the main avenues had been bricked up except for small portholes to fire from. The Special Forces had just the weapon necessary. They fired their Mk 19 (an automatic grenade launcher that spat out 40-mm grenades at the rate of 500 a minute) at the windows to suppress fire, while others moved forward to clear the building. Randy and others volunteered to go in to check for the wounded and dead, the most hazardous duty.

After clearing the building the team went deeper into the city, and found the Kuwaiti commandos it had first trained. They had been reassigned to capture the emir's palace. They excitedly hugged Randy and the others, and waved them inside to recount their exploits. None of the Americans had ever seen a Kuwaiti palace before, even one that had been picked clean by the departing Iraqis. Randy was agog to see it chock full of Russian surface-to-air missiles, SA–7s. "There are hundreds of these puppies," he exclaimed, as he went from room to room to make a rough count to report.

If the Iraqis had stayed to fight in Kuwait City it would have been a bloody war. Continuing through the city, the team saw that defenses in depth had been built, and every inch of the beach had been booby-trapped. Most of Iraq's soldiers were racing out of Kuwait, hiding or surrendering by the thousands, but a rearguard was quietly preparing to fight.

The Iraqis had stockpiled huge caches of ammunition everywhere—in the riding club where the team first stopped, and in the police station intended to be the Badr Brigade headquarters. The team decided to look for a different site because the police station was not in an easily defensible location. The Iraqis had been using schools as barracks, so the Americans went to check out one of the schools. Warren went upstairs. There were rust-brown stains on the walls, and the carpet was soaked with fresh blood. He nearly gagged, and then walked out. Someone decided to make it the communications center because it was the most secure room. Warren was not thrilled.

For the first couple of days, the team systematically cleared the city blocks around the Badr brigade headquarters set up in the school. Randy's team sergeant called him over to a cave-like opening in the ground. "Do you see that grenade right inside?" he asked. Randy nodded. "If we can see that, it probably means the whole place is rigged waiting for us to dismantle that one part," he said. Randy agreed, but had no time to say anything else, when the sergeant said, "Move back.

I'm going to blow it with one of these Iraqi grenades. Count three and start running for that hole over there."

Before Randy could respond, the team sergeant had pulled the pin and motioned to him to run for a nearby hole. They started running and then they were running in the air, just like in a cartoon, their legs moving but with nothing under them. They were blown past the hole they had been aiming for and came down in a heap on the ground. Randy scrambled for cover, his ears ringing. He thought he heard a sound like the beating of angels' wings. He looked up. Chunks of concrete and twisted metal the size of car doors were spiraling back down to the ground. He cowered in the hole, praying. After the debris stopped flying they gingerly returned to the place where the cave-like entrance had been. They found themselves looking at a tractor-trailer container that had been buried and used as an underground ammunition bunker. As he realized that they both should have been dead a hundred times over, Randy was jolted by a belated surge of adrenaline shooting through his body.

"I'm going to beat the bejeebers out of you, man," Randy yelled at the team sergeant. He was so furious that he did not care that his superior could demote him on the spot for talking to him like that.

The team's sergeants were divvied up in pairs and assigned to a company of the Badr Brigade. Each was given a sector and went about finding a defensible building where they could set up camp. Warren had the sector on one side of Randy and on the other was one of his best pals from Bragg, another wild man named Randy.

Randy was glad to have Warren, the team's resident genius, next door. Warren was without a doubt the most intellectually gifted man on their team, perhaps in the group. He was a natural linguist, he used words like mnemonic without thinking twice, and he was always the one they turned to for deciphering highly technical manuals. Sergeants who chose communications as their military occupational specialty tended to have mental styles that were literal, deductive, painstaking.

Warren's style complemented Randy's instinctive approach in one of those fortuitous combinations that regularly occur on teams. Problems that one could solve would stump the other and vice versa.

Warren was grateful that Randy treated him like a valued member of the team and not like a private first class with a Special Forces tab. He had been ribbed a lot by others, because he was the youngest man on the team. With his youthful, round-faced, blond, Anglo looks, Warren would still look like twenty-five when he was pushing forty. He had already learned he could count on Randy, day or night and in all weathers. At Campbell, Randy was the team's designated driver when the guys would go out drinking, because he had no tolerance for alcohol. Over the past year Randy had dissuaded Warren from some foolish hijinks that he would most certainly have regretted by the light of day. No one had Randy's breadth of experience and hands-on practical knowledge, from breaking horses and roping calves to taking down a roomful of shooters. He was the best shot that Warren had ever seen, no matter what the weapon. They all had been trained in martial arts for hand-to-hand combat, but Randy had been practicing judo since his days as a Wyoming sheriff. Above all, he had a hunter's sixth sense that told him when something was around that corner or bush—all of which was hugely reassuring as it became clear that Kuwait City would be the scene of some ugly urban warfare.

ODA 574 and the Badr Brigade had been assigned to secure the oil workers' neighborhood, which was predominantly Palestinian, and the nearby oil facilities. The 100-hour war had been won, but the Palestinians were mounting a sustained insurgency in the city. The Iraqis had cached and abandoned tons of arms and munitions. The Palestinians had cooperated with the Iraqi occupiers, in part because of their pro-Palestine stance. The Palestinians knew that, having colluded with Iraq, they likely faced retribution, so they set ambushes and picked off the returning Kuwaitis. There was also rampant looting in other empty neighborhoods—what the Iraqis had not carted off to Baghdad, the stay-behinds were now busily ransacking—from hubcaps to wiring to any available vehicles.

The first test for the Badr Brigade was to see if it could protect its own compounds. Had the Special Forces been able to impart enough skill and knowledge for their charges to successfully man the checkpoints around the brigade headquarters? They had a chance to find out before the first week was out. Hidden snipers targeted the guard shack on the main approach to the Badr headquarters in the school. The men stayed down behind the sandbags, returning fire but receiving a massive volley every time they appeared over the barricades. After a few hours, the head of the checkpoint unit saw that they were down to their last rocket-propelled grenade. He sent one of their group, a teenager, who took off running, shoeless, through the streets of Kuwait City to Randy's compound more than a mile away. When the youth arrived, his feet were torn and bleeding from the shrapnel and glass he'd run through. Randy was proud of the Badr troops, especially the young man who had crippled himself but kept going, like a Greek marathoner. They might be civilians, Randy thought, but they had shown what they were made of.

Randy and Warren and the rest of the team felt responsible for keeping their Kuwaiti allies alive. They were the only Americans inside the city. The Kuwaiti commander of the Badr Brigade was officially in charge, but it was the Special Forces who had the skills to protect them all. Despite best efforts, several dozen Kuwaitis were killed in the first three weeks after the ground war ended, a high toll that weighed heavily on the Special Forces soldiers.

"I don't know how many Iraqis I'm shooting at, but I sure am trading shots with lots of Palestinians," Warren commented to Randy.

It was often difficult to identify their attackers. Most often they were ambushed or sniped at, so they rarely saw the perpetrators. They only saw the flashes of their gun muzzles. As more and more Kuwaitis fell to the ambushes, the Kuwaiti resistance, feeling betrayed by the Palestinians, began to exact revenge on them, often taking the law into its own hands. The Special Forces tried to keep things from spinning out of hand

and set up stings to catch Kuwaitis who were engaging in payback sprees or taking advantage of the chaos to commit crimes. But it was difficult to police one side while engaging the other.

The men were living in a noxious environment as well as a deadly one. The oil wells around Kuwait City continued to burn out of control. Because they could not have Kuwait's wealth for themselves, the departing Iraqis had set fire to it. The air was full of acrid, choking smoke, and a fine mist of oil constantly rained down. It was so dark during the day that lights were needed. Day after day, the men wore camouflage uniforms that were soaked through with oil, as was the long underwear underneath. The uniforms' chocolate-chip pattern was no longer visible; the cloth was just a wretched sticky, stinky black. The air reeked of a horrible charred petrochemical smell.

Warren ruefully wondered what the long-term health effects were going to be. As if in answer, the team began finding dead camels and other sick animals wandering around the oil field sector where they had set up a range for firing and disposing of munitions. The order came down that they were to kill any sick animals they saw, in case they were contaminated or infected. There was definitely something wrong in that area, but no one ever figured out what was making the camels sick. Chemical weapons, oil smoke, depleted uranium shells, the possibilities were legion. It was another mystery along with the Gulf War sickness that would sicken many of the veterans.

After two weeks of patrolling their sector against guerrilla attacks, the men were close to exhaustion. They had been working nearly around the clock, snatching a couple hours' sleep at a time. After a succession of fierce ambushes, Randy was worn out. Although trained to function despite extreme fatigue, he was nearing his limit. He went inside their U-shaped compound, which had a gate in front, and lay down. For the first time since the war began he took his boots off. No sooner had he shut his eyes than shots were fired. He leapt up and went into the courtyard. His Badr boys erupted in a babble of fright and excitement.

"Hold on, one at a time," Randy said.

They explained that attackers had tried to storm the gate and then had run into the warehouse next door. About thirty yards of open ground stood between their building and the warehouse, the door of which stood open. Randy could not afford to let them stay in there, because they could easily come back that night. He had to go get them. The Kuwaitis were in a high state of anxiety, fearing that they would be overrun. Randy couldn't take them along to clear the warehouse; they simply did not have the room-clearing skills. One of his Badr boys, a teenager, was an extremely accurate shot but couldn't maneuver and shoot. He would have to do for backup.

"Here's what we're going to do," he instructed the young man. Pointing out the path he would take, he told the youth, "I'm going to run across this open ground to the warehouse. Watch for my signal, like this"—he waved once, over his shoulder—"and come forward. Then you cover my back, always stay behind me. Got it?"

The young man nodded and gripped his AK–47 rifle. Randy took a deep breath and exhaled slowly to get ready. Neither man had body armor. None of them did. He slid extra magazines into the vertical pockets of his ammunition vest, thin canvas pouches suspended from web straps, and tested the spring-loading mechanism of each cartridge with a quick push of his thumb. The preparations were second nature, but they had to be meticulous, not rote. Randy's equipment was not ideal for this kind of close-quarter battle. The M16A2 was a bulky rifle, unlike the collapsible models being deployed. Randy should not be going in without a reliable backup, but he had no choice. He focused his concentration. The training kicked in and he became all business. Point, look, shoot. Where the red dot of the aiming laser went, the bullet would go, if he pulled the trigger. As he went through this mental rehearsal, his body was pumping full of adrenaline. He turned to the boy and nodded.

Randy ran across the open ground in an irregular zigzag movement so that an attacker would not be able to foresee his course and draw a bead on him. He reached the wall of the warehouse building and flattened himself against the outside, waving once to the boy, who raced after him, mimicking his movement. He reached the building and Randy let him catch his breath.

"Stay here by the edge of the doorway 'til I wave you in," he whispered.

Randy swung around into the open entrance to the warehouse and saw that it was lined with individual rooms all the way around. He ran to the first one, to begin a systematic clearing of the entire building. He stopped, flat to the wall, at the edge of the first doorway. A black hole yawned inside, and Randy expected armed men to jump out. His heart pounded furiously. In the lower corner of his peripheral vision, just below the night-vision goggles' rims, he caught sight of his uniform. His heartbeat was moving it. Randy was as afraid as he had ever been. He took another deep breath and exhaled slowly, forcing his heart rate down. His finger steady on the trigger, he stepped inside.

Randy scanned the room, one eye looking through the rifle's sight at the laser's thin red beam visible only with the goggles, looking from one side to the other, up and down. It was completely empty, so his search was completed in seconds. But would the teenage Kuwaiti shoot him when he popped back out into the hallway? He knew how scared the young man was, and he would only have a split second to decide if it was Randy or an assailant coming out of the darkness.

When Randy first taught the Badr Brigade members to maneuver in groups, out in the Saudi desert, some would hit the sand and their fingers would slip onto the triggers, letting loose a burst of automatic fire. Randy, in their midst, had yelled at them furiously a hundred times to keep their index fingers pressed flat against the magazine, in the safety position. After one of these accidental firings, the embarrassed but insouciant Kuwaiti responsible had called out "Inshallah" (Allah willing) after the bullets narrowly missed Randy. Now, alone but for one untested teenager and an unknown number of the enemy, it was time to see whether God was willing.

Randy swung out of the room and the teenager did not fire. Randy waved him to his side and he came dashing forward low and fast, picture perfect, and got behind Randy just as he'd been instructed. The boy would have to cover them against whatever might come out of the other rooms. Randy prepared to enter the next room. It and the next few were empty. With each room, however, the tension mounted as the odds increased that the next one would hold the gunmen.

The anticipation of being shot can prove excruciating to the point of debilitation. Randy knew that the increasing strain would eat away at his young partner's self-control, because he had to exercise that same instantaneous judgment over and over, each time Randy emerged from a room. It was easier to shoot wildly to relieve the tension than to maintain one's discipline. Only years of practice could so perfectly synchronize perception, decision, and action so that the finger pulls the trigger only when the brain has identified an armed foe in the fraction of a second before he shoots.

The ODA had attempted a room-clearing drill with the Badr group in the desert, but the Kuwaitis had spun around spraying bullets wildly. The bullets were blanks, so no harm was done, but the issue was settled. There would be no room-clearing with the Kuwaitis. The risk of getting shot in the cross-fire was too great. There was no shame in this. Fighting in city streets amid buildings and civilians was a difficult skill, and learning how to fight inside buildings was even more difficult. Randy had first learned the techniques when he was with the SWAT team in Wyoming. It required constant training to master and maintain the skills. Close-quarters battle is a series of highly precise procedures for moving in groups, covering each other, discriminating among targets, and delivering lethal blows in hand-to-hand combat. It was a kind of mortal ballet to be performed only by professionals.

Randy's trepidation was entirely rational because he knew he was gambling with a lot of adverse factors. Room-clearing should be done by at least two commandos because the human head can only look in one direction at any given moment. In this case, he had to enter alone and use one pair of eyes to cover four corners of each room, and the night-vision goggles restricted his peripheral vision. Finally, he was extremely fatigued and the weeks of poor diet were beginning to catch up with him.

Clinical studies showed that Special Forces soldiers were uniquely prepared to handle extreme stress. Tested under the brutal conditions of their SERE escape and evasion course, their levels of cortisol, adrenaline, and neuropeptide-Y went much higher than those of a control group in the same conditions, and the levels returned to normal much more quickly than the other group's, which remained depleted. The tests provided a chemical portrait of what staying "cool under fire" looked like. SF soldiers also showed markedly less tendency to dissociate under stress, or have "out of body" perceptions that would inhibit their ability to react properly. These findings were indicators of behavior traits that were essential for these types of operations.

Randy steeled himself to enter the last room. Once again he prepared for the jack-in-the-box to pop up and shoot him. The chemicals were recharging in his body for the assault—the gunmen had to be in there. The whole operation had taken less than ten minutes. His perception had not been focused on the past or future but on each separate second of the immediate present. Randy sensed that his young partner was spent from the strain and motioned for him to stay against the wall.

Pivoting around the door jamb, Randy kicked the half-open door in a furious explosion of energy. He aimed across in a swift arc, then up across the ceiling, down around the floor and furniture. Eyeball on the red dot of the aiming laser, peripheral vision straining at the rims of the goggles to catch any movement, rifle butt jammed high into his shoulder so his eye went right along the barrel's scope. The red dot found no target. Instead, there was only an open window—the quarry had escaped. There had been no sound, so the window already must have been open for them to climb out.

He went back out to get the young man to help make a final search of the back area outside, to make sure they were not hiding anywhere. He felt sure they were gone. After they finished, Randy put an arm around the boy's shoulders and congratulated him.

"You did very well. Thank you for watching my back, soldier. Well done, my friend."

The young fellow shook his hand, blinking and smiling, proud but drained.

The general in charge of Kuwait City did not believe that the Americans were still encountering resistance so long after the war had ended. Randy, who was, in effect, the acting commander of his sector, the most volatile one, was called in to brief the general. From where the general sat, Kuwait had been pacified since shortly after the 100-hours war. Randy and part of his team traveled to the general's command post in one of the ambulance trucks, which wove its way out of their neighborhood's crowded warren of dilapidated apartment buildings. As they left their sector they were shot at despite the red crescent painted on the truck's doors. When they arrived at headquarters, they inspected the bullet holes in the Ford's hood, and decided that was a good Exhibit A for the briefing of the general. A few days later a busload of congressmen was brought into their sector, where it hit an improvised explosive device in the road. Randy had tried to tell them the war was not yet over.

By the late spring of 1991 it was time to leave Kuwait. Randy and his team bid goodbye to the Kuwaiti comrades that they had slept, ate, worked, fought, and laughed alongside. Randy and some of his young charges shed a few tears. Many of the Kuwaitis already had returned to their civilian lives, and they were grateful for these men who had shared their makeshift living quarters in the eerie gloom of the oil fires. The bonds among the Special Forces soldiers were strengthened by their common effort in the cauldron of war. After eight months of Desert Shield, Desert Storm, and the aftermath, the soldiers were dog-tired and ready to go home. They were brothers, but they needed a break.

CHAPTER 5

SOMALIA

Know the enemy and know yourself; in a hundred battles you will never be in peril.

—SUN TZU

DESERT STORM turned out to be the prelude to a long involvement in Kuwait. The 5th Special Forces Group would rotate men in and out of Kuwait for the next twelve years to keep Saddam's forces at bay and to prepare for a possible eventual showdown. After Desert Storm, the teams went through the inevitable reshuffling that occurs after wars and long deployments. Warren Foster did go off to Officer Candidate School the next year, with his wife's blessing and the certainty of at least three more moves before he got back to a Special Forces Group. Chris Conner met Polly, fell in love, got engaged, and then got married—all within nine months.

Randy Wurst moved over to ODA 534, where he teamed up with the crusty staff sergeant Steve Rainey, who joked about arriving late to the battle of Khafji with his reluctant Saudi partners, and other HALO freefall fanatics. A local Kentucky artist painted a portrait of a Special Forces soldier, the first in a series, using Randy as an anonymous model against the backdrop of Kuwait's burning oil fields. She named it *Job's Done*, but in fact they would not be done for many years.

ODA 534 headed back to Kuwait in early 1992, for Operation Southern Watch, to patrol the border for infiltrators from Iraq's army, which was still intact behind newly dug trenches. The soldiers observed as Saddam used the helicopters which had been returned to him after the end of the war to smash the uprising of the Shi'ite majority in the south and to drive the rebelling Kurds in the north into the mountains. The international coalition that had been amassed for pushing Iraq out of Kuwait, however, could not hold together to endorse the launching of a war against Iraq itself.

By 1992, Iraq was competing with another serious preoccupation: the mounting chaos in Somalia. Fifth Group was drawn in because its area of operations included the Muslim countries of the Horn of Africa. Somalia had begun to unravel on the eve of Desert Storm, when its long-time Soviet-backed ruler fled the country in January 1991.

Randy, Warren, and the rest of their team, which was training Kuwaitis in the Saudi desert, had been scrambled to evacuate the U.S. embassy in Mogadishu. It suspended the desert training and drew up a mission plan. The team would parachute into a drop zone ten miles from the embassy and, if necessary, fight its way through the city. The men grabbed advanced sniper rifles and an assortment of high-speed equipment that was suddenly made available to them, and boarded a C–130 transport plane in Saudi Arabia. The plane was taxiing down the runway when the call came to abort mission. The U.S. military command in the theater had decided that the situation was stable enough to wait for Marines who were steaming up the Indian Ocean en route to the Persian Gulf. They evacuated the embassy a few days later.

By the summer of 1992, the situation in Somalia had worsened. Famine was spreading and with it warfare among the country's armed clans. The United Nations' humanitarian effort was foundering, so the United States began Operation Provide Relief to help the growing mass of starving, displaced Somalis.

Starting in August, planes carrying teams from 5th Group's 2nd Battalion began circling over Somalia in twelve-hour shifts. It was a mission that rivaled the tedium of sitting in a hide site, but the Special Forces had to be nearby to serve as a quick-reaction force if the aid workers below were attacked. Whenever food shipments were to be delivered, the Special Forces C–130 would land first, opening its rear hatch as it rolled down the runway. A team aboard two armed Humvees would roll out, and the men would fan out to secure the airfield perimeter. Because there were no air traffic controllers, U.S. air force controllers attached to the team would direct the inbound planes carrying the grain and other humanitarian goods to a safe landing. This U.S. show of force was usually enough to keep the Somali militias from storming the airfield and stealing the food—but not always. After the aid was unloaded and transferred to trucks for distribution, the Special Forces would lift off and return to their base of operations in Mombasa, the capital of neighboring Kenya.

When 2nd Battalion's Bravo Company took over the duty in the fall of 1992, Killer soon figured out the patterns behind the chaos in Somalia. He had been made team sergeant of ODA 564, even though he had not yet been promoted to the rank of master sergeant. The team sergeant is the glue or anchor of the team; his job is to direct the other nine sergeants and oversee their daily work. The captain is the commander and the chief warrant officer does the long-range planning for operations and intelligence, so it falls to the team sergeant to plan the day-to-day operations and see that his sergeants form a well-honed machine, ready to execute the missions.

ODAs are far more consultative and collaborative than most army units because its members are peers, each with his own area of expertise, which dictates the division of labor. Because the team sergeant is the link between the directing and implementing functions of the team, his temperament and leadership style are indelibly stamped on the ODA. He is also responsible for the discipline and well-being of his nine sergeants, the Bravos (weapons), Charlies (engineers), Deltas (medics),

Echoes (communicators), and the Fox (intelligence sergeant). These nicknames derive from the military alphabet and their military occupational specialty designations: 18B, 18C, 18D, 18E, and 18F are the five individual specialties of the A-teams. The team leader or captain's designation is 18A, the team sergeant's is 18Z, and the chief warrant officer's is 180Z.

Killer pulled his share of the shifts above Somalia and on the ground. He preferred being on the ground to flying monotonously over the sun-baked coast of Somalia. The usual routine was to land with the air force controllers about seven or eight in the morning, and the planes with the food would arrive soon thereafter. Things would proceed relatively smoothly until about noon, when Piper Cubs and other small planes would land at the airstrip and offload bundles of *qat*, a narcotic weed favored by Somalis, Afghans, and some Middle Easterners. The workers who were unloading the grain would stop working and start chewing the *qat*, as did the militia members of various clans who hung around the airstrips. Within a couple of hours they would be thoroughly stoned and start shooting at each other, the workers, the planes, anything that moved. At this time—almost a year before the fateful Black Hawk Down battle—U.S. forces were charged with a strictly humanitarian mission. Their orders were to protect the aid shipments and aid workers, not to round up drug traffickers, warlords, or their militias. So when they had accomplished that mission as best they could, they would get on their plane and head back to Mombasa. But this early picture of Somali habits and the aggressive behavior induced by the *qat* gave Killer a premonition of the complications ahead.

Right after Christmas, which Killer and the rest of Bravo Company, 2nd Battalion spent in their hotel in Mombasa, they were ordered to move into Somalia on a permanent basis for the start of a new effort called Operation Restore Hope. Until then, they had been operating since August on an in-and-out basis, retreating to the relative calm of Kenya each night. They had been the only U.S. military forces inside Somalia until that time. Bravo Company landed quietly at the airfield of the southern city of Kismaayo while the television cameras were filming

Marines and SEALs coming ashore on the surf-pounded beaches. Over the preceding months, 5th Group had provided security for experts taking soil samples at airstrips around Somalia to determine what type of aircraft they could support.

In the days before Operation Restore Hope began, the 4th Psychological Operations Group, the only active-duty psyop unit in the military, prepared and dropped massive sheaves of leaflets from the C–130s over the most-populated areas. The leaflets told the Somalis that the American soldiers would be coming and defined the rules of engagement. The leaflets were written in the Somali language and contained hand-drawn pictures to explain the essential message, which was that Americans could confiscate any arms they found and could consider anyone carrying arms to be a hostile party. Although the mission was still a humanitarian one, the rules recognized that the soldiers had to at least be able to defend themselves.

The newest addition to Killer's team was a young, high-spirited engineer sergeant named Alan Johnson. He looked at the leaflets that had been dropped and gave his own rendition of the message, much to the amusement of his teammates. Alan's translation was, "Weapons are bad juju. Put weapons down."

No decision had been made to attempt wholesale disarmament, but Somalia's social order was essentially clans defended by armed militias. So there would be continuing modifications of the rules of engagement in the months ahead, as the U.S. government attempted to come up with a workable and effective policy. The first mandate to U.S. soldiers, in mid-1992, had been to protect aid shipments and relief workers, but by year's end it was clear that this strictly defensive task was not possible in the violent and chaotic environment. So the policymakers authorized the soldiers to disarm Somalis or otherwise dissuade them from carrying guns. Hence, the psyop message warning that Somalis with guns would be considered hostile by the arriving Americans.

Starting in December, the Special Forces' task was to find out who these clans were, what their allegiances and animosities were, and how disposed they might be to attack Americans and the relief effort. They were also to find out whatever they could about the health and infra-structure needs of the population. The six teams of Bravo Company, 2nd Battalion, and a few others added later, spread out across the country to make contact with clan leaders in the provinces as part of the U.S.-led multinational relief effort. Killer's team served as a roving reconnaissance unit while the other teams were assigned to provinces from Kismaayo in the south to the central Baardheere, Balli Doogle, and Beledweyne in the north.

The ODAs' most urgent priority was to find out which of the clan leaders, or warlords, had foreigners in their crosshairs, so that the conventional forces coming in to conduct this first of the decade's "humanitarian interventions" could plan how best to protect themselves. Understanding the alliances and rivalries between the clans could also help predict how the situation might evolve. The broader mission to

Operation Restore Hope, Somalia, 1992-93

Source: Association of the U.S. Army

assess security risks, population condition, and infrastructure needs would aid future mission planning. No one had yet determined what it would take to address the root causes of the starvation or to give Somalia some semblance of a government. Sending the Special Forces teams out to understand what was going on and who the key players were was the first step. For the teams heading off into the unknown hinterlands, it was an unquantifiable risk. But it was just what they had been trained for: to be sent out into the wilds to use their wits and figure out what made the place tick.

On one of the first visits that Killer's team paid to El Gal in the north, their little Humvee caravan pulled into a dusty crossroads and spotted a large anti-aircraft gun mounted on the back of a truck. Definitely bad juju. The gunners in the turrets of the team's two Humvees kept their fingers on the triggers of the .50-caliber and Mk 19 guns as two Somalis ran toward the truck and scrambled onto it. The gunners waited. Killer waited.

They watched to see what the Somalis were going to do. The soldiers would have been completely within their rules of engagement, which they carried on laminated cards in their pockets, to open fire as soon as the Somalis jumped on the truck. Instead of running away from their weapons, the Somalis were running toward them. The intent to fire logically could have been assumed.

Restraint proved to be the right decision. The Somalis were trying to wrestle a huge tarpaulin over the gun's big barrel to cover it up. They had apparently seen the leaflets and knew guns were now forbidden. The Humvees moved in, with the gunners still at the ready, and the team leader and Killer informed the Somalis that their gun would have to be confiscated. They made them take the weapon to the multinational forces' camp in Beledweyne.

At the outskirts of another village where the inhabitants said that they had no weapons, the team found fresh AK–47 casings. They presented the evidence to the villagers, who told them that an alligator had recently attacked a woman washing clothes there in the stream and that thereafter they had posted a guard on washing days. The team decided that keeping small arms was a reasonable proposition for people who were part of mother nature's food chain. The soldiers did not have to disarm everyone they saw; they were merely permitted to do so. Not every weapon in Somalia was being used malevolently.

The village where soldiers had confiscated the antiaircraft gun was a definite trouble spot, however. Reports filtered back to ODA 564 about holdups and robberies. One evening, after encountering a bus full of passengers who had been robbed at gunpoint, Killer suggested to his team that they drive up to the village checkpoint just to see what would unfold. The team drove up without lights, as is Somali custom, and three men came out of a small hut in the brush. One of them threw an antitank mine in front of the Humvee. Killer looked at it in amazement. It was a white M19 U.S.-issue mine. The white ones were issued for use in the Arctic. How it had ended up in the middle of Africa was surely a tale to be told. Perhaps some arms merchant in the global black market had thrown it in as a bonus.

When the "toll-takers" realized that their next marks were soldiers, they started running toward a dry riverbed—but Killer was ready for them. He had left Alan and the gunner back down the road, telling them to ready all the illumination rounds that they had on hand. Alan loaded their two grenade-launching weapons, the Mk 19 and the M203, and waited. As soon as they heard Killer's warning shot, they fired a tremendous barrage of star clusters and parachute flares that lit up the riverbed like a sports stadium. One of the Somalis jumped out of Killer's sight below the river bank and the captain went after him with his pistol. The other two high-tailed it across a 100-meter wide-open stretch of land. Killer trained his rifle on them.

"Come on, come on," he muttered, "let me see your gun."

One of the Somalis had held a rifle when he approached the Humvee, but now it was nowhere to be seen. So Killer carefully squeezed off rounds, placing them in between the running figures. If he couldn't shoot them then he might as well give them a scare. The bandits ran into the village, but when the team arrived the residents said that they had no idea who or where the men were.

The next day, Canadian members of the multinational coalition searched the village and found a large cache of mortars and heavy weapons. To Killer and his men, it seemed that the orders for weapons confiscation changed every few days. At first, any arms at all were to be seized, then it was only large weapons that took two or more people to operate. If the soldiers ever were asked to collect all the rifles and pistols in every Somali village, they would be there for many years to come.

ODA 564 then headed south to Kismaayo, where the Belgians and the U.S. 10th Mountain Division were based. The conventional troops had stayed close to the coastal ports, where good progress had been made in the first month of Operation Restore Hope. More than 40,000 tons of grain had been offloaded, along with 6,668 vehicles and 96 helicopters to distribute and guard it.

The 10th Mountain commander wanted the Special Forces to probe farther west and see what they could find out. Killer's team had already established contact with a band of fighters in a village outside Kismaayo who belonged to the militia of a dominant clan chieftain named General Mohammed Morgan. The team dropped in a couple times a day, and eventually were allowed to use the high-frequency radio to talk to the warlord in his outpost on the Kenyan border. They needed to meet all the warlords in their area to size them up, determine their intent, and find out how many armed men and what kind of firepower they had. Kismaayo was becoming more unstable by the day. The Belgians started receiving fire and decided to pull out of their camp, which the Special Forces had been sharing.

The 10th Mountain commander decided it was time to go meet General Morgan at his camp out near the Kenyan border. Getting there was no small undertaking; it would be an eight-day off-road journey across 300 miles of barren Somali wilderness. The men of 564 set out in their two-vehicle caravan on trails made for feet and hooves, not vehicles. Their Dumvees (as they called their desert model of Humvees) rubbed against the branches of the acacia trees, and broke off the long thorns, which were an inch thick at their base. These would drop into the trucks and jab the men, and squads of big black ants would pour out of the thorns' base and crawl into the men's uniforms and down their necks. When one Humvee got stuck—a frequent occurrence in the rough, rocky terrain—the other one would pull up with its winch to yank it out.

When the sun climbed up to its blistering pinnacle each day, the team would knock off for a few hours and seek refuge in the scant shade of the ubiquitous acacia trees. Most of the fauna had been poached by starving Somalis, so there was little wild game around. But during Killer's turn at guard one night, he heard the distinct sound of a lion's growl not far away. Any idea of sleep immediately flew out of his head, and Killer sat bolt upright on the Dumvee roof. Guard duty took on an entirely new meaning when it was wild lions that were after you.

The team hired two Somali translators to help them on the trek. The Special Forces training in Arabic did not help them in Somalia, with its African language. The team had been assured that these two men spoke good English by the Somali-American they had brought as an interpreter from the United States. He, Dharman, had to stay behind to help in Kismaayo. After the first day, it became apparent that the English of their two new hires was in fact quite rudimentary. The men realized they were getting the same answers in response to whatever question they asked. Only a few days into their trek, the men were becoming frustrated with their Somali "translators." Even the patience of the gregarious and good-humored Alan—who was greatly enjoying this Somali adventure—had its limits.

The villagers encountered along the way had begged the men to shoot the pigs that ran through their dusty streets. As Muslims, they considered the animals filthy and wanted nothing more than to be rid of them. For the ODA, it was a source of relief from the monotony of their packaged rations. There was no mess hall back in Kismaayo, no logistical chain that brought them fresh or imported food. They had been living on the rations (called meals ready to eat or MREs), and swapping the Belgians and Canadians for theirs. After the pig shoot, the men carted around a load of pork chops for several days, iced down, until finally it was time to cook them or dump them. Alan and Killer whipped up a pork chop and mashed potato feast. The cooking smells were divine, and as the men queued for their portions, the Somali translators sidled into line as well. When their turn came, Alan, who was temporarily annoyed with the Somalis, saw a chance to relieve some of the frustration they all were feeling. He reached behind him and thrust out an MRE ration for each one. "You're Muslim. It's pork. You can't have any."

The rest of the team was ready to leave the two translators by the roadside, but Alan calmed down and took on the role of cultural ambassador once more. He'd learned about Somalia's tragic history from Dharman, the Somali expat they had brought with them from America to serve as chief interpreter. Dharman's father had founded an exile group called the United Somali Congress. The Somalis had lived through two wretched decades. The ruthless dictator Mohammed Siad Barre had driven the country into chaos and destitution for fifteen years, and provoked a devastating war with neighboring Ethiopia. Alan hoped that the Americans could contribute to better days for Somalia, or at least make its struggle for survival less brutal.

Alan had wanted to be a Special Forces soldier for as long as he could remember. When he was eighteen years old he went to a tattoo parlor and got a green beret tattooed on his right shoulder. He spent four years in the air force, serving at the special operations wing at Hurlburt in Florida, which further whetted his appetite. He could not go directly into Special Forces selection when he joined the army a few years later, but his mind was made up when he met his drill sergeant, Sergeant Washington, at basic training. Washington had been a medic in the Special Forces. "I had never met anyone so squared away before," Alan recalled. Sergeant Washington showed up for graduation and encouraged Alan to pursue his dream.

Alan was assigned to the 9th Infantry Division at Fort Lewis in Washington, the same base where the 1st Special Forces Group is located. An informal mentoring program permitted aspiring candidates to attend

the Special Forces' training exercises. Alan had been told that no one
from his infantry unit ever had made it into Special Forces, but he was
determined to do so. He went along on 1st Group's training, scuba,
swimming, mountain climbing, and other outings, and after his Ranger
school slot fell through, he went straight to Special Forces selection.

He passed the Q course in 1990 and reported for duty at 5th Group at
Fort Campbell in January 1991. His first assignment was on the company
staff. ODAs with open slots check out the newcomers and then begin
courting the ones they think will fit in with their team. Alan, with his
sunny personality, was an instant hit. He'd aced Arabic, and he was an
extraordinary athlete. Both scuba and HALO teams, the two most physically demanding, were soon hotly competing for him.

Killer wanted the mission in Somalia to succeed as much as anyone, but
the daily realities encountered in the country filled him with pessimism.
The team stopped along the roadside in one of their journeys and talked
to farmers who were working in their watermelon fields. Killer asked
them why they did not take their produce into town to the market. They
replied: "What's the use? If we do, we'll just be held up along the way
and our melons will be stolen."

On their trek to see General Morgan, the convoy stopped at a vast
sugar plantation and mill, the construction of which had been financed
by the Saudis. It supposedly was the third-largest sugar mill in the world.
They entered the silent five-story complex and found that the gigantic
lathe for making milling parts had been totally destroyed. Some Somalis
were upstairs chiseling metal plates off the floors. And out in the fields
ten-foot sections of the giant irrigation pipes, three feet in diameter, had
been unbolted and rolled apart just for the hell of it. They lay there scattered across the expanse of fields, hundreds of thousands of acres that
once, briefly, waved with sugar cane stalks. "These people have worked
hard at destroying their country," Killer thought.

In the weeks and months since the Special Forces had been in Somalia, the militias had shanghaied at least half of the grain that had been

brought in. Even a new government would be unable to run the country because there was literally no infrastructure to reach, let alone service, the countryside. Somalia was an extreme case of Third World dysfunction, with few roads, no water or electricity, and virtually no government services. The drought and famine were the consequences, not the causes, of Somalia's ills.

ODA 564 arrived at General Morgan's compound after four days of driving through the bush— nearly reaching Somalia's border with Kenya. Alan thought the mud huts looked surprisingly tidy, considering that they were in the absolute middle of nowhere. As in the provincial capitals, the inner structure of these buildings was a woven skeleton of sticks. Mud was then smoothed over the sticks in a thick layer on both sides. When the walls dried they were painted bright blues and greens and looked just like cement. Because it never rained, the homes stayed intact for years.

The team was led to a tall, dignified man who introduced himself as General Mohammed Morgan. Killer thought he looked like a black Stonewall Jackson. He was not an uneducated man, and he had sent his two daughters to the United States where they were in school. Morgan was also a pleasant man, unlike one district chief they had stopped to meet en route—he had fed them milk from a charred wooden bowl that later made them ill. That chieftain's attitude clearly signaled that he did not like Americans.

General Morgan invited ODA 564 to dine with him, and when they finished the meal they sat and discussed the conditions along the Kenyan border. Killer already knew that Morgan had been using the Red Cross hospitals for free medical attention for his armed militia. The position of the Red Cross was that it would treat anyone who came in the door, and it was importing Kenyan doctors to treat the wounded. The wily general simply was taking advantage of the free humanitarian network that had come to his country.

Morgan then asked the team if it could place a call for him to the U.S. general stationed outside Kismaayo, who was in charge of all U.S. army troops in Somalia. With the team leader's assent, the communications sergeant set up the radio and strung the antennas.

Making contact from the outback was always a tricky affair. The communications sergeants' training course is the second most technical and extensive, after the medics', that the Special Forces sergeants receive. They are taught how to use and repair a variety of short and long-range systems, from the MBITR short-range multi-band radio to the PRC–5 and PRC–137 satellite communications systems and encryption devices. The sergeants are also trained in computer networking and a host of related electronics skills.

Encrypted SATCOMS were clearly the wave of the future, but in the early 1990s the relative scarcity of satellites overhead limited the windows of time when a transponder would be in the right position to transmit the call—especially in remote parts of the world. The Echoes—as communications sergeants are known—tried and true fallback was a high-frequency radio set called the TRQ–43, which can bounce transmissions, called "shots," off the upper atmosphere to other continents, if the radio operator was skilled at the stringing of special antenna wires.

The communications sergeant tuned in the U.S. general's frequency on the TRQ–43 in about ten minutes. The team leader made the preliminary inquiries to get through to the commander and then handed the radio handset off to General Morgan.

Morgan cleared his throat. "Hello, commander, I just want to let you know that my forces are in control of your city," he told the American general at the other end of the line.

Alan Johnson looked around quickly at the rest of the team. Barely raising an eyebrow, they reacted immediately, moving out of each other's line of fire, hooking thumbs into the loops on their grenade pins, and positioning themselves for flight or fight.

Morgan had decided it was time to make his move on Kismaayo, which until then had been dominated by the militia of General Mohammed Farah Aideed, a former general in Siad Barre's army and one of the country's most powerful warlords. General Morgan knew that Aideed was occupied with a four-month-long brawl with Ali Mahdi over Mogadishu, and would not have the forces to respond.

The wily Morgan had instructed his men to move in overnight, and they had, swiftly taking the city out from under Aideed's lax watch. The Belgians, already miffed about the shooting-up of their compound, were bound to be apoplectic. Now he was betting that the American general would accept his fait accompli. For Morgan it was a convenient bonus that these American soldiers had shown up now to help him deliver the news.

The 10th Mountain commander was not about to acquiesce in such a blatant power play, but he did not respond to the warlord. Instead, he asked Morgan to let him talk to the Special Forces team leader. The team leader blanched as he heard the American general's instructions, and requested permission to confer with his own immediate superior, the major commanding Bravo Company, before carrying out the order. The American general agreed.

The team leader and Killer excused themselves to talk in private. The communications sergeant placed the radio call to their superior officer as the team leader told Killer what the American general had said. "He wants us to tell Morgan to pull his militia out of Kismaayo or he is going to send gunships and everything he has to come out here after him."

Killer replied, "He wants us to deliver that message?"

"We're supposed to call the general back and he is going to deliver the ultimatum to Morgan while we are standing here."

"What does he think is going to happen to us after he tells Morgan that he is coming to get him?"

"Good question."

For the nine men of ODA 564, alone in Morgan's stronghold and several hundred miles from any other U.S. forces, it was not difficult to see the flaw in the plan. The team leader got on the radio to suggest an alternative: "Why don't we just give General Morgan the radio frequency and tell him to call the U.S. general's headquarters at a specified time that gives us enough time to get out of here?" The commander agreed, and everything was arranged. The men went back inside to see how Alan and the rest had fared in smoothing over the disrupted tea party.

The men had taken their thumbs out of their grenades, though their body language was still tense. Killer proposed they take pictures as mementos of the visit as they passed the word that it was time to go. To provide an excuse that would help get them out the door and on their way, Alan suggested that they take a look at a minefield they had noticed on the way in. "We might be able to help your men clear it," he told the general. Morgan accepted the offer, and appeared to think the Americans had conceded the new state of affairs. The team leader told him to call the American general in an hour, and gave Morgan the frequency.

They parted with waves and promises to return. When they reached the minefield, the team asked Morgan's men to wait while they checked something further down the road. As soon as they were out of sight, the drivers of the two Humvees floored it and their teammates urged them on.

"Put the pedal to the metal," said Killer.

"Make like the Baja," Alan shouted.

They bounced and jolted as they raced back the way they came, until they reached a checkpoint where Morgan's militia blocked the way.

"Hold your fire," Killer said, once more demonstrating his willingness to risk his men instead of shooting without necessity. Alan tossed them some matches and they gave them one of their five-gallon cans of water. That friendly exchange bought them some grace from Morgan, they found out later. The militiamen had radioed back to their boss, who told the rest of the militia checkpoints to let the men through. Nonetheless, the team was grateful to see a Black Hawk helicopter coming toward them. It was their company commander, who had come to provide an air escort out of Morgan's territory. The final leg of their eight-day, 300-mile round-trip trek passed without any further excitement than the wild lions growling in the distance when the men tried to get a little sleep.

Arriving back in Kismaayo, the team saw that Morgan's men had indeed taken the city. His armed militia were everywhere. But Morgan then backed down and accepted the American general's ultimatum—at least ostensibly. Killer and his team drove through Kismaayo the day after the deadline and spotted the very same militia who had been their contacts before they made their trek west. Upon realizing that the Special Forces soldiers had seen them, the men dove for cover. But as the days passed, they became more brazen and blasé, finally waving whenever they saw ODA 564 go by. As long as they were not brandishing their weapons, Killer did not see a reason to go after them. The team might still need to use them to communicate with Morgan. The Belgians, however, remained upset that Morgan's men had attacked their compound. One day, Killer watched as two armed men raced across a square, with the Belgians in hot pursuit. "They went thataway," he told the Belgians.

The eight-day trek had sharpened the team's sixth sense about Somalia. The men could round a bend and see a Somali with a G–3, Israel's standard-issue 7.62-mm rifle, and tell whether he was a farmer guarding his flock or a militia henchman; they could recognize the jittery, aggressive behavior of a man high on *qat*. Ever since the moment when they had first held their fire as villagers climbed up onto their antiaircraft gun, the Special Forces soldiers had come to realize that there could be at least two possible interpretations of any given scene. They would have to interpret what their eyes saw and compare hunches with their teammates. The more time they spent in the field, the more their instincts were honed, especially in an environment like Somalia. Here, they were not engaged in a conventional war with clearly demarcated battle lines, allies and foes. This was neither war nor peace, and each day they had to feel their way, with constantly shifting directives from above. After years of running around outbacks like this, the NCOs and the chief warrant officers developed remarkable radar that enabled them to quickly distinguish the odd sight or potential threat from an imminently lethal one. A small group of inexperienced soldiers thrown into this situation would most likely fire as soon as anything spooked them, which in turn would cause a diplomatic storm. The Special Forces operated in Somalia for more than six months, scattered all over the country, with day-to-day command exercised by a major, their company commander.

*

The United Nations assumed control of the operation in the summer of 1993, and the situation grew shakier as the warlords began challenging the new multinational force. The international community was still divided over the degree to which it should act to disarm the warlords' militias. After Aideed ambushed and killed twenty-four Pakistani soldiers in the UN force, the battle lines hardened. The United Nations Security Council asked for more troops and started a concentrated campaign against Aideed. The fighting escalated, Somali mobs began joining in, and UN soldiers were killed and wounded. A U.S. helicopter was shot down. All of this happened before the tragic events of October 3, when the U.S. Task Force Ranger attempted to capture Aideed. While 5th Group grieved over the loss of fellow Delta and Ranger special operators during that long and bloody battle after their helicopters were shot down in Mogadishu, they were not surprised. Unfortunately, Washington had not realized that the United States now was engaged in all-out war.

Fifth Group had been pulled out of the hinterlands in the summer. The men would wonder if they could have helped prevent the tragedy had they still been there to keep tabs on the warlords. At a minimum, the U.S. government had lost eyes and ears and the ability to predict what the bad guys were up to, and perhaps some ability to rein them in. The belated recognition that the warlords and not hunger were Somalia's main problem did not result in a sufficiently decisive approach to the problem, or provision of the necessary resources. The United States was courting disaster in Mogadishu when it denied the task force's request for gunships and other support before the fatal October 1993 raid—a decision that factored in the U.S. defense secretary's subsequent resignation. The reality that was so apparent to those on the ground seemed to elude the decision makers in Washington. Many months earlier, Killer had concluded that the warlords and their *qat*-fueled militias were the central obstacle to progress. In his southern drawl, he summed up the task: "Some of these guys are going to have to be forced into being good."

Killer was born in Ohio, outside Columbus, but after eight years in the south he had a bona fide southern drawl. The many southerners in the Special Forces spoke a medley of dialects with many shadings, lilts, and twangs. They could easily identify each other's home states from just a few spoken words, but to someone north of the Mason-Dixon line southernese had to be studied just like any foreign language. The flattest, longest vowels came from the deep south, the softer singsong ones from the middle south. They all understood each other, of course, even when speaking Arabic with a Kentucky accent.

Killer was smart, opinionated and well read, and knew a lot more Arabic than he let on. "Heck," he demurred, "I can barely speak English." Alan Johnson had mastered both Egyptian Arabic and Modern Standard Arabic; Egyptian was the most widely used in television and other mass media, so most soldiers learned it. Michael T. Swift, another Bravo Company soldier, claimed to speak Tennessean and allowed that he communicated very well with other southerners, like his best friend, Jimmy Newman, who spoke Louisianian. In fact, they also spoke their assigned foreign languages very well. Michael T.—as he was called— learned Egyptian Arabic, and Jimmy Newman learned Persian Farsi.

Southerners, who have a long martial tradition, might have a hidden advantage in the competition to gain entry to the Special Forces. They seemed innately suited, with their talking skills, charm, and good-old-boy routines that were invaluable aids in the diplomacy that the job required. The Special Forces' primary mission of unconventional warfare was equal parts diplomacy and combat. Much of their task was to decipher that "other"—whether it was a friendly guerrilla, a hostile guerrilla, a foreign government, or their own conventional U.S. military ally—and work with him to achieve the mission objective. Talking was just as important as trigger-pulling in the Special Forces.

Ribbing had a permanent "open season," however. Michael T. and Killer both witnessed the first time Alan was shot at, and they never ceased reminding him how funny it was—because he had not actually been hit. Shortly after they returned from their trek to General Morgan, they were given the job of making contact with General Jess, one of Aideed's allies. They called on him at his compound on the outskirts of Kismaayo. He was truly a thug, Michael T. thought after the encounter with the belligerent man. The team pulled back to observe his complex of mud buildings from a hill about three-quarters of a mile away. The rest of 564 was still exhausted from the long journey in the outback. For the first time in four days, Killer took off his boots and laid down to rest.

As Alan and Michael T. watched General Jess's camp from their hill-top perch, they noticed a growing number of Somalis coming out of the city on the road that led toward them. Soon hundreds of people were streaming by, passing between Jess's place and their hill. Michael T. got on the radio to find out what was going on. The Belgians informed him that at an American MP had shot and killed a civilian, which had sparked a riot, and people were fleeing the city.

A high-velocity round split the air. Alan was on watch, so he jumped up first. He heard the crack but no thump, which meant that the gun-man was very close. The time between the crack—the sound of the shot breaking the sound barrier—and the thump of the firing pin—the sound that reaches the ear later the farther away the gun is located—indicates the approximate distance away of the person shooting. If the thump was not heard then it was too close to the crack to distinguish as a separate sound, which meant the shooter was very near.

Alan strained to see where the shooting was coming from when another shot went off. "Game on," Killer thought as he got up. Trying to find his boots, he hopped and shouted as he stepped on the acacia thorns. He saw Alan race across the crest of the hill, hoping to find a bet-ter angle to spot the shooter. The gunman fired again. From the sound, the soldiers could tell it was a 7.62 round, but they still could not see the sniper.

Thinking that they might want to make a quick exit, Michael T. pulled the Humvees into a position where the men could hide behind the vehicles and jump in them to pull out at a moment's notice. A truck had pulled up on the road below. Michael T. thought the rounds came from the compound, but Alan believed they came from the truck. He thought he saw the silhouette of a machine gun mounted behind its cab, a setup called a technical in Somalia that was the favored tool of the militias.

Alan started down the hill toward the truck. Shots peppered the ground where he was walking, then he felt the bullets whiz by him in the air as the gunner found his range. This enraged Alan, who dodged and danced to evade the bullets peppering the air and ground around him. He was so obsessed with finding the gunner to return fire that he did not think about what it would be like to get hit. But he could not just fire blindly at the truck, because it was surrounded by a veritable human flood. The massive exodus swelled around them, containing people and vehicles, animals, and probably unfriendly armed militias—the chaotic swarm of humanity that was Somalia.

They could not fire on civilians, and had to allow themselves to be shot at unless, or until, they could find the gunman. The firing continued sporadically for a few hours, then, just as suddenly as it had started, it stopped. "That wasn't so bad," Alan said, letting out a deep chuckle.

It was the first time Alan Johnson had ever been shot at. He never did find the gunman, and his teammates laughed long and hard at his bullet-dodging dance. Even for Michael T., who had been with the Saudi army in Desert Storm, this was as hairy a situation as he'd yet seen in his SF career. Given the sea of people, there had been no way to take the offensive, which was always the preferred tactic. Killer praised his men's restraint. "You can't just fire on a hundred people," he said, shrugging.

It was a taste of the messiness of war amid civilians, the classic guerrilla warfare for which they had been trained. These were the types of "battles" that these young sergeants would commonly encounter, even though they were not battles by conventional definitions. The "low-intensity conflicts," as the Pentagon had started calling these Third World wars from Africa to Latin America to Asia, did not feature uniformed soldiers lined up in formations or bearing down in tanks. Instead they were characterized by potshots in the night, rampaging crowds, fighters mingling in the crowd, the sniper or the ambush waiting around the next turn. One minute the area would appear to be completely tranquil, in the next gunfire would erupt and the trap would be sprung.

Soldiers frequently are asked by civilians, What is it like to shoot someone or to be shot at? Many will rarely discuss the first except among their comrades. The answers to the second often are unmelodramatic. For the well-trained soldier it is a matter of reflex, as with Alan when he immediately focused on locating the shooter, avoiding the gunfire, and seeking a defensible position. The training produces an automatic response with a minimum of reflection or extraneous thought, and little emotion—the soldier is too busy reacting. But after the fact, emotions can well up as the mind tries to catch up to the reality of the life-threatening event. Some men react to trauma in extraordinary ways, above and beyond the call of duty, and those stories are worth telling.

The day after Alan's first experience of being shot at, Bobby Deeks was killed. It happened up north, outside Beledweyne. He was a Special Forces medic in their company, which was short of medics. Sgt. First Class Robert Deeks had been attached to ODA 562 when the teams were detailed to visit various warlords' turfs. Alan and Deeks had become friends during their first months in Kenya. They had flown overwatch missions together and had infiltrated on clandestine airfield surveillance missions. They had been dropped off one night in the middle of Somalia with another operator and a bag of weapons. They had laughed about it later over dinner back in Kenya.

When Deeks and ODA 562 arrived in the north, they went on patrol near Somalia's disputed border with Ethiopia. The two countries had fought a savage, decade-long war and had only a "provisional administrative line" in the sand to show for all the bloodletting. No territory on earth had more land mines per square mile. Deeks drove one of the team's soft-topped Humvees, following behind another vehicle. His left wheel drove right over a buried land mine, so his body received the brunt of the explosion. When his teammates saw his bloody, mangled form they thought he was dead, so they began giving first aid to the other two men wounded in the blast, one of whom had a broken back. Deeks had been their only medic, so they treated the wounded the best way they knew how.

As the men worked feverishly to stabilize their teammates, one of them saw Deeks move. His face was covered in blood. The land mine had ripped one leg off above the knee, the other below it, and he had lost one hand and an eye. Yet, despite all this damage to his body, Deeks regained consciousness and began instructing his fellow soldiers on what first aid to give the other two men and himself. He was the medic and his job was to save lives. The team frantically tried to contact Beledweyne, where the medical evacuation unit of a Canadian airborne regiment was located. The primary radio had been in Deeks' vehicle and was destroyed, but they finally got the backup unit to work. An hour and a half after the explosion, the helicopter arrived. As it lifted off with Deeks in the bay, he lost consciousness. He had done all he could for his teammates. He died as the bird landed about thirty minutes later.

No U.S. Army Special Forces soldier from 5th Group talks about Somalia without mentioning Bob Deeks. Their language lab in the second dun-colored building on the south side of the Fort Campbell parade ground is named for him. And out in the parade ground itself, in the simple memorial park where a tree is planted for each of their soldiers who has died in action or on a training exercise, there is a tree with a plaque for Bobby Deeks.

CHAPTER 6

CONUS*

That's not a risk we have to take.

—COLONEL ARTHUR "BULL" SIMONS

EIGHTEEN SOLDIERS were killed and another fifty-seven wounded in the October 1993 battle in Mogadishu, Somalia. The worst single battle toll since Vietnam jolted U.S. military leaders into the recognition that they had to do much more to prepare their troops to fight in cities. The trend seemed inevitable: frontal set-piece battles were becoming less common than skirmishes with irregular forces who were intermixed with civilians. The military's national training centers remained focused on the big East-West cold war–era battle scenarios until the grisly spectacle of the bodies of U.S. Rangers being dragged through the streets of Mogadishu was broadcast on worldwide television.

The training centers began designing and conducting annual exercises specifically for Military Operations in Urban Terrain (MOUT). In such battles, soldiers in armored and mechanized units had to dismount

---

* Continental United States.

in narrow streets to fight where the tanks could not. They often had to do without artillery, which was too imprecise for urban settings and could cause heavy civilian casualties. Even for infantry accustomed to fighting on foot, shooting and maneuvering tactics in cities differed from the standard light infantry tactics and demanded higher skill levels. Weaponry had to be altered for use at close range, because the back-blasts on many standard weapons would cause friendly casualties. The Special Forces were the first to receive the M4, the modified standard-issue M16, whose short, collapsible stock was far easier to maneuver with. They were the envy of conventional soldiers.

The Special Forces had always done more urban and close-quarter battle training than the conventional military because of the nature of their missions, but after Somalia they, too, increased and expanded their own preparation. Two of the five missions that Special Forces were required by doctrine to be prepared to conduct were particularly likely to involve urban combat: counterterrorism and direct action (the latter is a catch-all term for a variety of quick commando-style strikes). Special reconnaissance, while not intended to result in contact with the enemy, could require urban fighting if the team was discovered. Even the missions that involved training or fighting with foreign forces (unconventional warfare and foreign internal defense, the ungainly term that replaced counterinsurgency) at times required using or imparting those skills.*

Fighting inside buildings is an order of magnitude more difficult than fighting in city streets. All Special Forces are trained in these close-quarter battle skills, including hand-to-hand combat, but some units devote all or most of their time to achieving and maintaining those skills. In 1977, the secret Delta force was formed and devoted full-time to counter-terror missions; it deployed many times to the Middle East and Latin America in the 1980s. Additionally, elements of the five active-duty Special Forces groups are designated as crisis-reaction units that can be

---

* Unconventional warfare is used in this book to denote all training, advising, and fighting alongside foreign forces.

launched at a moment's notice by the regional commander for counter-terror or other emergencies. The Special Forces have developed an alphabet soup of courses (ASOT, SOTIC, SFARTEC) to perfect various individual direct-action skills, and their group training is called the Special Forces Advanced Urban Combat Course (SFAUCC).

Then Major General William G. Boykin instituted the SFAUCC training after Somalia, when he became commandant of the Special Forces school. He had a particular motivation to improve their urban combat training; he had been the squadron commander of the Delta force troops in Mogadishu in 1993. The training gradually was expanded until every Special Forces company went through the SFAUC course periodically. During a typical five-week course, a company fires nearly two million rounds of ammunition in some of the most intensive shooting drills in the U.S. military. The extremely high level of marksmanship required for indoor combat only can be attained and maintained through practice. Distinguishing targets from noncombatants is practiced in situational shooting exercises and stress tests with night-vision goggles and laser aiming devices. The soldiers also practice switching quickly from firing their M4 rifles at a distance to drawing their 9-mm pistols on approaching targets.

After these skills are honed on the range, the soldiers move to a more realistic setting for the next stage of the course. At a complex of white two-story buildings at Fort Bragg, soldiers practice breaching wood and metal doors and walls and moving into and through rooms, all the while distinguishing armed targets from noncombatants. For this phase of the training, the soldiers use not guns with bullets but a version of paintball, with equipment that registers whether the correct target was hit with a pellet of paint. The equipment is called simmunitions, meaning simulated munitions. Occasionally, live volunteers are used to people the target zone; in one day's exercise, a civilian was asked to stand beside a target, which was a poster of Bruce Lee carrying a gun. The soldiers entered the room and correctly splattered paint on the karate king and not the noncombatant.

At the end of the course a full-dress exercise is held in an actual urban setting, with the permission of local authorities. In one exercise in early 2002, one company of 7th Group planned an entire mission including infiltrating, attacking, and exiting the target, in this case an abandoned school in a Dallas, North Carolina, neighborhood. The local SWAT team served as the opposition force, and the SFAUCC instructors built extra barricades inside the school that the soldiers would have to breach.

The company infiltrated its surveillance and signals intelligence teams three days before the planned "assault." The night of the exercise, the company flew to a nearby airport in Charlotte aboard transport planes, and then loaded into Black Hawk and Chinook helicopters for the final leg to the school. Shortly before the "attack," neighborhood residents were forewarned and the fire department set up a cordon around the block.

The assault was carried out at night, as preferred by the Special Forces' for all their operations. The team leading the entry fast-roped down from a hovering helicopter (the technique is essentially rappelling without the mountain) while the remainder came in aboard Chinooks that landed just across the street, churning up a hail of dirt and gravel.

The objective was to reach a room where "hostages" were being held. Some of the barricades that had been built inside the school refused to yield to their explosive charges, so the soldiers had to seek alternative points of entry. The commander of 7th Group, Colonel Peter Dillon, glanced at his watch to see how the men would recoup from this delay. They had planned to be in and out in thirty minutes, but it was an hour before they found and identified their suspect.

The exercise controllers sprang another surprise on the men during the exfiltration. A crash landing of one of the Black Hawks was simulated in a nearby park, to test how the soldiers would react to the emergency. They would have to land the other helicopters and retrieve the men from the one that had been disabled. When they did land, the local SWAT team ambushed them (with blanks), while hiding in the woods across a pond, further complicating the rescue effort. Some defended the team while others loaded the wounded soldiers onto the functioning helicopters.

Dillon stood about fifty yards away watching through night-vision binoculars. He would offer his evaluation after the men had provided their own critiques. He had designed the exercise as much for testing their ability to plan, react, and improvise as a unit under high stress, as for evaluating their shooting and raiding skills. Dillon's mild and thoughtful demeanor deceived those who expected commandos to be brash, swaggering types. Nothing about his quiet, almost academic manner suggested his past service. This was not uncommon for Special Forces personnel: if one was looking for a commando in a crowded room, they would not likely be picked.

Like athletes, the lives of soldiers are mostly filled with training. It is key to any expertise and, thus, it follows that the most skilled soldiers have the most training. The Special Forces place supreme emphasis on training because they view the individual soldier and his brain as the key factor in the fight. A Special Forces two-star general, David Baratto, formulated four bedrock principles for special operations forces when he became the first chief of operations at the Special Operations Command, which was created in 1986 to give special operations forces (or SOF) an institutional structure similar to the conventional army, navy, air force, and marines.

The first "SOF Truth" that General Baratto coined was "Humans are more important than hardware." The three other basic precepts are: quality is more important than quantity; special operations forces cannot be mass produced; and special operations forces cannot be produced quickly after a crisis occurs. The Special Forces had been eviscerated after Vietnam and Baratto wanted to make sure that, in the future, forces that take many years to develop would not be hastily dismantled. (Baratto later developed corollaries to these truths, called "SOF Imperatives," when he was named commandant of the Special Warfare Center and School. The school selects and trains the U.S. Army Special Forces and writes their doctrine—the official writ that describes every step of their training to every tactic, technique, and procedure for all of their assigned missions. Baratto's imperatives encapsulate central tenets of their craft. "Know your operational environment," for example, reminds the operator to examine all factors of a situation, political as well as military.)

Some Special Forces soldiers describe themselves as simply very good and experienced infantrymen. It is not quite true, because the type of man who fits the SF mold is not likely to have found the conventional force a comfortable fit, and the Special Forces are not ever intended to be used as infantry in conventional battles. But what is true is that the Special Forces soldier must have a strong foundation of infantry skills. He is turned into an expert by relentless training and competition. He attends schools throughout his career and even competes for assignments. The commander commonly asks two or more teams to come up with plans for a given mission and then picks the best one. The Special Forces' lives may be one long Olympiad, but these men tried out because they had a desire to prove themselves, strive for excellence, and tackle enormous challenges.

Even with all this training, the Special Forces assume a great deal of risk both in the missions they are assigned and the techniques they use to carry them out. The training itself is dangerous, although every effort is made to minimize the hazards. But training, to be effective, must be as realistic as possible. The reason SF soldiers are comfortable with loaded weapons is because they frequently use live ammunition. Soldiers who are not accustomed to loaded weapons inevitably have more accidental discharges, which result in more injury or death. The huge variety of weapons and lethal material that Special Forces soldiers handle, however, increases the risks nonetheless, especially when deployed in remote areas.

Randy Wurst just happened to pick the individual and team specialties with the highest risks. He became a weapons sergeant on a team that specialized in high-altitude, low-opening (HALO) parachute infiltration. Randy spent a lot of time with weapons on ranges and in airplanes. If a team member had a malfunctioning weapon he would seek out "Rawhide the gunslinger" to fix it.

The hazards of their lives came home to Randy and ODA 534 when they were deployed to Kuwait as part of Operation Southern Watch in 1992, while 2nd Battalion was in Somalia. The team set up camp just south of the Iraqi border, near the main highway leading into Iraq. The Special Forces' main task was to train the Kuwaiti military and watch the border, and they disposed of some of the massive quantities of munitions and arms that the retreating Iraqis had abandoned. There was also a large amount of unexploded ordnance that had been fired or dropped by American tanks and planes.

On one of their first days patrolling in their Humvees, ODA 534 found themselves surrounded by dozens of bright yellow shells with parachutes scattered across the sun-baked ground. The munitions might have been sensitized by lying exposed to the elements in the year since the American warplanes had dropped them, and the vibration from a nearby vehicle's movement could be enough to detonate them. The team halted and debated how to extricate itself.

"If you think about it too much it is going to paralyze us, and then we'll be stuck here," decided Randy. "There is only one thing to do. I'm going to clear a path for us to get out."

He raised his gun and fired at the parachute end of one of the soda can-sized bomblets, about twenty-five meters away. No explosion. He aimed at the other end and fired.

The Humvee rocked from the blast of the resulting explosion and shrapnel flew in every direction.

"Man, you are going to kill us," one of the sergeants suggested.

"That stuff is bad to the bone," agreed Randy. "But do you have any better idea how to get out of here?"

No one did, so Randy shot another one. It exploded and fireworks rained all around them. A couple more, equally terrifying explosions and he had cleared a path out. The men all felt a new sympathy for those who had been on the ground when U.S. planes dropped their loads. These cluster bombs were especially nefarious because their parachutes scatter them widely and they linger long after the conflict is over, posing a lethal hazard to civilians. They were still going off in Southeast Asia thirty years after the Vietnam war, and an estimated 1.2 million bomblets were left after Desert Storm and caused hundreds of civilian deaths. There were periodic campaigns to urge that cluster bombs, and land mines, be banned, or at least fitted with self-destruct mechanisms so they would not lie in wait for decades.

By night, ODA 534 ran patrols on the border and watched the Iraqi forces on the other side. By day, the men dug fighting positions, trained and advised the Kuwaitis, and tested, destroyed, and trained on munitions at a range they'd built. One day, Randy and another sergeant were working alone on the range as the temperature climbed to more than one hundred degrees. Explosive ordnance disposal teams had come through earlier to clear out some of the larger munitions, but this had been a vast ammunition supply point for the Republican Guards occupying Kuwait. Randy and his teammate found a cache of small black Italian-made grenades and decided to dispose of them in a nearby pit. The sergeant threw one but it did not detonate. Randy, his pitcher's arm still in decent form, sent one flying into the large white pit.

Windows blew open and dishes rattled in the oil field complex twenty kilometers away. A guard post on the Iraqi side of the border collapsed. A large metal building near the range creased in half and several shacks collapsed as the shock wave swept outward. The windshields blew out of vehicles. A hurricane-force wind carrying shrapnel, debris, telephone poles, sand, and anything else in its path, swept away from ground zero. A huge orange mushroom cloud formed and rose up into the sky, visible for miles around. The captain of the team saw the cloud and ran to his Humvee to go to the scene. He knew his men were near the epicenter of the blast because they told him they'd be working on the range that day.

The sergeant, who'd prudently bent down behind an eight-foot wall as Randy had lobbed his grenade into the pit, was so stunned by the incredible blast that he was certain he had been maimed. He held his arms between his legs and duckwalked away from the site. He gazed back at the yawning hole about forty meters wide and two meters deep that had been created by whatever had exploded down there. A few dozen meters away he saw two of their teammates who had been knocked down, one on top of the other, by the explosion. As they stood up shakily, all three of them turned at the sound of a war whoop and saw Randy running toward them out of the pit.

The captain pulled up at that moment, leaped from his Humvee, and, counting four bodies standing, sagged with relief. The men all looked at Randy. His face was black and bleeding and sandblasted, but he was alive. The doctor at Camp Doha thought his lungs might have been damaged by overpressure but allowed him to go back to his team's camp. As scabs formed over his face in the coming days, his teammates set up a separate table and stool, facing away from theirs, so they would not have to look at the mess of healing skin as they ate.

This became known as the "nuclear grenade" story. Randy, who was never shy of making jokes at his own expense, often told it, as did his teammates, who could best appreciate the walking testament to the power of explosives that he became for a few weeks. Staff Sergeant Steve Rainey, who had joined 534 after Desert Storm, was down the road when the blast occurred but saw Randy at camp that night. "When the explosion went off, it pushed all of Randy's hair back and literally creased his skin. It looked like the cartoon character's face when the bomb goes off," Rainey recalled.

> For two weeks after that, he'd get up in the morning and get a big bucket and wash his hair and his face. As soon as his hair dried, it went right back like that. You could see the lines in his face for two weeks.... It was *funny*. Because he was still alive, you could make fun of him. I'll never forget that face if I live to be 120 years old.

Randy suffered his teammates' jibes and the damage to the property and vehicles was paid for. No one could explain how Randy had survived such a powerful explosion. His face was scarred slightly and his lungs may have been permanently damaged, but he had walked away from it.

Randy had joined a HALO team as soon as he arrived at 5th Group.

As a general rule, men with certain personality traits gravitate toward certain types of teams. The military free-fall parachute teams, the HALO teams, attract men who are thrilled by what Clint Eastwood's character in the movie *Heartbreak Ridge* called the unnatural act of jumping out of a perfectly good airplane. It bears little resemblance to recreational sky-diving. Teams make oxygen-assisted jumps at night, in full combat gear, from as high as 35,000 feet into enemy territory. The first combat HALO jumps were made in November 1970 in Vietnam by Special Forces. Casualty rates had grown so high on helicopter insertions along the Ho Chi Minh Trail that parachuting from the altitudes used by commercial flights was pioneered as a less detectable means of infiltrating.

Military free-fall is one of the most demanding and dangerous advanced skills the Special Forces soldiers acquire. The trainees already must be qualified in the static-line parachute jumps done by the Rangers and other airborne units, which is one reason so many Special Forces members come from those units. Static-line jumps are made from a few thousand feet, with a static, or fixed, line inside the plane, which deploys the round parachutes immediately upon exiting the door. The Special Forces developed the high-altitude, low-opening parachuting as a method of stealthy infiltration because the plane is so high that it is mistaken for a commercial plane and the jumpers are not seen. Another method is high-altitude, high-opening (HAHO) jumps in which the parachutists open their chutes higher up and navigate great distances before landing. The men are outfitted with oxygen masks and free-fall singly, in groups, or in formations down to about 2,500 feet before pulling the ripcord on the 360-foot steerable rectangular chute. Soldiers master these skills in a four-week school that starts at the octagonal wind tunnel facility at Fort Bragg, N.C. and ends at Yuma Proving Ground in Arizona, where they progress through mass exits, grouping exercises, night airborne operations, and jumping with full combat gear and oxygen. Only 500 students are trained each year.

Once a soldier graduates from HALO school, he must keep jumping on a regular basis to maintain his readiness status. He must have completed the full sequence of required jumps in recent months—a daytime jump, then a nighttime jump, then a night jump with oxygen, then a night jump with oxygen and full combat gear. No matter how many times a soldier does it, the dangers of jumping fully loaded from tens of thousands of feet never disappear.

HALO teams are often requested to jump with foreign militaries' elite forces or to teach them the skill. ODA 534 was on just such a mission in Jordan in 1993. The Jordanian special forces were better than most, but they were not experienced HALO jumpers. Their equipment flew off and men collided with each other in midair. After a couple of jumps like this, ODA 534 decided they would let the Jordanians exit the plane first and follow on at a safe distance. When Randy's turn came, a strap on his rucksack broke, throwing him into a wild off-kilter tumble for thousands of feet.

Steve Rainey looked up into the night and all he could see were the red, green, and yellow lights on Randy's leg, pack, and altimeter twirling through the night. Normally, the jumper's body would be firmly splayed in the frog position. Hurtling earthward at 125 miles an hour did not give Randy much time to correct himself. He finally managed to grab the pack and pull the rip cord before he fell too low. The chute unfurled, but the center panel ripped out and when the chute collapsed in on itself, Randy resumed his earthward dive. Now he was really sweating. He reached for the emergency chute, but its ripcord had been twisted out of reach by the pack's displacement. He finally found it and yanked, unfurling the spare chute just in time to land safely.

Jump disasters followed Randy like the plague. Alan Johnson vividly recalled his second jump with Randy. ODA 544, the team Randy joined after 534, had no jumpmaster, a soldier who is certified to oversee jumps, so Alan agreed to fill their vacancy for a planned jump. When they were airborne, he proposed that they practice a formation jump—he would link up with Randy and the rest would join arms and legs as they descended. Sergeant First Class Eric Olson demurred, "I don't think you should do that. Bad stuff happens when Randy jumps." Eric had been shaken by the Jordan incident. "Nonsense," Alan replied. "We're all HALO qualified here."

When the men left the plane's door, the planned formation fell apart. The men broke off into solo jumps, and Alan and Randy grabbed each other's wrists in a standard two-man formation. They fell, bellies down, arms linked, and all seemed fine. Then suddenly Randy began rolling over, his wrists crossing, until he faced skyward. Perplexed, Alan let go of one of Randy's wrists so he could turn himself facedown again, but instead Randy slid underneath him. Alan decided to release him altogether. At that moment Randy did a barrel roll, spinning around and kicking Alan in the chin with his boot. Alan waved him off and decided to finish the jump solo. Randy landed a short distance away with no difficulty. The team's medic come over to look at Alan's split chin, which was gushing blood. "Holy crap," he said. Alan, like most Special Forces soldiers, did not want to report any injury that could sideline him, so he asked a pal who was a medic to come to his house with his lidocaine and needle and stitch him up. The next day, Alan told Randy, who was on his way to the certification course to become an instructor for HALO jumping, "If you come back from that course alive, I'll jump with you. But not 'til then." Randy completed the course and became his team's jumpmaster for several years, and memories of the supposed HALO jinx faded.

Over the years, Randy attended courses in anti-terrorism, driving techniques, sniping, even detecting nuclear and chemical weapons. Because he could not bear the idea of leaving the team for a staff position on the company or battalion, he decided to become a chief warrant officer, even though it would require going to school for more than a year of intensive study. The warrant officer course turns a sergeant into an officer: first comes officer candidate school and then a nineteen-week-long course that includes advanced special operations training, military decision-making process, personnel recovery exercises, and regional studies. When the Special Forces sergeant completes this schooling he receives the rank of chief warrant officer 2 (CW2) due to his prior experience. He now has all the skills to lead a twelve-man ODA and plan multi-echelon operations.

The chief warrant officer usually serves as the assistant commander of the ODA unless there is no captain, in which case the "chief" serves as the commander. Captains come straight out of the Q course to lead ODAs for an average of eighteen months. Then they move up the hierarchy, never to return to a team. They are given staff jobs, then they go to majors' school, then they come back to company and battalion jobs.

During the 1990s, Randy's team went all over the Middle East, including seven times to Kuwait as well as to Jordan, Bahrain, the United Arab Emirates, and northern Africa and the Horn. While Special Forces train in the continental United States (CONUS) and abroad, virtually all of the missions that the Special Forces undertake are in foreign countries. Only a handful have been carried out in U.S. territory. Most of those were counter-narcotics missions carried out in the 1990s, but after 2001 the small numbers of Special Forces were refocused on traditional national security tasks. The Posse Comitatus Act bars the military from acting in a law enforcement capacity on U.S. soil. The longstanding consensus has been to keep the uniformed services (except for the Coast Guard) focused on national defense rather than any task remotely related to policing. Drug trafficking and terrorism are two problems that cross traditional lines of authority and divisions of labor, however, and assistance from the military has been deemed necessary to cope with aspects of transnational crime and threats to homeland security. The military forces, however, are placed under the control of civilian law enforcement entities.

In the 1990s, drugs were pouring over the U.S.-Mexican border and law enforcement agencies were overwhelmed by the volume of drugs and the increasing sophistication of the trafficking organizations—as well as by the corrupting power of their wealth. Officials on both sides of the border were being offered princely sums to look the other way. A multi-agency Joint Task Force 6 and the El Paso Intelligence Center had been formed at Fort Bliss, outside El Paso, Texas, to pool various federal and local agencies' resources to address the crisis. Special Forces teams were detailed to help the tiny Border Patrol, Customs agents and others stem the flow of drugs in the United States. The teams were used for surveillance and detection against foreign targets. Any arrests were to be made by those with policing authority.

In 1997, ODA 544 was selected for a special mission on the southern border of the United States. Randy was delighted to be chosen to participate. Seventh Group had been working on anti-drug assignments in Latin America for years, but this was something new for 5th Group. The team saw it as a chance to help protect America's borders and to reduce the drug trade and its attendant violence. It was also a challenge: the traffickers were sophisticated, well armed, and spent millions of their drug cash on the latest weaponry, encryption, and surveillance technology. The Special Forces were not surprised that America's policemen were coming up short against what was in effect an irregular army.

Joint Task Force 6 needed a HALO team to conduct a nighttime surveillance mission on a major Mexican trafficking organization that was shipping tons of cocaine into the United States monthly. The Mexican cartels had eclipsed their Colombian partners as the principal transporters of illegal drugs. Their methods were bold and inventive. They landed jumbo jets in the remote desert along the Mexican side of the border and ferried consignments via trucks, tunnels, small planes, and human mules.

ODA 544 was sent to White Sands, New Mexico, just across the Texas border, to prepare. The team practiced patrolling, hide sites, escape and evasion, and desert survival in the most realistic conditions they could devise. All went well, with one small problem. Randy had shingles, which had spread to his face and then into one eye. The medicine he was prescribed dilated the pupil. He could see out of his other eye so long as he wore glasses, but he had been putting off the surgery he needed to correct the vision in that eye.

The team's penultimate practice jump went fine; Randy wore glasses with flight goggles strapped over them on the outside of his helmet. The next night would be their last jump before the real thing. As jumpmaster, it was Randy's responsibility to decide whether he would participate. Another jumpmaster might have sidelined him, but he decided to go.

The team moved to Texas for its final practice jump in the desert outside El Paso. When the plane reached 15,000 feet, the light came on and Randy motioned for the men to line up by the open door. The team members bailed out on cue and Randy went last. This jump was "full mission profile"—the team was to replicate its actual mission in every detail. The men carried guns and rucksacks loaded with everything they would need. Randy's gear added 200 pounds to his bodyweight of 197 pounds. The parachute spun out behind him and gave a mighty yank as it reached its full extension, like a gigantic yo-yo snapping at the bottom of its arc. The more weight, the harder the yank—sometimes it is hard enough to knock the men out momentarily. Randy's goggles and glasses flew off; he could cope without the goggles, but losing the glasses effectively blinded him. He could barely make out the needle of the altimeter fastened to his wrist, and when it passed into the black shaded area of the dial, indicating the 1,000-foot mark, he could see nothing.

All he could do was follow the chutes in front of him and estimate the point at which he should turn and bank his chute for the landing. He saw the chute two men ahead of him make its 90-degree turn to land and counted the interval until the next one executed its turn. He then waited the same interval to make his turn. That should put him at 500 feet above the ground, if the other two had turned at the right altitude. The square HALO parachute tilted forward on the sharp turn, angling Randy's body forward. In horror he saw the ground coming up to meet him no more than thirty feet away. Each of the succeeding jumpers had turned at lower altitudes. He was roughly roof high and would slam into the ground in seconds.

Certain he would be killed, Randy immediately let up on the steering toggle to lift the chute and pull his body into a more upright position. He could see the earth coming at him.

"Oh God, this is going to hurt," he said. "My rucksack!" He remembered that his toes were still hooked into the strap of his rucksack. The standard technique was to lower the rucksack onto one's feet while high above the ground and then release it just before landing. This minimized the pack's impact and equipment breakage. But landing with his feet in the pack's strap would be disastrous. He freed his left foot before he hit the ground. He pitched forward and his helmet plowed a furrow fifteen- or twenty-feet long. His chin was jammed into his chest so hard that he expected his neck to snap at any moment.

"Lights out. That's it for me," he thought. His body hit something and flipped him onto his back. The years of training kicked in—the first thing a soldier is supposed to do is grab his gun and get into a fighting position. As Randy reached for his gun he heard his bones crack.

His huge pack was lying on top of his right leg, so he gently pushed it off with his left foot. He raised himself up slightly to look at his right leg and found himself staring at his boot heel. The leg was twisted backward 180 degrees. He felt nothing.

"Okay, God, I'm really going to need your help," he prayed. "I know I'm pretty messed up, so you're going to have to help get me through this."

The rest of the team had gathered at the assembly area and was preparing to move out on the patrol that was the next step of their mission. The team sergeant came up—he had seen the last chute turn. "I'm going to chew the ass of whoever made that low hook turn," he growled.

The men took a head count and realized that Randy was missing. He must have crashed. It took them a while to find him because he was covered in dirt. Randy lay there, feeling nothing. He knew they would eventually find him, just as he knew he would eventually feel great pain.

Finally they found him. Eyes bulged when they saw Randy's leg facing the wrong way. The team's two medics instantly went to work to stabilize him and splint the leg. The communications sergeant called for medical evacuation. The other teammates chatted to him to keep his mind off the damage and what was to come. As they got ready to move him Eric Olson asked him, "Hey man, do you wanna hold my hand?"

Randy gripped it.

"Do you want a smoke?" Olson asked.

"You bastards didn't even realize I quit smoking," Randy said.

"Bummer, dude. Bad time to quit," Eric replied.

As the medics hoisted him onto the stretcher, Randy decided to accept the cigarette.

Just as the helicopter arrived, a storm moved in, lashing the Texas plains with winds and lightning. The chopper heaved and pitched all the way to Fort Bliss, the army base just outside El Paso. Randy wondered if God had spared him only to have him die in a helicopter crash. The crew struggled with the bucking aircraft as Randy pitched in the back.

Two of the top orthopedic surgeons in the United States happened to be at the medical center at Fort Bliss doing volunteer work on veterans. They heard the emergency call. Former paratroopers themselves, they were waiting at the emergency room door when Randy was brought in.

Randy looked up at them from a gurney.

"Two things I gotta tell you," he said. "My left eye is dilated because it is being treated. The other thing is, I don't wear any underwear so don't cut my pants off."

They laughed and started asking him questions and taking his pulse. "Commando underwear" did not surprise them; it was common among soldiers in Vietnam. One doctor moved up by his head and the other one down to his foot. Randy thought: Something bad is going to happen here. They're planning something. Then the doctor grabbed his foot and tried to turn the leg around.

Randy came straight up out of the gurney like a mannequin, then slumped back down onto the cart. He nearly passed out from the pain.

"Doc, you don't have enough balls to do that again," Randy said, a cold sweat pouring off of him. The doctors knew they had to straighten the leg to restore the blood flow or he would lose the leg.

"Okay, Chief, we'll put you out," one of them said, and gave him a sedative.

He came to a while later and, seeing his straightened leg, assumed that they had done what they needed to do. In fact they had yet to operate on the badly mangled leg and were waiting for the anesthesiologist. He drifted to sleep again. When he next woke, he felt very cold. He was still in the hallway outside the operating room. A female anesthesiologist stood over him. She asked questions and told him that he would have to sign a waiver for a spinal tap. He realized why he was cold. They had cut his pants off. He lay there half naked, the sheet at his feet, but the doctor did not notice his embarrassment. "Please ma'am," Randy begged, "would you pull those covers up?"

The next day, after the operation, a nurse came into his room. The anesthesia had left Randy groggy, but at least he was alive. The nurse opened the curtains and turned to look at him. She said: "You must be someone very important. You've had calls from two generals and a colonel. They called to see if you were all right."

Chris Conner had phoned Fort Bliss as soon as he heard the news. He had just returned to 5th Group as the operations officer of 2nd Battalion. He had been to the Command and General Staff College at Leavenworth, the Naval Post Graduate School to learn Russian, the joint staff in the special ops division, and in the personnel command at the Pentagon. He and Polly had had their first children, cute, brown-eyed twins they'd named Sam and Maddy. Conner could tell from the medic's report that Randy faced a long and painful recovery.

Randy returned to Fort Campbell where his first weeks were spent in the base hospital. He knew he was lucky. He hadn't been killed nor was he a paraplegic. He had his wife and children. He told himself that he would be up and running in no time, but a month later Randy still was lying helplessly in bed. He stopped taking the pain medication. The shingles, a raging infection in his nervous system, had lingered on. He looked at his cast and the contraption that held it and suddenly lost hope. During his wife's visit that day, Randy broke down and cried in her arms. He had never done that before.

"I don't think I'm ever going to walk again," he said. "My whole life is done." Randy could not bear to contemplate what might be in store. The doctors in Texas had told him that he might be permanently crippled, but he had not been able to process that information. Now the reality was starting to sink in: he might never be on a team again. He knew two men in 5th Group had been left with club feet after HALO accidents. They were permanently assigned to staff jobs—that could be his fate, or he could be forced to retire on disability.

The only previous occasion that Randy had experienced comparable despair was when, as a young deputy sheriff, he had felt betrayed by his own department. That had been fifteen years ago, in Cody, Wyoming, his adopted hometown. He had discovered and documented abuses by a fellow deputy, but the sheriff had not backed him up. The deputy, who intended to run for election as sheriff, schemed to discredit Randy, even though he had the best uncontested arrest and speeding ticket record in the department. By enlisting local powerbrokers in his machinations, Randy's rival eventually succeeded in having him placed in charge of guarding the jail—the equivalent of being demoted to private in the law-enforcement hierarchy. Randy had majored in criminal justice in college and that had been his chosen profession. He wanted to raise his family in Cody and live the police and cowboy life, but the sheriff, who had been a mentor and father figure to him, had let this happen. Randy was heartbroken that other colleagues had not warned him what was afoot, even as he discovered and publicized other unethical behavior. While some members of the department were later fired and then charged, he was blackballed for whistle blowing. He wanted nothing more to do with the profession. He'd had a new baby and a large mortgage, but decided to quit his job and start over, in the army, at the age of thirty. He had taken a huge gamble then and it had paid off. Now here he faced another crisis of confidence.

His wife brought people from their church to visit Randy in the hospital. They said a blessing for him, and the minister told him that, after all he had been through, it was clear that he had not one angel but a host of angels looking after him. Randy felt less helpless after he returned to work, hobbling, about two months later. He was assigned to the company staff, but early each day and after work he headed to the gym to grind out the exercises the therapists had told him to do.

Randy remembered when his grammar school teacher, the same one who had nicknamed him "Rawhide," had told him that he had a warrior's spirit. Mr. Weir was not referring to his Blackfoot ancestry or his athleticism. He had seen him face down some students who were bullying a new classmate for playing with a GI Joe doll. Randy taunted the bullies and deflected their aggressiveness onto himself, earning the newcomer's gratitude. Mr. Weir had not seen many kindnesses among ten-year-old boys. He told Randy that his ability to empathize and his willingness to absorb physical and emotional hurt were the real traits of a warrior. Because their rural school was so small, Mr. Weir was Randy's teacher for many grades, and he taught him as much about the warrior's way as did his grandfather, his father, and the Greek legends that had captivated him. The shame was not in falling down, only in failing to get back up. If his calling was to serve and protect, he couldn't do that unless he got back on his feet.

Although Randy's rehabilitation went slowly, the two surgeons in Texas had done excellent work putting his leg back together. In less capable hands Randy almost certainly would have been crippled. After six months he was still limping, but he was better. His doctor warned him that he would likely suffer long-term effects from the injury. He had a bolt in his ankle and his entire lower right leg was thicker from the scar tissue that was forming. Eventually the scar tissue growing in and around the joints would restrict their movement and cause arthritis. The ankle had been most severely mutilated, but his knee and hip and been injured as well.

Randy kept at his therapy and tried not to pester the company and battalion commanders too much, but he periodically beseeched them to put him back on a team. In 1999, after a year of recovery, he was assigned to ODA 564. Despite all of the rehab, however, Randy steadily lost flexibility. An orthopedic surgeon at Fort Campbell proposed a massive orthoscopic surgery to clean out all the scar tissue that had accumulated over two years. He could not guarantee the results but he would try to restore as much mobility as he could. Desperate for any remedy that would put him back into action, Randy agreed. At a checkup after the operation, he said: "You did a beautiful job, Doc. Look how much better I can move it." He knew that he would not even be walking if it were not for three men—this surgeon and the two in El Paso. He got back to the team a few weeks later and finished 2000 serving on it.

The following year, Randy was asked to be the commander of ODA 563, which did not have a captain and needed an experienced chief warrant officer to lead it. Randy jumped at the chance. "Rawhide" the gunslinger was finally back in the saddle and ready to lead the charge. Alongside him would be 563's charismatic team sergeant, Alan Johnson. Soon their team room hummed with energy generated by their enthusiasm. The team room is like a one-room clubhouse where the men live from dawn to dusk. After morning PT the men change into their uniforms and start to plan future missions and training exercises, schedule range time, draw and account for ammunition and equipment, fix and clean weapons and other gear, and perform the myriad daily chores that occupy them between deployment and training.

Randy made practice at the firing range a high priority. The first time Alan saw him shoot he was duly impressed. Rawhide was a fitting nickname for a guy who could twirl his pistol, spin it sideways, forward, or backward, and still hit the target dead center, just like a sharpshooter in Buffalo Bill's road show. He was carrying on the tradition of Cody's famous founder, which was still very much present in that land of ranchers and sheriffs. To the easterners on 563, it was as if a cowboy from a spaghetti Western had walked right out of the Silver Dollar saloon in Cody's Irma hotel and into their 5th Group saga. Alan decided to forgive him the long-ago split chin. That did not mean he would stop reminding him of the kick in the mouth. By this stage of his career Randy had plenty of crash and burn stories, and Alan even gave him hell for the one that nearly killed him in the Texas scrubland. "Randy," he would say, "You are the luckiest unlucky guy I ever met."

Randy's crash had deprived him of his chance to participate in a counter-narcotics mission on the Texas border, but others had taken his place and spent long nights staring through their powerful scopes at small Cessnas landing in the desert, furtive meetings in the dark, and a generally depressing avalanche of illegal narcotics that poured into the country. The men reconnoitered the border passes with their night-vision goggles and high-tech sensors while others humped their packs through Death Valley's heat to observation sites among the cactus. These surveillance missions helped drug enforcement agents document deals and map the web of traffickers. Sometimes the agents would make arrests, but often they would follow the same suspects for months to reach the highest possible rungs of the organization. Accustomed to compartmentalized operations, the ODAs often did their part without ever witnessing the culmination of the hunt, which might terminate in a city or foreign capital. The effort might take years or, in some cases, never bear any fruit.

For the teams, the anti-drug missions offered valuable experience in what would soon come to be known as homeland security, and a first-hand appreciation of what those charged with stopping contraband already knew—just how porous and difficult to control the borders were.

As the 1990s ended, the government's attention shifted to terrorist threats, particularly Islamic fundamentalist ones, and many Special Forces were returned to their basic national security focus. The approaching millennium generated a host of concerns about systemic Y2K failures and possible attacks by extremists. On December 11, 1999, the State Department issued a warning about travel overseas and the possibility of attacks on U.S. citizens, troops, and allies abroad after Jordan arrested thirteen Middle Easterners who were found to be planning to attack tourist hotels. Three days later the spotlight suddenly shifted to U.S. soil when suspicious Customs officers stopped an Algerian man taking a roundabout border crossing from Canada to Seattle, Washington. The man, Ahmed Ressam, began sweating profusely and tried to run away run from the officers. They discovered 130 pounds of an explosive called RDX and timers made from Casio watches in his trunk, as well as maps of Washington, Oregon, and California.

Ressam's arrest set off alarms throughout the government, which scrambled to secure all border crossings in the face of this indication that a major terrorist attack was being planned in the United States itself. The Federal Bureau of Investigation took charge of the Ressam case and began a nationwide investigation. It requested the help of the U.S. Special Forces 5th Group with its Arabic expertise. This stateside mission was the Special Forces' first counterterrorism operation on U.S.

soil. The usual Posse Comitatus norms applied, and the FBI was fully in charge of the investigation, surveillance, wire-tapping, and any arrests that would be made, but it was critically short of Arabic language and cultural expertise. Because there was probably a higher concentration of Arabic speakers in 5th Group than anywhere else in the U.S. government, it was a logical if unprecedented request—one that has remained secret until now.

Six soldiers from 5th Group were chosen to help. Alan Johnson, one of the group's best Arabic speakers, and two others were detailed to the FBI in California while the other trio met its FBI bosses in Seattle. Bits of information began pouring in from U.S. and international agencies. Airline records showed that Ressam had flown to Los Angeles in February of 1999 from South Korea and made two visits to the Canadian-U.S. border from his Montreal home. The sense of urgency mounted in the coming days when two of his Montreal-based associates were arrested after crossing the border in Vermont, a third in New York after he had attempted to visit Ressam, and another in Canada. Leads from these interrogations and those in Jordan led to a narrowing focus on California.

Alan and the other special operators in Los Angeles worked in shifts around the clock to assist FBI agents. The FBI asked them to interpret and analyze Arabic-language conversations as well as printed material including documents and pamphlets. Some of the conversations were tape recorded or transcripts, but most of the time Alan and his fellow Special Forces listened to real-time electronic intercepts of individuals that the FBI had under surveillance. Alan would don a headset and provide simultaneous translation for the agents. He sat in a room filled with electronic equipment in a secure but nondescript building that would never be mistaken for an FBI office. As the agents were out in the field, in Los Angeles and Orange counties, monitoring their surveillance subjects, Alan would tell them what he was hearing.

During his live translation of surveillance intercepts, on several occasions Alan could tell them whether it was safe to move forward if the conversation indicated they had not been seen. More than once, when agents were hoping to watch suspects undetected, Alan realized they had been spotted and warned his counterparts. He could not control any agents or activity by the Posse Comitatus terms, so the FBI relayed the news into their colleagues' earpieces. "Hey, they've seen you. Pull back," they ordered, "Pull back."

The FBI followed and questioned dozens of individuals from around California as they traced a widening net of Ahmed Ressam's associates with the help of wiretaps. Not all were suspects themselves but may have had unwitting contact with him. Over the weeks that the men from 5th Group spent in Los Angeles, the effort led to some of Ressam's co-conspirators as well as exposing his money trail and the organizational structure of his cell. The soldiers were not privy to the theorizing because their job was to train a fresh pair of eyes and ears on the individual pieces of data coming in. Johnson spent hours studying the material and writing analyses and reports for the agents.

The investigation soon established that Los Angeles, and not Seattle, was the target of Ahmed Ressam, who was affiliated with a radical Algerian group. For more than six weeks Alan and the other 5th Group soldiers helped the FBI amass the informants, evidence, witnesses, and, eventually, an indictment. Working with co-conspirators from Canada to New York to Mauritania, Ressam had planned to blow up the Los Angeles airport on New Year's Eve of the millennium. As the investigation progressed, the FBI "red-flagged" individuals' names on a watch list at U.S. ports of entry and shared them with friendly countries' agencies. At the end of January one of the suspects, a Moroccan, was picked up when he tried to enter Washington from Canada at a rural border crossing.

Ressam was convicted in April 2001 and sentenced to twenty-seven years on nine terrorism-related charges. It was not until three months later, when he testified at one of his co-conspirator's trials, that the full import of the millennium plot became public. In July 2001, Ressam told a New York court in great detail how he had been trained in 1998 in the Afghanistan camps run by Osama bin Laden. He described how he had been recruited and paid by one of Al Qaeda's top lieutenants, Abu Zubaida. He was part of a far-flung, multinational network that included his cell leader, subsequently indicted, who was based in London. After Ressam's second stint at a training camp, where he was given a six-week course in advanced explosives, he had been sent back to Canada with $12,000 to mount an attack on U.S. soil. When his original cohorts did not arrive in Canada, he had recruited new helpers.

Alan Johnson and the other soldiers from 5th Group received a letter from the FBI supervisory agent in Los Angeles thanking them for their linguistic assistance in an international terrorism case. The letter said that Alan had been "instrumental in aiding around-the-clock surveillance on several individuals . . . and the successful monitoring of these individuals." He also received the Army Commendation medal.

The tendrils of connections from that case continue to this day, as co-conspirators and camp trainees are still being pursued. It was a fateful clarion call to U.S. officials that the United States itself, and not just overseas targets, were in the crosshairs of the terrorists.

Alan was gratified that he had been able to play a crucial role in the investigation. Each time he had been sent on a mission, he thought, "That's it. It's never going to get better than that." He had loved Kenya and Somalia and the Middle East, but it was hard to see how any mission could top the millennium assignment for its direct and ominous portent for America's security. His eyes had been opened to what looked like the tip of an enormous iceberg, a loose federation of worldwide terrorists of various nationalities and creeds but common purpose. The country had not been so rattled since the attempted bombing of the World Trade Center in 1993. Those who studied terrorism recognized the grim signs of sophisticated planning behind the 1998 bombings of two U.S. embassies in Africa that killed more than 200 people: it had taken more than a two-bit terrorist outfit to pull off such deadly and simultaneous attacks. A sinister force had been gathering strength, and the millennium plot in Los Angeles was just the latest try.

Alan's life did keep getting better. When he returned to Fort Campbell from the millennium mission, he landed the job of team sergeant of

ODA 563. This job is the apex for Special Forces noncommissioned officers. He became the leader of his own band of brothers. Their challenge was to become the best in the group: they would compete with their fellow teams in training, in exercises, for assignments, and during missions.

Alan and Randy were pleased with the synergy of capabilities and personalities on their team. With the senior weapons sergeant, SFC Roderick "Robbie" Robinson, they brought more than a half-century of frontline military experience. Robbie was a fighting machine, another iconic poster boy chosen for the Army's latest recruiting campaign. All three of them excelled at door-kicking as well as the more artful side of SF. The senior medic was a nimble and talented veteran named Matt Nittler, who assisted in Randy's last surgery. The two communications sergeants, Mark Reynolds and Rich Davis, were skilled and dedicated. Getting radios and SATCOMS to work in the outback was an absolutely essential but tricky and frustrating business plagued with glitches. As Randy often said, they did not make excuses, they made contact.

Alan agreed. The true hallmark of a warrior, in his view, was not giving up no matter what. In the spring of 2001 ODA 563 won a mission in Kosovo, which would be brand-new territory for them.

CHAPTER 7

THE BALKANS

In war the result is never final.

—KARL VON CLAUSEWITZ

OVER THE COURSE of the 1990s, Yugoslavia fragmented in a decade-long orgy of bloodletting that became known as the Balkans conflict. The disintegration began as part of the cascading breakup of the Soviet Union and its satellites and erupted into a murderous ethnic war in 1992, after Bosnia's Muslim and Croat majority voted to secede from the Serb-dominated Yugoslav federation. For several years the United States stood aside, hoping that Europe would find a way to stop the hemorrhage. Diplomatic overtures and arm-twisting by NATO (the North Atlantic Treaty Organization) failed, while the killing of 250,000 of Bosnia's population of three million proceeded apace.

The so-called ethnic cleansing was essentially complete by the time of the Dayton Peace Accords in 1995. The attempt to enforce the accords and prevent further killing fell to the Dayton Implementation Force (IFOR), composed of 60,000 NATO-led troops.

The U.S. special operations component of IFOR was led by Col. Geoffrey Lambert with Lt. Col. Charlie Cleveland as his deputy. Lambert had commanded the 10th Special Forces Group, which is assigned to operate in Europe, since the fall of 1994, and Cleveland was its executive officer. The two men had served together in 7th Group in Panama in operations Just Cause and Promote Liberty in 1989–90. Those who knew Lambert knew that the former Ranger was not the type to command from the rear. The towering redhead was going to be in the thick of the action.

A native of Kansas, Lambert had been commissioned as a second lieutenant in 1973 and had then hopped back and forth between the Rangers and the Special Forces. In his early years, he had led a long-range reconnaissance patrol platoon, a rifle platoon, and a detachment in the Rangers, commanded a Special Forces ODA, returned to the Rangers for three more assignments, and then rejoined the Special Forces in time for Just Cause.

Lambert and Cleveland flew into Sarajevo from Italy on December 8, 1995, six days before the formal signing of the Dayton accords in Paris. In Bosnia, acceptance of the accords was far from universal. Operation Joint Endeavor was the largest mission NATO had ever undertaken, and it was a muscular peace-enforcement, not merely a peace-keeping attempt. As part of the advance party, Lambert and Cleveland's job was to pave the way for the rest of the IFOR and its British commander, who would arrive shortly. Special Forces teams were to fan out all over the country as liaisons among the member countries to provide a common communications network. Later, the teams became observers and, with their experience and language skills, waded into the ravaged and deeply divided communities to develop contacts, gauge the public mood, and identify the various power brokers, from priests to hoodlums, and persons of influence. Once they had constructed a map of the society they worked those channels to resolve problems at local, regional, and national levels.

The people of Sarajevo began begging the world for help when their picturesque and ancient city came under siege in 1992. Ultra-nationalist

Serbs had taken over the surrounding mountains and relentlessly shelled the city, which had been a vibrant, multiethnic cultural center since the Middle Ages. It had hosted the winter Olympics in 1984 and charmed the world with its attractions, but that did not bring international help when the bombardment and slow destruction of the city began. The Serbs' heavy artillery reduced many buildings to husks, damaged power plants, and left the city dependent on generators and more sporadic fuel supplies.

Senad Pecanin was the editor of Sarajevo's newsweekly, the most balanced and trenchant publication in the country. A Muslim who cherished his city and its secular, tolerant tradition, he had dared to publish accounts of Muslim atrocities as well as Serbs'. After his parents' apartment was riddled with bullets, he and his wife Belma, a stunning brunette with the looks and grace of a 1940s movie star, decided to send their parents abroad. As the death toll mounted Senad persuaded her to take their newborn son and leave too. He might not be able to save his city, but he could keep putting out the magazine, if he could only keep the generator for the printing press running. Thugs broke into his office and held a gun to his head to demand that he stop publishing. The U.S. embassy tried to ward off attacks by publicly voicing its support for the magazine.

Senad, a gentle giant in his mid-thirties, began losing his hair from the tremendous stress. He could not stop the country's descent into barbarism, but he vowed that he would always walk, and never run, through the infamous avenue in the city called Sniper Alley, the deadly shooting gallery where so many Sarajevans bled to death. Snipers in the mountains would take aim at ordinary people crossing this exposed stretch of city blocks. It was the only route to the dwindling supplies of water. Terrified men, women, and children would dodge, weave, and dash, and try all sorts of stratagems to run the gauntlet unscathed. Senad always walked. He and his magazine had become a symbol, and this was one way he could give his countrymen heart. He was a huge target, a bear of a man, but he would never give the Serb snipers the satisfaction of seeing him run.

The sniper problem was breaking the spirit of the Sarajevans. It had become emblematic of the Serbs' utter disregard for the conventional laws of land warfare. Snipers would sit in their nests high in the hills and cold-bloodedly pick off civilians, not caring that the world's television cameras broadcast their atrocities.

The special operations compound in the Serb quarter of Sarajevo was also targeted; it had been sniped at twenty-four times. The gunmen fired rifle grenades at it and its vehicles day and night. The peacekeepers blacked out their building at night and ringed it with trucks, to no avail. The sniping went on. One soldier was shot through the hand, another one grazed on the neck. The snipers also shot holes into military planes as they landed at the airfield.

Under the Dayton accord, all the parties had agreed to stop shooting. Long-barreled rifles were explicitly banned, yet the Serbian snipers kept on. Colonel Lambert came up with an idea and explained it to his counterparts from the British and French special forces, who were working together in Europe's first-ever combined joint special operations task force, led by a British general with Lambert as the deputy. The task force decided to give Lambert's plan a try. He arranged for a Q–36 radar to be brought to the airfield. Although made for homing in on artillery rounds, it could also spot much smaller rifle rounds. Every time the planes landed, the radar locked on to the muzzle flashes to fix the snipers' location. Lambert also handed out night-vision goggles to British sentries on rooftop observation posts. French special operators stole out with night-capable cameras and took pictures of the muzzle flashes of the snipers in the hills and used the photos to pinpoint the coordinates of the sniper nests. They were now ready for the next Serb shooter.

One night, the French special operators shot the man who was sniping at the airfield, riddling his body with thirty-seven bullets. The corpse was then taken to the Serbian police station. British soldiers were assigned to this sector, so they delivered the body and the message. They pointed out that the Serbs had agreed to abide by the terms of the accord, which included no more shooting and no long-barreled guns.

The Serbs were furious. The Serbs claimed that the dead man was a guard at a factory, but the soldiers showed them the photographic and radar evidence they had gathered, and then calmly presented their ultimatum.

It was the Serbs' duty as policemen to protect this sector of Sarajevo, yet there were Serb snipers ringing the city and shooting at people daily. The peacekeepers asked that policemen assume their responsibility to address this matter. The British expressed regret for the killing of the sniper, but they said that more of them could be killed if the sniping did not stop. They said they had the imagery and the coordinates for all the sniper nests in the mountains and the high-rise buildings around Sarajevo. "We're going to let you handle this, because we know you can," the British commander told the Serbs.

The plan worked. The peacekeepers did not have to kill one more Serb sniper, but there still were disgruntled Serbs. Whether an act of retribution or another random and senseless act, Lambert's caravan was hit soon after this showdown. He was not riding in the same vehicle he normally used, however, but in the car in front. His radio telephone operator was in the seat usually occupied by Lambert, but was shorter than Lambert and so the bullet just grazed him as it passed through the car's windshield. For his trouble, he received a Purple Heart for being wounded in action, and his commander's gratitude for having taken a bullet meant for him.

At the same time that the counter-sniping campaign was unfolding, Lambert launched Operation Teddy Bear. The British thought both the name and the concept were most unsoldierly and refused to have anything to do with it. Someone had donated 1,000 stuffed teddy bears to IFOR, so Lambert decided to hand them out to all the Serbian children in the neighborhood. He put Lt. Col. Charlie Cleveland in charge of it. Special Forces soldiers walked the streets with teddy bears, giving them out to any children they saw. They went without helmets or body armor to show solidarity with the civilians, who of course had no such protection either. They wanted to show hostile Serbs that, while they would not tolerate the sniping, they had no animus toward the population.

Stopping the violence was only half the job; they had to find a way to get these people to live together again.

Senad Pecanin now had some allies willing to walk the streets and try to revive hope in his beleaguered and beloved city. The Special Forces teams rented houses and lived among the population in the country's principal cities and towns. They met with church leaders, businessmen, political and militia leaders, and even crime bosses. They fed all the information into their database, and each time the fragile peace was disrupted by a killing, a violent mob, an unfounded rumor, or a misstep by the peacekeepers, they would work their contacts to try to calm the situation and persuade the influential locals to step up to remedy the problem. These networks also yielded valuable information about the war's atrocities and who had committed them. In a separate operation, secret units of Special Forces and others were tasked in mid-1997 with hunting down the PIFWCs, as the seventy-four "persons indicted for war crimes" were known, to be brought before the international war crimes tribunal that was eventually convened by the UN Security Council at the Hague.*

Lambert remained engaged with the Balkans' for the rest of the decade. After leading the special operations element of IFOR, he commanded all U.S. special operations forces in Europe. That job came with a promotion to brigadier general and his first general's star. Cleveland spent the next four years coming and going from the Balkans as well. In 1996, he served simultaneously as deputy commander of the combined joint special operations task force and 10th Group. In 1997–98, he headed the Joint Commission of Observers in Bosnia. Tenth Group's 3rd Battalion, which he commanded, supplied most of the commission's observers. Other Special Forces groups also contributed some of the 22 total ODAs to assist the non-European peacekeeping troops: 1st Group teamed up with Malaysians and 5th Group with Pakistani and Arab contingents.

* See Richard Newman's article, "Living with the Locals," *US News & World Report,* July 6, 1998.

Cleveland's Alpha Company commander, Major Ken Tovo, was in charge of the American sector observers. From the American base in Tuzla, Bosnia, called Task Force Eagle, he helped his teams navigate some of Bosnia's most neuralgic hotspots. Brcko was the center of a major tug of war between the ethnic factions: as arbitrators agonized over its fate, ODA 076 lived in the city to monitor and manage its constantly brewing strife. The triumphs were few and hard-won and sometimes laced with bitterness, as in Srebrenica, the city whose massacre epitomized the conflict's brutality. There, as an elected Muslim city council gingerly moved to take office, they and peacekeepers were attacked and a helicopter crashed. The ODA there functioned as a quick-reaction and first aid force, as well as the best pipeline of information going out to Tovo and the rest of the peacekeeping commanders. Tovo came back for another tour as aide to the conventional American commander in 1998–99, as Bosnia gained a semblance of stability while Kosovo took its place as the new killing ground.

As the head of all the observer teams in Bosnia, Cleveland frequently visited them in their respective cities or towns while his staff at the battalion headquarters in Sarajevo analyzed and updated the massive databases that the teams collected. Out driving one day, Cleveland thought about how far they, and the country, had come. He recalled his first outing in the war-torn land in December 1995. He and a few staff soldiers had found themselves in a mountain tunnel blocked with vehicles. It was a dark, cold winter night and none of the locals had any idea who they were. His logistics officer had blanched when Cleveland asked if he had a rifle, afraid that his boss planned to go up against several hundred people. The handful of Croatian soldiers they had encountered let them pass without a fight, however. The logistician would not have been comforted had he known that, a few years before, Cleveland had blithely jumped into a van and driven, alone, to a camp of Panamanian insurgents to talk them into surrendering.

Even two years later, Bosnia's peace was still an uneasy one, to be sure. One of the observer team's houses had been attacked during a riot in Brcko in the summer of 1997, and one of the teams had been stoned

recently when they rescued some Croats from a Serbian mob in Der-
venta. But despite occasional flare-ups, the Special Forces network did
succeed in deterring violence, heading off confrontations, and working
out disputes before they erupted into fights. This low-key, low-visibility
job was tailor-made for Special Forces. They had the training and the
confidence to circulate in the communities that few other soldiers had.
The observers wore uniforms but no rank insignia and tucked pistols
under their jerseys, rather than walking around bristling with weapons
that would scare the civilians. They had to gain the trust of the locals to
do their job; exposing themselves to some risk was part of the bargain.

The Balkans taught the Special Forces a lot of lessons about how to
build credibility, defuse a deliberately orchestrated demonstration, and
win the confidence of the clergy. This environment was neither war nor
peace: the methods of the regular soldier wouldn't work, and civilians
tended to lack the necessary influence. The Special Forces could work in
these gray situations to try to jumpstart the society's own governing
structures. For Cleveland it was something of a deja-vu experience; he
had sent teams into remote towns in the months after the Panama intervention to mend the factionalized country, which had been a peaceful
democracy for the past eight years. Like many success stories, it had
gone largely unheralded. In the Balkans he and his men greatly refined
this basic approach by applying social science tools. They constructed
matrices identifying persons of influence in eight different spheres rang-
ing from politics to business to religion and even crime, cross-catego-
rized with the regional and ethnic scope of his reach. They developed a
very precise and useful map of a most complex society.

Lt. Col. Cleveland's former comrade from the Panama days, Kevin
Higgins, was not surprised that his friend managed to juggle all these
jobs in the middle of the festering Balkans mess, the longest-lasting crisis
of the 1990s and one of the largest Special Forces deployments in terms
of numbers of personnel deployed. Higgins had watched Cleveland
dream up plans and organizations from scratch in Panama and Bolivia.
Higgins compared him to the type of individual profiled in historian
Daniel Boorstin's book *The Creators,* someone who is endowed with the

fresh perception and imagination that is the artist's hallmark. "Many SF men could follow along and execute an already established mission quite well," said Higgins, "but Charlie would be the guy most likely to have thought of it in the first place. When we were staring at a blank piece of paper, he would figure out what to do." After leaving the Balkans, Cleveland went to a mandatory joint assignment at the Pentagon overseeing Special Forces personnel matters. Chris Conner worked with him and recalled him being there at eight or nine o'clock at night, trying to find the right man for the slot. He never wanted to assign a man to a job he didn't want or wasn't suited for. After a year at the army war college, Cleveland was promoted to full colonel and, on a high-mountain summer day in 2001, he took command of 10th Group at Fort Carson. The Balkans' ever-brewing troubles still were not over.

The Dayton Accords had ended the fighting but also essentially rewarded the aggressors by permitting them to keep territory they had "cleansed" of unwanted ethnic groups. The political will had been lacking in the American and European capitals to enforce a return to the status quo ante. That lesson was not lost on the Serbian leadership, which wagered that the same methods could be used to clear ethnic Albanians out of the province of Kosovo, even though they comprised 90 percent of its population.

Kosovo had lived an uneasy existence in the fraying Yugoslav federation since Belgrade revoked its autonomy in 1990. In mid-1998, the Serbs began using police raids, artillery and helicopter attacks, and executions to push hundreds of thousands of ethnic Albanians out of the province and into neighboring Macedonia and Albania. Another fruitless chapter of diplomacy and saber-rattling ensued. NATO fighter jets conducted exercises and Marines were moved into nearby countries, and NATO approved air strikes but they were not launched. For months Serbian leader Slobodan Milosevic toyed with international negotiators and ignored their ultimatums. By the time NATO issued its final deadline there were 11,000 dead and a million refugees.

Finally, in the spring of 1999, U.S. and European leaders decided to employ force. They were haunted by having stood aside so long in Bosnia, and history was repeating itself in Kosovo. NATO began a limited air bombing campaign and escalated it until Milosevic acquiesced, seventy-eight days later, in June 1999. Fifty thousand peacekeeping troops moved in under United Nations auspices to stop further violence and to keep the conflict from destablizing the neighboring countries, especially Macedonia, where ethnic frictions were mounting. Kosovar Albanians were rumored to be sending arms and men across the border to their ethnic kin. The Special Forces played much the same role as they had in Bosnia, moving around in teams to gather information, win friends and influence people, and keep tabs on the troublemakers.

The accord reached on Kosovo was a bare bones affair with no road map for resolving the status of the province, the return of refugees, or any other core issues. This may have been the key lesson of the decade's "humanitarian interventions": they were always too little, too late. The impulse to save lives was laudable, even if it was galvanized by television cameras broadcasting scenes of dying or starving people, but it did not constitute policy. Acknowledging the suffering did not suffice as a diagnosis of its cause or what would be required to remedy it. The application of military power in the absence of an accurate diagnosis and adequate solution was bound to result in confusion and impotence or, at worst, tragedy and failure.

The United States and the United Nations had pulled out of Somalia entirely by 1995, and the U.S. defense secretary had resigned, but that lesson had not been learned. Other humanitarian interventions were attempted nonetheless, without much greater success. U.S. troops were used to restore Haiti's elected president to office, but the overriding goal was a casualty-free short-term occupation rather than lasting governability. Special Forces ODAs from 3rd Group were sent all over the country but were withdrawn before they had a chance to cement their progress. The Balkans experience combined ineffective diplomacy with halting interventionism that left the majority of victims displaced, key war criminals at large, a lingering international constabulary, and no clear end in sight a decade later.

A road map for Kosovo would have helped everyone involved, but the Special Forces were better prepared than most to deal with such murky situations. Kosovo's conflict featured unconventional tactics, a separatist guerrilla army, a popular revolt, and nationalist and regional dimensions—a stew of complexities. As part of the UN mission, the ODAs worked to disarm the belligerents, protect the civilians, and keep ethnic strife from breaking out again or spilling over the borders.

Although 10th Group provided the lion's share of Special Forces manpower to the Balkans effort, 5th Group lent its expertise at various junctures to work with Bosnian Muslims, Arab countries who provided peacekeepers, and the Kosovar Albanians, who were also Muslim. Alan Johnson had been in 5th Group's first deployment to the Balkans in 1994, when a half-dozen Special Forces soldiers were sent to Bosnia. He spent a bleak Christmas there, another one away from home. His split team was assigned to gather information on the warring parties and to advise and assist the commanders of a Pakistani battalion, which was part of the earliest, fledgling, and ultimately unsuccessful United Nations effort to help shield Muslims in five "safe havens" from the Serbian attacks. The massacre of 7,000 men and boys in one of the safe havens, Srebrenica, in July 1995 finally jolted the United States into concerted diplomatic action that led to the Dayton Peace Accords.

For the rest of ODA 563, the team's deployment to the Balkans in the summer of 1999 was an entirely new culture and experience. Even the physical environment—wooded, mountainous, and temperate—was a sharp contrast to the desert or subtropical regions where it usually deployed. A handful of teams from 5th Group was sent there to work with the Arab members of the UN peacekeeping force UNMIK and to serve as a liaison between those countries and American forces. Randy and Alan's team worked with the United Arab Emirates and the Jordanians. The teams were also to use their cultural skills and understanding of

Muslim norms to engage the Kosovar Albanians. The Kosovar Liberation Army had agreed to disband and assume the role of a domestic police force, but some of its members were reportedly helping foment irredentist sentiments across borders. Macedonia looked unstable, perhaps the next Balkan domino to descend into bloodshed and fragmentation.

Mule trains had been bringing in arms from Albania, across the mountains that formed the western border, from the bottomless cache of the Soviet-backed regime that had collapsed almost two years earlier. On the southern side of Kosovo, arms were being funneled across the border into Macedonia to arm ethnic Albanians there. One of ODA 563's jobs was to help interdict these arms flows and uncover weapons caches hidden in the mountains.

The longitude and latitude might have been new, but Rawhide knew just the solution to deal with this terrain. He had used pack horses and mule trains for years in his family's outfitting business. For years he, his father, and his cousins had led elk hunts in the mountains outside Cody. They did everything for the city slickers who came to bag big game: tracked the animals, set up camp, cooked the meals, and packed the gear. After the paying customers got their elk, they were free to get theirs. The cowboy life was where Rawhide started, and where he intended to end up one day.

By sheer luck, Rawhide's team had been working with horses over the past year at Fort Campbell. ODA 563 and a few others had updated the field manual on pack animals and practiced packing techniques. Some people had criticized their little project as a lark and a waste of time. The command had disagreed and dipped into the discretionary funds so the team could train on horse-related skills at the post's stables and local facilities. The men had argued that one never knew what kind of techniques might be needed in the Third World—or even in Europe, as it turned out.

In Kosovo, ODA 563 used pack horses so they could stay in the mountains for days at a time, running continuous interdiction operations. It also solved the problem of the Arab partners' unwillingness to hump 100-pound packs. Their allies from the United Arab Emirates had never been in the mountains, so the team showed them how to use and care for the horses, even how to shoe them, and how to navigate and camp in the terrain. The team scored numerous successes against the arms smuggling, turning up caches and stopping mule trains loaded with Soviet-made AK–47s, pistols, and ammunition from Albanian stocks.

One day, the communications sergeant, Mark Reynolds, was tinkering with his SATCOM radio and antenna at their base camp in the mountains. The faint sound of a motor's whine made him prick up his ears.

"Did you hear that?" he asked Alan.

"No, what?" Alan said.

"I think a helo just went down. Sounded like a Kiowa."

Reynolds was well suited for the communications job; he had extraordinary hearing and an analytical mind, and paid attention to details. His guess was confirmed a few minutes later, when the pilot's distress call came over the radio. Realizing that they were the only soldiers in the area and that it would be difficult for a heliborne search-and-rescue team to spot the pilots in the heavily wooded mountains, Mark, Alan, and a couple of other sergeants set off to search for them. Mark's sharp ears and keen sense of direction led them to the site. The pilot and co-pilot were uninjured, but their little Kiowa scout craft was wrecked. They walked down the mountain to where the medic, Matt Nittler, and a few men were standing by as a quick-reaction force. They drove the pilots back to their headquarters at Camp Bondsteel, the American base for the peacekeeping operation.

The team's orders were issued from Bondsteel, as were its supplies, but otherwise ODA 563 stayed out roaming around. It was assigned with its Jordanian and UAE partners to search an area surrounding Pristina, Kosovo's capital, that contained seventeen villages. ODA 563 knew the rules when it came to dealing with Muslim families: one dealt with the men, not the women. If the head of the house was not there, the sons, no matter whether they were the youngest people present, were the ones to talk to.

The armed resistance, the Kosovo Liberation Army (KLA), had not been keen to give up its guns, despite the formal agreement to do so. The Kosovars were still smuggling guns in because they believed they would have to fight the Serbs again, and many of them remained committed to the cause of independence. They would not give up their goal of seceding from Belgrade, by force if necessary. A referendum on Kosovo's status had been promised but no date set. From the standpoint of the international community, independence in the short term would provoke Serbian violence anew and send the Russians into orbit, as they saw ominous parallels between the Kosovo experience and their own breakaway Chechen republic. Those were the geopolitical realities—but on the ground the Special Forces were trying to stabilize the country one village at a time.

The village searches were tricky affairs. There was a good chance that the teams might stumble on dedicated KLA fighters who would shoot rather than surrender their arms. The population was not neutral; they were generally ardent supporters of their militia. The Serbs, for their part, had left booby-trapped buildings everywhere and were still ambushing people in the countryside and near the borders. Randy and Alan, both experienced in close-quarters tactics, knew they had to be executed precisely to avoid injury. They meticulously planned every operation and made sure each man knew his part. Everyone had to stay alert for that hair-thin wire attached to a grenade behind the door, a stack of strategically placed debris blocking their path, and a thousand other things. The vehicle was checked every single time before they got into it. One moment of casual inattention was all it took to end up dead.

Doc Nittler, the medic, was compact and extremely agile. His teammates called him "carni" because he could do flips and walk on his hands like a carnival entertainer. That made him the obvious candidate to be heaved into crawlspaces, attics, and barn lofts as the team searched the villages and countryside of Kosovo. It was a dangerous job, because an armed man lying in wait would likely have his gun trained on the opening, watching for someone to come through. In the close-quarter training, the instructors call this the "fatal funnel" because the target is perfectly silhouetted by the light behind him. This was Nittler's lot, time and again. They were not at war and there were civilians everywhere, so the men could not shoot before entering or throw a smoke grenade inside. They just tossed Doc into the void, to land and react as best he could. Day by day the entire team became more proficient. They would move quickly and quietly into a room or building, covering each other from every angle, and search their pre-determined quadrants with text-book precision. They did so well that the soldiers were handed another slice of territory as soon as they finished the first seventeen towns.

The extensive close-quarters searches welded the team into a fine-tuned machine as few other assignments could. The men learned to read each other's facial expressions and body language, making speech and the standard hand signals almost superfluous. Their skills kept getting better, team members bonded and the esprit de corps solidified. This was the epitome of what an ODA should be, and Randy and Alan were immensely gratified to see how well their mix of new and old blood, intellectual and instinctual types, acrobats like Doc and giants like Alan and Roderick Robinson, had come together. Their second communications sergeant, in addition to Mark, was a smart newcomer named Rich Davis. A few months before he had walked into Alan's office and announced that he'd been assigned to his team. "Don't I know you?" Alan asked, then recalled that he had encouraged Davis to try out for the Special Forces when he was a young soldier in the 101st Airborne Division. A friend had asked Alan to talk to Davis about the Special Forces, and here he was, three years later, on Alan's team. Al had been mentored the same way. This is the most successful means of recruiting Special Forces candidates, because the soldiers themselves can often spot who has the right traits to fit in. Davis was one of them.

The team was humming, but Randy found Kosovo to be the most depressing place he'd ever been. The wholesale extermination of civilians had no possible justification. People had been driven from their homes and everything they owned was burned and pillaged. One day, as he watched from the road, a woman tilling a field was killed when her hoe struck a mine. It was a senseless, random death, which he had been powerless to prevent, but he felt terrible nonetheless. He knew many places where the law of the gun prevailed—much of the world, in fact—and he knew the Arab world's strongmen, the chaos of Africa, but nothing so troubled him as this place. Education and wealth and "civilization" had not impeded this country's descent into violence in the least. The Albanians and Serbs were still teaching their children to hate each other just because they were different, breeding the next generation's war as he watched. If this could happen in Europe, he wondered, could it happen at home? What would it be like if war came to America?

Randy, Alan, and the rest of ODA 563 were at their compound on the army base, Camp Bondsteel, outside Pristina when they heard the news. It was mid-afternoon on September 11. Alan was outside with other team members, preparing their vehicles for a border patrol. Someone called him to come into the team's operations center, where CNN was always on. He watched as the second plane hit the World Trade Center in New York City. Randy, who had been asleep on his cot, resting for the night shift, was awakened. Alan, who had been reading up on Al Qaeda since his millennium mission, instantly guessed that it was them and his team would be going after the perpetrators. He told the sergeants to pack their gear. Within twenty-four hours, while they were still in Kosovo, ODA 563 had initiated its mission planning process, set up target folders, and drafted concepts for operations. The way Special Forces works, the team with the best plan gets the job, and 563 intended to be ready. It seemed to Randy that everything in his life had been a preparation for this moment. It was the first time the United States had been directly attacked in almost sixty years, and he was sure that the country would retaliate, and soon. They would be called on to defend their country, and this was the war they would tell their grandchildren about.

Back at Fort Bragg in North Carolina, Major General Geoffrey Lambert had taken the standard bearing the colors of the U.S. Army Special Forces Command from his predecessor four days earlier, on September 7, at a ceremony on the parade ground of Meadows Memorial Plaza. His new job came with a second star. Standing in front of a towering sculpture of a Special Forces soldier known as Bronze Bruce, the first Vietnam memorial, Lambert made a short and simple speech. "It's great to be home," he said. He thanked the soldiers from all seven of the Special Forces groups gathered for their work in the "dark, wet, and cold, in strange and lonely far-off places."

They had no idea where he was about to send them, and neither did he. But Lambert had more than a premonition. All summer long he had been reading top-secret intelligence reports and intercepts that convinced him and his colleagues that Al Qaeda was going to strike somewhere, soon. For the past two years, he had been the director of operations, plans, and strategy at the U.S. Special Operations Command in Tampa, where terrorism was the number-one topic that he woke up to and went to sleep with every day. They "war-gamed" the most likely scenarios, the worst scenarios, and what they might do to stop them. They knew an attack was imminent—there was just too much chatter on the bad guys' networks. But they did not know where and they did not know when.

On the morning of September 11, Gen. Lambert was holding his first staff meeting at his headquarters in the three-story Robert L. McClure building on Desert Storm Drive just off Yadkin Avenue. An aide came in and said there was something on television that he should see. Lambert stepped out of the meeting, saw the smoke billowing from the first World Trade Center tower, and said simply, "They got us." He stepped back into his meeting and announced to the colonels and majors and captains assembled in the conference room: "We just got hit."

CHAPTER 8

AFGHANISTAN

We sleep safe in our beds because rough men stand
ready in the night to visit violence on those who
would do us harm.

—GEORGE ORWELL

ONE OF THE Special Forces captains had moved to Fort Campbell in July 2001 and bought a house with a deck. It was his second tour in the Special Forces; previously an enlisted soldier, he had returned as an officer to lead a team. On the morning of September 11, 2001, the captain dropped off clothes at the Gate Four cleaners, next to the U.S. Cavalry store. When he got back into his SUV the radio said a plane had hit the first World Trade Center tower. As he crossed Fort Campbell Boulevard and drove through the gate, the news report said it sounded like a Cessna.

When he walked into the chow hall he found out that a second plane had hit. The men stopped eating and looked at each other. Because their careers had been spent in the Middle East, their minds all followed the same chain of reasoning: mass attack on civilians equals terrorism equals Middle Eastern radicals. If it turned out to be true, the soldiers would almost certainly be sent to war. Still, it could take days for the machinery to grind into action and turn out the warning orders that told them to prepare to move. So the captain, who had discovered rot in his deck, asked the company commander for a few days' leave to fix it. He tore out the deck the next day and that night received a call to report for a command brief the following day. He knew he would not be rebuilding his deck in the near future.

The men of 5th Group gathered in the conference room, which doubled as the group's museum. Gas masks, Soviet-made rifles, land mines, battalion flags, and other mementos of Desert Storm, Somalia, Operation Southern Watch, and the Vietnam era were crammed into glass cases in the anteroom. The memorabilia overflowed into the conference room, where uniformed mannequins and a DShK antiaircraft gun sat in the left corner of the stage area where the group commander stood in front of a screen. A handful of team leaders were seated in a semicircle before him around a three-inch-thick varnished blond wooden table the size of a pool table, which was inlaid with the crossed-arrow insignia of the Special Forces in darker wood. It had been made by a retired sergeant major who was an expert woodworker. Colonel John Mulholland, who had just assumed command of 5th Group over the summer, gave his men a one-sentence brief: "Gentlemen, you have been selected to infiltrate Afghanistan."

The commander reshuffled soldiers to fill the vacant slots on the teams—the captain with the rotten deck was assigned to lead ODA 555. Each team would need to have every position filled for the job ahead. With twelve men the team would have two qualified commanders, a captain and a warrant officer, and a pair of each specialty: operations and intelligence; weapons; engineer; medic; and communications. That would enable it to split into two units of six and retain the full complement of skills in each. It could also break down into four- or even two-man elements if circumstances required because the senior sergeants were cross-trained in more than one specialty. In all likelihood, the team would be called upon to perform all five of the Special Forces' doctrinal missions: special reconnaissance, direct action, unconventional warfare, counterterrorism, and, if the plan to replace the Taliban with a new government was successful, foreign internal defense. The pace of work was going to be relentless. Every team would be under enormous pressure to deliver quick results and a constant stream of intelligence to the eager eyes of senior Washington officials, including the secretary of defense and even the president. The weight of the country's response to September 11 rested on their shoulders.

A few of the longtime senior NCOs had been in Afghanistan and along the Pakistan border in the 1980s when the U.S. government armed and helped the mujahedeen who were fighting to push the Soviet military out of Afghanistan. Since the Soviet withdrawal a decade earlier, however, the United States had had very little to do with Taliban-governed Afghanistan. As a result it had very little intelligence, contacts, or infrastructure in place to mount a quick response to the September 11 attacks.

The military decision-making process is a highly refined procedure that calls for exhaustive analysis of various courses of action and their likely consequences. With little reliable intelligence and even less time, however, Colonel Mulholland kept his orders simple and to the point. The basic document known as the commander's intent, which is the basis for subordinate units' planning, was one page long. It laid out the purpose of the mission, the key tasks, and the end result he instructed his troops to achieve. Mulholland could not have been more succinct in framing the goal: they were to capture Kabul. Nothing else mattered. The SF were to accomplish the commander's intent, no matter what flawed assumptions, unworkable plans, or casualties they encountered. They were to fulfill the mission one way or another.

This bare-bones plan ended up to be the blueprint essentially for the entire U.S. operation in Afghanistan. No one in the military command or upper echelons of the government had a contingency plan sitting on the shelf, so the Special Forces stepped up to the plate and said: let us send our troops in to link up with the Afghan resistance, take down the government, and root out the Al Qaeda organization it was known to be harboring. They had all the necessary skills—the Special Forces had been advising and training foreign forces for its entire history, albeit, since Vietnam, mostly on a small scale and with a low profile. Insurgency and counterinsurgency were long-term propositions that required months or even years. Could the Special Forces produce results faster if they were given every tool in the U.S. arsenal and made speed their primary goal? Nobody knew, but no one had a better idea. So they were given the green light.

The first Special Forces teams packed and flew halfway around the world to an airfield in Uzbekistan, code named K2, which served as their staging base. The idea was to infiltrate a handful of teams into Afghanistan to join forces with the Northern Alliance in the Panjshir Valley and other anti-Taliban fighters, and train and arm them for a spring offensive. By October, the winter snows had already begun to close the mountain passes.

Just getting into the country proved to be a monumental challenge. The first team loaded up to fly into the Hindu Kush, a 16,000-foot-high mass of rock and permanent snow stretching across northeastern Afghanistan. A couple of U.S. intelligence operatives who had managed to get into the country further south said that the weather there was clear. But Afghanistan has enormously varied topography and climates, and the winter storms sweeping south had stacked up against the Hindu Kush and created an impenetrable wall of weather. Three times the helicopter pilots tried to get the men in, once taking fire from dug-in Taliban fighters on the ground below. The captain of ODA 555 offered to march his men in. Someone had to get there, and he knew his experience would be needed. He had served eighteen years in the army, including as an intelligence specialist and radio operator, and he spoke fluent Russian.

ODA 555 and another team were flown into Afghanistan on October 19. ODA 555 joined up with the Northern Alliance commander General Fahim, but a few days later one of the team's sergeants fell seriously ill. The medic tried to stabilize him and gave him morphine for the excruciating pain, but he was unable to diagnose what was causing the sergeant to suffer even from light and noise. An air force helicopter tried to fly in and crashed in the attempt. The captain, frantic, knew his sergeant needed to be evacuated to a field hospital and fretted that whatever he had might sicken the others. Finally a helicopter managed to fly the man back to K2, where tests revealed he had meningitis. In three weeks he had recovered and rejoined them.

Once another half-dozen teams got on the ground in northern Afghanistan, things began to happen very fast. The decision was made not to wait until spring but instead to launch the offensive right away. Supplies were air-dropped when weather permitted, and jet fighters were placed on alert to bomb targets as the men on the ground called for them. Teams were attached to various Afghan tribal leaders and their fighters to attack cities to the east and west, on foot, on horseback, and in anything that rolled.

The main effort, led by ODA 555 and General Fahim, drove south toward the capital. Their first fight was for Bagram airfield, which was littered with the rusted steel carcasses of Russia's war. ODA 555 took the control tower to use as an observation point for calling in bombs on some 7,000 Taliban troops and their Soviet-era tanks and artillery on the other side of the airfield.

The Afghans watched in wonder as the Special Forces soldiers set up their secret weapon, a dark gray box called a laser target designator, and pointed its lens toward the Soviet-made tanks and artillery. Its laser marked the target and the range finder calculated the distance. The men on the ground called on the satellite communications to the unseen pilots in the sky and to their intermediaries, who were sitting in Saudi Arabia thousands of miles to the south. Master Sergeant Tom Rosenbarger was one of the Special Forces liaisons manning the Combined Air Operations Center at Prince Sultan Air Base in Saudi Arabia. Rosenbarger and other Special Forces soldiers were there to help translate the army and air force's different terminology, equipment, units of measure, and any other communications problems that came up.

The resulting barrage of bombs and two days of fighting cleared the Taliban from Bagram. Fahim and the Special Forces then set about resupplying their troops and planning the attack across the Shomali Plains and into Kabul. They launched the attack on November 11 in a

two-pronged movement—south with an envelopment to the west. The
Taliban scattered and the capital fell on November 13, less than a month
after the first teams had set foot in the country.

Meanwhile other ODAs were scoring successes across northern, eastern, and western Afghanistan with a rapidity that astonished military
planners and the spellbound American public. The Taliban fled in the
face of the binational cavalry and the awesome power of U.S. air support. No one had ever imagined that fewer than one hundred Special
Forces soldiers and an indigenous militia could overthrow a government
so quickly. Kabul was theirs, but the job was not finished. The Taliban
was still holding out in its southern stronghold of Kandahar and in the
eastern border regions, and Osama bin Laden remained at large.

Shortly after the fall of Mazar e Sharif, a key city in northern Afghanistan, the command center at K2 received urgent news: the top general of
the Taliban, his bodyguard, and the governor of eastern Paktia province
had been captured. To date, this was the biggest "catch" of the war; in
fact, except for the Taliban leader Mullah Omar or the very top Al
Qaeda leadership, these were about the "highest-value" targets out
there. Both the general and the governor were close to the top leadership, so it was hoped that they would provide the critical intelligence to
lead the Americans to the top men and to other nodes of the international terrorist network in Afghanistan. The general's capture would
demoralize the Taliban fighters and make it harder for them to regroup
and counterattack. The governor was equally valuable because Paktia
was a Taliban and Al Qaeda stronghold where many training camps had
been located, and where many of the remaining fighters had fled. The
K2 operations center surveyed the available manpower to find the best
men to bring these "high-value targets" out.

Master Sgt. Alan Johnson and four other members of ODA 563 were
chosen to fly into Afghanistan to pick up and deliver the important prisoners. Alan couldn't believe their luck—the men had been itching to
leave the frozen canvas tents at the airfield in Uzbekistan and get into

the fight. The teams of 3rd Battalion, 5th Group, had been the first ones sent into Afghanistan and, as the war front widened, other teams were being called upon. Teams joined with anti-Taliban forces in Herat, in the Taliban stronghold in the south, and in the critical eastern provinces which were Al Qaeda bastions and corridors to Pakistan.

Alan and his teammates flew to Mazar e Sharif in an MC–130 transport plane and were met by the team and intelligence personnel as soon as they landed. The Taliban general was a hefty man dressed in a baggy, belted brown uniform. He walked on a wooden leg with a barely detectable hitch in his step. Many veteran Afghan soldiers had lost limbs in the decades of fighting in a land ridden with mines, and many had become quite adept with their prostheses. The governor and the bodyguard were Pashtuns of slight build, dressed in loose-fitting olive drab shirts and pants; the governor's ensemble was topped by a suit vest in typical Afghan style. The prisoners' hands were bound but they were not blindfolded or shackled at the legs so they could walk up the rear ramp and into the hold of the plane. As the hatch began to close, the three Afghan men suddenly decided to fight. Perhaps they had expected a last-minute rescue attempt, or perhaps they had only then realized that they were likely to be going away for a very, very long time. Whatever was going through their heads, they fought as though for their lives.

Alan and Robbie reacted immediately. Sgt. First Class Roderick Robinson, called "Robbie" by his friends, was 563's weapons sergeant. He was a massive man who could have been a professional football player. He grabbed the general and bounced him on the floor in what looked like a smackdown scene out of the World Wrestling Federation. Alan had less bulk than Robbie but he was a black belt in jiu jitsu and one of the "combatives" instructors for 5th Group.

The Special Forces have developed their own course for hand-to-hand combat that is a hybrid of techniques drawn from martial arts, grappling, and boxing disciplines—as well as ultimate or street fighting, which is bound by no rules except the last man standing wins. They also learn how to disarm attackers armed with knives and pistols. Each discipline is effective for a certain type of fighting, but each has its weaknesses—a martial artist can be beaten by a boxer, and a grappler can beat them both if he gets them onto the ground. So for those interested in the practical applications of such fighting skills—i.e., fights to the death—they must learn them all.

Alan subdued the flailing governor and the bodyguard with a few quick blows. Neither Alan nor Robbie used excessive force—but they were not about to let these men get away. After this brief demonstration of martial arts skill the prisoners evidently decided against further resistance. The team took no chances, however, and bound their feet and blindfolded them with cloths. The soldiers strapped the Afghans into webbed seats bolted to the inner wall as the plane taxied down the crater-filled runway. Their destination was Pakistan, which had granted the United States the use of three airbases for logistical support of its operations in Afghanistan.

Once airborne, Alan and Robbie searched every square inch of all three Afghans to make sure that nothing, no weapons, information, or anything of use, had escaped the previous, no doubt thorough going-over they'd already been subjected to. Alan and the intelligence sergeant interrogated the men to determine whether any time-sensitive information might have been missed by the previous interrogations. Suddenly Robbie said, "Hey guys. Take a look." He crumpled the gray-striped suit vest that the Taliban governor was wearing over his shirt and heard the faint sound of crinkling paper. "I think there's something in here." The bearded Afghan said nothing but his brown eyes glowered at them. From the black sheath fastened to his thigh with Velcro straps, Alan pulled his Kershaw knife—which opened with the touch of a finger for one-handed use. The Afghan became very still as Alan brought it up to his vest, then carefully slit open the seam.

While Alan did this, the intelligence sergeant took a series of photos with the team's digital camera to document the discovery. He photographed the vest, the slit, the paper halfway out of the vest, and the paper itself. It was one sheet of handwriting in Arabic; although it was phrased elliptically, it appeared to Alan to be instructions for handling money and supplies, and large amounts of both.

The men were sure that the document contained valuable information about the terrorists' operations. Why else would it have been so carefully concealed? As soon as they landed they would hand over the evidence and their photos; they would also give their own headquarters copies. They landed at a well-guarded air base in Pakistan; it was full of Marines, but the U.S. presence was being kept as low profile as possible because Pakistan itself had a large population of Islamic fundamentalists, some of whom worked in the government. Alan and the other members of 563 handed off the prisoners, who did not put up any resistance this time, to the waiting arms of U.S. naval intelligence. They also handed over the document they had found in the governor's vest and their documentation of the discovery. Their mission accomplished, they refueled and flew back to K2.

When they returned they gave copies of the digital files to their commander and the intelligence section of the ops center, which sent the information through their own channels for analysis as well. So often in their highly compartmentalized business, Special Forces teams play a frontline role in some critical event but never learn of the eventual outcome or consequences of their work, unless they are assigned to follow through. The men learn to take satisfaction from what they know they have accomplished, and not to wonder too much about what happened next. In this case, ODA 563 learned later that the document had indeed proven to be extremely valuable. It led investigators to an important funding source for al Qaeda and helped them unravel some of the supply mechanisms and surrogates that the group used. Tracking Al Qaeda financial networks was a monumentally complex task because the funding streams crisscrossed the world and came from such diverse sources as Saudi royal coffers, the precious-metal trade, religious entities, and Afghanistan's largest cash crop, opium.

ODA 563 was pleased that its first assignment in Operation Enduring Freedom had yielded important intelligence. In the wake of September 11, the Special Forces, like others in the military, felt personally responsible for defending the United States against those who had sworn to carry out a jihad against the country, and those who had caused the deaths in the rubble of New York's financial district, the Pentagon, and the cornfields of Pennsylvania. The soldiers keenly felt the urgency of their assignments in Afghanistan. They would climb the highest peaks barehanded if their commanders ordered them to, which is exactly what ODA 563 was ordered to do next.

ODA 563 waited anxiously with the other teams at the K2 base to see what mission it might be next assigned. The teams did not wait long. In late November, 563 was one of three teams sent to a place called Tora Bora—a vast cave complex in the mountains along the border with Pakistan, just north of Paktia province. Al Qaeda and Taliban fighters had been spotted heading into it. The mountain range was named Spin Ghar, or White Mountains, because the peaks were snow-capped year-

Operation Anaconda

round. This formidable redoubt was a legendary refuge which had withstood Soviet efforts to penetrate it and overwhelm the mujahedeen fighters holding out there during Russia's decade-long war of occupation. This region had also been a killing ground of the British the century before. The advantage in this terrain lay overwhelmingly with the defenders.

It was cold, even at the lower elevations where the men made camp. The first thing that the three teams and the company commander did when they arrived at Tora Bora was to hold a memorial service on a flat-topped steppe. The firemen of New York City had sent some of the ruins of the World Trade Center to the 5th Group commander, Colonel Mulholland, who parceled out pieces of the wreckage to the units as they fanned out across Afghanistan. When the teams arrived at their destinations they held simple ceremonies of remembrance and dedication and buried their piece of stone or twisted metal in the rugged land where they had come to fight. On their windswept hilltop, ODA 563 and the other teams dug a hole and put the piece of the New York building into the ground. Each man filed by and placed a rock on top of the pile. They leaned a flat rock against the shrine and Randy wrote on it with a marker:

9–11

NYPD NYFD

USA

They bowed their heads and said a prayer. When they finished, Randy slipped a pebble from the hilltop into his medicine pouch. In the days to come, he noticed that the Afghan allies they had recruited kept a respectful distance from their small shrine.

Before leaving K2 the teams had been given the latest satellite imagery of Tora Bora, which they analyzed along with daily feeds of new information from the intelligence agencies. Unmanned aerial vehicles, Predators, flew over the mountain range to search for signs of the hidden fighters. Jets arrived almost daily to drop massive bombs on the caves that were located. But however sophisticated and powerful the American technology was, the search had to be carried out by human beings, one remote cave and mountain peak at a time.

Most of the caves were small, crude affairs, little more than indentations in the rock that could hold a few men. The search was laborious work, but the SF could not dally, because bin Laden and his fighters were likely either to dig in and erect heavy defenses or slip through the mountain passes that were not already sealed shut by ice and snow for the long winter. They would not be passable again until the spring thaw in April, giving bin Laden a four-month head start. Just across the border lay Pakistan's autonomous tribal regions where the ultra-conservative population sympathized with Al Qaeda and probably would give it safe haven. No one knew how many fighters might be hiding in the mountains, but there were reports of large caves and huge caches of ammunition that had been stored in underground bunkers built to fight off the Soviets.

The three teams on the Tora Bora mission each were assigned to work with a different band of Afghan mujahedeen who had been fighting the Taliban for years. The fighters were loyal to a warlord named Hazrat Ali, who held court in the provincial capital of Jalalabad. ODA 563 was assigned to a group with a chieftain named Colonel Malik. To procure quick assistance in this land of ever-shifting loyalties, the Special Forces and the Central Intelligence Agency were authorized to pay the Afghans for their help. That clearly colored their motivations, but the simple fact was that the SF needed the help of locals who knew the impenetrable mountains, and needed it before bin Laden got away. The soldiers had no hope of finding their way quickly through such difficult terrain without guides. That did not mean they were unaware of the complications, however, and Randy and the others realized that they would have to guard against attempts by the various chieftains to use the Special Forces' firepower against their rivals, as internecine warfare was a long-established feature of Afghan life. This region was especially rife with warlord rivalry because it was prime opium-growing territory. In sum, this was an extreme real-world example of the Robin Sage exercise:

the Special Forces had to enlist little-known allies in record time and manage the known deficiencies on a mission of the utmost urgency and importance.

The team made its base camp in the Tora Bora foothills in an abandoned stone-and-mud-walled school they dubbed the "Alamo." It was a small, one-story, U-shaped building with a wall in front of it that had an opening just wide enough to drive their borrowed Toyota trucks and, later, all-terrain vehicles (ATVs) into the courtyard. The ATVs were lashed to pallets and dropped from C–130s. They were the only motorized transport that proved useful in chasing down suspects in the foothills. In the mountains, travel was strictly by foot and mule train. To haul supplies from the drop zone to the Alamo or to staging areas they used small six-wheeled flatbed trucks called gators, which were also airdropped.

The men built a plywood shower stall and hung their canvas shower bucket from it. The water in it would freeze if they did not bathe quickly. When they washed their clothes, they would turn into stiff frozen boards on the clothesline. Their Afghan partners, about a hundred of them, camped nearby. One day the Afghans and U.S. soldiers bought some live turkeys at a local market and demonstrated methods of killing and trussing fowl to eat; the Afghans always bled theirs facing Mecca.

Whatever Randy's reservations about their allies' loyalties, he soon came to appreciate their mountaineering skills. On their treks, which often lasted for days, the Afghans would scamper along the treacherous footpaths like mountain goats, never out of breath even when climbing at altitudes near 10,000 feet.

On December 4, the teams in Tora Bora received grim news from Kandahar province in the south. The Green Berets had suffered their first fatalities in Afghanistan. ODA 574, which had been fighting a fierce battle in Mullah Omar's hometown area, had been the victim of a deadly friendly-fire accident. Someone on the ground had given the pilot the wrong coordinates and re-confirmed them. Apparently the controller had misread the GPS's output sequence, confused the locations of the team and the target and called a 2,000-pound bomb squarely onto the team. Two members of 574 and a signals intelligence sergeant attached to the company were killed, along with three Afghans, and several others were wounded critically. The Afghan leader with them, Hamid Karzai, gazed in shock at the carnage around him. He had just learned that he had been selected as the interim head of the new post-Taliban government.

The men in Tora Bora were devastated. They were in a war and knew that some among them could die, but the deaths hit the small, close-knit community hard. It was especially bitter that the deaths had been self inflicted. ODA 574 had been Randy's very first team, and Alan had been close friends with its team sergeant, Master Sgt. Jefferson Davis—he and "J.D." had served on 564 together until 1999. Then he and J.D. had become rival team sergeants of 574 and 563 respectively, trading friendly jibes and jokes between their team rooms. Now he was dead. Alan's next thought was of a conversation he'd had with J.D.'s wife just before he left Fort Campbell for Afghanistan. J.D. had already left, and Alan and his wife had run into her at the shopping mall. She had asked him: "J.D. will be okay, won't he?" Alan had reassured her and said that her husband was well prepared and more than a match for the fighters they were going to encounter.

The Tora Bora hunters had no time to stop and grieve, however, as intelligence intercepts had just picked up a voice that analysts were sure was Osama bin Laden's. The teams rounded up their Afghan allies and prepared to head out to different destinations. They would go in split teams, and Randy would lead one that included Alan. The team had been given a quick lesson in Dari, the Afghan language that was related to Arabic, but they'd had no time to learn more than the rudiments. Malik, the Afghan chieftain assigned to ODA 563, only spoke Dari, but one of his men also spoke Arabic so Alan used him as their interpreter.

ODA 563 was ordered to head for a high-mountain hamlet called Jangaley, a few kilometers from the border of Pakistan. In the pre-dawn darkness, the men tied their packs onto mules and donkeys draped with multicolored ropes and blankets. Randy watched the Afghan mule skinner, a gnarled fellow in thin garments and the traditional hat that looked like a wool soufflé, to see how he arranged the pads and boards and tied them onto the animals' backs. Randy would have done it differently, but the Afghans wanted to use their men, so he adapted to their system. The skinner came along to care for his animals and act as a Sherpa. Randy was awed to see the leathery man, who was only in his forties but looked like sixty, splash knee-deep through icy streams while wearing only flip-flops. Many of the SF had started wearing the local hat and the warm woolen blankets as capes over their layered long-johns, flannel shirts, and vests. A few of the men swore by pantyhose with the feet cut out as a perfect thin, heat-trapping layer for the legs. But they were all sworn to secrecy and no one outside of the team would ever be told who wore them.

From studying their maps, Randy and Alan knew that the journey to Jangaley would be arduous. It was about forty kilometers out and back as the crow flies, which meant probably twice that, given the terrain. They would ascend to elevations over 10,000 feet. Thus far, the teams had only fought running gun battles with a few Taliban fighters they had encountered in the mountains, but as word of their tactics spread they might well face ambush or concerted resistance. They could never be confident of their Afghan allies—they had only themselves to count on. Randy and Alan were grateful for the Kosovo mission; it had proven to be the ideal prelude to the challenges they faced here. Their team had been forged into a solid, tested unit, and there was not a weak link among them. This was what a team ideally should be. Robbie, Alan, Randy, Matt, Mark, Rich, and the rest knew they could count on each other's strength, competence, and courage. In circumstances like these their lives wholly depended on each other.

Tora Bora soon revealed its most formidable terrain. The team entered gorges so steep that the sun never shone on the walls of ice. Randy had never seen mountains like this. It looked like Shangri-la. Some men walked below with the mules while others flanked them on the high trails to defend against ambushes. At clefts too deep for the animals to cross they stopped and built stone bridges. The footpath wound around sheer mountain walls that rose straight up for hundreds of feet, and plunged downward for thousands more. The paths were not wide enough to stand with two feet planted. The Afghans led them on, and the Americans summoned their willpower and blocked out the sheer drop, the frigid wind, and any tremor that could cause a fatal slip. If the mind does not admit the possibility of failure, the well-trained body obeys.

After traveling for a day and a night, they reached the outskirts of Jangaley, which lay in a crevice of the mountains. Important Al Qaeda members were supposed to be hiding there, perhaps including bin Laden himself, according to intelligence reports. The team was hunting strictly "high-value targets" to find and capture them. The preferred scenario was for them to call for a helicopter and fly the captives out, so the men had scouted for possible landing zones (LZs) on the way in. They named the three LZs they found Tina, Lydia, and Deanna after three of their wives. "It might be our last chance to tell them we love them," said Alan. Getting a helicopter in would not be easy, however; first the communications sergeant would have to make contact, which was itself difficult in the remote and jagged terrain.

Randy, who was commanding the split team, wanted to go into the village as soon as they had eaten and rested. Malik, or the G-chief (guerrilla chief) as the team called him, insisted on sending his own advance party to scout Jangaley and would not let any U.S. soldiers go along. Randy was suspicious and wanted his own men to go. The situation grew tense. Everyone was armed, and Afghans rarely hesitated to resort to their weapons if their honor was insulted. Randy and Alan both knew that the situation could quickly go from bad to worse, deep in these mountains. The Afghan commander, deeply angry at Randy for doubting his intentions, called a halt for the night. He took some of his men and went into an old dungeon with mud walls four-to-five-feet thick.

The language barrier had complicated matters. Randy believed that the Afghan fighter Alan was relying on as an interpreter was not translating accurately. The Americans did not speak Dari so they could not be sure what he was saying to the commander, but Randy felt that something was amiss. He considered whether the interpreter or Malik might be working for the other side. Might someone have paid them off? In the 1980s, all factions of mujahedeen, including what would become the Taliban, had fought together against the Soviets. Shifting loyalties were part of the landscape that made Afghanistan so treacherous. Malik had led them off into the unknown, and Randy had to be alert for any signs of a trap. In this remote and perilous place he felt keenly his responsibilities as commander to protect his men.

Randy and his men sat outside under the moonlight and weighed their options. Alan went down into the dungeon where the commander and his men had gathered. It was filled with acrid smoke from their cooking fire. Alan was invited to sit down. He did, and tried to mend the breach. He listened to their stories and ate the pita they offered while they roasted a goat. It was hacked into pieces and laid out—this was what the SF called a "goat grab." In less-primitive settings the goat would be surrounded by rice and peas. Then each man would reach into the pile to pick up a piece of meat and some rice and peas with a bare hand. Alan broached the topic at hand. The G-chief explained his refusal to send Americans on the patrol to Jangaley: if anything happened to the U.S. soldiers, then the big boss, Hazrat Ali, would kill him, no questions asked. Malik said he could not risk their involvement in a firefight.

Alan, careful not to impugn Malik's authority or imply that his men were incapable of acting on their own, described his own men's combat experience and training in raid and ambush tactics. He explained that Rawhide, their commander, was qualified to lead up to a battalion of men. This impressed the G-chief. Alan told him how Randy had led a company of Kuwaitis in combat in Desert Storm, and how sometimes the chief warrant officer was frocked with a higher rank so foreign troops would understand the level of expertise that they possessed.

Alan also described his sergeants' training. The medic, Doc Nittler, was qualified to perform field amputations and other surgery. No other medics in the U.S. army had such extensive training, which included rotations in emergency rooms to learn trauma care. The medics were treating both old and new land-mine injuries all over Afghanistan, which has one of the highest densities of mines in the world. Amputations in the developing world often required repeated operations to cut away the dead and rotting tissue. One Special Forces medic performed dozens.

One by one the G-chief invited the SF into his den. Finally he invited Randy inside. Randy went warily and sat down. Their split team included a young TACP, the tactical air control personnel sent by the air force to help the Special Forces call in air support. This young fellow had never seen anything like these Afghans, this terrain, or this entire surreal experience. The Afghan fighters lay sprawled in rope beds they had hung from the low ceiling. The choking smoke nearly filled the room, so the Americans bent low to suck in the less acrid air. The TACP was already dehydrated and suffering from altitude sickness, and after five minutes inside he had to leave. He climbed out to rejoin the communications sergeant who stood watch up above.

Alan had cracked the code. The G-chief was now prepared to accept the team as equals. Randy realized that they had to mend fences to get through this mission. At this point, they really had no other option. Then the G-chief revealed that his advance patrol had captured prisoners.

"You have captured prisoners?" Alan said, taking the lead as his relationship with the chief was still the strongest.

"Don't worry, they will be beaten," the chief assured them.

"Uh, beaten?" Alan had a sinking feeling.

"Really. Don't worry, they will be beaten *very* badly."

"Umm, where are the prisoners?" asked Alan.

"They are in the mountains."

Alan thought, "Well, we're not likely to see those guys again." Everyone had the same feeling, yet there was nothing they could do without precipitating a showdown with their partner. It was decided that they would all go into the village at first light and see what they could find.

The G-chief was now kidding around with everyone—as far as he was concerned, they were now all one happy family. Randy remained doubtful. He was also very concerned about the TACP. If the young man went down then they would need a helicopter to evacuate him. He had dragged himself along valiantly so far.

Randy decided to have a talk with the interpreter. He did not want to take the team into Jangaley without greater confidence that they would not somehow be double-crossed. Randy told him a story, speaking slowly and plainly. He told him that the team had been dependent on a translator in Kosovo. When they searched homes, the translator's job was to enter first and tell the people inside what was going to happen, then the team would go in. The translator could have set them up if he had wanted to, and the team would have no way of knowing whether he had tricked them until it was too late. They had to place their trust in him.

"You are an essential part of our operation, and we have to trust you, but that trust must be earned," Randy said. Then he delivered his punch line. "This is what I told our interpreter in Kosovo: 'If you set us up, you'll be the first one I shoot. It's that simple.'"

The Afghan stared at him, then looked at Doc Nittler.

"He's not kidding," Nittler assured him.

"If you earn our trust, you will be part of us," Randy said, finishing his speech. "Then we will put our lives in jeopardy to protect you."

Randy curled up against a rock for an hour's sleep, his 9-mm pistol cradled in his hand. The interpreter kept his distance. He stayed in the rear when they set out before dawn, only coming forward once they entered the village and his services were needed. Randy hoped his speech had had the intended effect.

Randy had wanted to enter the village by night, the time that all special operators prefer to strike. Their night-vision goggles and laser-aiming devices gave them a critical advantage over adversaries and a mantle of protection, especially when the enemy knows the terrain. But the G-chief had insisted on waiting. Was he giving time for others to escape through a back route? They would never know for sure, Randy thought grimly.

The soldiers and the Afghans searched the town's few mud buildings. The house where the Al Qaeda operatives were supposed to have been was empty. The men searched the rooftop patio where they had reportedly been living for any clues. They talked to villagers with the help of the interpreter and learned that a drug shipment had gone out that night. They gathered the village leaders to see what information they could elicit from them. They said that foreigners had left that night for Pakistan. Arabs. Randy knew that would have been impossible if the G-chief's patrol had been blocking the pass as they were supposed to have done. This convinced him that they had been duped. Alan shared his fears.

Had the Special Forces been outbid? They were feeling the double-edged sword of expediency in a culture of double-dealing, in the heart of the high-stakes opium business. Randy wished they'd gone in unilaterally the night before despite their orders to rely on Malik. If the G-chief had been paid off by others, however, he would not have hesitated to attack the soldiers. After the Herculean effort they had made to reach this place, this defeat was bitter indeed—and they still faced the hair-raising journey back.

The team would never see the prisoners that Malik said he had taken, and it would never know if bin Laden had been there that night. The thought that Al Qaeda's leaders may have been in the team's grasp haunted the men. The soldiers were not permitted to cross into Pakistan in pursuit. All that was left to do was to proceed with the secondary objective of the mission, which was to try to ensure no one else went through that mountain pass into the wild netherworld of Pakistan's tribal provinces. Trying to seal this passage required diplomacy, bargaining, and more reliance on Malik. The stratagem was to use Malik's stature as a lieutenant of Hazrat Ali, backed by U.S. force and money, to convince the population that it was the winning side. If the villagers could be persuaded that rewards would come their way if they cooperated, and punishment would ensue if they did not, they might be recruited into a local watch network. The soldiers would also try to play on the fact that many Afghans did not like Arabs.

The team stayed for two days while the G-chief received the village chiefs from miles around. The Special Forces tried to reinforce the message that the villagers would gain from turning in any Al Qaeda or Taliban figures who came through these mountains. The G-chief was the best bet for building a functioning network of informants, so anything the SF could do to shore him up and help him build rapport with these people would serve their interests. That did not mean the team's reservations had vanished, but it had to work with what was available. Improvisation and compromise were the central lessons of unconventional warfare, and tough moral choices were often involved. Randy did not like the strategy of buying help and overlooking the rampant drug-trafficking around them, but that was the deal that had been struck. The mission was to find the leaders of Al Qaeda who had plotted and directed the attack on the United States, no matter what. But here the trail was cold.

On the return trip, the men radioed for permission to search some caves they'd seen on the way in. Outside one cave, the team spotted a few Afghans who eluded them and fled into the rocky byways. These caves were big enough for ten or fifteen men at most, but some were as large as a single-car garage, with fireplaces and reinforced concrete slabs shielding the front entrance. About 90 percent of the caves they'd found were empty, although many held caches of ammunition, and sometimes AK–47s or other weapons. They had even found documents and laptop computers—whose hard drives yielded troves of information about Al Qaeda's operations. The team also found some underground caves, but never the vast, elaborately outfitted underground complexes that some experts had alleged existed in these mountains.

On the final leg of their descent from Jangaley, Alan was riding one of the donkeys—a comical sight, for the 190-pound master sergeant was the same size as the donkey and his legs nearly dragged along the ground. Despite his load, the donkey must have realized it was near home, and it began to run. Randy, on a mule, challenged Alan to race the last stretch to the Alamo.

"Hucha," Randy shouted, which was Dari for giddyap.

Alan's barnsour donkey ran for all it was worth. Suddenly stumbling on a rock, it shuddered to a halt, pitching Alan forward. Alan regained his balance midair, hit the ground at a run, and beat Randy and his mule to the finish line. The tired and discouraged warriors returned to the Alamo. The mission was not accomplished.

The team did not get to rest. A few hours after its return, the team received urgent orders to search a cave atop another mountain—it was another bin Laden alert. The men strongly doubted that this would be a fruitful probe, however; they had seen no trails into this area and their contacts in the nearby village told them no one went up there. But the team had no say in the matter: the targets were selected by the intelligence community, which was relying on Predator footage, signals intelligence, and other means. The exhausted men shouldered their gear and set off. When they reached the base of the mountain they stared upward in disbelief. It was an almost vertical climb. This was going to be brutal. Alan attempted to lift their spirits. "The longest journey begins with the first step," he intoned in his best stage voice.

Despite their skepticism about the assignment, the men had their orders and it was a point of honor to fulfill them to the letter. They would leave no stone unturned and no cave unsearched.

The Afghan allies sped ahead, while the Americans, less acclimatized and weighed down by more ammunition and equipment, toiled on behind. They clambered amid the scree and boulders and slid on icy rocks. Randy, two months shy of his forty-ninth birthday, humped his pack alongside men almost half his age—who were amazed at his stamina. Randy gave thanks for his Hanwag boots.

The men pulled themselves up with ropes in the final steep approach to the summit. They used their GPS to find the location that matched the coordinates that intelligence had provided—it appeared to mark a point in midair off the mountaintop. But ODA 563 was not one to leave it at that. The newest member went the final extra meter: Sgt. First Class Rich Davis volunteered to verify that there was no cave opening on the sheer mountain face that lay just out of sight. He edged out on a ledge and swung himself out onto a lone scrawny tree that had somehow taken root thousands of feet above timberline. He craned his shaved-bald head in its black fleece cap to see around the rocks. Dangling in space with a thousand-foot drop-off below, Davis confirmed: "No cave." They'd come up empty-handed once again.

The team had been promised a helo ride off of this mountain, but it did not materialize. The title track of the rock-and-roll CD they had burned for the war in Afghanistan took on new meaning. A favorite of the HALO jumpers, the U2 song "Elevation" would henceforth be associated with Tora Bora.

Between December and mid-January the teams searched more than 200 caves. ODA 563 chased fleeing Al Qaeda and Afghan fighters, most of whom did not make a stand but preferred to slip away into the mountain recesses. One of their fellow hunter-killer teams did strike it big, however, capturing an Al Qaeda lieutenant who ran the training camps. Several hundred Al Qaeda fighters had remained behind as a rearguard but, as December wore on, the soldiers grew increasingly convinced that bin Laden and his top aides had slipped across the border. The searches continued to net some low-level people, a lot of ammunition and weapons, and bags full of documents apparently left behind in haste.

Some of the cave complexes had been sealed off by bombing, but the preference was to search them for all the possible intelligence they could yield, and then record the coordinates so they could be monitored by Predators and spy planes or their Afghan allies in case any of the terrorists returned. The promise of the $25-million reward just might buy bin Laden's capture. One day, as their stay neared its end, the SF came upon two Afghans who were digging holes to plant mines in the road outside their camp. The soldiers chased them down in their ATVs, shooting one and capturing another in a village where he had hidden in a market stall.

"Christmas in Tora Bora. Sounds like a name for an album," Alan joked as the holiday arrived. The team made a cardboard sign with greeting-card script that read: "Merry Christmas from Tora Bora" and took a group picture to send home. Everyone was thoroughly weary of the wretched, fly-blown Alamo. Austere environments were nothing new to them, but Afghanistan was literally a few centuries behind the rest of the world.

Just after Christmas, one of 563's medics was sitting in the courtyard sewing his pants, which were in tatters after all their mountain climbing. A soldier ran out of the compound, vomit spewing out of his mouth— like in the scene from *The Exorcist*. "Drink more water," the medic

calmly counseled the soldier once he'd finished retching. Gastrointesti-
nal disturbances were an everyday affair, and a virtual certainty if one
ate locally prepared food. The link between sanitation, hygiene, and disease was not understood by the rural Afghans, whose mud huts scarcely
demarcated the place for food preparation from the place for defecation.
The medics tried to explain, to no avail, that the flies traveling from one
to the other ensured sickness, dysentery, and many early deaths. Yet,
diplomacy often required eating food prepared by their hosts as a way of
establishing rapport. When the soldiers visited the villages tucked into
the mountain crevices in search of current information, if they refused
the traditional hospitality—which always involved tea and often food as
well—they would offend the very people they sought to cultivate.

Tora Bora would be one of the most-debated episodes of Operation
Enduring Freedom. Bin Laden had slipped through the net. Many pun-
dits and observers criticized the reliance on dubious allies, which was
not news to the men who had to work with them, but there had been no
promising alternative. The soldiers were certainly willing to proceed
unilaterally, but they would have been unlikely to find their way as
quickly without any guides. And once they were in a position to strike
unilaterally, as at Jangaley, they ran the risk of having to fight on two
fronts. In a briefing at the Pentagon, a general tried to explain the difficulty of manhunts in layman's terms. "It is like trying to find one particular bunny rabbit in the whole state of West Virginia," he said. The odds
were overwhelmingly against the Special Forces: the lack of intelligence
assets, the terrain, the lack of reliable allies, and the limitations of technology. The men had done their best in unbelievably harsh conditions,
but had come up empty handed. There were two additional purported
sightings of bin Laden but, by Christmas, most of the men on the
ground felt the trail was long cold and it was time to move on.

Although it was small comfort, there were some lasting benefits to
the effort: the U.S. military had gained firsthand knowledge of the area
and its population, and a huge store of intelligence had been collected
for analysis. Hundreds of caves had been demolished or located and
marked and, by one estimate, 300 Taliban and Al Qaeda fighters had

been killed, mostly in the bombing. In the capital, a start had been made in forging substantive alliances with new leaders based on common interests—always a stronger foundation than alliances of convenience. The struggle against terrorism was going to last a long time, and it was quite possible that Tora Bora would be the setting for a future chapter. In all likelihood the U.S. forces would do better the next time.

The first three months of the war had been conducted by Special Forces on the ground with U.S. air force, navy, and marine jets overhead, along with the coalition and local allies. By early 2002, U.S. conventional forces had taken charge of the overall military effort. They planned Operation Anaconda when intelligence indicated that enemy fighters were concentrating in Paktia's Shah e Kot valley. ODA 563 and other teams were assigned to accompany troops from the 101st Airborne and the 10th Mountain divisions, while other Special Forces would join several hundred local Afghan fighters driving in from the west. The plan was to seal the valley in the south and force the Al Qaeda and Taliban fighters to flee north, where a company of the 101st would await them.

Geography indicated a basic weakness in the plan. The men would be dropped by helicopter into the valley floor, which had an elevation of about 4,000 feet. The surrounding mountains on either side of the valley rose to 10,000 feet. In the middle of the valley was a mountain they called the "whale." The military planners didn't know it then, but the Taliban had emplaced machine guns, artillery, and mortar tubes on all of these steep overlooking heights. One of the cardinal rules of warfare formulated by the Chinese strategist Sun Tzu was to fight from high ground to low ground—and the U.S. forces would be doing the opposite.

ODA 563 was split into two halves and assigned to accompany different elements of the 101st to two different landing zones in the valley. The team gathered for a final briefing before boarding the helicopters for their staggered departures. The operations officer pulled Alan aside. He did not look happy. The basic concept of the operation was to step on the puddle and see what came out. "We really don't have any idea how many of them might be up there," the worried officer told him. "It could be twenty, it could be 200. It could be 700." The officer in charge of loading the men repeated the orders one last time, emphatically: everyone had to wear their protective gear. "Helmets and vests?" Those words sent a chill up Alan's spine. "Holy crap," he thought. "Something bad is going to happen."

And it did.

The first helicopter lifted off with the captain of ODA 563, Doc Nittler, Mark Reynolds, three other sergeants, and a platoon of 101st soldiers. Upon landing they came under immediate fire. The mortars landed very nearby, which indicated that they had already been registered to home in on this location. Normally, several rounds of mortar fire are required to fix, or bracket, the target. The men scrambled to get organized and find cover in the open valley. High-velocity bullets rang off the rocks around them. Mark Reynolds estimated that it came from a heavy gun that had been fired about four kilometers down the valley. The team had nothing that could reach that far. The team had two M240 machine guns, Mark had a sniper rifle, and the 101st troops carried 90-mm mortars but their maximum range was 3700 meters. The commander of the battalion turned to Mark for advice. Mark could see anxiety in the faces of the young infantrymen around him. The first time under fire is a searing experience for every human being—and they were in the middle of a kill box with weapons pointed at them from all directions.

There was nothing to do but run and hide, so Mark led the way to shelter behind some rocks. It would be a few minutes before the Afghans adjusted their fire and homed in on them again. Mark offered up a plan. They would have to drop their rucksacks to be able to move fast enough and dodge the fire. They could come back for them at nightfall, but first they had to find cover. The men always carried supplies in a small kit so they could drop the large packs in emergencies like this. They were going to have to run, and at this altitude, they could not run far with those monsters. The guns were closing in on them again, so the troops returned fire as they prepared to seek new shelter.

They didn't know it yet, but one part of the plan already was falling apart: their Afghan allies entering the valley from the west also had come under heavy fire. One of the Special Forces teams' chief warrant officers was killed, and the Afghans had withdrawn.

The next four hours was a running firefight, as Mark and the other soldiers in his group moved north to a wider part of the valley, running and zigzagging from boulder to boulder. The Afghans used their antiaircraft guns as artillery, pointing the heavy 12.7-mm guns right down at the men in the valley. The U.S. soldiers fired back, mostly in vain, at the fighters high above them, but also skirmished with fighters as they moved north through the valley. They searched a cluster of recently deserted huts and found a large arsenal of heavy weapons. The 10th Mountain soldiers, fighting hard at the other end of the valley, took about two dozen casualties and were then pulled back. This disheartened some of the young men still fighting. Finally, Mark and his group reached a *wadi*, a small slit in the steep cliffs of the mountain, and dashed into it. It was no more than forty feet wide. The men had run about eight kilometers under more or less constant fire. It was a miracle that no one in the group had been hit.

They set up a defensive perimeter about twenty feet in diameter and the men took turns guarding and resting. Mark sat on a rock, facing his team leader. Suddenly, a mortar exploded about twenty feet behind Mark, and sent him sprawling onto his face. The captain was catapulted backward but quickly rolled to his feet, pistol in hand and covered in dirt. The men shifted to a new spot farther into the *wadi* as dusk arrived. The 101st was not used to fighting in the dark—but was about to learn. With binoculars, the team pinpointed some of the Afghans' dug-in guns and radioed for air support. While waiting for the air strikes, the 101st troops set up mortars and began firing rounds at the mountainsides. They could see the Afghan and Al Qaeda fighters ducking into holes or caves as the bombers arrived. As soon as they dropped their loads and flew off, the Afghans' heads reappeared. The soldiers on the mortars saw this pattern and timed their own barrages to hit the Afghans when they came back out. The fighting went on through the night, so the soldiers could not go back to retrieve their packs and their kevlar vests. The next day they would eat snow.

All night long, Alan, Randy, and Robbie were frantic for news of their teammates. They had been held back and recalled to the planning shed to assess other options, after the first half of 563 encountered such heavy fire. They finally settled on a plan to fastrope from a helicopter onto a hilltop at the far end of the valley, and then fight their way down to link up with their team and close off that end of the valley. Alan was worried about the condition of the men on the ground; nothing had been heard from them in a while. While they debated, one of the signals intelligence soldiers who had been with the 10th Mountain troops came into the command post. His hair was singed from rocket fire, and his equipment was back in the valley. After hearing his description of the battle, Alan was convinced that they needed to pull ODA 563 out.

"If our guys are in this kind of shape they won't be much use when we get to them. Why don't we pull them out, refit, and then go back?" Alan suggested. The commander, Colonel Mulholland, agreed. Although he was not in command of the overall operation, he retained ultimate control over his troops. Alan was grateful for his intercession, as he'd helped quash some of the hare-brained suggestions that were being floated now that the operation obviously was in deep trouble.

The evacuation plan was radioed to ODA 563. It would not be easy; the men would have to cross the valley floor to the far side, because it was the only place a helicopter could land and not be in the heavy guns' crossfire. They would have to retrieve their packs and cover about three kilometers in an hour. At almost 5,000 feet elevation and with 100-pound rucksacks, this was going to be a smoker. It might even be impossible. But it was their only way out, so they'd have to try.

As the stranded men hoofed it down the valley, dodging gunfire, Mark saw a Chinook helicopter go by, then another. "Hey, is that our ride?" someone asked. It was, but the helicopters had been diverted to another developing disaster on a southern mountaintop. A team of SEALs had attempted to land to take out the enemy's artillery, but the helicopter had come under heavy fire and one of the men had fallen out. The damaged helicopter limped to another peak, and the focus turned to rescuing the captured SEAL from the heavily fortified command post. More SEALs, Rangers, and helicopters were sent into the ferocious battle, which lasted until nightfall when they were extricated, with eight dead.

During the SEALs rescue attempt, the men in the valley dodged bullets, returned fire, and ran for cover throughout the day. Finally, they were told they had a half-hour to travel two kilometers to a pickup zone. "We can't do it," Mark said. The answer came back, "You've got to. It's the only chance you've got."

Exhausted after more than a day and a half of running and fighting, the men summoned their final reserves. As darkness fell on the valley, the men exited to the south and ran for the pickup zone. They watched one helicopter of the 101st Division take off without them, then set down in a different place. They missed a second one that landed in yet another place. Finally, on the third try, they got out.

The tide finally began to turn for the operation on its sixth day, after troop reinforcements numbered 2,200 and bombers rooted out most of the entrenched positions manned by the Al Qaeda fighters—who were much more formidable and tenacious than the Afghans. In the first week, eight Americans and an estimated 450 enemy fighters were killed, and it took another week to secure the valley. The U.S. forces had confronted at least 700 hardened and well-trained Al Qaeda fighters, who had used their advantages adroitly and employed innovative tactics in one of the war's largest battles. After such ordeals men tend to develop a penchant for gallows humor. Sergeant First Class Mark Reynolds was droll even before he became a veteran of Operation Anaconda. Mark was especially piquant when the official historians came to interview him for the formal after-action reports that are done after significant engagements. He said that the lesson he learned was, "If you get shot at, run."

Anaconda marked the end of Operation Enduring Freedom for ODA 563 and much of 5th Group. By March 2002, they had been deployed for more than five months, and had been fighting and living in the harshest winter conditions that the U.S. army had encountered since the Korean War. The team went back to Bagram and by April the men were home.

The 5th Group and its partners had toppled the Taliban government. Al Qaeda had not been destroyed, but it had been hit hard—dislodged from its sanctuary and scattered. Osama bin Laden's whereabouts were unknown, but one of his top lieutenants, Mohammed Atef, had been killed and another one, Abu Zubaida, had been captured. A video of bin Laden sent to Arab television suggested that he may have been wounded, possibly in the bombing at Tora Bora where the chief of his training camps had been captured. Hundreds of bin Laden's fighters had been killed and hundreds more taken prisoner. Intelligence collected had led to more than 1,000 arrests worldwide.

The troops in Operation Anaconda might have fared even worse if a little-known operation had not been carried out to curry support among the villages in the Shah e Kot and surrounding valleys. A few weeks before Anaconda began, Maj. Simon Gardner of the 96th Civil Affairs Battalion flew from Bagram down to the nearest airfield, in Khost, with sixty Civil Affairs soldiers. He organized the delivery of truckloads of food and other aid to the area. The goals were to stop the local population from supporting or joining the Taliban's fight, and to encourage it to support the pro-American Afghan resistance. Gardner and his men were 150 miles from any American support network, and they provided their own security at the airfield. There were no humanitarian organizations in the area, so they mounted the operation from scratch. They pushed 100 truckloads of 600 metric tons of food out to sixteen different tribes, including 5,000 Cuchi gypsies. The aid was distributed by local leaders who the United States wanted to legitimize as reliable partners. Home Depot donated building materials including hammers, nails, and wheelbarrows for another distribution; wheat was also delivered.

The population of Khost had never seen such largesse. "The idea was to flood the region with goodwill so they would be less friendly to the fleeing Taliban," Major Gardner said. Gardner also hired interpreters and drivers, which generated income in a desperately poor area. All this created a less-hostile environment for the Special Forces' advance patrols before Anaconda was launched.

Gardner only wished he'd been able to arrive a month or two before the operation to have had even greater impact. The men kept working through Anaconda and lent their C–130 planes to support the soldiers pinned down in the valley. Most of the villagers fled the fighting and few provided sanctuary to the mostly Al Qaeda force.

The Civil Affairs soldiers stayed on after Anaconda. They dug wells and hired fifty or sixty workers every day to fill sandbags at their fire base at the Khost airfield. They paid 200 rupees or about $2 a day, the best wage in the province. They worked with the local police and extended the range of their own patrols to reach more people and develop more sources of information.

The 96th Battalion is the only active-duty battalion of Civil Affairs soldiers. Its Charlie Company performs the tactical, i.e., battlefield, Civil Affairs missions that directly support the Special Forces, as opposed to the reserve Civil Affairs units that come in after the fighting is over. Tactical Civil Affairs units work directly in support of Special Forces' missions; they are, in essence, the arm that is devoted full time to working with the population. They are also trained and equipped to operate in active war environments. Until recently, the noncommissioned officers who comprise three of the four men on each Civil Affairs team were even Special Forces–qualified soldiers who had passed the Q course and, in many cases, served on ODAs.

Tactical Civil Affairs teams very often are attached to Special Forces units to expand their capacity for working with the population and civilian leaders during wartime, insurgency, or counterinsurgency. They have key non-combat roles to play in each of those scenarios. The common principle that unites Special Forces, Civil Affairs, and Psychological Operations is that the population is the center of gravity, and the key to winning in any war.

Simon Gardner, at age 42, was one of Civil Affairs' rising stars. He had led two Civil Affairs teams and been the deputy operations officer for the joint special operations task force to help the Kurds in Operation Provide Comfort II. A spunky, articulate man, he had enlisted in 1986 before attending Officer Candidate School. Born in England, Gardner could summon up a perfect British accent at will. He'd recently completed a master's degree at a program designed for special operations officers at the Naval Postgraduate School in Monterrey and written a thesis on Central Asian conflicts that had dissected their mixture of nationalist, territorial, and religious causes.

Civil Affairs was a growth industry, and not only because small wars had proliferated and, with them, U.S. engagement. Gardner and his commanders at the 96th Civil Affairs Battalion realized that the nature of modern warfare made Civil Affairs an increasingly vital actor on the battlefield during conflicts, and not just in the postwar stabilization and reconstruction phase as was often presumed. In wars like Afghanistan, there are no uniformed fighters. The only way to identify the adversary was with the help of the local population. The U.S. forces, or their allies, can gain access to the locals only if they have rapport, credibility, and legitimacy.

A few days before September 11, 2001, Gardner had become the Civil Affairs planner at the Joint Special Operations Command, which conducts the most secret missions, so he was the logical choice to head the civil military operations task force sent to Afghanistan. Gardner arrived in Bagram in December, and found hundreds of refugees camped in tents just south of the airport on the Shomali Plains. For years it had been the frontline of the war, and it was about to become the scene of a humanitarian crisis. Ten people died in the first month after he arrived, and his medics estimated the malaria rate at 40 to 50 percent. The team dug a well and winterized some shelters.

Gardner also turned out to be an able ambassador to the male population. He is an accomplished rider, has a degree in equine management and has family in the horse business. The Afghan national sport, *buzkashi*, is a type of polo played with a headless goat. Gardner, as short as a jockey, played very well. He also earned a thank-you from the secretary of defense for personally unblocking a miles-long traffic jam in the icy waters of the dysfunctional Salang Tunnel, a vital artery north of Bagram, on the day a humanitarian field hospital was to be inaugurated—a major media opportunity to showcase progress in Afghanistan.

Throughout the spring and summer of 2002, the effort in Afghanistan moved into a new phase. Special operations professionals like Gardner and others knew that if the effort waned now the United States would likely have to return within the next decade. The vital task was to build a stable government and prevent the country from becoming a terrorist sanctuary again.

The conventional military was in control, but the Special Forces had important missions such as training a new national army to replace the warlord's militias, and continuing to hunt down Al Qaeda and Taliban remnants. One of the last 5th Group soldiers to leave Afghanistan was Sgt. Major Jim "Killer" Kilcoyne, who had been the sergeant major for the Joint Operations Center (JOC) since October. In March, he moved from K2 to Bagram with the rest of the special operations apparatus. He was ready to go home and would be gone by April, but meanwhile he carried on with his usual impeccable and stoic aplomb.

The JOC was the nerve center for the day-to-day operations of the Special Forces teams and their associated units. The JOC prepared them to go into the field, supported them in the field, and tracked their operations so that at any moment they could brief the commander on their actions.

The 3rd Special Forces Group took over the SF mission after 5th Group went home. Third Group was also assisted by 2nd Battalion of 7th Group and a Special Forces Group of National Guard soldiers that had been activated, the 19th Group. The activation of the two National Guard groups, the 19th and the 20th, indicated how much in demand the Special Forces had become for missions around the world. The 19th Group assumed the job of training the new Afghan National Army.

At Bagram, the JOC was located in a large quonset-shaped tent about forty by seventy feet. The JOC chief sat at the front with the operations officer and sergeant major at his side. The commander and his two subordinates, the deputy commander and the executive officer, were given information and updates whenever they requested them. Otherwise, the JOC chief ran the show. There were screens for projecting briefings on the front wall of the tent and a cluster of buffet tables for planning meetings. Around the circumference of the tent sat desks for every component of the special operations task force, from weather, intelligence, communications, and legal advice, to every special operations force from the army, navy, and air force. Liaisons from the conventional force also had desks, as did the noncommissioned officers and the foreign special operators in the coalition.

Seventh Group had been loaning officers for missions around the world since September 11, even though it had its own growing war in Colombia to tend to. Its commander, Peter Dillon, joked that 7th Group had become SF's strategic reserve, with some of his best officers flying off for months at a time to Djibouti, Afghanistan, and elsewhere. First Group could spare few men because it was chasing down Abu Sayyaf in the Philippines and standing on permanent alert for Korea.

Dillon's intelligence officer, Major Tony Martin, jumped at the chance to be night operations chief in the JOC in the summer and fall of 2002. He was a pugnacious, take-charge personality with coal-black hair and brown eyes. His nights were spent advising the younger officers in the field on their proposed operations. Unlike the top-down army, about 80 percent of all the Special Forces' operations are proposed by the teams; the higher echelons then help them develop the concept or steer them away if it is not a worthwhile project. One night a team ignored Martin's counsel and tried to fly in from Uzbekistan without a flight plan. He was unsympathetic when they were called on the carpet by the commander. Martin's main duty was to keep the teams safe by keeping track of them: all requests for fire on the battlefield, whether from aircraft or ground forces, had to be cleared through him. He made sure that the small units of hard-to-detect special operations forces were not in the target area.

Martin had been going through the Q course for the second time, as an officer, when he broke his back for the second time. Two previously crushed vertebrae and a herniated disk—the legacy of his first parachute injury in 1985—gave way. He made it through the Q course, but his injury forced him to make a career shift into military intelligence. It was a bitter disappointment because he had been an able platoon leader, winning the top awards named for the Darby Rangers and the Merrill Marauders, and he had demonstrated bravery in recovering his commander's body in Just Cause in Panama.

Perhaps fate had steered him to a new career, however, to take advantage of his sharp intellect. Martin served successive tours as intelligence officer and taught at West Point while finishing a doctorate at Duke University. His dissertation critiqued the strait-jacketed military decision-making process and proposed that teaching game theory to officers would enable them to think and act strategically on the battlefield. Because intelligence officers typically take the role of the opponent during war-gaming exercises, they develop excellent contrarian and critical thinking skills.

During his long nights in the JOC, Martin analyzed the operations unfolding in front of him in Afghanistan. He saw that, while the current Special Forces units continued to find caches of weapons, ammo, and documents, they were not finding live targets because they were failing to analyze their quarry's habits—to predict their movements and stay one step ahead. It was a perfect example of the type of training that his doctoral thesis had argued that officers needed to adapt and win on a fluid battlefield. Despite all the rhetoric about military transformation Martin believed the army would only change gradually, not radically. One day, he was pleased to see a dramatic affirmation of the Special Forces' value demonstrated by their conventional army brethren. Five days after an ODA had pulled out of a firebase in a risky corner of Afghanistan, the conventional battalion commander pleaded with the joint special operations task force to send the team back. The position of his 120-man infantry company at the remote outpost had become untenable without the Green Berets.

When his night shift was finished, Martin would send his wife a characteristically uninformative email—as security requirements dictated—

and head to his tent for a few hours' sleep until the un-airconditioned tent reached an unbearable 120 degrees about 9:30 A.M. Then he would get up and work on editing his dissertation. His friends joked that he would never finish it, but he finally defended it, successfully, in the fall of 2004.

The fight for Afghanistan and against Al Qaeda would continue for a long while yet, but the battlefield successes of the Special Forces in Operation Enduring Freedom had won an assured place in military and popular history. Military experts thought that the rapid and unorthodox overthrow of the Taliban government constituted a model for a powerful new kind of warfare. Special Forces allied with local fighters and high technology, such as precision bombs, could replace large numbers of troops and tanks in certain scenarios.

The war in Afghanistan had a stunning effect on the public profile of the U.S. Army Special Forces, most of whose previous successes in Panama, El Salvador, the Balkans, and elsewhere had gone largely unnoticed and unheralded. Not since 1968, when John Wayne starred in *The Green Berets* and Robin Moore helped write the popular "Ballad of the Green Berets," had the SF been thrust into the spotlight with accolades from every quarter. For twenty-five years they had been virtually unknown to the average American, who had seen many movies and documentaries and books featuring Navy SEALs and Delta Force commandos, some more fiction than fact. The men who wore the green berets were not unequivocally pleased with their status as media darlings, however. Some feared that it would cause a variety of negative repercussions from the rest of the military and for their families' safety, and that exaggerated expectations would result from sensationalistic coverage. They worried that it would destroy their mystique and erode their stealthy effectiveness. Their concerns were valid, but it was the beginning of their heyday nonetheless. The Special Forces, allied with 18th-century-style fighters on the ground and a powerful 21st-century airforce overhead, had seized the country's imagination. That cowboy on horseback with a laser target designator could have leapt out of a Marvel comic book or a Greek legend, but he didn't. He was real.

The recognition that the Special Forces had won in Afghanistan also gave them an opportunity to communicate their insights about war, which went beyond the image of the man on horseback with a laser. They hoped that those ideas would resonate with others in the military and national security circles and influence strategy and thinking about future wars. The essential insights included the core principle of working through and with other countries' forces which, for the Special Forces, is at the heart of unconventional warfare. It has the practical benefit of reducing the number of U.S. forces required but, more fundamentally, it is a collaborative approach that recognizes the local actors' stake and their knowledge of the adversary, the terrain, and the culture. They were most effective when permitted to "go native" and adopt unorthodox approaches based on the circumstances they encountered. Their effectiveness also increased if they were permitted to react quickly to the developing situation. Such autonomy cut against the grain of traditional military hierarchy, but held the promise of truly revolutionizing military operations to cope with the most elusive and shape-shifting types of threats.

The Afghanistan experience was rich in lessons for the future, and the Special Forces set about culling what had worked and what had not. By the summer of 2002, it seemed increasingly likely that Iraq would be the next battlefield. Preparations and training were under way by August. After returning from Afghanistan, the soldiers of 5th Group had a few brief months to make up for lost time with their wives and children. The school year was almost over, and another one would go by if, in fact, they went to war in Iraq. The soldiers also gathered in the parade field to remember their comrades who had not come home from Operation Enduring Freedom, in a somber ceremony where new trees were planted in the memorial grove.

A contingency plan for war in Iraq, codenamed 1003 Victor, had been sitting on the shelf since the 1991 war. The military's job was to prepare and rehearse plans that the civilian leadership might order to be executed. While there was a view within the services that the ongoing bombing campaigns of Iraq had sufficiently reined in Saddam Hussein,

President George Bush and his counselors determined that this containment policy failed to address the regime's latent threats. As 2003 approached the planning process revved up in the two key operational hubs, the Joint Staff in Washington and Central Command in Tampa.

Unlike Afghanistan, Iraq would be fought mostly with conventional forces, but the Pentagon's civilian leadership pressed for it to be fought as innovatively as possible. If the Special Forces could demonstrate their utility as unconventional partners in a war led by their conventional brethren, they would have made another giant leap forward in the space of two and a half years. In the end the special operations forces were given their biggest role in any war the United States had yet fought.

CHAPTER 9

WESTERN IRAQ
The Battle of the War Pigs

What is of supreme importance in war is to attack the
enemy's strategy.

—SUN TZU

O N MARCH 19, as soon as darkness fell, soldiers from 5th Group's
1st Battalion, Bravo Company, and the Florida National Guard
began digging down the berm on the Iraqi border with shovels. It was
the quietest way for the Special Forces to enter western Iraq before the
war's official start. Bravo Company commander Maj. Jim Gavrilis
watched the progress anxiously. When the wall of sand was low enough,
his men piled into their Humvees and trucks and started their engines.
The Guardsmen planted the American flag and the Florida state flag
atop the broken berm and waved the Special Forces through. A few
hours later, farther south, Charlie Company had determined through
surveillance that there was no need to be discreet. The breach team,
ODA 531, dynamited several concrete pillars to open a passageway
through the twelve-foot-high berm, and each team followed behind,
radioing its password once it was inside Iraq.

First Battalion Commander Lt. Col. Chris Haas breathed a sigh of relief when all fifteen teams cleared the two breach points. The border crossing was the single most vulnerable moment of their entire operation because the forces were bunched up and could have been decimated with a couple of missiles. As soon as they passed through the berm, the men dispersed across the wide-open, bowling-alley flat desert, hoping that all the ground surveillance radars had been knocked out as planned.

First Battalion's two companies of ODAs had left their secret bases in neighboring countries to launch the first operations of Iraqi Freedom. Speed became all the more vital to the success of their mission in the western desert of Iraq when hostilities began ahead of schedule with the attempted "decapitation strike" by F–117 stealth bombers and sea-launched missiles that targeted Dora Farm, where Saddam Hussein and his sons were thought to be, in the pre-dawn hours of March 20. Fortunately, the teams were already inside Iraq.

First Battalion's assignment was to slip into Iraq early to stop the launch of any missiles into neighboring countries, especially Israel. A missile launch would instantly complicate the conflict, and quite possibly would trigger a wider regional war. During the first Gulf War the coalition had failed to prevent the launching of missiles from the western desert. Israel had refrained from retaliating then, but this time it vowed to strike back if hit. One missile could unleash this course of events, so Lt. Col. Haas told his men that this was a "zero defect" mission.

It was no simple matter to stop the launch of any Scud or other medium-range ballistic missiles from Iraq's western desert. This territory, about the size of New Jersey, was known as the "Scud box" because missiles fired from it could reach Israel, Jordan, and Saudi Arabia. Dedicated Iraqi launch teams lived, slept, and worked together and were on call around the clock to drive the mobile Scud missiles into the desert from the city of Ar Ramadi, military bases, or other hiding spots. International inspectors and intelligence agencies estimated that Iraq still possessed anywhere from a dozen to eighty or more missiles of this range.

Behind the wheel, Sgt. First Class Jason Latteri of ODA 521 stepped on the gas of his 13,000-pound heavily loaded Humvee as the convoy raced across the rough ground. The soldiers had spent months learning how to drive these monsters at top speed in pitch darkness wearing night-vision goggles. The latest generation of nods, as the goggles were called, was much improved, but depth perception was still limited. Latteri concentrated on the moonscape unfolding before him. Would he see an obstacle too late to swerve? Would he drive into a *wadi* that had never been mapped? He gripped the wheel and pushed the vehicle close to its maximum speed of seventy miles per hour. They had more than 300 kilometers to go to reach their assigned areas in the Scud box.

The Special Forces soldiers on the teams were well aware of the magnitude of the stakes. Fewer than 300 men had been tasked with controlling the ground of an entire theater of the war. It was a seminal mission very much in the tradition of their military history, an appreciation reflected by the movie they chose from their DVD collection the night before leaving their secret base, *Day of Days,* about the Special Forces' forebears who jumped into Normandy behind enemy lines. More than one soldier went to sleep hoping the next days would prove him a worthy member of that lineage. One of them, a giant blond Alabama man named John Pace, was a newly minted chief warrant officer on trial in his new job as assistant commander of ODA 523. He had fought in Desert Storm in the 101st Airborne and, after joining 5th Group, had been mentored by the likes of Michael T. Swift, his former team sergeant, and Randy Wurst, who had shared his close-quarters shooting tips. Chris Conner had also known Pace for years, and saw in him the potential to become one of the group's standard-bearers.

This war was a defining moment not just for the men of 1st Battalion, but for all Special Forces. Their success in Afghanistan had led the conventional military to appreciate what they could do. Whereas they had been restricted to a small set of missions in the first Gulf War, General Tommy Franks, the Central Command four-star in charge of Operation Iraqi Freedom, was willing to entertain any proposal they made. The secretary of defense was also an enthusiastic supporter of special operations forces. While they had barely been allowed into the command center during the first Gulf War, now the Special Operations commander for the Middle East, Brig. Gen. Gary Harrell, sat a stone's throw from Franks in the U-shaped brick building of the main quarters at Qatar's As Saliyah base.

Franks accepted many of Harrell's proposals, with the result that all the services' special operations forces were sent to every corner of Iraq on a wide variety of missions. They went in before the conventional forces, they would fight alongside them, and they would stay behind to deal with the populous south as the main army force raced to Baghdad. And in two major theaters, the north and the west, they would be the principal or sole forces on the ground. Their day had truly arrived, and now they had to deliver.

In the western desert, the secret to success lay in preparation. Fifth Group's 1st Battalion closely studied Desert Storm to learn what it could from that experience. The Scud threat had been underestimated and the methods used to counter it inadequate, resulting in the launch of eighty-six Scuds at Israel and Saudi Arabia. Aircraft had not been able to find all the launch sites, and the Patriot air defense system had not stopped all the missiles. A handful of Scud-hunting teams had been dropped in by helicopter and moved on foot, but their range was limited and their vulnerability high. One of the British Special Air Services commando teams, the famous Bravo Two Zero, had been captured and tortured.

The key lessons that the Special Forces drew from the first Gulf War were that the Scuds could not be identified and stopped by air power alone and that the ground force had to be mobile, stealthy, and large enough to cover all the territory from which missiles might be fired. Stopping the launch of missiles would hinge on the Special Forces' ability to flood the potential launch area and dominate the key points of the territory. The new strategy developed essentially was a deterrence strategy: if they could convince the Iraqis that they owned the Scud box, then the Iraqis might not even try to launch any missiles. Three things were required for this strategy to work: the Special Forces had to be sufficiently mobile and survivable; they had to identify every key node of the Scud system; and they had to take their partnership with the air force from Afghanistan to a new level of hand-in-glove cooperation.

In the mid-1990s, 1st Battalion's Charlie Company had begun calculating what it would take to put an entire company on wheels to fight in unison on the battlefield. Chief Warrant Officer 3 Ray Brady became the point man for building this capability. What Brady did with a 2.5-ton truck had never been done before. He cut off the cab to lower its profile and installed an M240 machine gun up front and a Mk 19 automatic grenade launcher in back. He mounted racks for tires, fuel and water drums, ammunition, and food, and calculated the load variances for all kinds of conditions. Finally he added all the antennas for the various radios and SATCOMS, and camouflage nets. The result was a mobile, defensible command vehicle that could resupply and direct all the ODAs that would be running around the desert in their Humvees, hunting Scuds. The group arranged a joint exercise in 2000 at the National Training Center to test their concept. It worked brilliantly. Brady and the rest of Charlie Company kept adding refinements and new capacity. Their strange but effective creations were baptized the "war pigs."

Two hours after Major Paul Ott had assumed command of Charlie Company in July 2002, the company had gone into isolation to prepare for the Iraq war. As the wider plan developed, the group command realized that it needed a second mounted company. First Battalion's Bravo Company was the logical choice, because Alpha Company was 5th Group's crisis reaction element for emergencies in the Middle East.

Bravo's new commander, Major Gavrilis, was ordered to duplicate Charlie Company's model in just six weeks. Gavrilis was a fortuitous choice in several respects: he had just come from the command and general staff college at Fort Leavenworth, where he had studied, among other things, past desert operations, and he had been in 3rd Group, where he had gained experience in Africa's deserts. He was meticulous and fiercely competitive; one of his hobbies was racing in triathlons. He welcomed the heady assignment to lead troops on the frontlines, where every commander wants to be, but getting there would require a Herculean effort.

The transformation of Bravo Company involved much more than duplicating Brady's "war pigs." Trained to operate on foot, it did not even have Humvees of its own, which meant the unit did not regularly train on them or their .50-caliber and Mk 19 weapons, let alone the extra array of antitank and anti-air missiles that would be needed for killing any Scuds or hostile aircraft encountered.

More 2.5-ton and 5-ton trucks were sent to the welder to be shaped into fighting vehicles, and Brady shared with Bravo Company his store of accumulated knowledge about tire pressure, tire sizes, load variances, weight limits, and every square inch of the trucks' mechanics. The manufacturer could not turn out all the Humvees the company needed, so it borrowed some from fellow teams and other units. Many of the vehicles were aging and in need of extensive repairs. With no time to lose, Chief Pace, Sgt. First Class Andy Brittenham, and other operators got on their backs under the Humvees with 5th Group mechanics to change brakes, weld parts, and fix transmissions.

Bravo Company then went to the U.S. and Jordanian deserts to practice fighting maneuvers and learn the limits and quirks of the Humvees' 400 cubic inch, 190 horsepower, 6.5 liter turbocharged diesel engines. Empty, a Humvee weighs 9,800 pounds, but with extra ammunition, weapons, and food packed into every nook and cranny they top out at around 13,000 pounds. The teams also had to adopt new tactics, because as the lone ground force they would have to fight through to the finish. The company staff had to become equally nimble driving and fighting from the "war pigs."

At the end of exercises in the Jordanian desert, Bravo Company was put through a live-fire nighttime drill that tested all their newly acquired skills. Through the grainy green light of his night-vision goggles Gavrilis watched Chief Pace and his men move from Humvee-mounted weapons, to personal rifles, to setting up and firing a mortar—executing it all flawlessly in minutes. They were ready. When Gavrilis arrived at 5th Group he had recognized Pace—they had attended both Ranger school and the Q course together. Over the ensuing weeks Gavrilis came to appreciate the energy that Pace, with his bottomless well of enthusiasm, lent to the company.

First Battalion also burned the midnight oil to design a battle plan.

The men divided the western desert into sectors and assigned a team to each one, then each team researched that sector to find out what sites had been used in the past to hide, prepare, or fire the missiles. They identified every node of the missile-launching infrastructure including roads, rails, fuel dumps, and oxidizers that prepared the liquid fuel. They obtained current satellite imagery and studied every square inch of their territory. In the end, each team came up with a prioritized list of hundreds of targets to search or seize.

"We spent many Visine-laced nights on this," Andy Brittenham said. "These target sets were not handed to us; we developed them." The teams even measured bridges and culverts on the imagery to determine if they were large enough to hide missiles. They prepared target lists and did their usual terrain study to plot infiltration and escape routes and features that could be used for defending or attacking, as well as their trademark study of the local population demographics, tribal affiliations, and political and religious history. In the final dress-rehearsal briefing, Gavrilis watched Sgt. First Class Lee Linville take his turn at the map board. The quiet intelligence sergeant on Pace's team, with little fanfare and no notes, spun through a detailed review of how they would get in, array their forces, and neutralize the missile threat.

The third piece of the strategy was to marry their mobile ground force with the U.S. air force in a far closer coordination than had occurred in Afghanistan. A force of F–16 fighter jets, A–10 aircraft, and B–52 bombers would be on call in the western desert twenty-four hours a day. If the Special Forces spotted a target or got into trouble, they would call on their friends in the sky. A fleet dedicated to the western desert was vital for the quick reaction needed to prevent missile launches.

To forge this tight coordination, the Special Forces went to Nellis Air Force Base in Nevada and practiced with the pilots. The two sides learned what each could and could not see from its vantage point. The pilots did daytime and nighttime runs over the men in their Humvees, who painted targets with their laser and infrared devices so the pilots could see what they looked like. The pilots showed the soldiers what their Humvees looked like through their FLIR (forward-looking infrared radar), lantern system, and lightning pods (guns with cameras and self-lasing capability). To ensure that the air force would not mistakenly bomb the tiny clusters of Special Forces, they worked out a keypad system that would "turn on" a sector when Special Forces were inside it. That "black" sector would then become a no-go zone for aircraft unless called in to aid the teams. This innovation would, they hoped, prevent any friendly casualties and ensure maximum coverage of the territory, because the planes could concentrate on searching other squares in the grid. Pilots and ODAs then would trade information about what they found. They also worked out a common-sense recovery plan for rescuing downed pilots that was approved by the chain of command.

As the two companies of 1st Battalion raced across the desert on March 19, they were about to discover whether they could pull all three pieces of their strategy together successfully. The teams needed every hour of darkness to get to their assigned sectors.

Major Ott led Charlie Company, with its thirty-five vehicles and seven ODAs, into the southeastern half of the desert to their priority targets, which were bases and airfields clustered around the towns of Nukyab, Habbariya, and Mudyasis. ODA 534 went to Nukyab, which was deemed one of the highest-threat launch sites because it housed the base closest to the Saudi border where U.S. troops were encamped. With that special loyalty reserved for the first ODA a soldier serves with, Randy Wurst and Warren Foster wished these men well in their high-stakes mission, remembering how they had gone to war to the strains of Pat Benatar in ODA 534 twelve years ago.

Bravo Company's principal targets were the central desert town of Ar Rutba and a sprawling airbase west of it called H3. Major Gavrilis and his company staff tucked their war pigs into a *wadi* south of Ar Rutba, while the six ODAs fanned out to their first targets. ODAs 521 and 525 each cleared abandoned airfields and, in the wee hours, the latter team pulled up outside Ar Rutba. Noticing that a large radio directional finding complex for detecting and jamming enemy communications had not been bombed, the team called in its grid coordinates to the AWACS (advanced warning and control system) plane overhead, which relayed the information to F–16s standing by. Soon, precision guided munitions destroyed the complex, but left nearby residences intact.

The tremendous explosions told all 17,000 inhabitants of Ar Rutba that the war had begun. What they did not yet know was that they were being watched by a twelve-man team a few kilometers away. Farther west, ODAs 523 and 524 searched a cluster of buildings called the Southwest Storage and Mine Facility but found no missiles. After the teams cleared their first set of targets, Maj. Gavrilis ordered them to lay low and observe the Iraqi forces' reactions, locations, and movements. The Special Forces teams were going up against much larger forces, so they needed to preserve their anonymity until the most advantageous time to announce their presence.

Sergeant First Class Andy Brittenham came from hardy Scottish stock, but the weather was harsh even for him. The rushing thirty-knot wind found few obstacles in the barren land and the temperature slid below freezing as night came on. His team, ODA 525, split into two halves to surveil Ar Rutba and the two highways leading from it. ODA 525 was a scuba team, known for years as "the Sharkmen," so the men continued the theme and named their three-man vehicle crews for sharks. Brittenham's split team, Bull and Hammerhead, watched the highways, while Mako and Great White crept close to the city and dropped two men on a hilltop to observe at close range. One was the team's chief warrant officer and the other was the junior communications sergeant in his first war. Amid the barking of Bedouins' dogs they set up a hide site in a rocky outcropping and waited for dawn on March 21.

Early the next day, the hilltop duo thought it spotted an armored personnel carrier in the folds of the desert. Brittenham offered to take his split team out for a look, even though it had just returned from searching an abandoned prison. It was no surprise that he volunteered his crew despite the men having had no sleep since they began their infiltration two days before. Brittenham would see it as a point of honor to be the last man standing in most circumstances, let alone wartime. A short, muscular man with black hair and the gift of gab, he displayed the brio typical of scuba team members, who did not let their fellow Green Berets forget that they had been among the first teams into Afghanistan. The common riposte was a gibe about the utility of scuba skills in a land-locked country.

Brittenham was a passionate talker, but he was also extremely proficient technically. He had two military occupational specialties (MOS). Currently he was the team's 18F or "fox," the intelligence sergeant, a job that requires a separate operations and intelligence course. His original MOS had been 18E or communications, which he had also taught at the Special Warfare school. He understood the finer points of radio wave propagation, and when a new piece of equipment arrived he would take it apart and dream up new uses for it.

On its excursion Brittenham's crew found no armored vehicle, but on the way back it encountered some bedouins. That was inevitable, as the special operators had discovered in Desert Storm, because the desert is never empty but, rather, full of nomadic herders. Just then, the team leader called for the team's return to camp: higher headquarters had reported that an Iraqi special forces unit had been sent out to hunt for it. Brittenham and his men left the bedouin encampment, but the chief warrant officer continued to watch the tribesmen through his powerful scope from his hilltop perch a few kilometers away. He saw one of them get into a blue pickup truck and drive straight into Ar Rutba. The chief drily commented to the young communications sergeant at his side, "How long do you think it's going to be before someone rolls out of the city?"

As his vehicle crew pulled into camp, Brittenham realized he was famished. He unfastened the Velcro tabs on one side of his desert camouflage kevlar vest, slid it off, and tossed it into the back of his Humvee. He was rummaging for an MRE in the back footlocker when the chief's voice came over the intra-team MBITR radio: "Hey, you guys need to get ready. You've got five pickup trucks full of jackasses coming your way."

It had been less than thirty minutes since the hilltop surveillance team had seen the blue truck enter Ar Rutba. A large, white, late-model

Army publication, January 1992

WHAT MAKES SPECIAL FORCES SO SPECIAL?

Master Sgt. James "Killer" Kilcoyne (back row, left) standing next to General Mohammed Morgan, and Staff Sgt. Alan G. Johnson (front row, second from left) and ODA 564, in Somalia in early 1993.

Master Sgt. Michael T. Swift (left) and Chief Warrant Officer 3 James Newman, ODA 554, in Herat, Afghanistan in 2001.

(Then) Captain Warren Foster, 96th Civil Affairs Battalion, in Operation Iraqi Freedom; Special Forces veteran of Desert Storm.

Major Simon Gardner (foreground) and Major D. J. DeJarnette, deputy and company commander, 96th Civil Affairs Battalion, handing out school supplies to sheikh in Az Zubayr.

Major James Gavrilis (commander of B Company, 1st Battalion, 5th Group), accepting capitulation of Iraqi officer in Ar Rutba, western Iraq, April 2003.

Chief Warrant Officer 3 Randall Wurst, outside Nasiriya, Iraq.

ODA 523: Chief Warrant Officer 2 John Pace, 1st row, second from right; Sgt. 1st Class Lee Linville, second from left.

Master Sgt. Tom Rosenbarger (standing) holding GPS at Iraq-Iran border. (On his right is SFC Luis Rojas, of the 4th Psychological Operations Group.)

Lieutenant Colonel Bob Waltemeyer, commander of 2nd Battalion, 10th Group, on Jeep hood, consulting with Colonel Charles Cleveland, 10th Group Commander before entering Mosul.

ODA 081 and PUK pesh merga militia (Operation Viking Hammer).

Lieutenant Colonel Kenneth Tovo (3rd Battalion, 10th Group Commander) and PUK Kurdish leader Jalal Talabani in northern Iraq.

Members of ODA 081— Yellow Prong of Operation Viking Hammer (awarded Silver and Bronze Stars for battle against Ansar al-Islam in Sargat Valley). From left to right: Medical Sergeant, Team Leader, Weapons Sergeant, Team Sergeant, Weapons Sergeant.

Sergeant First Class Mark Reynolds of ODA 563 in vicinity of Tora Bora, Afghanistan.

Master Sergeant Alan Johnson of ODA 563, 5th Group, in Tora Bora.

ODA 563 at the "Alamo" in Tora Bora, Afghanistan.

Some of ODA 563 at Tora Bora, Afghanistan. In the back row middle are CW3 Randy Wurst and Master Sergeant Alan Johnson, and in the front row are, left, SFC Rich Davis and SFC Matt Nittler, right.

Lieutenant Colonel Chris Conner, commander 2nd Battalion, 5th Group.

Dodge pickup truck led four "technicals" out of the city and followed the blue truck back to the bedouin camp. A "technical"—a term adopted in Somalia—was a small pickup truck with a large-caliber weapon, typically a .50-caliber machine gun or a DShK, mounted behind the cab. The chief watched through his long-range optical scope as men in black uniforms got out of the white trucks and inspected the ground. They spotted the Humvees' tracks and got back into their trucks to follow them.

ODA 525's camp became a flurry of activity. In little more than a minute, the four Humvees, Bull, Hammerhead, Mako, and Great White—minus their two hilltop sentries—were peeling out of the *wadi*, thanks to the soldiers' habit of repacking whatever they used as soon as they were finished with it. The team leader jumped into one of the passenger seats and punched up Falcon View terrain maps on his tiny laptop computer as they bounced through the desert rubble. They turned away from their pursuers, east and then south. The team made for a fingerlike ridgeline and u-turned behind it. The men set up in a hasty ambush formation and waited, expecting to see the pursuing Iraqis at any moment. Finally the four Iraqi pickup trucks, loaded with about forty armed men, came into the team's view. When the Iraqis were within range of the Humvee's heavy machine guns, the weapons sergeant opened up. The cold temperature prevented his .50-caliber gun from switching to full automatic, so he had to recock it after the first round. But even the first shot, which hit the lead pickup truck with a flash, threw the Iraqis into a panic. One of them tossed a rocket-propelled grenade launcher into the air. Two of ODA 525's Humvees, Mako and Great White, which had been covering the rear approach to the ridge, spun around and joined the attack. The Mk 19 gunner fired a hail of grenades that enveloped another pickup in a cloud of smoke. The .50-caliber bullets tore holes in the trucks. One truck inexplicably began driving in circles, and then all four beat a hasty retreat. The Dodge quad cab, the command vehicle, had not followed into the fray but had stayed behind to call for reinforcements. As they fled, the Sharkmen raced back toward the hilltop, hoping to extricate their two teammates before whatever happened next.

Before they could get to the hill, trucks began rolling out of Ar Rutba. They headed straight for the hill's base and stopped, and men began piling out. "They're jumping into the ground and disappearing," the chief radioed to the rest of the team, which had pulled up about two kilometers south.

As he watched the developing scene, the chief realized that there was a trench line ringing the southwest side of the city and that it had been covered to make a tunnel-like structure with sand-bagged strong points. The Iraqis had been prepared for the Americans' arrival. He stopped counting after one hundred Iraqis got out of the trucks, and radioed again: "These guys are moving on us. If we don't get some air right now, they're going to be all over us in about ten minutes."

The chief did not think their hilltop site had been spotted, only that the troops and militia were logically deploying to take the high ground. More technicals lined up at the base of the hill, in what looked like preparation for an assault.

The chief and the sergeant had only constructed a partial hide site from rocks and their camouflage nets. Digging a proper hide site would have required most of a day. If the hill was overrun they would be discovered. They set out their kit, their fragmentation and smoke grenades, and extra magazines of ammunition—in preparation for a last stand.

Brittenham got on the satellite communications channel that they called the "air net" or the "Scud net." It was to be used only for sightings of missiles or similar emergencies. The battalion and the air force had worked out codes for a variety of contingencies. Brittenham radioed the code word that meant, "If we do not get air immediately, Americans are going to die."

"Say again?" the AWACS pilot asked, sounding stunned.

Brittenham repeated the code slowly, three times: "Sprint. Sprint. Sprint."

"I copy," said the pilot.

"Do you currently have any air flying CAP?" Brittenham asked, using the acronym for combat air patrol.

"That's affirmative," the pilot assured him.

Up on the hill, the young communications sergeant watched Iraqis pouring like ants out of the vehicles and into the trenches and up the slope toward them. He thought to himself: "Well, thank goodness they haven't seen us yet." He looked over at the chief, who at that moment pulled the sniper rifle up to his cheek and began deliberately squeezing off rounds. He was using a Mk12 SPR or special purpose rifle, with a Leupold scope and a suppressor that dampened the sound of the high-velocity 5.56 rounds. It was a weapon developed specifically for special operators and had the range, weight, and stealth they required. As the chief started shooting men about 800 meters below, the Iraqis realized they were in someone's crosshairs.

Brittenham would be the team's radio operator for the battle. From the number of armed men that the chief had described pouring out of the city, he could tell this was not going to be a fifteen-minute skirmish. He got back on the air net. "We are going to need every available aircraft you can give us for the foreseeable future," he said. "Roger that," the pilot responded.

The team called 521, its nearest sister team, which had been clearing sites east of Ar Rutba, and said, "Get over here at best speed."

When the "Sprint" code word first came over the radio, the 1st Battalion headquarters in a neighboring country fell silent. As Brittenham repeated the code, the place erupted into a hive of activity. Men clustered around the blue force tracking monitor, which allowed commanders to determine their teams' locations instantly. Lieutenant Col. Haas and Maj. Gavrilis did the hardest thing for any commander to do when his men are in a life-or-death situation: nothing. Asking for a situation report or attempting to micromanage events on the ground would have been worse. So they all just stood by to provide whatever help they were asked for, and prayed.

This was the first battle of Operation Iraqi Freedom, although, as with so many of the Special Forces' exploits, it would remain unheralded to the outside world. Nonetheless, it was the moment that these soldiers had trained for their entire careers. Brittenham described it as a matter of "clicking on," saying, "You just become all business."

Ar Rutba Battle, 21 March 2003

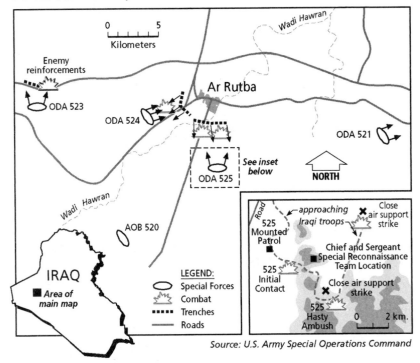

Source: U.S. Army Special Operations Command

Within minutes the AWACS had given him a sortie of F–16 fighter jets. The immediate goal was to put enough ordnance onto the ground to shock the Iraqis into halting their advance, so no effort was made to match bomb to target. The planes dropped whatever they had, laser-guided JDAMS or dumb bombs, 500-, 1,000-, or 2,000-pounders.

In the middle of this emergency, the men worked out a seamless close air support (CAS) system that became their standard procedure for the rest of the war. Andy became the "get and grab" guy who talked to the AWACs to procure the aircraft. He passed them to the "marshaller," the air force combat controller who was attached to their team, who stacked the planes in holding positions. Then he passed them one by one to the chief on the hilltop, who directed them onto the targets.

The team overheard the U.S. AWACS pilot explain the situation to his

British counterpart, who was also circling high above Ar Rutba to communicate with his Tornado jets: "We have SOF operators on the ground. They are dismounted on the ground. We need to get these guys out of there."

The air force passed the team sortie after sortie of aircraft. At one point four planes were stacked up waiting to make bombing runs. The air force flew tankers into the area to refuel the jets.

Hours passed, and still the Iraqis showed no sign of surrendering. A fighter pilot asked for permission to go below the "hard deck"—the lowest altitude the planes are permitted to fly. The deck had already been lowered to 5,000 feet for this battle. He was granted permission and roared down to a mere 200 feet off the highway as the astonished soldiers, American and Iraqi, watched in awe. He landed a 2,000-pound bomb squarely on top of a technical that was barreling toward the hill. The U.S. soldiers cheered the pilot's skill—and his bravery, because he was flying well within the range of the air defense artillery that bristled all around the city.

For four hours the battle continued, as more technicals and armored trucks came out of the city. The rain of bombs from above and the teams' heavy weapons tore up the hillside and reduced vehicles and Iraqi guns to smoking, twisted wreckage. As more aircraft showed up to join the fight, the AWACS pilot told Brittenham what was available. Andy would look at the battlefield and ask, "Can you get us this?"—and he would. The air force spared no effort or hardware in this, the war's first big fight.

At about 2 P.M., the fighting lulled and 525 decided to attempt the retrieval of its two teammates from the hill. Two F–16s and two Tornadoes covered the men's approach. ODA 521, which had fought alongside them, went too. All eight vehicles raced to the back side of the hill as Brittenham radioed to the chief that they were on their way. Some vehicles faced outward while two Humvees drove up to the hill. The chief and the communications sergeant came running down and dove into the back of the vehicles. "Glad to see you," Brittenham radioed on the MBITR as they all turned south. The chief and sergeant had alerted the team to the initial pursuit and the team had returned the favor, so it was a day of Sharkmen saving each other's skins—with the help of their airmen comrades. A B1 bomber flew over the team for about ten kilometers until it joined Maj. Gavrilis and the rest of the company command.

Andy Brittenham, his team, Gavrilis, and the entire company were jubilant over having prevailed in an extended, intense battle and, particularly, over the perfect orchestration of ground and air fighters. "It was smooth as glass!" Andy crowed. The air force was equally pleased, all the way up its chain of command to General Michael Moseley in Saudi Arabia, who had listened on the satellite communications as precision air strikes were repeatedly delivered on target within a few hundred meters of friendly forces on the ground by virtually every bomber in his fleet.

This was a quantum improvement over Afghanistan, where delays and friendly casualties had occurred through miscommunication between ground and air. Here, the chief had been able to locate the exact targets from his hilltop perch and help the pilots positively identify them before releasing their loads onto the desert floor. It was an auspicious start to the western desert campaign, the success of which would depend on such well-choreographed warfare.

Another innovation was that the command and control arrangements were located near the battle—not in Saudi Arabia as was the case during the war in Afghanistan. The control node, called a joint fires element, was located at the Special Forces command center in charge of the western desert, with a duplicate node at the battalion command center. They were staffed by both air force and Special Forces personnel, with the sole purpose of ensuring that AWACS, fighter pilots, and soldiers on the ground were in communication, understood each other, and all knew where each was located. This model was likely to be embraced by both services for future warfare. It was another step toward that seamless joint operation that all the services championed but rarely achieved.

In this case, the air force, which was the conventional force in charge of the western mission of countering the ballistic missile threat, was in effect following the Special Forces' tactical direction while maintaining its official authority. In the formal organizational flow chart, the Special

Forces reported to an air force general, but all were less concerned with which group technically was in support of which, and more intent on developing a system that won battles and kept men alive.

Successful air-ground collaboration was important to the resolution of a bigger lingering dispute as well. The air force had asserted its right to place an air force controller with every Special Forces team, and those personnel brought detailed knowledge of aircraft, the ordnance they carried, and their payloads. But the Special Forces retained their authority to issue the final instructions. The senior team members generally had far more experience than the young air force controllers, many of whom were reservists, and CAS had been part of the Special Forces' repertoire since Vietnam. They had done it in Panama, where Kevin Higgins called down a rain of fire a hundred meters from his men on Pacora Bridge. They had called in strikes across the Iraqi border in Desert Storm. And they had toppled the Taliban in Afghanistan by calling in precision bombs.

How CAS was to be conducted was an enormously important issue. The bombs were lethal, the technology was automated, and the small Special Forces teams could easily be mistaken for guerrilla fighters. Casualties most likely would be the result of any errors. If the wrong coordinates were loaded into a smart bomb, it would go to that destination regardless. The Special Forces' deaths in Afghanistan had been due to such mistakes, so they were especially motivated to make sure the system worked. The key was to use both services' knowledge in a synergistic way, and that is exactly what the "get and grab" three-part system that ODA 525 developed did. The premium for getting this right was enormous, because it was evident that a new era in small-unit warfare had begun. As Chief Pace put it:

Can you imagine what the bad guys think? They are looking for twelve guys with heavy rucksacks and radios and batteries hanging off them. Instead, they get rolled up on and smoked by twelve guys in four gun jeeps with big guns and any kind of missile you want, and air power overhead. The lethality that we were bringing to the battlefield was unmatched.

The teams remained with Gavrilis's company command overnight to replenish depleted stocks of ammunition and brace for a possible Iraqi counterattack. The night passed uneventfully, and it appeared that the severity of the day's pummeling had given the Iraqis pause. At least 100 had been killed in action, and the chief had counted more than twenty vehicles destroyed in the desert plain around his hill.

Equally fierce fighting had occurred just north of the chief's hill while ODAs 525 and 521 were under siege. ODA 524 arrived shortly after the battle began to protect the northern flank against the trucks pouring due west out of Ar Rutba. The team was fired on by four technicals on a hill and counterattacked, destroying the vehicles and overrunning the position. For the next three hours, ODA 524 held that hill and repelled three attacks by about seventy Iraqis and a half-dozen technicals. When 524 needed air support, it radioed ODA 525, which sent some of the mustered aircraft.

Farther west, ODAs 522 and 523 had also fought Iraqi reinforcements that were headed to the Ar Rutba battle. ODA 522, ambushed by Iraqis under a bridge, called in an air strike and fought through, captured documents and moved on. When ODA 523 heard the bombs falling to its east, Chief John Pace took his team to the highway and saw two trucks loaded with soldiers. He quickly prepared his men to attack; they were authorized to shoot upon identification of the Iraqis as soldiers. But Pace waited to give the order until he saw one holding a gun, then he yelled, "Engage!"

The gunners in the Humvee turrets let loose with their heavy guns and the others with their M4 carbines and the M240s. Suddenly, amid the flashes of impacting rounds and tracers, the echoing booms, and the general Dantean hell of the firefight, the intelligence sergeant, Linville, saw a station wagon packed with people, apparently civilians, driving into the firing zone from the west. He called out, "Cease fire. Cease fire. Cease fire."

The soldiers stopped shooting just as the front bumper of the car reached the rear bumper of the last truck in the convoy and stared in disbelief at the car with several children jammed into the rear. How had this man failed to hear the din or see the battle he was driving straight into with his family? As soon as the car passed from their target area, the team resumed firing.

Master Sergeant Tom Ray, Chief Pace, and Sgt. First Class James Smith then decided to approach the trucks on foot. Ray headed to the rear and Pace and Smith moved to the front of the convoy, where they saw a man lying on the ground about 100 meters away. He was armed, so Pace fired, and the body lay still. Then they saw a man crouched in the wheel well of the lead truck. They decided to hold their fire, because they could not see if he had a gun and they had lost sight of Ray. "*Arif adik!*" (Hands up!) Smith and Pace shouted in unison. The quivering man came out from the wheel well. Pace covered Smith, who went forward to search the Iraqi. Pace felt sorry for him—a few minutes ago this guy was seated in his truck, maybe getting ready to drink some tea with his buddies. The next thing he knew, he was in a hurricane of bullets and two big white guys were standing in front of him screaming. When Pace and Smith determined he was no threat, they took him to the roadside and made him lie down where the rest of the team could watch him.

They found Ray, the team sergeant, stuffing documents from the truck into a bag. Cars were streaming down the road in both directions, and the team captain radioed for them to pull out. A few minutes on the target was long enough. They brought their Iraqi prisoner back to the Humvees. His pantlegs were in tatters from the bullets and shrapnel, but only the tip of one finger had been shot off. Randy Smith, the medic, bandaged his wound and gave him water. Then they released him. Pace said: "Go home. If I see you again with a weapon, I'll kill you." The man seemed as stunned by his unexpected freedom as by the violence that had engulfed him. He set off walking west into the desert.

A few minutes later, ODA 522 radioed that two armed vehicles were coming their way. ODA 523 lined up in ambush formation and the men saw an SUV and a Toyota quad cab truck hurtling toward them at about ninety miles an hour, both packed with men and guns. The Iraqis' eyes widened when they saw the men, but it was too late. At 300 meters, Sgt. Jake Spring shot the front tire off the SUV with a .50-caliber round, causing the truck to swerve off the road and crash. Sergeant Jeff Ruble stitched down the side of the Toyota with his .50-cal and hit the gas tank, which caught fire. Men jumped out of the back of the pickup. It was all over in a few minutes: fifteen Iraqis were dead, one survived.

Later that day, John Pace reviewed his and his team's performance in its first Iraqi engagement and was satisfied with the balance of aggression, judgment, and compassion used. It was often difficult to make the right decisions in the microseconds that war allowed. Years before, Randy Wurst had counseled him not to second-guess himself because that instant of hesitation could cost him and his teammates their lives. He had also sought to shield Pace from the post-battle doubts that can gnaw at a soldier for the rest of his life. The more experienced and skilled a soldier, the more restraint he can safely exercise, but when he determines that the situation calls for firing his weapon, that decision must be made without looking back.

It is a hard thing for a man to take another man's life, even under oath in the service of one's country in indisputably hostile circumstances. He can only try to make absolutely sure that it is necessary. That was why John Pace waited to give the command to fire until he saw that the soldiers were in fact armed, and why they spared the man cowering behind the truck. This was the way that many soldiers seemed to come to grips with the dreadful task of killing: you do it if you must, and then you move on. A wise retired general recognized that it is easier said than done, especially when the killing is at close range. "That is why we give men medals, to make them feel better about the killing," he observed.

Pace's personality was an interesting mixture. He was 200 pounds of muscle who loved to fight. A natural gunslinger, he had begun his Special Forces career as a weapons sergeant and served in the crisis-response Alpha Company, which spent most of its time on "door-kicking" missions. Pace reveled in the commando work, the comic-book stuff of boys' dreams, and marveled that he actually got paid to learn advanced shooting, demolitions, and special tactics at their SFARTEC school. But he was also a natural politician who loved people and loved to talk, and this tempered his aggressive side. He had been groomed by Michael T.

Swift, who was a demanding team sergeant, a model of exacting prudence and quiet authority, but one who also inspired people to go the extra mile.

Pace kept reaching for more training, which seasoned him. He took the ASOT course and became an intelligence sergeant and, after another promotion, became a team sergeant. When told that he would only have eighteen months as a team sergeant before being relegated to staff jobs, he protested: "I'm not done yet. I've got plenty left!" Pace chose to become a chief warrant officer, but the lengthy course meant that he missed Afghanistan, so wild horses could not have kept him out of Iraqi Freedom. Pace had matured without losing his youthful enthusiasm. At age thirty-six, he might still appreciate pure shooting prowess, but he was just as proud of his team's restraint and compassion.

Major Gavrilis reminded the company that it still had hundreds of sites left to search and miles of roads to shut down. Gavrilis's objective was not Ar Rutba, not yet. He had no intention of getting bogged down in an urban battle when his main mission was to prevent missile launches. His plan was to systematically shut down the road networks, airfields, the ammunition dumps and secure the desert around the city and the H3 airbase, to convince the Iraqis that any attempt to send out a missile team would result in its capture. Then he would tighten the noose on H3 and the city, and force the armed combatants to leave.

H3 was the primary military installation in the western desert, which Pace's team, ODA 523, and ODAs 522 and 581 were assigned to surveil. They captured an Iraqi soldier who told them that the base had once held 500 troops but that only 100 remained there. The sprawling base was vast, with a triangular airfield, barracks, bunkers, and several satellite airfields. The teams knew that their command was eager to neutralize any threat from the base, so they radioed Lt. Col. Haas for permission to move onto the base and clear it. He granted permission, then decided to send two of the teams to check out another threat instead. It would turn out to be a serendipitous change of orders that almost certainly saved the men's lives.

Instead of assaulting the base, Pace's team set up a reconnaissance position six kilometers southeast of H3, behind three sandbagged observation posts that were the only hiding spots in the open landscape. With the additional resources that the Afghanistan war had brought its way, 5th Group had invested in powerful long-range optics as well as more laser target designators, two items that had been in great demand there. As the team observed H3, the men discovered that it was, in fact, crawling with soldiers—about 1,000 of them—and also was heavily defended. The team identified an array of well-protected antiaircraft guns: ZPUs, ZSUs, and 57-mm cannons. That night, March 23, the Iraqis fired these air defenses in a lengthy display of saber-rattling, but whenever the coalition aircraft roared overhead they fell silent.

The next day, March 24, Lt. Col. Haas granted permission for calling in air strikes on the base. Sergeants Linville and Clayton identified and plotted the targets. The combat controller lined up the aircraft and, after the target data was checked by the supervising senior operator, the Special Forces called in the strikes. The method used for calling in close air support varied depending on the target and the equipment available. If the target was physically isolated or prominent, the operator could often give verbal directions and geographic reference points to the pilot: this was known as "talking the pilot onto the target." Alternatively, laser or infrared signal devices might be used, especially to distinguish a specific target in a cluster of structures or at night. The best one was the SOFLAM laser target designator, which could send the target's coordinates directly to the plane or to the bomb itself if it was a laser-guided munition. The IZLID infrared pointing device, which resembled a flashlight, was more portable, but its infrared beam could be seen by anyone wearing older generation night-vision goggles, which many Iraqi units had. By contrast the SOFLAM beam could not be seen by those older nods. The team did not take any chances, because if the Iraqis could see the beam it would point directly back to them. Because they were well within range of the Iraqi antiaircraft guns, the Iraqis would only have to lower the barrels to quickly finish off the team.

The team directed planes to drop bombs onto the antiaircraft batteries, the command post, and guard formations. When the Iraqis moved to a different building on the base, the team called in more bombs. After twenty-four hours of this lethal hide-and-seek, the Iraqis started digging holes in the ground to sleep in, away from the buildings. Then a serious sandstorm kicked up, which greatly reduced the team's ability to call in targets to the pilots. Team sergeant Ray stayed glued to the scope and caught a glimpse of frenetic activity on the base. He shouted: "There's a convoy lining up! It looks like they're leaving the base."

As the storm ebbed to a brief halt, the team counted ten, twenty, then dozens of vehicles lining up. The Iraqis had marshalled anything on wheels: civilian buses, military trucks, motorcycles, flatbed trailers with antiaircraft guns—they were trying to rescue them from the attack. The team called on every radio and satellite frequency they had to spread the news. "We've got bad guys trying to pull out of here," the 525 captain said. "Looks like everyone's making a run for it."

The convoy, by one count fifty-four vehicles long, with perhaps another thirty in a second string, drove out of H3 and barreled east on Expressway 1, the six-lane divided highway that ran from Jordan to Baghdad. The task of stopping the convoy fell to ODA 521, which had been searching another suspected missile site outside Ar Rutba. Sergeant First Class Latteri picked up the call and collected the team to reboard the Humvees. It was about 5 P.M. and what little light there was would soon be gone. The team reached Expressway 1 and parked on high ground on its northwest side, where they could see the eastbound traffic.

Within ten minutes, Latteri spotted the lead truck in the convoy through his binoculars. An antiaircraft ZPU artillery piece was mounted on its back. On Latteri's signal 521's gunner began firing the .50-caliber machine gun at the truck's engine block and stopped it in its tracks. Someone in the Humvee beside them took aim at the next truck in the convoy with one of the Javelin antitank missiles. The teams had practiced with non-explosive training models, but this was the first time they had actually fired a Javelin, which had a greater range, better aim, and more power than the AT–4. With a boom, the missile left its firing tube. It dipped down toward the earth in front of Latteri's Humvee until the motor kicked on with a whistling sound. The missile then picked up speed and hurtled into the truck it was aimed at. Civilian cars had stopped with the first shots, and onlookers watched as the missile hit the truck and exploded. At that moment, Andy Brittenham and ODA 525 pulled up on the opposite side of the highway and saw the smoking truck rolling, driverless, down the freeway. The entire convoy halted just as aircraft began to arrive. Hearing the jets overhead, many Iraqi soldiers panicked and poured out of the buses and trucks, knowing that their vehicles would be the first thing bombed. One truck, however, leveled its antiaircraft guns at ODA 521. A pilot saw it through his forward-looking infrared radar and warned the team to pull back. The pilots were soon stymied by the worsening sandstorm, but the convoy never made it farther east, and most of the vehicles and fighters scattered into the countryside.

Bravo Company gathered overnight to weather the storm and repel any Iraqis that might regroup. Icy rain blew sideways and mixed with the sand flying through the air. The men put on every piece of clothing they had and hunkered down. The next day, March 27, with the storm still raging, they began to search the giant H3 airbase. They captured some soldiers and a vast quantity of weaponry. They found a Roland—a French-made antiaircraft system that had painted the planes with its radar two nights before—and disabled it with a few well-placed charges. They found fifty multi-barreled ZPU and ZSU artillery and about thirty single-barreled 57-mm cannons, plus huge stocks of SA–7 portable antiaircraft missiles, AK–47s, machine guns, and more ammunition than they had ever seen in one place. H3 had more bunkers than Fort Campbell, packed with rounds for rifles, mortars, RPGs, anti-air, antitank, land mines, and C–4 and other explosives, with hundreds of pallets more lying out in the open.

Major Gavrilis's company staff had been working around the clock. By night the soldiers received supply drops or ferried out prisoners that the teams had passed to them. By day they resupplied teams who came in for fuel, food, mechanical repairs, or just to have someone to stand guard while they got a few hours' sleep. In addition to his ten Special Forces soldiers, Gavrilis had a three-man chemical reconnaissance detachment and a four-man SOT-A signals intelligence unit, a mechanic, and an air force tactical air control personnel or TACP, who is the most highly qualified air force ground personnel trained to do everything from the terminal guidance for bombs to opening and running airports.

The supply drops either were parachuted from planes or brought in by Chinooks in the dark. The massive bundles weighing anywhere from 500 to 2,000 pounds were dropped from just a few hundred feet above ground, giving the chutes barely time to open before the load crashed into the ground. While an ODA secured the perimeter, the company would unpack the bundles and load the supplies onto the war pigs, a task that would take all night. The fifty-five-gallon barrels of fuel and water were the most vital supplies needed to keep the mission running and the most unwieldy cargo of all. In their final months at Fort Campbell, Chief Ray Brady, the genius of the war pigs, had figured out how to handle them. He had ordered a commercial off-the-shelf crane and had mounted it on a truck. Together with the winch they installed on the rear, they could hoist a half-dozen or so barrels onto each truck and pump the contents into storage cans or directly into the vehicles.

The labor was back breaking and the sandstorm seemed endless. There was no escape from that wind: men huddled wherever they could to study their maps. It was impossible even to make coffee. The biting cold of the desert sank into their bones. By the end of the ninth day the men were miserable and utterly exhausted; one soldier fell asleep using a rock as his pillow.

Gavrilis stretched out on the rocks in his sleeping bag and covered himself with his poncho for a nap. He awoke to the sensation of small rocks pelting him—it was hail. He started laughing at this latest escalation in weather war. What else could possibly come? He folded his arms over his face, under his poncho, and went back to sleep. An hour or so later, amid the rain and hail and swirling sand, a resupply helo landed with a meal of hot steaks. It was 3 A.M. The men on duty were torn between letting their tired comrades sleep and giving them their first treat since the war began. They roused the men, who ate the steaks with numb hands.

Seizure of H-3 Airfield, 27-28 March 2003

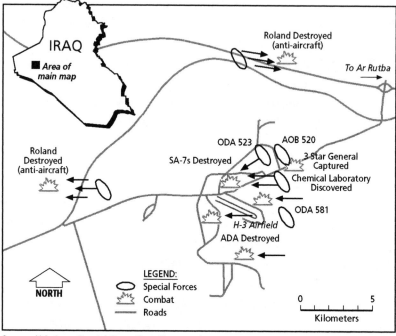

Source: U.S. Army Special Operations Command

This trial of discomfort and endurance reminded Gavrilis of the miseries of the Q course. He had learned there that exhaustion was just another state of being, like winter was one of the four seasons. It also had given him a new perspective on the simple pleasures like food. As he ate his steak in the howling wind, Gavrilis remembered how he had once dropped his pound cake into the mud during a long trek in the North Carolina wilds. He had picked it up and eaten it anyway—with pleasure. During survival school at Bragg, he and his little band of survivors had lost weight and foraged for days. Then one sunny afternoon, after a heavy rain, they had come upon a blueberry patch, with its fat blue fruit glistening in the clearing. He had eaten a half a canteen cup of berries and it had seemed to him a banquet.

The next day, March 28, they caught the Iraqi three-star general who had been in charge of the H3 base—the first general to be captured in the war. Pace's team and ODA 581 had set up a checkpoint outside the base and caught him trying to sneak away in the backseat of a taxi, dressed in civilian clothes. Another Iraqi identified him. It was a great morale boost for the men. Later, ODA 523 discovered samples of biological and chemical weapon agents in a lab on H3: they were not weapons-grade but diluted materials used for training purposes to familiarize soldiers with mustard gas and nerve agents. Although they were not the much-sought-after weapons of mass destruction, they indicated that the Iraqi soldiers at H3 had been trained for a battlefield in which such weapons would be used.

It was becoming clear that 1st Battalion's strategy had deterred Iraq from attempting missile launches. The soldiers still had many places left to search for Scuds, although it was quite possible that Iraq might have had fewer missiles left than supposed, and may have withdrawn those based in the desert as the war loomed. The final accounting would have to await postwar intelligence assessments, but for the moment what mattered was that not one missile had been launched from the Scud box. 1st Battalion had accomplished its primary mission and was also well on its way, with the help of the National Guard airmen overhead, to controlling the entire western theater.

In early April, Bravo Company turned to Ar Rutba, population 17,000, the one major outpost in the area still in regime hands. After the March 21 battle outside Ar Rutba, many of the governing Ba'ath Party officials and black-uniformed Fedayeen militia had fled the city, but surveillance indicated that at least 800 Fedayeen were still in charge.

The campaign for Ar Rutba would be very different from that against H3. Bravo Company used a more classic Special Forces approach of working with the population and a variety of other tools. The soldiers talked to Iraqis as they came out of Ar Rutba, emphasizing that only the regime was a target, not the population. They also sent the psyop team close to the city to broadcast the same message from the speakers mounted on their Humvee. A cache of food that they had discovered on the H3 airbase was delivered to the city. Gradually they cross-checked information they gathered and won over some helpers. The brother of an Iraqi who had been killed by the Iraqi state security organization volunteered to go into Ar Rutba to find out where the Ba'ath leaders were, where the arms were stored, and which buildings were being used for military purposes.

The Special Forces also spent a lot of time in the Bedouin camps drinking tea and eating pita bread cooked over an open fire. They gained some allies and information there too. This was what the Green Beret life was about, at bottom. If a man did not find Arab culture fascinating in some respects, he was not going to be very happy in 5th Group. Those who had followed Andy Brittenham's advice and read T.E. Lawrence's *Seven Pillars of Wisdom* had gained some knowledge and appreciation of tribal life. These "bedous" as they called them had lived here for centuries, much as their ancestors had, and to many of them it really didn't matter who was in charge of the central government.

The Iraqis used unconventional tactics of their own. From the first days of the war the Iraqi military had changed to civilian clothing. Since the battle outside Ar Rutba, every vehicle on the road flew a white flag, even if it carried fighters who would open fire on them. The Iraqi Fedayeen also used the Bedouins and civilians to gather information on the U.S. soldiers, and threatened them. The Special Forces found that one of the biggest hurdles they had to overcome was the Iraqis' fear of them. The Iraqis had been told that they would be summarily shot and killed. They believed that the Special Forces wanted the names of the civilian administrators who ran the waterworks and power plant in order to assassinate them, even though the soldiers were just compiling a dossier of those whose help would be vital to restart city services.

Bravo Company slowly squeezed the city. As Fedayeen came out to fight or escape, the ODAs skirmished with them or detained those who surrendered. They called in air strikes on the 57-mm cannons defending the city's perimeter, and set up observation posts to positively identify the buildings that the residents said were being used by the Fedayeen and remaining militia who controlled Ar Rutba. Each team had been issued three Javelins, which they used on targets like the Ba'ath Party provisional headquarters. Their selective approach required exacting marksmanship. One sergeant was so adept with a Mk 19 grenade launcher, which is normally used to cover a wide area, that he could drop a grenade round through a window a kilometer away. Other gunners could hit targets a kilometer and a half away with their .50-caliber machine guns—at night using nods with no illumination. The precision, effectiveness, and amount of the Americans' firepower led many Iraqis to believe there was a brigade or more of soldiers laying siege to their city.

On April 8, Maj. Gavrilis decided they were ready for the finale of their campaign. He arrayed the nine teams and assorted units attached to his company around Ar Rutba to block the major roads, and commenced a day of selective bombing on the remaining targets being used for military purposes. They exempted the hospital, mosque, and schools even though they were also being used by the militia. The hospital was inadvertently damaged, however, when an ammunition storage point next door was struck and exploded. Apache helicopter gunships showed up to provide some of the precision fire. A few hours into the bombing, a delegation came out from the city and pleaded with Major Gavrilis to stop. He agreed.

"We will do this as a goodwill gesture," he told them. He repeated the message they had been delivering for the past week: "Our fight is with the regime and not the population."

Bravo Company pulled back to the fire station on the city's outskirts that it had occupied as a temporary base. That night the soldiers discussed the situation and offered opinions. Finally Gavrilis decided it was time to enter the city. The communications sergeant called the air net and asked their friends in the sky to provide the company with the most intimidating escort they could muster to accompany Bravo's entry into the city the next morning.

At 6 A.M., they entered the city with a B–52 bomber and F–16 fighter jets roaring overhead. Then A–10 fighter planes came in low, dropped flares, then circled continuously for the rest of the morning. With such an overwhelming display of force, not one shot had to be fired. Pairs of Humvees drove to each of the major regime buildings, including the

Ba'ath Party headquarters and the intelligence service and others where they had seen shooting or military activity. Some Iraqis cautiously approached the soldiers, mostly welcoming, although clumps of men stood glowering at them from a distance. A few residents came forward to tell the Americans where arms caches were hidden in the city.

Gavrilis took two ODAs to the police station in the center of the city. It was a British fort built in 1927, with large steel doors that had to be blown open with explosives. After searching it, Gavrilis set up his command post there. Through an interpreter, Gavrilis broadcast a message on the psyop team's loudspeaker, calling for all of Ar Rutba's tribal leaders and civilian administrators to report in one hour. Once they had gathered in the police chief's office, Gavrilis asked each man to identify himself and his position. Then he explained his intentions: "We want you to choose an interim mayor. Civilian administrators, we want you to come back to work, and we will help you get the power and water and services going. The first order of business is to collect all the weapons. We will be in charge of security."

With that short speech, the campaign for the western desert entered a new phase. Gavrilis did not need to ask what to do next: he knew that as soon as major combat ended, they had to provide security and governance. The Americans wanted to prepare Iraqis to take charge of their affairs as quickly as possible. The Special Forces were not numerous enough to do the job, and turning over control to competent Iraqis would speed the transition—the faster this occurred, the less opportunity for anarchy and resentment to set in. It was not until the end of that busy day that Gavrilis heard the news from the rest of Iraq. U.S. troops had entered Baghdad the same day, April 9. And Ar Rutba already had a new mayor. Gavrilis felt pretty good about that.

In a few short days, Gavrilis had erected an entire interim governing structure. He quizzed the interim mayor closely to ensure that he was a respected figure from a prominent tribe. The Iraqi was a lawyer who had served as mayor years before until he had a falling out with the regime. The police chief had disappeared, so Gavrilis named a police lieutenant as the interim chief. The ODAs began to put the infrastructure and security force back together. Within a few days the teams had restored power to 60 percent of Ar Rutba using some generators they found outside the city. They discovered a water main that had been broken by bedouins seeking water for their herd and started to repair it. They reopened the market by letting the merchants use their satellite phones to place orders for fresh vegetables and food from Jordan. They began joint patrols with the police force, which they had brought back to work, and started a neighborhood watch network. Ba'athist officials and mid-level officers could join the interim government if they forswore their party affiliation and signed a capitulation document. An Iraqi brigadier general from the border guard came in to help.

The progress was remarkably smooth. There were some protests and demonstrations against the U.S. occupation, but Gavrilis viewed it as a healthy sign of people exercising their newfound liberty. Some civilian officials, like the fire chief, had been fearful that they would be taken away to prison. But, on the whole, the city seemed grateful for the rapid return to normalcy that Gavrilis was pushing. The Americans reopened the bank and allowed city officials to be paid from government accounts. Some of the tribal elders wanted to hold definitive elections right away, but Gavrilis said they could not get ahead of the national process. They did elect an interim city council and held an assembly in the largest mosque, which reconfirmed the mayor in his interim post.

At age thirty-six, Gavrilis was overseeing a city's administration, and running his company's resupply operations as well as the ODA's ongoing security missions around the western desert. He was a determined, detail-oriented individual who managed all these operations with the same laserlike focus with which he had conducted the company's preparation and combat. The Pittsburgh native had earned a master's degree in international studies with a near-perfect GPA and had submitted his application for the Special Forces selection course the first day he was eligible in 1993. His brother, two years older, was already in the Special Forces and a role model. Jim Gavrilis just seemed to thrive on continual competition and excelled at virtually everything he did. As a young soldier, he had placed second in his division's Best Ranger Competition, made the commandant's list at the Officers Advanced Course, was an honor grad in the Q course, and then tested out of language school early so he could get to the excruciatingly difficult pre-scuba and scuba course, which he also finished with honors. This was a man who could not find enough challenges.

One problem in particular continued to plague the western desert. Scores of foreign jihadists were streaming in from Syria. In a typical incident, ODAs 521 and 525 stopped two buses outside Ar Rutba, both full of young men of military age. A couple of the men reacted very belligerently when the Special Forces ordered them off the bus to search it. Andy Brittenham guessed, from their tone of moral authority and the deference of the others, that these were religious leaders or mullahs. When he searched the back of the bus he found large and suspiciously lumpy pillows, which he cut open to find stuffed with uniforms, pistols, and ammunition. The soldiers ordered the foreigners back on the bus and announced in Arabic that they would be escorted back to the border, minus their weapons. If they tried to return to Iraq, they were told, coalition aircraft would bomb their buses.

There were also reports that Saddam Hussein himself was in the desert, trying to slip across to Syria. The Iraqi border guard had dissolved and the border crossings were entirely unmanned. Some ODAs were sent there to restore order. Bravo Company sent the cooperative brigadier general to try to restore some of the collapsed system. Brittenham and ODA 525 went to the main crossing into Jordan. Charlie Company also had teams to spare as the southeastern sector was less populous and less well traveled. ODA 531—Steve Rainey's old team from Desert Storm and the battle of Khafji—was sent to Ashakat on the border with Syria. Sheep smugglers shot at the team and, in the ensuing firefight, some bedouins were wounded. The team's medics patched them up and tried to win them over as sentries against the jihadis pouring into the country.

At the end of April, Jim Gavrilis was called back to the battalion headquarters to oversee the extraction of the two companies and their replacement, in early May, with a conventional unit, the 3rd Armored

Cavalry Regiment. On the noisy night flight aboard the Chinook helicopter, he allowed himself a moment of bursting pride for what he and his men had achieved. They had not found any Scuds, but none had been fired, and that meant mission accomplished. They had set a new standard for company-size mounted operations, thus adding one more powerful variation to the many uses of Special Forces. His company had worked like demons every day since the previous July. They had conducted some of the most effective and well coordinated close air support assaults in memory. The bombs would fall and minutes later the ODAs would be charging across their targets. They put Ar Rutba back on its feet in days. This was a story they would all tell their grandchildren one day.

CHAPTER 10

SOUTHERN IRAQ
Sneak and Peek

All warfare is based on deception.

—SUN TZU

WHILE 1ST Battalion commander Lt. Col. Chris Haas was keeping tabs on his Special Forces teams in the western desert, Chris Conner's 2nd Battalion ODAs were scattering throughout southern Iraq. Each morning before dawn, Conner awoke in his tan canvas tent and walked a few hundred feet, crunching the fist-sized gravel underfoot, to Hangar 17 of Kuwait's Ali al Salem base. The warren of offices ringing the hangar's open bay contained his forward operating base and was the hub for all special operations being conducted out of Kuwait.

Conner had a dizzying array of action to monitor: two companies of teams, including a handful that went in early on secret missions, from Basra in the south to Karbala, one hundred miles outside of Baghdad. Charlie Company, led by Jonathan Burns, with Randy Wurst and Jim Kilcoyne as its senior NCO, was moving straight up the highway from Kuwait to Basra, Iraq's second-largest city. The job was to provide intelligence and targeting data to British forces, the principal U.S. partner in the war and the group that would control the sector after the U.S. Marines had passed through. Bravo Company was bound for south-central Iraq, where it would command and control ODAs from the outskirts of Najaf. Together these two companies and the teams assigned to them would carry out the Special Forces' missions in the most populated part of Iraq, the famed cradle of civilization between the Euphrates and the Tigris. Alpha Company's commander was attached to the army's V Corps, to keep the main conventional force apprised of where the SF teams were and what they could do for it.

The men of 2nd Battalion would have the closest contact with the conventional ground forces, so they would have daily opportunities to attempt to reduce the friction that existed between the two communities. Most of the discord was the product of perception rather than reality, but because the SF activities were conducted in secrecy, apart from the regular army, there had been little opportunity to correct such perceptions.

A complicated relationship, it was marked at the lower levels by envy of the elite troops and at higher levels by disdain or ignorance of what SF could offer in a "heavy-metal" tank-on-tank war. Some took the Special Forces' focus on "unconventional" warfare to mean that they were out of control, or that "conventional" was pejorative rather than merely different. This was aggravated by small issues like the Special Forces' penchant for wearing baseball caps—a seemingly innocuous matter to civilians, but one which violated the army's regulation dress code and sent conventional commanders around the bend. Conner told his men to appear in standard uniform whenever they were around "the big army," and Haas went farther, and confiscated his men's caps at the border.

The overall war plan called for the U.S. Marines and the U.S. Army to sprint through southern Iraq, avoid the major population centers, and reach Baghdad as quickly as possible. The theory was that the rapid capture of the capital might prompt the rest of the country to cede without a fight. There was no way to predict how much of Saddam Hussein's army would stand and fight, but most of his best Republican and Special

Republican Guard units were positioned around or in Baghdad. War planners did not expect a cakewalk, even in southern Iraq, where the population of largely Shi'ite Muslims had been brutally repressed for more than a decade and would presumably not rush to the regime's defense. A crushing blow would be dealt to the first units the troops encountered, coupled with a massive "shock and awe" air campaign, in a demonstration of power that might break the others' will to fight. The battlefield of southern Iraq, with its cities and complex politics, was tailor-made for Special Forces. They would help speed the conventional forces' passage through the battlefield and deal with the population until follow-on forces arrived. As in western and northern Iraq, they would be holding down the fort in large areas while the conventional effort was bent on Baghdad.

Basra was not only the second-largest city but also was the site of the country's largest oilfields and a vast gas-oil separation and pumping infrastructure. A major concern of U.S. war planners was that Saddam would set the oil wells on fire as he had in Desert Storm in 1991. The special operations command proposed an ambitious scheme to secure the sprawling Rumaila oilfields, the pumping stations, and oil terminals of southern Iraq in the war's opening hours. One of Conner's teams— ODA 554—was selected for a part in it.

Michael T. Swift and the rest of Special Forces ODA 554 were tucked in among the vast ranks and snorting machinery of U.S. Marines at the Kuwait-Iraq border in the pre-dawn darkness of March 21, 2003, the day that the ground war started. The team was easily distinguishable from the Marine tanks and armored personnel carriers: its twelve men rode in two Humvees and two pickup trucks, which would help them blend into civilian traffic once they headed off on their own. Their uniforms also set them apart: they wore the army's standard desert camouflage pattern while the Marines wore digitized camouflage that was the latest in concealment clothing. At seven crossing points, bulldozers plowed dirt into the giant tank ditches—four meters deep and four meters wide, topped by electrified wire—that separated Kuwait and Iraq. At sunup on March 21, the troops crossed over, and Operation Iraqi Freedom's ground war began.

A few hours before, the Navy SEALs had seized the two oil terminals on the Al Faw peninsula, Iraq's tiny finger of waterfront territory. The SEALs then began securing the waterways just west of Al Faw around the Umm Qasr port, which held the main pumping station of the terminus. They searched every vessel and seized mine-laying ships in round-the-clock operations. Just west of Umm Qasr, ODA 554 and the Marines made straight for Safwan Hill, the high ground of southern Iraq. From there the Marines were to sweep down into the Rumaila oilfields, assault through them, and then be followed by the British forces that would secure the fields, the pumping facilities, and two gas oil-separation plants.

First, however, ODA 554 had to sprint ahead to carry out its part of the plan. The team was to drive to the outskirts of Basra to pick up four Iraqi oil technicians who had been recruited to help secure the oil infrastructure. Insiders were needed to guide the troops into the oil complexes and to tell them which valves had to be turned off to prevent or minimize spills, fires, and sabotage. At Safwan Hill ODA 554 split into two parts, and one part boxed around the west side of the hill and then drove east to the highway to Basra.

This half of the ODA 554 team was composed of Chief Warrant Officer 2 Jimmy Newman, Master Sergeant Michael T. Swift, and four other NCOs: a gunner, an engineer, a communicator, and a medic. Conner had selected them for the mission because the combination of Newman and Swift was the best chief–team sergeant duo that he had ever seen. Jimmy was a gifted, charismatic soldier who led by instinct, while Michael T.'s bent was more rational and calculating. Their combined talents frequently allowed them to outguess and outmaneuver the rest. Michael T. loved to play "dumb as a fox," as Conner put, when in fact he was the sharpest tack in the box. Conner had known the wry Tennessee native since Desert Storm, and since then Swift had been all over the Middle East, Central Asia, and North Africa. In fifteen years of wearing the green beret he had raised a new generation of sergeants, including John Pace, and had served on scuba, HALO, and mountain teams.

Swift had joined ODA 554 in January 2000 at the same time as Chief Warrant Officer 2 Jimmy Newman, who served as team leader until a captain filled the slot. The two men became fast friends. Jimmy, a Cajun from Louisiana, did the talking, and Michael T. made it happen. When Jimmy was hell bent on a wild scheme, Conner knew that Michael T. would rein him in. Few could resist the twinkle in Jimmy's eye, which helped him to transcend cultural and language barriers almost effortlessly and to enlist friends, spies, and allies with a few jokes. "Jimmy's calling in life is to make friends," Michael T. often said. Like his other close friend and fellow charmer, Alan Johnson, Jimmy was a schmoozer of epic stature.

Jimmy and Alan had gone through the Q course together thirteen years earlier and the two extroverts had hit it off. On one hot day during Robin Sage, they stripped down for a swim, and then dressed up in loin-cloths and sprang out of the bushes when their "guerrilla" partners came along. The scare gave them a psychological advantage over their allies. Thereafter, the two would frequently resort to the unexpected—a tactic at the heart of unconventional war. One time, for example, Michael T. and Jimmy had faced several hundred hostile militiamen in Herat, Afghanistan—and won them over with the help of a toy bear that danced to the song "Wild Thing," a gift sent by Jimmy's wife.

It took ODA 554 three hours to drive around Safwan, longer than Swift had estimated. The team's vehicles kicked up tremendous clouds of dirt that obscured the men's vision and coated them in fine brown silt. When ODA 554 reached its pre-arranged meeting place, the four Iraqi technicians were waiting. So far, so good. As they climbed into the back of the Humvees, Michael T. noticed that none of them carried an overnight bag or knapsack. Someone had neglected to tell them that this was more than a one-day job, but there was no time to send them back home. The team backtracked south on the main highway toward the advancing Marines and British forces. The Iraqi technicians were visibly scared; the war was now in full swing all around them. Explosions rang out as Marine tanks and artillery blasted any enemy formations spotted. Many Iraqi tanks had already been abandoned by fleeing soldiers.

Michael T. knew the risks of driving straight toward friendly forces, but also knew that the team's movement was being monitored by Conner and other commanders who had access to the Blue Force Tracker. The boxes mounted in their Humvees sent out signals which showed up on the commanders' computers, which were equipped with special software, as square blue dots. Michael T.'s original specialty had been communications, so he understood the technology better than most, but still he did not place too much confidence in the "Ouija board," as he called it. It was a seductive gizmo that could lure some officers in the rear to micromanage their troops in the field. Swift knew that Conner would never do that because he, too, appreciated the limits of technology. A moving dot presumably meant that a team was still alive, although it would look exactly the same on screen even if enemy forces had killed the men and commandeered their vehicle. At any rate, it did not enable Swift or the Marine tanks barreling north to see each other.

The team reached the highway overpass where it was to meet a Marine lieutenant and hand over the Iraqi technicians. They parked under the overpass and waited. Ten minutes later, a burst of gunfire erupted several hundred meters to their right—they were under attack. They could hear the sounds of several AK-47s and at least one rocket-propelled grenade launcher firing, but, so far, the shooters had missed their marks. The team's gunner immediately engaged with the .50-caliber, the medic fired the M240, and the other two waited holding their M4 carbines. Michael T. and Jimmy wanted a better look at their attackers, so they climbed up the sloping embankment to the top of the overpass, staying low so they would not silhouette themselves against the sky.

"I can't believe they're firing at us," Swift said to Newman as they climbed the hill. He was amazed that they were under attack not by a heavy Iraqi army unit but by a few lightly armed militiamen. It was a taste of things to come. Michael T. wrinkled his leprechaun's face, pursing a bow-shaped mouth that was too small for its teeth. He was genuinely puzzled why a small band was foolish enough to stand and fight when an entire Marine division was bearing down on it and the regular Iraqi troops were fleeing.

"Can you believe they are shooting at us? What are they thinking?" Michael T. said, as they reached top of the overpass. "We can talk about it later, Mike," Jimmy said. True to form, he was far less interested in analyzing why they were being shot at than in how they were going to shoot back.

The two men hunched down and surveyed the scene. The Iraqis were only about 100 meters away, just off the highway. So far, they were not attempting to flank the team to come up behind them. The team's guns were more than a match for their assailants, but Swift was concerned that the .50-caliber bullets, with their much longer range, would hit the civilians, including children, who were milling around a cluster of buildings about 600 meters behind the shooters. Michael T. decided to call off the .50-caliber gunner and have the men use only the rifles and the M240. He climbed down to tell them, while Jimmy stayed on the overpass to see where their shots were landing.

All the teams had been issued the new multiband intrateam radio (MBITR) but, in a classic example of Murphy's law—which Michael T. firmly believed in—the radios were not working at the moment. The MBITR was a great asset, but they had already found out that aboard the vehicles it was very easy to get out of range. Swift's teams always rehearsed their maneuvers assuming that they would have no ability to communicate, and learned how to react jointly as a situation developed. They had to be able to do it the old-fashioned way. So, Swift went down in person only to find that the gunner had already switched to his M4 rifle.

The sergeants knew their business, but Jimmy was always ready to teach them new tricks, as he knew all the individual specialties. While he loved mentoring, Jimmy's primary role on the team was planning for operations beyond forty-eight hours. Michael T. coordinated current operations and, with the intelligence sergeant, handled intelligence preparation of the battlefield. Jimmy and Michael T. had a good-cop/bad-cop routine based on the time-tested parental model. The sergeants could come and complain to Jimmy, the good cop, while Michael T. cracked the whip.

The two men never quarreled—almost never. Right before the war, Michael T. became upset when Jimmy left on a special assignment. Even though Jimmy was laying the groundwork for the team's mission, it took him away from the team's own preparations. Soon after Newman left, Swift emailed to apologize for getting mad. When Newman reappeared in Kuwait, 554 was reunited again. The men were like brothers, and the team, ever like a family, drew especially close in wartime. The delicate assignments they had drawn simply intensified the dynamics.

The Fedayeen militia, dressed in black uniforms that resembled pajamas, traded fire with the team for nearly an hour and a half. The Iraqis did not advance, but they also did not retreat—even after ODA 554 shot and killed three or four of them. The team was only interested in holding the Iraqis off, not chasing them down. The team had to wait for the Marine who was due to pick up the technicians. He finally arrived, but spoke no Arabic; nonetheless Swift handed over the Iraqis and wished them luck.

The men had to hurry to rejoin the other half of 554 for their next assignment. They were going undercover, with a friendly Iraqi sheikh, to help the British target enemy forces around Basra. As the team headed north, Swift tried several times to make radio contact with Charlie Company, but he got no answer.

Charlie Company was busy dodging artillery and tank fire outside Basra. During mission planning, commander Jonathan Burns had chosen a compound near Basra to use as a safe house. There the company would relay all the teams' communications back to Kuwait and perform the other control and resupply functions. As it approached the site, the company found the British First Armoured Division engaged in a fierce battle with Iraqi forces, and U.S. Marine Super Cobras flying overhead. British soldiers were wounded when a small Tiger tank and a Land

Rover were hit by Iraqis. The Charlie Company convoy watched as some Iraqis ran into their would-be safe house. A British Challenger tank swiveled its main gun around and fired, demolishing the building. "I guess we'd better go find a new hooch," Randy said over the MBITR.

Randy Wurst was delighted to be in the gunner's turret of his Humvee on the frontlines of his fifth and probably final war. Until the very eve of the war, it had not been decided when the company command would move to the front. While the teams prepared back at Hangar 17 in Kuwait, Randy told Alan Johnson that he worried that he might be left behind, stuck at a desk. The men had brought Randy their guns for final fine-tuning, until he was forbidden to touch another weapon. His job now was operational planning and intelligence—an important job—but Randy couldn't help pining for a last stint as gunslinger. When the company command had decided to convoy in on day one, Randy had been so pleased that he gave Alan a hug.

Charlie Company's convoy set off into the night to its fallback choice, Basra International Airport. Major Jonathan Burns led the way; then came Jim Kilcoyne, who was now the sergeant major of Charlie Company, followed by their SOT-A signals intelligence team and a Civil Affairs team, led by Randy's Desert Storm comrade Warren Foster—now a captain in the 96th Civil Affairs Battalion. Randy Wurst and a psyop team brought up the rear. Rawhide, Randy's call sign, was painted on the bumper of his Humvee.

Major Jonathan Burns was a reserved man, but his call sign, "Wildman," stenciled on the bumper of his Humvee, hinted at his bachelor days. His staff, however, quickly learned that he was a selfless person who listened to his men and really cared about them. Like Major Gavrilis, Burns had come from 3rd Group. He had taken command of his company in the summer of 2002, just days before the Special Forces' planning for war in Iraq began in earnest.

Basra International Airport sat beside a small city called Zubayr, which was just west of Basra. To reach the airport, the convoy doubled back on the highway and then took a side road lined with high-walled industrial buildings. It looked like a perfect place to be ambushed and, sure enough, after the first vehicles of their convoy passed what turned out to be an Iraqi military post, several Iraqis appeared in the road, armed with machine guns and rifles. Standing in the gun turret, Randy watched the attackers through night-vision goggles and the .50-caliber gun's scope while drawing his pistol. "Drop your guns!" he shouted. They did not move. Randy fired a shot into the ground. Still no response. He and the other soldiers with him let off another burst of gunfire.

Hearing the shots and seeing tracers, Burns got on the radio. "What's happening, guys? Give me a sitrep." He got no answer to his request for a situation report, because the men had left their Humvees.

The psyop sergeant, Luis Rojas, had spotted men with guns near the military post and fired.

"Repeat, give me a sitrep. Do you need backup?" Burns asked again impatiently. No answer.

Warren Foster turned his Humvee around and drove to the scene. He was the best Arabic speaker in the convoy. He pulled his unarmored Humvee behind Randy's armored one and got out. "If you do not drop the bloody weapons right this instant, we will blow your heads off," he shouted at the Iraqis, adding a few choice curse words that were sure to shake them out of their stupor. "Get out of here and don't come back."

The Iraqis dropped their guns and ran. Randy was glad to have Warren and his 3+/3+ Arabic by his side again. In these early hours of the war, it was impossible to gauge the level of resistance that Iraqis would mount. Disarming them without killing them was the preferred course.

Killer counseled restraint on the part of some of the company's young sergeants who wanted to shoot at everything that moved. "Not everything out there is necessarily a threat," he advised. "See if you can determine whether it is before you shoot." In a few days, however, they would be less inclined to let pass anyone who demonstrated hostile intent. Several British soldiers were shot in the same stretch of road, which became known as ambush alley.

After their confrontation in the alley, Burns turned the convoy around and joined a British unit camped along the highway. The U.S. soldiers tucked themselves into the British formation for the night. Iraqis continued to shoot at them in the dark with AK–47s. The British armored vehicles were impervious to the small arms fire but the open Humvees were not, so some of the U.S. soldiers dismounted and went to find the culprits. They did, and disarmed them. At sunup, the convoy again set off for the airport. With luck, the Marines and the British would have seized it overnight. The company needed to set up a communications node so it could begin doing its job.

ODA 554 had reached the farm of the friendly Iraqi sheikh and his clan on the edge of Zubayr. The Iraqis insisted on giving the team their home and moving to a neighbor's. The house was a humble mud-walled affair with a tin roof and a curtain for a doorway. Jimmy Newman hated to sit in the Humvee to type his sitreps, but there was no room in the tiny home for an office, so he set up his collapsible chair in the chicken coop out back. One of the hens had several new chicks and fought ruthlessly to defend her domain. Michael T. Swift returned from a patrol to find Jimmy ensconced in the coop, smoking a cigar and typing away calmly. The mother hen perched on top of the portable coffee maker he'd brought in. "We have an agreement not to bother each other," Jimmy said. At the sight of his friend living among the chickens, Michael T. laughed until he cried.

ODA 554's sheikh, who had been recruited before the war, had plenty of information on enemy targets around Zubayr, where the British were running into considerable resistance. When the team failed to make contact with Charlie Company, which was supposed to pass on its information to the British command, the team sought another way to get the job done. It was war, and the intelligence on enemy positions could be outdated in a matter of hours. The team stopped a British tank and asked the soldiers the location of the nearest command post. The regimental commander was delighted to receive 554's information.

Two things quickly became clear. The Iraqis were putting up more resistance than expected, especially near Zubayr, and they were adopting guerrilla-style tactics. Rather than stand and fight, they were melting into the population and using homes, schools, mosques, and hospitals instead of military bases. They took off their uniforms and resorted to ambush, deception, infiltration, and various rearguard tactics. Iraqis waved white flags and then pulled out guns—they had little compunction about violating the laws of land warfare. It looked like Saddam's forces had planned to resort to unconventional tactics from the start.

The British had expected to roll right through Zubayr and on to Basra. Michael T. Swift was surprised by the amount of resistance, too. The first barricade the team had come to was manned by an Iraqi—at least fifty years old—who stood his ground and fought. He and about ten other men held their ground boldly and traded fire with the Americans. A division of U.S. Marines had passed through and now a British division was parked on their doorstep, and still they fought on. This first contest was ended when the British brought in their heavy artillery. Michael T. thought that the rest of the barricades leading into the city would then crumble, but they did not. Day after day it was "smash-mouth football" as the combined forces took down the barricades one by one. Swift concluded that the Iraqis' tenacity was due to the fact that some men knew that they would be shot by their commanders if they did not man the barricades, and others knew that their power and privilege would vanish with the regime. Both groups had every incentive to fight as long as Saddam's command structure remained intact.

Instead of arriving in Basra by the second or third day, ODA 554 remained at the farm, eating pita and drinking tea with their Iraqi partners. The men ate as little of the food as was possible without alienating their hosts—because the food was making them sick, one by one. Nonetheless, the patrols had to continue.

An urgent order came from a general to search a compound in the area where Kuwaiti POWs from Desert Storm might be held. Jimmy Newman grabbed a couple of available sergeants and went off at dusk. They reached the walled home, but no one opened the doors. Given the priority attached to the mission, Jimmy was not about to give up. He hailed a passing British tank and persuaded it to ram in the door. They found only an indignant squatter family inside.

That was a miss, but the team had plenty of hits. Each day it would send Iraqis into the city or receive runners coming out with current information on where the underground headquarters of the leaders were, where the arms were being stashed, and where the men who manned the barricades were sleeping. The team used several methods to cross-check the information, then delivered it to the British. A couple of men from ODA 554 would hop onto their tanks—there wasn't enough room inside—and lead the way to the locations. This collaboration worked well until the British division commander found out that information was not flowing up through his chain of command but laterally. He delivered an ultimatum to Maj. Burns that the improvisation be stopped. All information had to come through his command.

Major Burns and Charlie Company had set up shop in the maintenance quarter of Basra International Airport. The mechanics' bays served as garages where the teams could park their Humvees out of sight. Just a kilometer away was the Zubayr canal and enemy snipers. One of the Civil Affairs sergeants hot-wired a bulldozer and built up a six-foot berm around the complex. At night they made sure no light gave them away. There was no power or water in the buildings, which were slightly damaged from bombs, but the soldiers hooked up a generator in the main office and one in the Civil Affairs bay. The Civil Affairs soldiers cooked group rations for dinner and invited those not out on missions to watch a nightly movie they projected on the wall. One night's offering, *Gladiator,* was a 5th Group favorite: it had adopted the motto "strength and honor" as its own after the September 11 attacks.

The British division commander had moved into the control tower and terminal building about a quarter mile from Burns's camping spot but, to the U.S. soldiers, the security around the airport remained curiously lax. British tanks were parked at intervals around the perimeter, but Iraqi tanks remained in place and had not been rendered inoperable.

As always, the Special Forces pulled their own security watches, which paid off one day. In broad daylight, some Iraqis were sneaking across the fuel dump that separated the canal from the airport. A shout went up, and several SF soldiers grabbed their guns and climbed the berm. They caught and detained the Iraqis, then turned them over to the British—who released them shortly thereafter. When Randy found out, he was furious; these men had seen the layout of the American and British positions and were now free to report it back to the black-robed Iraqis who stood along the opposite bank of the canal. The snipers and artillery would now be able to zero in on their positions easily.

Randy set up a map board and began logging all the incidents and information as it came in, creating a real-time intelligence update that all the teams could look at day or night. They had been taking incoming mortar fire nightly. The British would fire up their artillery, drop some illumination rounds for a while, and then start shooting. It did not stop the mortars, yet the British balked at letting the Special Forces call in air strikes on targets they'd identified, for fear of collateral damage. The SF operators failed to convince the British that the laser-guided munitions were actually more precise than their tank and artillery rounds. One night, a team got an AC–130 gunship on station to take out the most bothersome mortar position. The Special Forces were all for fire discipline and minimizing casualties, but many of the men believed that the restraint was emboldening the Iraqi resistance.

Daily, Maj. Burns went over to see when they might move. "Once we set the conditions" was the vague reply. By day, the British pushed forward over Bridge Four, the last of four bridges across the Zubayr canal, and the one closest to Basra—at the doorstep of the city. But, each night, the British would pull back so that they did not have to defend the territory they'd taken. They were either hoping that the city's defenses would collapse or waiting until Baghdad fell to move on Basra. It was a strategy designed to minimize casualties on both sides as well as collateral damage, but it could take a while. The unintended consequences of the strategy had yet to be fully appreciated: armed Iraqis might just disappear to fight another day.

The Special Forces were not allowed to enter Basra without the British, so they concentrated on Zubayr. They collected intelligence that enabled the British to round up about 170 regime leaders in the area; Saddam Hussein's Ba'ath Party loyalists and the Fedayeen militia were directing much of the unconventional tactics being employed. The Special Forces discovered a Ba'ath Party phone directory in the airport, so the soldiers began tracking them down and detaining them.

One team had been trained to use a new unmanned aerial vehicle (UAV), an experimental model called the Pointer. It looked like a model airplane, made of gray plastic and about five feet long, with slotted wings and a tail fin that packed into two suitcases and assembled in minutes. Team members could guide it through a box-shaped visor that was pressed to the face. It helped the team gather information, in one case about the layout of a petrochemical complex and armed men who had holed up there. The team then helped conduct a forced search of the premises. The Pointer was also ideal for seeing into the walled compounds that were the standard architecture of Iraq and reconnoitering dangerous routes like ambush alley.

The best intelligence came from Iraqis—particularly from the tribal clan that ODA 554 worked and lived with. The team wanted to reciprocate with something that would help the clan and enhance the sheikh's position as a leader in the community. The Civil Affairs unit attached to Charlie Company was already working on it. Right near the sheikh's farm a warehouse had been discovered, packed with pallets containing imported clothes, food, machinery, and paper goods. Major Simon Gardner, the Civil Affairs deputy commander, found documents in the warehouse showing that the imports were part of the United Nations "oil for food" program, which had allowed Iraq to sell oil and import non-military goods.

The contrast between this abundance and the poverty of most Zubayr residents suggested that the imports were hoarded for distribution to select government loyalists. Gardner and his men filled up their Humvees with paper, books, and other school supplies and drove them over to a one-room school near the sheikh's compound. By agreed plan, the sheikh was not there, so he would not be visibly linked with the Americans. They left the supplies for him to distribute.

The warehouse also contained medical supplies, which the Civil Affairs teams intended to distribute to clinics in poor areas rather than through the central, regime-controlled hospital in Zubayr. It would help them establish direct links to civilians to encourage their support for the American presence and cultivate additional sources of information—not to mention ensure that aid got to some of the neediest of the Shi'ite population. But first they had to find out where the clinics were. Gardner and the CA commander, Major "DJ" DeJarnette, decided that they would visit the central hospital director to see if he would give them that information. Warren Foster's medic, Eric Anderson, went inside the hospital along with Gardner and an interpreter. DJ and the rest stayed outside, each plugged into his MBITR headset. The director, a tall elegant Iraqi, spoke perfect English but was decidedly hostile.

Gardner kept prodding but got nowhere. Anderson tried the good cop routine, but that didn't work either. Gardner led the way out, pointing briefly to a framed portrait of Saddam Hussein that still hung over the door of the director. His loyalties were clear. As the Civil Affairs soldiers walked toward the front door they saw that its metal gate had been locked. They were trapped inside. DJ's perturbed voice came over the radio. "Come on guys. We've been on this objective for thirty-seven minutes. Let's go!"

Walking quickly toward the gate of the hospital, Gardner—all of five-foot-five, but grim-faced and with his M4 rifle raised at the men standing guard—made a convincing case that he was about to open fire. The men unlocked the gate and the Civil Affairs soldiers quickly parted the crowd that had gathered out front. DJ and Warren stood by their armored Humvees.

"Come on, come on," DJ urged. He had seen plenty of combat, so he knew when a situation was on the knife-edge cusp of turning violent. The Civil Affairs guys jokingly called themselves the "geriatric squad" because they were a good decade older than the average sergeant on the ODAs. Their four-man teams, called CAT-As, were often misperceived as aid workers in uniform, but these sergeants had all passed the Q course and many of them had served for years in the Special Forces.

The British armored division continued to probe Basra and to prepare for its eventual full-scale assault on the city, which would occur the day that Baghdad fell. In addition to using the ODAs for intelligence, the British tapped the skills of the psyops team that was attached to Charlie Company. It was a three-man team led by Sgt. First Class Luis Rojas. The 4th Psychological Operations Group, like the active-duty Civil Affairs battalion, is used during combat operations. The group creates, prints, and drops leaflets, and scripts and broadcasts messages from speaker-mounted Humvees or the EC–130 Commando Solo aircraft. It is among the most powerful combat multipliers in the military—an effective psyop campaign can persuade entire divisions not to fight. Psyop can also make its side's forces seem larger and more formidable.

Sgt. Rojas, a genial Cuban-Dominican from New York City, was thirty-eight years old with sixteen years of military service and a firm grasp of his craft. Tactical psyop, aiding combat operations, required fast work. The window to swing the tide of battle and popular opinion can open and close with little warning.

In preparation for their push on Basra, the British asked Rojas to prepare a recording to induce as many surrenders as possible. They had already seen him carry out a successful deception operation—his team snuck forward into enemy territory and played a recording of tanks and artillery that fooled the Iraqis into believing they were under attack there, when in fact the British were moving across one of the other bridges.

Rojas rejected the British draft script as too nuanced. He wrote a new one and recorded it using an Arab interpreter. The Iraqis who were still fighting were hard core. What was needed was a blunt message that clearly spelled out the choice and the consequences. One never promised or threatened and then failed to deliver that undermined the effectiveness of any subsequent message. Rojas burned a CD with a simple message: "If you give up now, you live. If not, you die. We are coming in."

When night fell Rojas drove to the British command post at the airport's control tower and followed their tanks out of the gate. Randy went too, with his vehicle crew and armored Humvee, because Rojas's

Humvee was unarmored and armed only with a light squad automatic weapon. The two large speakers mounted on his roof took up most of the room and restricted his gunner's field of fire. Although Rojas was a veteran soldier, it was only the first war for each of his two young sergeants.

It was a wild ride. The road to Bridge Four, their destination, was heavily cratered and littered with hunks of twisted metal and asphalt that loomed up out of the darkness. The tanks sped ahead at nearly thirty miles an hour, while the Humvees could only do about half that and still avoid the obstacles. The tanks were equipped with infrared sights and not night-vision technology, but they could roll over or through most obstacles. As they neared Basra, two of the tanks opened fire after a dozen or more Iraqis started shooting from a compound. The buildings and nearby fuel tanks erupted into a blazing fireball that blinded the Americans, who were wearing night-vision goggles. The devices work by greatly magnifying minimal light from the stars and moon, so when bright lights appear they "flare out" and the wearer can see nothing.

Randy, in his gun turret behind the .50-caliber machine gun, tore off his nods and cursed. The operations sergeant Marty Moore, a ten-year veteran who was riding shotgun down below, yelled up to him: "We're blind here. You've got to tell us which way to go." The young medic at the wheel, Rosco Evans, strained to see the next obstacle before him. "Stop!" Randy shouted.

The Humvee teetered at the edge of the road on the brink of a seven-foot ditch. Rosco inched back and picked his way slowly as the tanks got farther and farther ahead. One tank vanished and Randy tried to see where it went. "Stop!" he called out. "Do NOT follow that tank."

The big Challenger tank had driven over a ledge and tipped over. Its gun barrel jammed into the ground, so it did not flip onto its top and trap the men inside. Rojas's Humvee was stuck in the dirt where the pavement had ended. Everyone pulled back to regroup, while Randy's Humvee waited by the overturned tank. The U.S. soldiers' radios could not communicate with the British tanks, so they waited until the men climbed out of the hatch, unharmed. With help on the way for the over-turned tank, the mission proceeded. The tanks reached the canal on Basra's outskirts and lined up in an inverted V facing the Iraqi frontline. The psyop Humvee drove into the V where it would be protected but close enough for its broadcast to be heard.

Rojas calculated that the sound would carry two kilometers in the cool night air; it was nearly 3 A.M. His sergeant turned on the speakers and loaded the CD. The first response to the recording was a burst of gunfire. The tanks returned fire. They moved to a different spot on the canal and repeated the process. At the end of each broadcast Rojas' interpreter made a live follow-up appeal. He did not announce exactly when the final assault on Basra would occur, only that it was imminent.

While the psyop team did its work, Randy scanned the canal banks through his nods. He saw a small boat launch through his sniper rifle's scope but, at 1500 meters, he did not have a clear enough shot. He watched the team's perimeter to make sure that no one was flanking to attack from the side or rear. The soldiers in the tanks were protected, but it was up to him to keep the rest of the team alive.

Randy fingered the green plastic tag that hung from a chain on his neck. It was another talisman of sorts, like the ones in his doeskin pouch. This one had a practical purpose too: it marked him as a volunteer for the new fibrin bandage that had been rushed into the field for this war. The Special Operations Command had begun developing it when one of the Rangers in the 1993 Mogadishu battle had bled to death after his femoral artery was severed. The bandage was made of real blood fibers that would clot the wound as soon as it was applied. If it worked as hoped, it would be a revolutionary advance in trauma care and would eventually be in the kit of every medic in the army.

The soldier's oath to serve and protect comes into sharp focus in wartime. Randy had always been conscious of his vow—it was what had given his life meaning for the past two decades. He could not help but feel every mission was doubly important to him in this war, knowing that it was likely to be his last time on the frontlines.

Dawn broke his reverie. As the first light peeked over the earth's rim, through his binoculars Randy spotted a compound with armed Iraqis outside. They were three kilometers away, far out of range of the Iraqi AK–47s, but that did not stop them from firing at the U.S. and British forces lined up on the canal. They are taunting us, Randy thought. We have called for surrender, we have held off assaulting Basra, and this is their response. They believe they can shoot with impunity. The tank driver nearest to Randy had the same reaction. "Let's call the artillery in on them," he suggested to Randy. Randy checked the coordinates and the British soldier called them in. Minutes later they watched the compound disappear in a few flashes of light and a cloud of smoke.

The British command reported that Iraqis were starting to come out of the city at Bridge One, about eight kilometers away, and asked the psyop Humvee to come help manage the crowd. Marty Moore was also a fluent Arab speaker: as a bachelor for five of his ten years in SF, he had spent his time burnishing his skill to a 3/3 rating. The U.S. forces were directed to a spot on the city's edge. Rojas parked under an overpass and broadcast a new surrender message he had quickly scripted. He told the Iraqis to gather on the left side of a building opposite them. White flags began popping up, but before the people could approach, an Iraqi tank drove in between them and began firing. The British tanks fired back and the white flags went down. Rojas was crestfallen.

The British commander called them to the arched entryway to the city, where other Iraqis were coming out on foot and in cars. Randy and Rojas drove their Humvees to the intersection and set up security. Marty began working the crowd. He stopped cars and looked for men of military age and anyone who might have useful information—those he sent back to the British collection point a few hundred meters away. Randy stood guard while the others searched the vehicles. Some of the trunks were stuffed with uniforms. It was the first time that the British had moved to the edge of the city and stayed, and it was paying off. They collected dozens of people to interrogate, and the military intelligence team with Charlie Company helped cull information about the remaining defenders, mostly Fedayeen militia, and the location of their hit teams in the city. Randy watched the growing flood of people and vehicles. There were not enough forces to control all the avenues of approach, and a wooded area nearby was a prime spot for snipers. Even though the crowd was mostly peaceful, there still was intermittent gunfire.

"We've got to pull out. I cannot provide enough protection on this road," Randy told Marty, who agreed. As they left for the airport, a shrapnel fragment struck Randy's arm. He pocketed the hot metal, to add to his medicine bag. He had been lucky again. He'd never been shot—not in five wars. He had been hit during a test fire in Kuwait before the war started, but that did not count; a grenade fragment fired by some Arab allies had hit him in the chest pocket, right on his Zippo lighter, which had stopped the shard. Another time, an Mk 19 had misfired and blasted his thighs into hamburger. And he'd been hit by a ricocheting bullet during one of their many room-clearings in Kosovo. Randy would always consider himself lucky.

That night Maj. Burns announced that they were leaving. They had a new assignment. Only Michael T. and Jimmy's team would stay on to keep working its contacts. At the Basra airport, Chief Newman sat outside the maintenance bay, smoking a cigarette and chatting amiably with the other teams as they packed up. He had grown a bushy mustache and his hair was shaggy. Like Randy, Jimmy had served twenty years in numerous conflicts. He was extremely proud to be a Special Forces soldier, but he had already made up his mind to file for retirement when he returned. Jimmy was forty years old and ready for a new chapter of life. He wanted to spend more time with his German-born wife and their five children and brand-new grandchild. In just a few months he would be going home to them for good.

CHAPTER 11

CENTRAL IRAQ
Masters of Chaos

The ultimate in disposing one's troops is to be without
ascertainable shape. Then the most penetrating spies
cannot pry nor can the wise lay plans against you.

—SUN TZU

T HERE WAS ONE blue dot that 2nd Battalion commander Chris
Conner kept a particularly close eye on. Back in the United States,
generals with access to the system, including Geoffrey Lambert, also
were checking for the same dot the first thing every morning. Other military forces could only speculate when they saw the lone blue dot, blinking, far ahead of all the others on the Blue Force Tracker screen. One
Special Forces detachment had embarked on what would turn out to be
the longest wartime special reconnaissance mission in the history of the
Special Forces. To Conner, this was no disembodied blue dot. He knew
from Desert Storm exactly what they were going through, hundreds of
miles away from help, with Iraqis all around them. They were in the
maw of the beast.

ODA 551 infiltrated the critical Karbala Gap, a narrow strip of land
that the conventional forces would have to cross to reach Baghdad.
Below the gap, the ODA's of Conner's Bravo Company, would fan out to

cities in the south-central region. Although the conventional forces planned to avoid populated areas as much as possible, the army would have to pass right by Najaf on its way to Karbala, and the Marines would drive north through Diwaniya. As with Burns's Charlie Company teams farther south, these ODAs were charged with providing intelligence on threats to the conventional forces' flanks and assisting in whatever fighting might develop in or around these cities. They would raise resistance forces against the regime wherever they could, and be the eyes and ears on the urban front.

No one knew how quickly the army would reach the Karbala Gap, but what was crystal clear was that it was the key chokepoint. This seven-and-a-half kilometer strip between the vast Milh Lake and the city of Karbala was the most direct route to the capital for the forces sweeping up from the southwest. It was the obvious place for Saddam Hussein to try to stop the 3rd Infantry Division, the ground force leading the assault. If he did not stop them there, it was a mere 100 kilometers to the capital. Only the fight for Baghdad would remain between him and utter defeat.

The Russian-speaking captain who had torn out his rotten deck before he led a team into Afghanistan had still not rebuilt it by March 2003. But he did land the special reconnaissance mission at Karbala Gap. His eighteen years of military experience was one factor that led Conner to pick him for the job. He had served in the military four times longer than most ODA captains. Before joining the Special Forces he had been in the military intelligence branch, so he knew in great detail what kinds of information the conventional forces needed before they reached the gap. The team's senior half also was made up of seasoned soldiers in their late thirties, who were mature enough to sit in a hide site for as long as required and to carry out the mission even if just one man and one radio were left.

Conner had sent two other teams on early special reconnaissance as part of their mission set, but SR was 551's sole assignment. The Karbala Gap was the spot where war planners expected Saddam Hussein to throw his best forces and deadliest weapons into stopping the U.S.

forces' wall of iron and steel. They needed to know his every move around the clock.

ODA 551 had been reunited in the summer of 2002, after the war in Afghanistan, where its members had been dispersed to fill out teams that had fewer than twelve members. The captain had given them the option of staying where they were, but they all opted to come back to ODA 551.

As the team began war-gaming its mission, it estimated that it could last anywhere from two to ten days but most probably from three to five. Conner drilled the men on how they would make decisions at key junctures. Would they abort their mission if they were discovered by children? By adults? By an armed group? How large an armed group? What were their recovery options? Could they make it to a pickup zone? The answers that emerged from their planning process were sobering. It would take ten hours for a helicopter rescue, starting from the time the team was notified. The team also learned the little-known fact that, as a matter of policy, helicopter rescues occur only when the pickup time falls during the hours of darkness. So if the tenth hour did not fall during nighttime, the rescue time would grow even longer. Somalia had demonstrated, and Anaconda had driven home, the high risk of helicopter shootdowns during daylight hours. The air force's emergency response time worked out to anywhere between forty-five minutes and three hours. The team members realized that theirs was not really a recoverable mission. No one would be able to get to them anytime soon that deep into enemy territory in the middle of Iraq. The team would have to prepare to evade and, if it could not, to fight.

The battalion, along with many U.S. forces, went to Jordan in the winter for a dress-rehearsal exercise called Early Victor. By early 2003 they were in Kuwait—if and when the United States went to war, they were ready.

On March 15 the team did a dry run at the Ali al Salem base in Kuwait. The soldiers drove their Humvees and "nonstandard tactical vehicles"—pickup trucks outfitted with guns—onto the MH–53J Pave Low helicopters and the MC–130s Combat Talon planes to weigh them fully loaded and gassed up, and to check how fast the team could mount the guns and drive them off the birds. On March 19, when the war kicked off a day early with the "decapitation strike," the operations officer asked the captain how soon he could be ready to go. "Two hours," the captain replied. As they rushed to gather men and equipment, a sergeant came to the captain, saying, "Hey, sir, someone just briefed your mission on CNN."

A retired general providing television commentary had told the world that the Karbala Gap was the critical land mass that the 3rd Infantry Division would have to punch through to reach Baghdad. Otherwise it would have to detour west around the huge Milh Lake or go east through the marshes. The military, he said, would have to put a Special Forces team in the gap to get eyes on it and confirm or deny the enemy's chosen course of action.

The captain was ashen-faced. Their mission had seemed dangerous enough before; now it had been broadcast in Baghdad and every other city in the world. It would be a miracle if they evaded detection.

From 10 P.M. to 4 A.M. on March 20, during the first wave of "shock and awe" bombing, the air force imposed a ban on anyone flying above 300 feet or under 3,000 feet. This required a change in 551's original flight plan. The men flew into Iraq with the night exploding above them. By the time the team was deposited in the undulating desert terrain southwest of Karbala, the helicopters were bumping up against their deadline of reaching the border by daylight. The helicopters crossed back into Kuwait with only fifteen minutes of fuel in their tanks.

It had been the longest infiltration and heaviest load that the special operations helicopters had ever flown. 551's captain, who had worked in a helicopter unit, knew the risks the pilots and crew had run to get them in. They had pushed their equipment to the limit and waived rules on mixing loads of fuel and ammunition. If they had crashed, they all would have gone up in a giant fireball.

Once on the ground, 551 had to move fast: the 3rd Infantry Division might reach Karbala in as little as thirty-six hours and needed to know what was in that seven-and-a-half kilometer strip. A few hours of darkness remained. The team members drove like demons toward the Karbala Gap, staying well to the west of the populated areas. They could not avoid being seen by the bedouins, just as Lt. Col. Conner had predicted. As the miles brought them closer and closer to the strategic gap, they grew increasingly jumpy.

"Is that a tank?"

"No, it's a bush."

The men talked back and forth on their MBITR headsets, comparing notes. It was hard to see at a distance through the nods. If two of them agreed it might be a tank, they halted for a better look. Twice they mired down in the soft sand of the downwind side of dunes, but they had practiced how to tow each other out. They tried to keep a straight course, although the *wadis* channeled their direction of travel. Every man kept his GPS device handy. Just before dawn, they reached the *wadi* they'd selected to hide in for the day. As the sun rose, they saw the ubiquitous bedouins, some trucks, goats, and kids playing soccer. For those on guard duty, the "what ifs" they'd discussed before suddenly came into sharp focus. What would they do if that woman or child got close to their hide site? Colonel Conner had shared his views on this greatest moral dilemma of the reconnaissance man but had said that each man would have to wrestle with his own conscience. Would he capture or kill a man, woman, or child who discovered their site in order to save the mission? It was one of the worst scenarios they had to contemplate, and it would be up to the sergeant who was awake to make the call.

Luckily they did not have to make such terrible choices. The day passed uneventfully, if nervously, and they set off at dark for their final dash into the gap. The captain laughed at what they found, and didn't find. It was true that the gap was full of tanks, as the intelligence reports had said. But they were fuel tanks. It was also true that the gap was heavily mined. But the mines they found, at least initially, were stone quarries.

The soldiers chose one of the quarries along the lake's edge to hole up in. From this piece of ground they could see the surrounding approaches and most of the city. They chased a 110-pound female hyena away when she tried to come back into what had been her den. She was a good sign, because if a hyena lived there it meant the area was fairly deserted. The team settled in and started the observation and reporting process. Its job was to paint the most detailed picture possible for the 3rd Infantry Division, from the weather, wind, temperature, and road quality to all the different types of forces that the team could identify. This was the essence of "ground truth": it did not matter what the imagery, overflying pilots, defecting Iraqis, or intelligence analysts said was there. The men were to report exactly what they could see, measure, and collect empirically. There is no substitute for eyes on the target. It was immediately clear that there were no Iraqi divisions sitting astride the gap, and no burning oil trenches. If Saddam was going to pick this place to make his defense, he had not yet moved.

The first morning after ODA 551 reached the gap, Conner woke up earlier than usual and went to the ops center in Hangar 17 to check on the blue dot. It was not there. His heart sank. The ops center immediately radioed a message—Were they there?—Yes. Change your batteries, Kuwait instructed. The satellite was not picking up the Blue Force Tracker. He checked again—No dot. They called back. Change batteries again, maybe those were duds. The captain figured out what was going on. They had parked in such a deep hole that the tracker's signal was not getting picked up. He fixed that.

The next day a sandstorm struck. For hours on end, the soldiers lay exposed to fifty-knot winds driving sand into their hole. The men donned their choice of goggles—Oakley ski goggles or Wiley-X goggles were favorites, or army-issue HALO goggles, or anything else that did the job. They continued reporting on three-hour shifts. One-third of the team slept for three hours while another third manned the observation posts and scopes or patrolled, while the other third relayed the reports by radio.

The sandstorm stalled the northward advance of the main army force, the 3rd Infantry Division, which decided to make a "strategic pause." This caused the captain to reevaluate his mission, as well—it now might last beyond the three to five days they had expected. Rations were cut to one meal a day, and water was only for drinking—no shaves and no bathing. In the daily communications, Conner asked whether the men needed a resupply, but the team decided that it would be just too risky to pull out of its hole at night, go to the desert to retrieve an air drop, and expect to make it back in again undetected. The soldiers would keep going until they were down to one five-gallon can of water. Their "bug-out" packs, of course, would never be touched. These packs had food, water, and essentials that they would take if they had to flee on foot.

The men had been wearing their full charcoal-lined chemical suits since they arrived. They'd taken off their gas masks when they saw cars and trucks on the roads—if civilians were moving around, then there were no chemicals in the air—but kept the masks and gloves within reach at all times. The consensus of U.S. and allied intelligence agencies was that Saddam Hussein still possessed the chemical weapons that the United Nations inspectors had deemed to be there in 1995, so the military prepared accordingly.

The captain of ODA 551 was taking no chances, especially because Karbala had been identified as a point on the "red line" where it was deemed likely that Saddam would use chemical weapons as his last line of defense on the approach to Baghdad. Both the captain and his intelligence sergeant believed that Hussein was far more likely to launch a chemical attack here than to send his heavy divisions across the Euphrates, because there they would be cut off from the capital if the bridges were bombed.

The team did see plenty of assorted troops: forward observers, the Karbala garrison, and dozens of plainclothes Fedayeen and other Iraqis out patrolling in military trucks, Nissan pickups, and cars. They were obviously conducting an intensive search that went on around the clock. The team later found out that Iraqi TV had indeed broadcast the possibility of its presence, so the frenetic activity was directed at finding them. Strangely enough, none of the patrols approached the hiding place; but after the fifth and sixth days of observation from the abandoned mine, it was getting weird—there were not even casual, unwitting approaches by civilians. The soldiers were within 400 meters of all sorts of activity, but they might as well have been on the moon. They had figured out that the Iraqis did not like to leave their trucks at night, but the men were genuinely puzzled that no one had come poking around during daylight hours.

On the night of day six, the 11th Attack Helicopter Regiment began flying patrols into the gap in preparation for the 3rd Infantry Division's assault. The patrols had no idea that the Special Forces were there, and for a few gripping moments Major Jeff Smith, the officer in charge of deconfliction, feared that all their efforts to avoid fratricide might fail. He scrambled to get the helicopters recalled. ODA 551 began talking to every plane that went overhead, to let them know the men were down there so they would not be bombed, and to offer their services to recover any pilots who got shot down. The next day, an Apache was shot down by a farmer with an antique bolt-action rifle. To its great regret, the team was on the other side of Karbala, so it could not reach the crew. The eleven men could not hope to fight through the entire defenses of the city to rescue them.

On day eight, the probes from the 3rd Infantry Division forces began, and ODA 551 could see its special reconnaissance coming to an end at last. It had one major challenge left. The most dangerous part of special reconnaissance is exfiltration. The team had escaped detection so far, but it ran the greatest risk of discovery while pulling out. The team had to leave its site and then successfully fold itself into the ranks of the approaching U.S. forces without being shot at. On day nine, the men debated and prepared to depart. To minimize the danger of discovery, the captain wanted to pull out and link up at night, but the 3rd Infantry Division wanted to do it by day. They settled on a plan to pull out of the gap right before the conventional assault began. At ten P.M. on the night of day ten, the men of ODA 551 quietly rolled out of their hole, started their engines and, when they reached the designated spot, flashed their headlights. The team briefed the 3rd Infantry Division commanders, and then continued south, retracing its original infiltration route.

The Special Forces team's company commander, Maj. Andy Lohman—

who had set up camp in the desert outside Najaf—informed it that its services had been requested by the conventional army in Karbala, so ODA 551 turned around and headed back. There, the team learned the secret of its hide site. Some captured Fedayeen prisoners said that it had been used for years as a firing range for every kind of artillery, missiles, and other ordnance the Iraqi army had. Unexploded shells littered the area. The team unwittingly had chosen the perfect hiding spot, albeit a very dangerous one.

While ODA 551 was staking out the Karbala Gap, the other teams under Maj. Lohman's command had fanned out to aid the 3rd Infantry's advance. Their first priority was Najaf, about seventy-five kilometers south of Karbala, because the 3rd Infantry Division would pass by just west of it en route to the gap, followed by the 101st Airborne Division. Najaf was a well-guarded population center and the unofficial capital of Iraq's Shi'ite majority. ODA 544, the "pilot" team that went into Najaf first, had to provide intelligence on the regime forces in the city and other potential threats. The team was to seek local Iraqis inclined to rise up against the regime and ferret out Hussein loyalists who went underground. Last, but not least, it had to try to encourage pro-U.S., or at least neutral, sentiments among Shi'ite leaders.

Master Sergeant Steve Rainey, the team sergeant of ODA 544, was now a gray-haired veteran. He, the chief warrant officer, the intelligence sergeant, and the senior engineer had a combined total of nearly sixty years in the Special Forces. The most junior sergeant had four years in SF. A team this seasoned was best used in a complicated assignment with high stakes and a lot of unknowns. Rainey had been in the military for twenty years, with a Special Forces career bracketed by Desert Storm and Operation Iraqi Freedom. He liked the symmetry of it. Like Randy, Michael T., and many of his cohorts, this was the last war he was likely to fight. He had been dreaming his retirement dream for a while; he wanted to start a tandem skydiving school. You can take the man off a HALO team, but sometimes you can't keep him from jumping out of airplanes. The crusty master sergeant was looking forward to the next chapter of his life, once he had finished this war.

Rainey's team was flown into Iraq at night on two MC–130 Combat Talon planes, the mainstay of the Air Force Special Operations Command (AFSOC). The night after the first troops crossed into Kuwait, two MC–130s lifted off with Rainey's team, two Humvees, and two commercial pickup trucks. The pilot, co-pilot, and navigator wore night-vision goggles on the blacked-out flight. They had no running lights. Behind the cockpit another crew member sat at a tall board of electronic hardware, watching a screen, ready to release the chaff and flares that would divert any heat-seeking missiles that might be fired. Only a faint red light glowed in the cargo hold, where men rested or put on finishing touches of camouflage paint.

The big birds touched down in total darkness on an abandoned airfield at Wadi al Khirr. It had been bombed in Desert Storm and Operation Southern Watch, but the pilots found enough of the taxiway intact to land on and braked to an abrupt halt. The crew quickly released the Humvees from their tiedowns as the back hatch yawned open. The AFSOC boys waved another team down the ramp and into the dark night, and then quickly powered up for takeoff. They had several more flights on the night's schedule. Between dropping in SEALs, Delta and Green Berets, and resupplying the Special Forces' war pigs out west, they would work throughout the night for weeks to come.

Rainey's team drove seventy-five kilometers toward Najaf on the first night. It saw sporadic machine gun and rocket fire in the distance, and war planes making bombing runs to the north and west. At daybreak the men laid up to rest, covering their vehicles with camouflage nets that were fastened to one side of the roofs. In late afternoon, they started off on the final leg to Najaf. As they drove, the communications sergeant found out that the 3rd Infantry Division was moving faster than expected as its westernmost elements bolted unopposed through the desert west of the populated areas. ODA 544 had intended to precede them by a day, so the team would have to hustle.

The team's company commander, Maj. Lohman, was traveling with

the western prong of the 3rd Infantry Division and would set up outside Najaf in a gravel plant. His job was to feed information to the conventional command as his teams collected it, and guide and resupply
the teams, much as Maj. Burns was doing to the south. The battalion's
third company commander, Maj. Jeff Smith, was the liaison attached to
the army V Corps commander, Lt. Gen. William Wallace. Smith's job
was to keep the army command apprised of the Special Forces' whereabouts so the corps could plan accordingly, and to funnel the teams'
threat assessments and intelligence to the corps. With so many Special
Forces teams running around all over the battlefield, behind enemy
lines and crossing friendly lines, Maj. Smith had his hands full. One
friendly-fire incident could set back the unprecedented degree of collaboration that was unfolding between the conventional and special operations forces.

V Corps pitched its tents alongside Lohman's gravel plant, opposite
the 3rd Infantry. Soon afterwards, the Iraqi military started firing
artillery and missiles at them. Prudent military planning dictated that
each attack be treated as a possible chemical attack, so most of the
troops dashed for the sand pit bunkers in full chemical regalia. Major
Smith opted for black PT shorts and tan regulation T-shirts in the baking
heat. Smith and his men had no special foreknowledge that Saddam
Hussein would not end up using any chemical weapons if, indeed, he
still had any—they were just hot.

Others chose not to take any chances. Master Sergeant Alan Johnson
and ODA 563, who had arrived with Maj. Lohman, wore their chemical
suits over their shorts, and when the sirens sounded they headed for the
nearest pits. Their gas masks were strapped to their sides in canvas
pouches. Each man readied one of his atropine cartridges, which contained a spring-loaded needle and a chemical antidote. Most nerve
agents cannot be seen, smelled, or tasted, so the soldiers watched each
other intently after hearing the warhead's impact. If the paper in their
kits or the sensitive tape on their suits changed color, or if any man
started drooling or foaming at the mouth, that would be the signal to
inject him or oneself.

The first task for Steve Rainey and ODA 544 was to find out what kind of threat Najaf might pose to the force gathering in the desert just to the west. The men set up checkpoints on the outskirts of Najaf and selectively stopped traffic to see what could be learned about the intentions of the Iraqi forces and the population generally. Some of the drivers and passengers had heard that the Iraqi command had ordered the Fedayeen militiamen in their "technicals" to attack the U.S. forces, which it believed to be the light 101st Airborne Division. The Fedayeen sallied out that night and found instead the heavy tanks of the 3rd Infantry Division. They crept close, unaware that the soldiers inside were watching their every move through the tanks' thermal sights and waiting until the Iraqis aimed their weapons before blasting the unfortunate militia to smithereens.

The next day, ODA 544 returned to the checkpoints as more Iraqis left the city. Some were fleeing because they feared that the U.S. forces were about to attack the city; others were merely curious and wanted to confirm that the troops were indeed there.

Najaf was tightly controlled by government forces to keep the Shi'ite population subjugated. For weeks ODA 544 had studied Najaf's physical, social, and economic makeup in detail and analyzed the satellite imagery. The team had already plotted the coordinates of the city's heavy gun emplacements, and Ba'ath Party and Fedayeen headquarters and barracks. But it would not call for air strikes without positively identifying the locations and confirming that the regime was still using the targets.

It soon became clear that the regime loyalists would fight to keep their grip on the cities and would lay siege to the lengthening supply lines, which now stretched from the Kuwaiti border through the southern half of Iraq. The Iraqis shelled and mortared the army as it paused in the desert west of Najaf and fired on coalition aircraft passing overhead.

The commanders decided Najaf had to be taken, and the information that the ODAs were digging up gave them their best chance of fighting back. A scheme was hatched: they would try to draw the Fedayeen out of the city and then selectively target their key command and troop sites, so that when the U.S. forces did enter the city the threat would be largely removed. They would avoid fighting street by street and getting bogged down in the kind of punishing urban warfare that had occurred in Somalia.

The plan's success depended on Lohman's ODAs providing accurate and current intelligence. ODA 544 worked about twenty hours a day, retreating to the relative security of the company command for about four hours' sleep and then returning to the checkpoints east and west of the city. When the Iraqis shelled or mortared the checkpoints, the Special Forces identified their location and called in air strikes. When the men were fired on by approaching cars, they returned fire. The 3rd Infantry Division had to resume its march north, so the capture of Najaf fell to the newly arrived 101st Airborne Division commanded by the hard-charging Lt. Gen. David Petraeus.

Coincidentally, 5th Group's neighbor and the chief tenant of Fort Campbell was the "Screaming Eagles" (as the 101st was known). Those soldiers were the "big men on campus" back home—they got preference on range time and training schedules, and had the biggest budget and the best facilities. Out here in the middle of hostile Iraq, however, everything would be different.

The captain of ODA 544 and Master Sgt. Rainey were stunned at how Gen. Petraeus received them. He gathered his assistant division commander and staff around the team's Humvee to hear what it had to say. As Rainey spread out the map on the hood of his truck and pointed out the various sites the team had identified, the three-star general said to his subordinates: "Are you getting this? I want you to get a battalion on this tomorrow. What time can you be there?"

The captain of 544, who had served in an armored division two years earlier, knew that the only time a general speaks to one of his own captains is when the latter is in trouble. "Here I am, a snot-nosed captain, and the general wants to know what I think," he thought in wonder. Petraeus was an intimidating man—on the eve of the war he challenged a private to a push-up contest in front of reporters. The general was more than fifty years old, but he could still outrun and outperform most of the men in his unit, as befitted a former commander of the 101st's hypercompetitive Rakkasan brigade. It was clear that Petraeus would be one of the star generals of the war, yet here he was treating a Special Forces team like a valued partner and keenly soliciting its advice.

The fact was, the Special Forces provided exactly the kind of intelligence that Petraeus's division would need to take control of the city. He could tell a good plan when he saw one. ODA 544 worked its checkpoints and conducted surveillance to locate the enemy forces, and each morning at 7 A.M. Major Lohman would nominate their newly confirmed targets to the general's staff. By noon they would be striking them. From Iraqi civilians leaving the city and from newly captured prisoners, the Special Forces would find out how much damage had been done and pass the battle damage assessment up to the 101st. In all, the SF nominated about thirty targets, of which twenty were hit. In another fifteen or so cases they called in emergency close air support when they and the 101st came under attack. The 101st could have called its own artillery or mortar sections, but it was usually faster and more accurate for the teams to call on the air force.

Every member of the ODA knew how to call for close air support or CAS. The senior engineer had fought in every war since 1983, and the entire team had once or twice a year trained with fast movers, as the fighter jets are called, for a week. One night, low-flying coalition jets were fired upon from Najaf. Using the range-finder, Rainey determined that the fire came from a site the team had already mapped. The team's air force controller called for air support and two FA–18s arrived. After a brief delay due to ground haze and refueling, Rainey vectored them in to hit the 57-mm cannons and military trucks. They also had the grid coordinates of a ZSU 23–4 antiaircraft battery, but it was too close to residential areas to bomb.

At the end of March, Lt. Gen. Petraeus decided it was time to assault Najaf. He launched a spoiling attack on March 29 and the next day made a thunder run straight into the city. ODA 544 accompanied one battalion and called in air strikes when it came under artillery fire. ODA 556 entered the city from the north with another unit of the 101st. In a widely televised image, the 101st pulled down the statue of Saddam Hussein; Najaf was the first Iraqi city to fall. ODA 544 camped out in a schoolhouse for a couple of days and then moved with Major Lohman's company command into an agricultural college on a bluff overlooking the city.

Petraeus believed that the strategy used for Najaf should be the template for the rest of the cities the U.S. military would have to enter. He had to keep moving north, but left one of his brigades to hold Najaf for two weeks until reinforcements arrived. He thanked the Special Forces for their help and promised to speed up the ground-breaking on their new barracks when they returned home.

The battle for Najaf was not over, however. The regime's Ba'athist Party officials, who had much to lose, and the arch-loyalist Fedayeen continued to wage a hit-and-run fight. For this phase of the campaign, ODA 544 adopted its "unconventional warfare" approach and linked up with a group of Iraqis led by Abdul Munin. The day that the 101st moved into Najaf, Munin, also known as Abu Hattar, had publicly called for an intifada against Saddam Hussein. It was a risky move because it was by no means clear that the United States was the winning side, but Abu Hattar had taken risks before: he'd been arrested and tortured for dissidence in the past decade. A former army officer, he had joined an opposition group, the Coalition for Iraqi Unity, after Desert Storm. He had lost a leg in the Iran-Iraq war and walked on a prosthesis, but it hardly diminished his mobility or his martial zeal.

The captain of ODA 544 sought out Abu Hattar the day the team entered Najaf and found that the rebel had about 125 armed followers. To demonstrate his bona fides, Abu Hattar took his men to the main mosque to capture some Ba'athists and Fedayeen who had barricaded themselves inside. He then led the team to the hideouts of key regime figures in Najaf, including a senior general. When the team caught the general, it also found payroll records for men trained and paid to be suicide bombers and the names and addresses of Fedayeen militia members. It was exactly the information needed to roll up much of Najaf's hardcore resistance. The team nicknamed Abu Hattar and his men

"Bulldog and the Regulators," and he was made the provisional mayor and police chief.

ODA 544 also worked on its delicate assignment of reaching out to the Shi'a leadership and Shi'a population. The team had made several overtures to the reclusive senior cleric of Najaf, Ayatollah Sistani. As the spiritual capital of Shi'ism, Najaf could influence the entire Shi'ite majority of Iraq, and the U.S. government hoped that Shi'ites' loathing of Saddam Hussein would translate into active or at least passive support for his removal. The Shi'ites also held the key to a successful postwar transition to a government that would represent all of Iraq's ethnic and religious components. For fifty years, the Sunni minority and Saddam's brutal rule had dominated everyone else. If the Shi'ites insisted on a theocratic state which they would dominate as the numerical majority, the new Iraq would be torn apart.

As part of this daunting task, ODA 544 was assigned to safeguard a moderate Shi'ite cleric named Abdul Majid al Khoei who returned from exile in early April. Team members served in shifts as his bodyguards. Khoei's father had been killed by the Hussein regime, and it was expected that the son would wield significant influence—he was thronged by crowds in Najaf. As they got to know Khoei, the captain of ODA 544 and Rainey thought that the young cleric seemed genuinely concerned for the Iraqi people's welfare and convinced that a secular state was in Iraq's best interest, as did Abu Hattar. A serious debate was brewing, however. Prominent Shi'ite leaders wanted to follow Iran's lead and establish a fundamentalist state, and Iranian-based Shi'ite exiles were beginning to come across the border in droves, many of whom embraced that view. A local cleric in Najaf, named Moqtada al-Sadr, seemed to be both radical and ambitious. He had approached the 101st's remaining brigade, the 327 Brigade, to see if he could be the conduit for dispensing aid, which would enhance his stature, all the while railing in his sermons against the U.S. invasion and agitating for a theocratic state. Khoei had asked Sadr to hold a joint press conference with him to present a united Shi'ite front and patch up differences the two young clerics had had before Khoei had gone into exile.

April 11 was going to be a busy day. A city assembly had been organized to vote on whether Abu Hattar should continue in his role as mayor and police chief until elections could be organized. More than one hundred lawyers, teachers, tribal sheikhs, and other community leaders had been invited in an effort to convene the most representative collection of voices in the city. The commander of the 327 Brigade chaired the assembly, which was held at a hotel.

The soldiers of ODA 544 thought that Abu Hattar had accomplished a great deal in a short time. He had helped round up the key Saddam loyalists. He had put 200 policemen back on the streets to keep order and found cars for them. He also had persuaded city administrators to come back to work with the promise of future payment. There was a mounting murmur of opposition, however, from residents who said that Hattar was from outside Najaf and not one of them. Team members had pressed people for specific allegations of wrongdoing, but heard none; they surmised that the ire stemmed from those who had lost positions of favor or power.

The team had moved into Abu Hattar's temporary police headquarters, so it could monitor his daily activities. He looked like a valuable and trustworthy ally. The team had watched the proceedings to reconfirm him from the sidelines, but was happy when the debate concluded and the representatives unanimously ratified Abu Hattar as the interim mayor and police chief.

While the city assembly was convened, Khoei paid a visit to the grand mosque downtown. That morning, the captain and Rainey had asked him if he wanted an escort and he had declined, saying, "My people will protect me." The team was uneasy, but the captain acquiesced. For the past five days, ODA 544 had been reinforcing Khoei's own security but had stayed clear of religious sites to avoid inflaming Shi'ite sensitivities. As the captain and Rainey left the meeting at the hotel, they got the news: Khoei had been slain on the steps of the mosque. Not just killed, but hacked to death. Devastated, the soldiers rushed to the area. The atrocity shocked Najaf to the core and, as word spread, the streets filled with grieving, angry Iraqis.

The captain of the 544 felt personally responsible, because the team had not gone along to guard him. He berated himself bitterly. "If we'd been with him, he'd still be alive." He had no doubt as to the perpetrator, saying flatly, "Moqtada Sadr had him butchered."

In the days ahead, Sadr would claim that he fired the two bodyguards who'd slain Khoei prior to the murder, and that he had no control over them. The men of ODA 544, however, were convinced that the young firebrand had seen the returning cleric as a mortal rival. The loss of Khoei weighed heavily on the team. The captain thought that he should have listened to the team and overridden Khoei's own wishes. The men had taken very seriously their responsibility to protect Khoei, and feared that his loss significantly darkened the prospects for Iraq to find a peaceful moderate path into the future.

ODA 544 fully grasped the Clausewitzian maxim that war is politics by other means—and the converse. The team had handled tricky political situations involving Afghanistan's neighbors, but the ferment in Najaf was a major challenge. As the assassination had shown, the bloodshed was far from over. Weeks went by and the team had to be ready to turn on a dime from the fence-mending diplomacy to commando-style responses when violence flared. Rainey's team was skilled in raid, ambush, and strike tactics. Many of the team members had been to a shooting school favored by Special Forces, called the Mid-South Institute. Rainey had not but, even with a few of his fingers missing (the result of a long-ago accident), he was an excellent shot.

Rainey's reflexes were tested one day in May, when the team discovered an arms bazaar in full swing in a village north of Najaf called Kifl. As he stepped out of the Humvee, Rainey saw a man get down behind a low wall and raise an RPK machine gun at him and his gunner, Sgt. First Class Tim Kreier. At ten feet apart, one of them would certainly be killed. Rainey's gun came up and a bullet hit the Iraqi's head, killing him instantly. A dozen other Iraqis behind the wall began firing AK–47s. Rainey, the chief warrant officer, and the sergeants systematically shot them one after another. The team's ferocious response caused the crowd of about 200 armed men to scatter. It also bought the soldiers enough time to quickly search the arms dealer's car, take his record books, and make their exit.

From the bodies and blood trails, men estimated that they had killed six Iraqis and wounded four. No one was proud of killing: the team had been attacked and had fought back. But it was justly proud of the text-book execution of basic commando principles: shock, surprise, speed, and violence of action—the only way a small force can temporarily stun and prevail over a much larger one. The records proved to be a gold mine of information. The Iraqi had been selling weapons from Basra to Mosul, and his customers and sales were exhaustively documented. It was a stark reminder of how easy it was to get arms in Iraq, and of how long the fighting was likely to go on.

Conducting raids with an indigenous force is immeasurably more difficult, but the team worked frequently with Abu Hattar and his men. The "Bulldog" led from the front. In one raid, he planted himself in front of the door to the compound they were assaulting and stood his ground, prosthesis and all, as bullets rained around him. He leveled an RPG at the door and blew it down.

The most hair-raising battle that ODA 544 fought tested both its commando skills and its ability to deal with the vagaries of indigenous alliance. The fight occurred one week after the team had entered Najaf and forged its alliance with Bulldog and the Regulators. Early on April 7, the team received a tip that the second-highest Ba'ath Party official of Najaf province was hiding in a place called Abbas. The 101st was still fighting in Najaf, and no U.S. forces had yet been to this isolated town of 30,000 people that was located about twenty kilometers northeast of the city. The top party official had been killed in the bombing of Najaf, and the deputy was reportedly organizing the rearguard resistance effort.

Master Sgt. Rainey and half of ODA 544 drove to Abbas with twenty of Abu Hattar's men to capture the Ba'athist leader. Upon reaching the neighborhood, they directed some of the Iraqis to cordon off the block. The rest entered the walled compound from the front and back, led by

Rainey and the chief warrant officer. Rainey nearly collided with the suspect as he fled out the front door. The men quickly cuffed him and brought him out into the narrow street in front of the house. They had just put the Ba'athist official into the lead Humvee when gunfire erupted from a wall across the street, about fifteen meters away. Rainey spun around to see men's heads sticking over the wall and the muzzles of AK–47s peppering them with bullets. He immediately returned fire and ran over to Hattar's men, yelling and motioning for them to flank. Rainey wanted them to circle the house that held the shooters and then enter from the side. Instead, the flustered Iraqis ran off, thinking Rainey had called for them to evacuate. They left their truck behind, blocking the Special Forces' Humvees in the dead-end street. At the open end of the street, about twenty-five meters away, another set of Iraqis appeared behind a parapet on the rooftop of a house and began firing at the U.S. soldiers. In the middle, out in the open, in a very small area, were Steve Rainey and his split team. They were in what the military calls a kill box; in vernacular terms they were fish in a barrel.

The men were pinned down under a rain of withering fire. They knew that quick action was necessary to change this dismal equation. The chief warrant officer moved toward their closest assailants to reach the M240 machine gun mounted on the back of the Humvee. At the same time, Rainey audaciously stepped out from behind the Humvee into the middle of the street and, began firing on full automatic, at the Iraqis behind the wall and on the rooftop. These bold moves gained just enough breathing space for the weapons sergeant, Tim Kreier, to run to the Regulators' truck, jump in, and throw the vehicle into reverse. He backed down the street, shooting all the while, and careened around the corner, past the rooftop where the Iraqis were firing down on them, and out of the kill zone. Then Kreier ran back through the street to rejoin his teammates.

Rainey was still in the middle of the street. He had a better shot at both sets of attackers from there, but he was also making himself a bigger target. Keeping watch on both walls, Rainey carefully aimed each time a head popped up. The Iraqis' heads came up less often, and then they just poked their rifle barrels over the wall and sprayed bullets. The Humvees were riddled with holes, and one of the AT–4 anti-tank weapons strapped to the side of the roof took a direct hit on its warhead but fortunately did not explode.

Kreier jumped into the rear Humvee and the rest of the team loaded up. As the two Humvees backed out of the street Rainey followed behind on foot, still firing. Once they were out of the "kill box," Rainey hopped into the front passenger side of one of the Humvees and they took off. A few miles away, they rejoined a unit of the 101st and began organizing the Iraqi militiamen to go back and search the site. Rainey needled the Iraqis about their hasty retreat, saying, "You guys made like Fred Flintstone—all we saw was dust."

They returned less than an hour later but found no bodies, only a few blood trails, some of them leading to car tracks. The house that had held their attackers was still under construction and now sat vacant. Inside the house, on the roof, in the street, every single brass casing had been picked up. Rainey was astonished. His team had fired at least 200 rounds from the .50-caliber gun, eight or nine 40-mm grenade rounds, and several thousand .556 bullets from their M–4 automatic rifles, yet they found nary a shell in either house. The Iraqis did not want to leave any sign of a gunfight, apparently out of a fear of retaliation.

It was equally surprising that not one of the U.S. soldiers or their militia partners had been wounded in the extremely close-quarters battle. Some of it was pure luck—a bullet had passed through the sleeve of the chief's uniform and come out the back without even grazing his skin; the antitank missile did not explode when hit—but it was also the level of skill, gained over years of training, that explained how the Special Forces consistently won battles with few or no casualties. The accuracy and volume of the team's fire and its bold, unexpected actions had turned the tables on their attackers. Facing down the attackers while trapped in a cul-de-sac also required the team to summon an extra measure of bravery, but the men did not beat their chests about it. While they talked about the firefight among themselves, it was not until much later that their commander heard a blow-by-blow account. When he learned what they had done, he nominated the chief, Rainey, and Kreier for combat awards for their heroism under fire. Steve Rainey, his usual sardonic self, swore that it was the last near ambush he ever planned to be in.

Master Sgt. Alan Johnson and ODA 563 helped Rainey's team while they waited to head east to Diwaniya, which lay astride the main highway into Baghdad. Working the checkpoints gave ODA 563 a very clear picture of what kind of war it was going to be. The Iraqis came at them in pickups, buses, even ambulances and opened fire as they drew near. It was guerrilla warfare from the start. ODA 563 set out for Diwaniya once it made contact with some tribal sheikhs who were reportedly willing to help bring down the Iraqi forces in the area. The team didn't have a minute to lose, because the Marines were heading north.

ODA 563 met the five tribal sheikhs secretly in the countryside south of Diwaniya near Highway 8. The Marines were taking heavy mortar and artillery fire. Over the inevitable goat grab at one of the sheikh's compounds, the team learned that all of the tribal chiefs in the area had pledged their support. Each of the five sheikhs had a few dozen armed men. The Iraqis proposed capturing the nearby city of Qwam al Hamza first, because it was their home. This smaller target made sense to the team to test how effective its Iraqi partners would be. The Special Forces arranged for the Marines to drop a couple of bombs on the Fedayeen and Ba'ath party headquarters as the sheikhs and their men entered Qwam al Hamza.

At 2 A.M., the Marines sent their jets and F/A–18s to destroy the building. One of the Iraqis, Sheikh Bassoun, called Alan on the satellite phone they'd given him. "We've got it! The city is ours," he announced. ODA 563 entered Hamza from the west. The team drove past the wheat fields and ditches where Chris Conner had scouted and hidden for three long days and nights during Desert Storm twelve years earlier.

Alan used a loudspeaker to tell the assembled sheikhs and their men that they would move on to Diwaniya at first light. He asked if they wanted to send any of their armed men, knowing that they would not necessarily be volunteers. Iraq's tribal system was essentially feudal; the sheikhs were the equivalent of dukes or barons. With their inherited position came a certain number of clan members who were essentially serfs. A couple dozen men in dish-dashes, the long shirt dress of Iraqi men, came forward. Each had an AK–47 with one magazine of bullets. It remained to be seen whether they would actually fight. The Marine reconnaissance team that had been working with the ODA was eager to come along.

The next day the soldiers approached the bridge outside Diwaniya. Alan was prepared to roll right into the city. The Marines were nonplussed. "Are you just going to keep moving forward until you draw fire?" they asked him. "Yep," he said. "That's how we'll know where they are." The Special Forces had more latitude to decide when and how to act than the young Marines who followed along. The little band seized the bridgehead at daybreak and, almost immediately, mortar rounds began landing around the men. Their position was less perilous than it looked or sounded because the mortars had not been pre-registered to hit the bridge. Alan knew it would take the Iraqis a little while to adjust.

It was time to see what their allies, Iraqi guerrillas, could do, so they put red armbands on them and sent them off in the direction of the fire. Dissidents in the Iraqi army unit stationed in Diwaniya were waiting to rise up on cue. The team cross-checked its targeting data and called for the air strikes to begin. The bombers systematically began dropping bombs on all twenty-one targets the team had identified: the general's house, the tank yards, and multiple headquarters of army, militia, and the Ba'ath party. When they finished, Alan had the bombers strike at the same targets again, because the Iraqis would reoccupy targets in the belief that the U.S. forces would only hit the same spot once.

The team thought that the strikes had gone well, but it was not until the next day that the soldiers could see how well. Upon entering the city, they saw the general's house demolished but a power plant and another house next to it perfectly intact—current intelligence and precision munitions were an unbeatable combination for urban warfare. They had requested the smaller 500-pound JDAMs, laser-guided bombs, to minimize the collateral damage. In Desert Storm, only eight percent of the bombs were precision munitions, but Iraqi Freedom used more than 90 percent of such weaponry. As long as the right information was fed into the GPS device on the bombs, the objective would be achieved with the least amount of collateral damage ever. The pinpoint accuracy also had a devastating effect on the Iraqi army's will. It fled Diwaniya for Baghdad, chased by Marine pilots all the way. The team estimated that about 200 regime personnel had been killed in the city. Diwaniya had been taken by an ODA, a psyop team, a couple dozen Iraqis, a handful of Marines, and their friends in the sky.

The team moved into a medical school that had recently been closed. The doctor there warmly welcomed the men as a deterrent to looters. The doctor became a valuable ally as the team moved into the phase of putting Diwaniya back together again.

The real work for the ODA had just begun. The sheikhs' network informed it that the Ba'athists were forming an insurgency to fight for the city, and criminal gangs began robbing banks. The team began working in shifts, and the men slept only about five hours out of every thirty-six. One Humvee with four operators would be on guard duty at the base while another was out working in the city, and the third stood by as the quick-reaction force. The SF were trying to ferret out the resistance, get the city services restarted, and establish some governance. After one week, the team received help from the 82nd Airborne, which set up some checkpoints around the city. Ten days after that a Marine squad was assigned to guard their compound, so the team could concentrate on the work in the city.

Only one of the sheikhs and his band of fighters proved to be of much use in this phase. Sheikh Bassoun and his two dozen "redbands" took over guard duty of several banks. The sheikh was aggressive and was the only tribal chief who actually cared to lead his men personally. One day, several different bank robberies were reported, so Alan's crew pitched in to help. Driving around, they saw a man emerge from a hole in the wall with a bag in his hand. Like a flash, Doc Nittler was out of the Humvee and into the hole, with the communications sergeant right behind him. They hauled out a half-dozen Iraqis who had blown a hole in the wall and then tunneled into a next-door bank vault.

A few days later, Alan's team answered another call for help and, to reach its destination, turned down a street bordering a river. Alan did not like the street at all: the road dropped straight down to the canal and the buildings formed a solid wall to the right. Ahead, Alan saw sandbags laid out across the street—their vehicle would have to slow down to cross them—it was a perfect setup for an ambush. As they slowed, someone might pop up with a rocket-propelled grenade and take them all out. For the first time in his twenty-three years of military service, Master Sergeant Alan Johnson felt the chill of mortal fear. Then a machine gun started firing—they were in an ambush.

"Go, go, go!" he shouted to Nittler, who was driving. The medic knew what to do. He spun the Humvee around in the narrow street, backing the 10,000-pound beast into the quickest three-point turn he'd ever done, and then raced back to the bridge over the tributary. They zoomed over it and found Sheikh Bassoun's fighters, who were involved in a firefight of their own. Alan's crew joined in and helped finish it before returning to the compound. Alan would remember this as the first time in his long career that he had been afraid he might be killed. He had figured his way out of many life-threatening spots over the years, but he had to admit that he had finally felt the fear of death in that trap.

Sheikh Bassoun's role in helping ODA 563 in Diwaniya came to an abrupt end one day at a town meeting intended to select temporary authorities for the city. Bassoun, who was from Hamza, was being heckled by a crowd that had gathered outside the city hall where the meeting was under way. The mob grew unruly and began throwing large rocks at the sheikh's trucks. Perhaps fearing he would not make it out alive, the sheikh burst out of the meeting and fired into the crowd, killing an old man. The 82nd Airborne soldiers, who had been trying to keep the crowd back, pointed their guns at Bassoun and hogtied him. Alan came outside and saw that the enraged crowd needed to be calmed immediately.

Walking over to the sheikh, Alan said, "Look, we are going to have to arrest you and your men. We will cuff you and take you out of town. Then we will take you to Hamza. Okay?" The sheikh looked at him and nodded. He knew he'd be lucky to stay alive in the face of this mob. "You can stay in Hamza and help the Americans from there. Okay?" Alan continued. "Inshallah," the sheikh replied.

The cardinal rule of unconventional warfare was to be adaptable. Alan was exceptionally good at thinking on his feet, and it was clear that Sheikh Bassoun had become an untenable ally. What mattered was creating a functioning city, not promoting a particular leader. In the end, the doctor of the medical school that ODA 563 had made its base was chosen as the interim mayor.

Because it had become the Special Forces' compound, the medical school was referred to as "the embassy." People came day and night, seeking help. Women came to report rapes, men came to report adultery. One man informed on his brother, a former intelligence agent. Another man claimed to know where "nuclear grenades" were hidden. If ODA 563 was the embassy, Alan was its chief ambassador. His efficiency, lively personality, and fluent Arabic made him a favorite among the locals.

The whole team buzzed with energy. Sergeant Rich Davis set up a 600-man police force for all of the province. The engineer struck a deal with the city's wealthy residents who had generators to wire them into the electrical grid, and in return they received free fuel. The team scrounged for additional generators, and within two weeks 80 percent of the city had electricity for more hours of the day than they'd had under the old regime. Within three weeks, schools and hospitals were reopening, and one of Alan's buddies in the Civil Affairs unit outside Najaf trucked over medical supplies. It was the fastest return of city services to occur anywhere in Iraq.

At the same time, ODA 563 still had to maintain security, and the Ba'athists seemed determined to mount a serious insurgency against the U.S. soldiers and whoever supported them. These officials of the former regime stood to lose everything in a post-Saddam Iraq. The Special

Forces first had to identify and locate the Iraqis, and then seek to change their calculus. It was far more efficient to persuade them to abandon their fight than to try to capture or kill all of them.

Sometimes, however, the team had to do it the hard way. One day it learned that a top Ba'ath official whom it had believed had fled was still in Diwaniya. Alan, Robbie, and their vehicle crew set off for his house, a three-story mansion with marble floors, in a cul-de-sac in the city. The house was still immaculate—no looters had dared go near it.

Alan and his team had developed a method to deal with Iraq's ubiquitous walled compounds. They crouched on the roofs of their Humvees and, when they reached their destination, they simply jumped off over the wall and into the compound. It saved them the time and trouble of breaking down the door. After two sergeants leapt into the Ba'athist's yard to begin the search, Robbie saw an Iraqi cross the wall into a neighboring compound. Robbie "tagged" him with a shot. The man didn't stop, and the chase was on.

Robbie jumped over the adjoining wall while Alan went around through the entrance. The two men dashed in and out of several compounds, over rooftops, into neighbors' yards, until they lost the Iraqi's trail. Outside one home, Alan bent down and looked at a footprint in the dirt. Talking into the MBITR radio he asked, "Was he barefoot?" When the affirmative answer came back, Alan started to break down the door.

An Iraqi appeared in the street and said it was his house, assuring the two soldiers that no one was inside. "Open the door," said the team sergeant. "There is no one there," the man contended. The soldiers threatened the man with jail, and still he refused. Seconds ticked away.

Suddenly Alan noticed a tiny smudge on the wall and leaned closer—blood. He turned and grabbed the man's wrist and cranked it. The man went down on his knees. "He went in," cried the man. Alan yanked him up, and the man fumbled with the key to open the door.

Al and Robbie searched one room after another, guns at the ready. Nothing. Out back was a bathroom, a sort of outhouse, inside which they found a sink with fresh blood and a bloody rag. The Iraqi had obviously dressed his wound here.

Back-tracking through the house, they reached a bedroom with a large German closet, a wooden armoire big enough for a man to stand in.

"Check the doors," said Robbie.

"You got me?" Alan said.

"You know it," replied Robbie.

Just as Alan flung open the door, Robbie yelled: "Freeze!" Oh crap, thought Alan, and he spun around and saw Robbie's gun aimed under the bed. "Don't scare me like that!" Alan complained, as they hauled the Iraqi out from under the bed and put flex cuffs, plastic handcuffs that look like zip ties, around his wrists.

By the time they brought the Iraqi out of the house, a large crowd had gathered in the street. People began to beat themselves and scratch their faces, wailing and shouting. It was turning into a riot.

"Let's give him first aid," Alan suggested. Doc Nittler got out his kit and began to patch up the man, pulling out lots of bandages for extra effect. The crowd quieted down just enough for the team to load their charge into the back of the Humvee and take off.

One of their old 563 gang was missing, and Alan knew that if Randy Wurst had any idea of the time they were having up here in Diwaniya, he would eat his heart out. Alan also knew that the time was approaching for them to leave. The team had restarted and run an entire city almost single-handedly for more than a month. Now, the conventional forces were taking the baton, but the team had one last hurrah. A warehouse full of equipment to repair the region's electrical grid was being looted, so Alan grabbed two of his sergeants and two from a Civil Affairs team—Special Forces-qualified men. Twenty minutes after arriving at the warehouse the five men had it cleared of looters and under control. They radioed the 82nd Airborne to come and collect the detainees. When the soldiers arrived they looked at the forty-nine Iraqis sitting cuffed on the floor. The officer looked at Alan and asked the obvious question: "You five did this?"

Operation Iraqi Freedom gave thousands of conventional soldiers their first look at Special Forces in action. Even those who shared the same bases at home, as the 101st Airborne Division did with 5th Group, and the 82nd Airborne did with 7th, did not have any first-hand information about how the Special Forces operated in the field. The media images of men in beards or exotic garb did not really tell the story. This incident did. The Special Forces had the technical capability, the maturity, and the institutional autonomy to act on a moment's notice to solve problems that blew up around them.

ODA 563 in Diwaniya and ODA 544 in Najaf had orchestrated and guided the only two Iraqi uprisings in support of the coalition of the whole war. However lamentable Sheikh Bassoun's grand finale, he and the sheikhs of Hamza had risen up against Saddam and supported the United States. ODA 563 then rolled into a counter-insurgency mode to find and neutralize Iraqis plotting against U.S. forces, while simultaneously putting the city back on its feet with the help of willing allies.

In the Shi'ite capital of Najaf, ODA 544 had also performed an array of missions, from obtaining key intelligence and targeting data for the conventional forces, to grappling with deadly Shi'ite politics, to jumping into the breach with direct-action raids. The teams did what teams always do: ate pita with the politicos, went to goat grabs with the clans, and drank tea with the clerics—all to understand the complex local politics and devise solutions that all the factions could live with. As 5th Group commander Colonel John Mulholland had told them on the eve of going to war, they were "masters of chaos."

CHAPTER 12

NASIRIYA
Warriors, Spies, and Diplomats

> Therefore when I have won a victory I do not repeat
> my tactics but respond to circumstances in an infinite
> variety of ways.
>
> —SUN TZU

LIEUTENANT COLONEL Chris Conner had seen it coming. Messages were flying back and forth between the various military component commands and the Pentagon about fielding a group of Iraqis to fight alongside the U.S.-led coalition. Anything that involved indigenous forces would almost certainly land on the Special Forces' plate.

No one seemed quite clear, however, just who these Iraqis were and what they were supposed to do. All that was known was that several hundred Iraqi exiles and opponents of Hussein had been gathered in northern Iraq in the Kurdish autonomous zone. Some of the confusion stemmed from the fact that the United States was training a different group of Iraqis at a military base in Hungary for postwar stabilization missions—a kind of Civil Affairs unit for police and reconstruction tasks. It was called the Free Iraqi Forces (FIF), yet that name was also applied to the new Iraqi group.

Conner was asked to have his battalion assess the new group's potential utility. The idea was to get the group into war in some fashion to show that Iraqis were fighting to liberate their own country. The basic concept made sense. Indeed, the Special Forces' original plan had been to raise resistance forces throughout the south, until it became clear that the regime's grip remained too tight. Saddam Hussein's extensive internal intelligence network would almost certainly detect and quash any attempt at an uprising. The arrival of the U.S. military might make Iraqis more willing to take risks. Unconventional warfare, the business of sponsoring foreign fighters, was often marked by improvisation and intrigue, and this particular rendition would turn out to involve the competing agendas of top officials in the Pentagon, the CIA and the U.S. State Department, and ambitious exiled leaders.

Major Burns, Randy Wurst, and the rest of Charlie Company got the assignment. The fledgling Iraqi force was to be flown into Tallil airfield outside the southern city of Nasiriya. Burns sent one of his ODAs ahead to scout for a place near the airfield where they could set up a new camp. The team quickly packed its Humvees and the ten-foot-square trailers they towed and headed out of Basra and into one of the bleakest landscapes imaginable. The desert, littered with tanks, shells, and unidentifiable hunks of rusted metal, looked like the set of the movie *Road Warrior.* Southern Iraq bore the scars of nearly thirteen years of bombing.

The lead Humvee turned off the eerily deserted freeway into the desert, which was not sand, as in Kuwait, but dirt that was the consistency of talcum powder. The men pulled their kaffiyehs and neck gaiters over their noses as they were enveloped by clouds of silt. They halted at a pile of rubble that turned out to have been an air defense site, a few miles from the Tallil airfield. The cement roofs and walls of the main buildings were caved-in or heavily cracked from bombs, and iron bars jutted from the broken slabs at crazy angles. It was a scene of utter destruction—no windows, no power, no water. Nearby, a forlorn row of barracks stood; only the cement skeletons remained. Only one building in the entire complex was essentially intact, with an undamaged roof and a sliding metal door to shut out the dirt-filled wind. But, as the team quickly discovered, it was already occupied.

A prominent exiled politician named Ahmed Chalabi, who had arrived that morning with his retinue, claimed the building, and unfurled a carpet on the bare concrete floor. He had flown in on the same U.S. military transport plane that brought the 700 Iraqis that Charlie Company was supposed to assess from northern Iraq. The Special Forces had not been told that Chalabi was part of the package.

The leader of the Iraqi National Congress, Chalabi was the first exile figure to appear in Arab Iraq, obviously to position himself as a future leader of the country—even though the war was barely a week old. He had a U.S. military colonel as a liaison and they had managed to board a U.S. military plane, so the Special Forces soldiers had to assume that Chalabi's presence had been blessed by some senior official of the U.S. government.

The soldiers went about securing the area and setting up camp. Their location had, in effect, been chosen for them, as the Iraqis they were supposed to assess, and possibly train and lead, already were moving into the barracks. All that was left were the bombed-out air defense compound of three squat cement structures, which offered only the barest shelter from the elements. The inscription over the doorway was less than comforting: "the martyr is the most blessed one of all."

The media's attention had been riveted on Nasiriya since the first week of the war, because the heaviest fighting had broken out there and U.S. soldiers had been captured. Both the army and the Marines had run into resistance as they passed the city's outskirts. On March 23, the fourth day of the war, the tail end of the army convoy, the 507th Maintenance Company, had driven mistakenly into the city instead of continuing on the highway, and had been ambushed. Sixteen soldiers were dead, missing, or captured, and a dozen Marines had been killed so far.

Much of the drama in and around Nasiriya would remain a secret even as a full-blown media circus developed around the rescue of Private Jessica Lynch of the 507th Maintenance Company. The Special Forces had been in Nasiriya before anyone else, but their activities were unknown to the world. From the high-wire early infiltration of ODA 553, to its untold role in discovering the POWs' whereabouts, to the deployment of an Iraqi militia in record time, Nasiriya was a very busy place for Chris Conner's men.

Two days before the ground war began, ODA 553 flew in to conduct reconnaissance on the bridge outside Nasiriya that the army planned to cross. What the team did not count on, however, was its helicopter crashing. The air force special operations MH–53J Pave Low helicopter has the most sophisticated avionics and terrain-avoiding radar of any aircraft made. The chopper came in low and fast, and somehow the tail rotor clipped a rock outcropping and flipped the bird over.

Conner watched it happen live from Hangar 17 on video feed coming from a Predator unmanned aerial vehicle that hovered over the landing site in the desert west of Nasiriya. It was a sickening, helpless feeling to watch his men go down behind enemy lines in the dead of night. He immediately got up and walked down the hall to the operations center, where he alerted the battalion's quick-reaction force. The ops officer tried to make radio contact.

The helicopter and most everything in it was a total loss, and three men were injured. Luckily, the flight crew had not yet released straps holding the pickup truck to the chopper's floor. The intelligence sergeant of 553 sat in the truck bed, and the chief warrant officer, the team sergeant, and the medic were all squeezed into its cab. The chief was thrown hard against the truck's roof as the helicopter flipped. The soldier in back was thrown out of the truck, as gas and fuel spilled everywhere. Guns, ammunition, and packs and radios were soaked in the flammable mix. All of the men were bruised and cut, and they had to free one of the pilots from the wreckage. The intell sergeant had a concussion and back injury. The most seriously injured was the chief, who had herniated four disks. The two sergeants dug their guns out of the oozing jumble and stood guard while the chief radioed Conner. The chief said they were proceeding with the mission. The helicopter had to be destroyed to protect its classified technology.

When ODA 553 reached its observation site the men discovered that it was too far from everything they needed to see. As quickly as possible, the team had to answer three critical questions for the army: Was the bridge intact and usable by heavy vehicles? Had it been rigged for destruction by explosives or other means? Was it defended and, if so, how heavily? Moving in to conduct the surveillance, the team had a hair-raising fight with the Fedayeen, but it accomplished its mission. The team went to find the Marines and army units it would escort across the bridge and, after that, it began working undercover in Nasiriya.

At its bombed-out base outside Nasiriya, Charlie Company had only a matter of days to get the Free Iraqi Forces group up and running. Training, fielding, and leading foreign forces was the Special Forces' raison d'être, but their doctrine envisioned unconventional warfare as a seven-phase process taking months or even years. It was April 1, 2003, and the U.S. military was charging toward Baghdad. Time was short.

Each team member started on a different task. Randy and Killer scoured the supply channels to get the Free Iraqi Forces equipped with uniforms and guns, and tried to get a handle on just who these Iraqis were, vetting them for obvious undesirables. The ODAs plunged into assessing, organizing, and training the Iraqis. ODAs 565, 546, 543, and 542 each took on a group and formed a platoon with squads. As the commander, it fell to Maj. Burns to deal with the ever-present politics of the venture in the form of his camp neighbor Chalabi. After the frustrations of Basra, the major was eager for a new challenge. He had come prepared for their classic mission with a stack of books on insurgency, including texts on Che Guevara and Mao Zedong, because the Middle East did not have much guerrilla warfare literature.

Burns was no stranger to weird places and complicated politics. He had led an ODA in Les Cayes, Haiti, in the 1994 U.S. intervention to reinstate President Jean-Bertrand Aristide and restore some semblance of order in one of the planet's most chaotic, benighted countries. Its brew of poverty, violence, strongmen and paranoid politics, spurred by a long history of U.S. intervention, made for stiff odds. The Special Forces teams had lived in provincial towns and attempted to nurture democracy at the grassroots while U.S. forces had hunkered down in the capital. In the end, the U.S. government, opting for a speedy exit over protracted nation-building, declared victory and brought the troops home. This was a Middle Eastern version of the same basic ingredients: a population that had known neither lawful order nor self-rule, and a U.S. government that was divided against itself.

Chalabi's Pentagon backers were pitted against the State Department and the Central Intelligence Agency, which had their own favorite exiles. Burns was philosophical about the situation, saying, "You can never be sure what you're going to get." He had been given a group of Iraqis who wanted to help remove the regime, and his orders were to put them to work in the service of the U.S. goals of winning the war, finding the leadership figures being sought, and laying the groundwork for postwar security and stability. Jonathan Burns would navigate the complications as best he could.

Chalabi, dressed in business slacks, a blue shirt with silk tie, and a kaffiyeh knotted around his nearly bald head, paid Burns a visit. The Iraqi walked into the compound with a slow, regal gait, his head held high as he stepped through the craters and debris. Sweat trickled down his face. It was only April but already scorching hot. Part of Chalabi's retinue, his general, four bodyguards, and the U.S. colonel, came along. His daughter, an American, and his own traveling press corps and spokesman stayed behind.

Major Burns, a calm and soft-spoken man, listened politely as the INC leader said that the Iraqis must be deployed immediately, to show that the U.S. intervention had Iraqi support and would result in Iraqi rule. Burns agreed; that was certainly the plan as he understood it. It also became clear, however, that Chalabi regarded the Free Iraqi Forces as his personal army, a praetorian guard that was to do his bidding, and he intimated that the Special Forces should do the same. The fact that U.S. money was paying for raising of the FIF, or that Burns had his own chain of command, did not seem to cross Chalabi's mind.

Under the Iraq Liberation Act which Congress passed in 1998, the INC was receiving $340,000 a month to help unseat the regime and provide information to the United States. Chalabi's perception that he was in charge may have been encouraged by the access he enjoyed at the Pentagon. He had only to dial his Thuraya satellite phone to get its number-two official, Paul Wolfowitz, on the line, which he did nearly every day.

Randy watched the exile leader walk back across the compound. Chalabi made the hair on the back of Randy's neck stand up. His poor opinion of the man was formed when Randy saw how rudely Chalabi treated his subordinates. In Randy's book, a general—or any leader— was nothing without his troops, or followers, and should never forget that. He was glad that his job was handling the *jundies* (Arabic for soldiers) and not the politicians.

The *jundies* were a disparate lot: young and old, illiterate and educated, fit and infirm, Kurd and Arab—even some Syrian and Iranian nationals. Two military intelligence interrogators attached to Charlie Company took pictures and collected basic data on the recruits. Many of the Iraqis had lived in exile in Iran for years, and had apparently brought their friends along. But there were also intelligence reports that foreign militants were infiltrating Iraq. Chalabi complicated matters further, unbeknownst to Burns, by telling local sheikhs to send recruits to swell the force. Some of those who showed up at the unguarded, fly-infested camp were immediately denounced by the original group as spies. Some confirmed as Fedayeen militia were taken away to a detention center that had just been set up at Tallil, the only secure foothold, which eventually became the army's major logistics hub for southern Iraq.

On the second day, U.S. army trucks rolled into the camp and dumped pallets containing non-pork rations for Muslims, uniforms, boots, belts, T-shirts, and sundry supplies in front of Charlie Company's compound; another convoy parked eight Maersk containers in back.

Killer stepped out the broken rear window of the compound, walked over to the closest container, and yanked the lever to open the door. Out tumbled crates of rocket-propelled grenades, mortars and fuses, and boxes of ammunition, right onto his feet. Killer stared in disbelief at the unholy jumble of lethal material and then gingerly began stacking. It was a miracle that the whole thing had not exploded. The word had gone out that Charlie Company needed guns and ammo, so the materiel had been loaded—obviously in haste by non-experts—at an Iraqi base that had just been captured.

Randy helped Killer survey the remaining containers. There was enough weaponry to equip a division for heavy combat: mortars, mortar tubes, antiaircraft and antitank guns, sniper rifles, RPK and PKM machine guns, pistols, and AK–47 rifles, and enough ammunition to start another war. The SF only planned to give the Iraqis arms for light combat and policing—AK–47s and one light machine gun per squad—but now that they were sitting on an arsenal, it would have to be closely guarded. Randy was familiar with every item there, except for some suspicious-looking yellow plastic grenades filled with powder. As long as the fuses were kept separate, he hoped they were harmless. Gas masks and tin cans of unlabelled powder already had been found in their compound in a room labeled "bio-chemical room," so it was anybody's guess what was in there.

The ODAs spread out to different areas of the bombed-out base. The medics gave first aid classes while other sergeants taught the laws of land warfare, squad movement drills, and checkpoint and house search tactics. The men set up a crude firing range with tires and plastic bottles for targets. Many of the Iraqis were excellent marksmen, and the best were made machine gunners. One young man denied he had been a soldier but the ease with which he handled a weapon indicated that he'd been a fighter of some sort. Another wizened man claimed that he had been a general in the Iran-Iraq war. Most of the rank and file had no political affiliation, but each platoon had a leader assigned by Chalabi and an overall commander named Aras Karem Habib who were supporters of the Iraqi National Congress.

The platoon leaders thus had two sets of leaders, INC and their Special Forces captains. How much politics would interfere remained to be seen. It was time to roll out the FIF to see what it could do. Burns chose the city of Shatra, north of Nasiriya, because an Iraqi general nicknamed Chemical Ali (for his gassing of the Kurds in 1988) reportedly had a house there, and some of the FIF militiamen knew the terrain. The Marines had bombed a large air defense site that sat on the northern edge of the city, but the town itself had not yet been entered.

Charlie Company borrowed a few trucks from Tallil and loaded up the FIF. The Special Forces taped a fluorescent orange square onto their Humvee hoods, the symbol to the aircraft overhead that they belonged to the coalition, and interspersed themselves among the trucks of Iraqis. The soldiers hoped that the Marines they encountered along the way would see them first, not the Iraqis with AK–47s. The rules of engagement allowed soldiers to open fire on armed Iraqis immediately.

Conner flew in from Kuwait to observe the FIF's maiden operation. Burns ran the show from a command post on the outskirts while the ODAs and the *jundies* went into the city. Randy stood by with a quick-reaction force in case there was trouble. The FIF platoon leader, who knew the city, asked the town's elder sheikhs to come out, and explained the soldiers were going to tour the town and question some of the residents. The sheikhs were reluctant but, after a half-hour of discussion, they understood that they did not really have a choice. Two teams had set up checkpoints on either side of the city and had started questioning people as they passed. Two other teams drove in slowly, with most of the soldiers and all of the *jundies* on foot.

The city was a squalid place with open sewers in the streets. To Conner the thing that would always identify Iraq was its smell, the smell of burning. The smell of cooking fires, burning garbage, and sewage—the smell of the Third World, which certainly described southern Iraq. They visited the hospital and found it had no anesthesia, little oxygen, and few antibiotics. Some of the wounded patients accused the Marines of firing on civilian buildings, and denied that they had been firing back at the Marines with antiaircraft guns placed on the roofs.

Outside, the streets grew packed with cheering men and children, while women peeked over rooftops or waved from doorways. Rojas and his psyop truck told the crowd the purpose of the visit was peaceful, but the INC agenda crept in when the FIF platoon leader and his friends began exhorting residents to back Chalabi.

In practical terms, Shatra was a modest success. The SF did not find Chemical Ali, but ODA 543 learned that weapons were hidden in a school—and the next day the Special Forces found more than 200 Milan antitank missiles in two different schools. Considering that Charlie Company had inherited the FIF only four days before, the battalion-size operation was an amazing accomplishment. In Special Forces' history, no foreign militia ever had been organized, trained, equipped, and fielded in only four days.

The soldiers continued to work in Shatra. The Civil Affairs officers, Maj. Simon Gardner and Capt. Warren Foster, took a 2.5-ton truck full of medical supplies to the hospital, and the sheikh who had been most helpful was asked to join them. The donation served to bolster support for the United States and its allies, and enabled solicitation of further information.

Even though Civil Affairs could not win wars on its own, Gardner believed that no military operations could succeed without the Civil Affairs projects. Civil Affairs soldiers could gain and maintain access, legitimize their operations and partners, make the environment safer for soldiers, and provide detailed assessments for postwar aid and reconstruction. Policymakers had recognized how Civil Affairs could make a dramatic impact on local sentiment and had decided to double its ranks, but much of what Civil Affairs did had never been codified in any doctrinal manuals. So Gardner was using the operations in Afghanistan and Iraq to create a template for the roles that CA played during the Special Forces' seven-phase unconventional warfare.

Conner flew back to Kuwait and let Burns take his plan to the next stage. He had no desire to stay in that God-forsaken camp of theirs. In Basra, malarial mosquitoes had feasted on the men, but they were all taking their medicine. Here, no amount of repellent would stop whatever was biting them. The soldiers were being eaten alive by some kind of sand flea or fly; red welts and rashes were cropping up all over their bodies. Killer kept spraying insecticide, to no avail. The last thing they needed was a parasitic epidemic. At least they had folding cots so they could sleep off the ground.

The staff had made a few improvements since moving in—digging a latrine and, later, erecting a three-stalled plywood outhouse over it. A waist-high plywood shower stall also was built, with a pole for hanging a shower bag. Occasionally, the men washed clothes in a bucket, although they were blown full of dirt within minutes afterward. Each morning, Randy fired up his camp stove and battered coffee pot to heat water for coffee. When no one could bear the sight of another MRE, Rosco Evans drove over to Tallil to pick up hot T-rations.

Burns' plan was to send the ODAs with their platoons of *jundies* out to cities in southern Iraq. The Marines' manpower was stretched thin, as most of their ranks and the army's had headed on to Baghdad. "King" Chalabi, however, had other ideas—he wanted the FIF to escort him into the capital. Burns's pale face reddened, and his noncommittal smile froze into an uneasy grimace; he was not about to buy off on Chalabi's agenda. Burns did not believe the purpose was to supply the INC with a private militia, to enhance his standing vis-à-vis other Kurdish and Shi'a would-be leaders who had their own armed bands. Once severed from the Special Forces' tether, there was no telling what mischief the FIF might create.

Burns repeated that his orders from Conner and the army command were to use the FIF to man checkpoints and run patrols to augment the thin U.S. ranks here in the south, to gather information, and to put an Iraqi face on the urban operations. Burns had no official orders yet for what would come next, but one working assumption was that the FIF might form part of a reconstituted Iraqi army. Someone would have to take over the job when the U.S. forces left, and the sooner they started building some security structure the better off they'd be. A patchwork of politicized militias would surely take Iraq down the wrong path.

Chalabi was livid. He marched back to his building and rang up Wolfowitz. His press aide called reporters, who within hours were milling around the camp. Burns radioed his chain of command to report the latest turn of events. The army command in Kuwait would have to determine exactly what the intentions of their civilian bosses were.

In the end, Chalabi got one platoon of the FIF to escort his convoy to Baghdad, and Burns sent ODA 565 along to look after them. He considered it a success, under the circumstances. As the men packed to go, a big sand—dirt—storm blew in and the sky grew dark. The *jundies* began ransacking the place for everything they could carry off, and Randy worried that the arms containers would be next. He donned his sniper uniform, mask, goggles, and gloves, then grabbed an SPR rifle and went out hunting. He looked scary enough that none of the FIF dared approach the compound.

At the same time, Burns sent the other ODAs and their FIF platoons to other cities. ODA 543 left for Hilla, after an overnight mission to a town called Nasir. Aside from narrowly escaping obliteration by Marines surprised to see a band of armed Iraqis, that outing had gone well. The tough-talking team sergeant, Chief Warrant Officer Tony Goble, and Captain Matt Erlacher had sensed something fishy the minute they rolled into the town. The army had fled, the Ba'ath Party headquarters had been ransacked, but a tribe had barricaded itself in the police station. It had been forcibly collecting arms, money, and cars from residents ever since being installed by a liaison agent working with U.S. intelligence. The team quickly sent the tribe packing—after letting them sweat, tied up, for a night. The next morning Goble told them: "Go back home and don't return, and nothing bad will happen to you."

Goble and the team sergeant had more than thirty years of military experience between them. They worked well together—the team sergeant was a feisty ball of fire, and Goble was a steely, terse man. He was nicknamed Lil Tony because he was only five foot nine, but he was a hard-core scuba man and combat dive instructor. His wife Lisa called him "secret squirrel" because he never talked about missions, especially those in the crisis response unit where he served for years. Few operators discussed even the unclassified parts of their work at home; the

Goble home was typical in that talk revolved around family, the three children they each brought into their marriage and their new addition on the way.

When the team reached Hilla it quickly found a civilized solution to living quarters at the Babylon Tourist hotel, rehiring its old staff and fixing its generator. The team started gathering information and patrolling with the FIF to stop the looting that had begun across Iraq. Because Saddam Hussein and his henchmen had gone underground, Central Command issued a deck of fifty-five cards naming the most-wanted figures of the regime.

Receiving a tip, Goble and his men went to search a hamlet outside the city and met resistance from the sheikh there. The team considered a surprise midnight raid, as it had done in Nasir, but opted instead to show the sheikh the deck and explain that rewards were being offered. The next day, the sheikh's men approached Goble, saying that they had one of the wanted men and demanding $200,000 to hand him over. Goble said that they had to deliver the suspect to get the money. They returned with Number Nine, the former deputy prime minister—and the first man on the deck of cards to be apprehended. Because the payment process had not yet been determined, Goble wrote up a certificate and presented it to the Iraqis. He was especially pleased with that little innovation; one Number Nine, free of charge. A month later, ODA 573 nabbed the head of the Special Republican Guard. By year's end the Special Forces would be credited with helping to find more than half of the Iraqis depicted in the "deck of cards."

In early April, Master Sgt. Tom Rosenbarger and ODA 542's 158-man FIF went to Kut, a major city east of Baghdad near the Iranian border. A ferment of Islamic fundamentalism was bubbling up throughout the south as the lid of the repressive regime came off. Iranians were flooding in as well as Iranian-based Iraqi exiles, including the Badr Brigade. That group had taken over Kut's city hall and staged demonstrations denouncing the United States and calling for an Islamic state. The Marines had moved north to Kut to try to pacify the roiling city.

Rosenbarger gathered his sergeants for a little talk: ditch the baseball caps, look sharp, ride herd on the FIF, and don't give the Marines any cause to complain. The ultimate "team daddy," Rosenbarger ran his team like a benevolent patriarch. The name and his blond hair might not come from the Sicilian side of his family, but his ability to control people and defend turf did. The Louisville native oozed southern charm but was as territorial as a rottweiler. He'd flash his white-toothed smile and tell his sergeants how it was going to be with the same decisiveness that he had picked out his bride as soon as he laid eyes on her in high school. A fourteen-year veteran of the Special Forces, Rosenbarger was in his element, having wangled a second stint as team sergeant. It was the best time he'd had since his first ODA in Panama.

When ODA 542 reported to the Marines at Kut airbase, outside the city, the Marines were not happy in the least to see the FIF Iraqis with AK–47s. Another Marine contingent was ensconced downtown by the Tigris River, next door to an ODA, but the two Marine colonels did not talk to each other. Rosenbarger let the captain navigate the politics and kept his men busy. The airbase around them was littered with arms caches that were stacked with bombs. The team set up its mortar tubes and shot off round after round to dispose of them, and by day the men wired and destroyed the caches.

The chemistry on 542 worked because Rosenbarger delegated authority to his rock-solid senior sergeants and left the chief to advise the young captain. He encouraged his sergeants to exercise initiative, but if they got out of line, the iron fist would come out of the velvet glove. The two senior men were the engineer, Del Magana, who was teased as the old man, and a somber intelligence sergeant who rarely cracked a smile. They were the perfect ballast for the rambunctious younger sergeants, including two men fresh out of the Q course. After its long Afghanistan deployment, the team could recite the entire dialogue of movies like *Joe Dirt,* which the men would do to entertain themselves on long drives. Like every ODA, it had its own personality and resembled a family as much as a military unit.

The next day, upon learning of a disturbance at city hall, ODA 542 led its FIF platoon into town unarmed to see what it could find out. The

Iraqis could mingle unnoticed in the demonstration and find out whether the crowd was paid, organized, or merely curious. Conversely, the Marines' response to the city hall takeover was to buzz it with Cobra attack helicopters, which only incited the mob to more furious demonstrations. The Marines quartered downtown in a hotel on the banks of the Tigris were taking RPG and machine gun fire most nights, so they began probing and buzzing the factory across the bridge. The Marines regarded the Special Forces' practices of mingling with the population as risky. Their concerns about force protection were heightened by their experience in Nasiriya, and in their view the best defense was a good offense.

The Marines relented and allowed the team to move to the edge of town. It found an abandoned complex next to the hospital, with a mural painted in its entrance that said, "Jerusalem Jihad Academy." The place had been gutted and burned, so there were only shards of documents to determine whether it had indeed been a school for suicide bombers. The 158 FIF soldiers, led by a fat man named Ali and a thin man named Abbas, moved in next door.

Relations with the Marines turned around a few days later. Armed Iraqis took over the hospital next to the jihad academy and began a gun battle that spilled out into the street. ODA 542 and the FIF responded immediately. The FIF leader Ali, a former colonel in the Iraqi army, took his men to the rooftop where they could fire on the gunmen. Rosenbarger took the junior engineer and senior medic to the front of the hospital and dug into positions for what turned out to be a three-hour firefight. When the Marines arrived and saw they had the situation well in hand, they decided to see what else this odd combination of Iraqi militia and Green Berets could do.

The team divided into three cells and launched into action. Each cell took a different job: security, city administration, or unexploded ordnance. The next day the intelligence sergeant set up fourteen checkpoints to begin collecting information and weapons, using the FIF members as manpower and translators. They also ran patrols to the Iranian border to see who was coming across. Another cell led by the chief and the engineer worked on putting the city back in business. It restarted the propane factory, shut down a black market in fuel, set up a first aid station, resupplied the hospital, and reopened the bank.

Rosenbarger, originally a demolitions engineer, led the ordnance disposal work. Each day they blew up a dozen or more caches of 500 pounds of munitions. Ridding Iraq of its vast quantities of arms would take years, but each detonation meant fewer weapons that could be used to destabilize the country. The ordnance disposal units were completely overwhelmed and there were not enough troops to guard all the vast depots that had been discovered. The amount of weaponry located around Kut alone was mind boggling. Day after day they carefully wired cases of RPGs, mortars, and other ordnance with detonation cord and charges constructed out of C–4 wrapped around a mortar. The charges would be strung together and then positioned to blow the lethal material down into the ground rather than up into the air. Some Marines had been killed shooting off the lethal RPGs at the airbase.

For nearly a month, ODA 542 labored to secure Kut and gather detailed information on the Iranian influx and Shi'ite agitation. In early May, Maj. Burns told ODA 542 to return to Tallil with its men. The team had been ordered to demobilize the FIF—a decision that was the product of many factors.

The FIF platoon that had gone to Baghdad with Chalabi had run amok and joined in looting and pillaging, along with much of the population. The two FIF platoon leaders were shot and killed. Chalabi had moved into a palace and seized a large stash of government documents that would certainly prove useful both in hunting down regime opponents and as political currency. These factors were all that Chalabi's opponents at the State Department and CIA needed to be able to regain the upper hand and check his ambitions.

Demobilization is the seventh and most difficult phase of unconventional warfare. Armed men never want to give up their weapons. Some of the *jundies* cried; they were now unemployed and without protection. Rosenbarger's platoon was angry, but he quickly quashed the incipient rebellion. He didn't even lose his big white smile as he brought out the

Sicilian hammer. "You all need to settle down right now, or those Marines will take care of you," he said in his Kentucky drawl. The threat worked immediately; the *jundies* had had enough close encounters with Marines.

ODA 542 thought it had accomplished a great deal with the FIF platoon. There were some bad apples, but compared to the Afghan militia that the SF had trained for three weeks to serve as a blocking force in Operation Anaconda, the FIF was more proficient militarily and no less disciplined or trustworthy. The rule of thumb in unconventional warfare, as Maj. Burns had said at the outset, was to do the best one could with the cards that were dealt. Burns had done so, and when the short-lived FIF came to an end he did not complain. He even laughed at the news accounts and a caricature that depicted the FIF as the Keystone Kops.

The balance sheet on the FIF was mixed, and its ties to Chalabi were problematic as far as being an impartial security force and possible component of a future Iraqi army. But the militia had provided Arabic speakers and much-needed manpower. Something, for better or worse, was needed to replace the men, and soon. At some point the Iraqis would have to take over their own country. Introducing Iraqis into the equation early would help diminish the perception of the U.S.-led coalition as an occupying force. Already, in western Iraq, Gavrilis and 1st Battalion had turned the Iraqi soldiers who forswore allegiance to Hussein into guards.

To the men on the front lines, it was obvious that anarchy would soon prevail if nothing was done to stop it. But two fateful decisions were made by U.S. policymakers: Iraqi army salaries would no longer be paid, and a "de-Ba'athification" campaign would bar former administrators from reassuming their jobs. These decisions in effect dissolved the army and civil service. If the old institutions were not going to be reformed and used, as had occurred in Panama and other postwar scenarios, then new ones would have to be built from the ground up. This would take years, and in the interim U.S. troops would have to shoulder the burden.

★

The FIF had not been Charlie Company's only job. Other teams scattered from Amara to Samawa had to be overseen, resupplied, and coordinated. Every day Randy combined the teams' intelligence reports and sent a fused portrait of southern Iraq's threats, problems, and progress to Conner and the other special operations and conventional commanders. In rare quiet moments, usually at the end of the day, Randy retreated to his Humvee for some solitude and a respite from the dirt and wind. He chewed on his antelope jerky and made notes in his diary.

Killer and Randy also spent a lot of time mentoring the unusually young company staff. A few of the sergeants were experienced, like his former 563 teammate Mark Reynolds, who had helped the conventional soldiers through the deadly barrage in Operation Anaconda, but several operators were brand new and one was a "snowball"—a seriously below-par operator. This snowball was lazy, forgetful, and arrogant. Randy and Killer rode him hard, but he seemed impervious to the notion that he was not making the grade. No one wanted him on their team; his attitude and poor judgment could get someone killed. One senior sergeant invited him outside for an ass-kicking within a half-hour of meeting him.

The snowball frequently talked about the fact that he'd shot a man in Basra, which had been his first kill. He reviewed every detail of the scene, as if making a movie in his mind. Most of the men exchanged stories, sometimes making light of the firefights as a way to dispel the horror of killing, and then purged them from their minds, or attempted to. The prevailing attitude was that you do what you have to do, and then put it behind you. The snowball seemed to revel in his deed, believing it had somehow enhanced his stature. There were several possible futures for this sergeant, who had been a reservist. His immaturity would surely be reflected in his evaluation. He could apply for further schooling which might shape him up; he could be kept on a staff on a short leash; or he would be forced out. Despite the extensive selection and training process, some people made it through who fell short or simply were not suited to the Special Forces.

Just down the road in Nasiriya, ODA 553 had burrowed into the city since the end of its prewar reconnaissance mission. The chief's neck, injured in the crash, needed medical attention, but he refused to leave until the team's job was done. The men of 553 had studied Nasiriya as exhaustively as Swift's men had studied Basra and Johnson's men Diwaniya and Rainey's Najaf. With their Iraqi partners they located arms and fighters and called in AC–130 air strikes. They discovered that a nearby city was pumping new fighters into Nasiriya via the marshes. In Nasiriya, the regime made a stand to test whether inflicting heavy losses on the U.S. forces would cause them to quail. The capture of the 507th Maintenance Company had dealt a psychological if not strategic blow, and all the publicity had increased the propaganda impact.

The Marines initially had looked askance at the ODA 553 soldiers, who were dressed as Arabs and ran around in their civilian pickups with very little protection. Once the Marines saw the precise intelligence and accurate picture that 553 had of what was going on in the city, however, they welcomed the strange unit into their midst. The team moved into their compound in the city and worked with them for a month. The chief and team sergeant felt protective toward the young Marines, most of whom were younger than their own children, and who mostly were tied down in guard duty without much sense of the environment beyond the checkpoint where they were posted. One Marine platoon lived for weeks in a mud hole next to the main bridge running through the city. In contrast, the Special Forces knew the landmarks, infrastructure, geography, and tribal demographics—the chief knew its streets better than Clarksville back at Fort Campbell. The team could even tell the Marines which streets had cement dividers that would impede U-turns during their operations.

As the Fedayeen went underground, the ODA 553's intelligence network followed them. The network also won the team a certain notoriety. One day, an Iraqi approached the compound, saying that he'd been sent by a mutual acquaintance. He told the team that the blond American soldier was in the local hospital. This was the first accurate intelligence about the location of Private Jessica Lynch that U.S. forces had received.

The team's contact was one of two sources who came forward, and his information proved to be the most reliable and useful. The second, less accurate source, a lawyer named Mohammed Odeh Rehaeif, became the focus of media attention. Much of his story was later discredited, but not before he was given "humanitarian parole" to take his family to live in the United States and signed a six-figure book contract. The team had no desire to attract any publicity and never sought to correct the record. But the truth was, it was the team's informant who was equipped with and trained to use a concealed video camera, and then sent back to the hospital to tape the entrances and a route to the POW's room. He was paid for his services but remained in Iraq.

When the entire Lynch affair—the concocted story about her effort at self-defense, the noble lawyer, and the filmed rescue—was whipped into an overblown propaganda spectacle with the eager assistance of the media, ODA 553 became even keener to let sleeping dogs lie. The rescue itself was a successful mission, but the media criticized it as having been hyped—and the media itself was the primary engine of the hype. The Lynch story dominated the media coverage for weeks on end, even though it represented little about the war, and much of the story fed to the public was actually untrue.

The Special Forces' role in locating the POWs extended beyond providing the key—and unheralded—informant who produced the most detailed information about Lynch's whereabouts. Because ODA 553 knew Nasiriya and the forces there better than anyone on the scene, it identified the command and control structures that had to be eliminated before going in to rescue Lynch. Charlie Company had been compiling all of 553's reports and adding its own intelligence, including that of the signals intelligence unit attached to it, so it was the fullest intelligence picture developed for the operation. The Special Forces also analyzed the information and conducted ongoing patrols to deduce likely locations of the other POWs.

Nine of the other POWs' bodies were discovered at the hospital where Lynch was rescued on April 1 in a special operations raid that included Navy SEALs, Rangers, and air force pilots. The rescue party was criticized for entering the hospital prepared for hostile resistance, but it was prudent standard practice. Had the raiders been mowed down in an ambush, there would have been far more serious consequences and outcry. As it was, the armed Iraqis had fled and the doctors were only too happy to turn over the badly injured and frightened patient and to lead them to the corpses of the other soldiers. Charlie Company and other troops scoured the area around Nasiriya for the other POWs, and finally on April 13 the five soldiers were released.

One man still was missing. In the unending waves of publicity and fiction spinning around Private Lynch, this casualty went almost entirely unnoticed, but not by the missing man's mother and not by Major Jonathan Burns. Specialist Edward John Anguiano was presumed dead, although his remains had not been recovered. His mother Juanita believed he was still alive.

Burns made it his personal mission to find this soldier and return him to his family. Charlie Company got one of the detainees at the Tallil detention camp released to its custody. Burns believed they could persuade him to talk, and they had a strong suspicion that he knew what had happened to Anguiano. They told the man that they could guarantee his release if he would help find the missing soldier, who was presumed to have died in the initial firefight. The Iraqi insisted he knew nothing. They decided to release him anyway, thinking that he might spread the word and churn up some new leads. They left him at a roadblock in town. He did not walk toward his home but instead in the opposite direction. The next day, a young boy approached the same checkpoint and told the Marines he knew where the last American was buried. He took them to the spot where the man had gone the night before.

Anguiano's remains were found on April 24 and confirmed with DNA testing. His mother learned on Easter Sunday that her twenty-four-year-old son was dead. Like ODA 553, Burns had no interest in receiving credit for the discovery; he was extremely reluctant to acknowledge his role. But he felt sorry for the family, which had waited without word while the fate of one soldier was treated as somehow hugely important and their son's as not. The family's pain would be increased by the lack of information Burns could provide about the young soldier's death, even with dogged effort. No one knew why Anguiano had not been found along with the other bodies. No one knew what had happened in his final minutes. His grandfather had thought he would be far from the front lines. It was only the barest form of closure that the family was offered, his remains packaged and sent home. It may be that Burns felt this more acutely because he was await- ing his own homecoming with great longing. His first child, a daughter, had been born while he was at war. He had not even seen photos yet. But his longing was joyous, not the sorrowful vigil of the bereaved mother in Texas, whose wait had just come to an end.

CHAPTER 13

VIKING HAMMER (AND THE UGLY BABY)

Although everyone can see the outward aspects, none
understands the way in which I have created victory.

—SUN TZU

WHEN CHARLIE CLEVELAND left home, on January 17, 2003, he
told his wife that he would be gone for ten days. He did not
return until May 22. After twenty-four years of marriage to a Special
Forces soldier, his wife was not entirely surprised; she had been through
it before. Most Special Forces wives soon learn, if they don't know going
in, that they must hold down the fort at home, often for months at a
time. A SF wife may not know where her husband is going, what he is
doing, or when he will return. The limit for overseas deployment was
supposed to be 183 days a year, but after the September 11 attacks all bets
were off.

Colonel Cleveland flew from Fort Carson, Colorado, to Germany to
attend Internal Look, the generals' table-top exercise of the Iraq war
plan. It assumed that the forces destined to fight in northern Iraq,
including the 10th Special Forces Group which Cleveland commanded,
would deploy through neighboring Turkey. But Turkey, despite being a

close U.S. ally and opponent of Saddam, had not yet agreed to allow its territory to be used to invade a fellow Muslim country. Its greatest fear was that the Kurds in northern Iraq would rise up and declare statehood, and ignite Turkey's own restive Kurdish population. U.S. officials were convinced that their ally would bend if enough aid was offered and pressure applied. But as Cleveland and other officers shuttled to and from Turkey for closed-door meetings with its generals and special forces, he saw how high sensitivities were running in the country's unsettled electoral climate.

If Turkey did not budge, then the entire conventional plan for the north would collapse. There was no other way to get heavy armored forces into northern Iraq. If conventional forces could not make it in, then the Special Forces would have to handle the theater on their own. Few people believed that it was even possible for a Special Forces task force to do the job of some 60,000 U.S. troops—the size of the entire 4th Infantry Division that was slated for the north. The colonel, a curious blend of personal modesty and intellectual boldness, might blush at the drop of a hat, but he never doubted that he could find a way to do it—just as he had as a young captain when entrusted with planning the Special Forces' missions in Panama.

Cleveland's first task was to figure out how to get his troops into Iraq. He drew a circle around Iraq that represented the range of the U.S. MC–130 Combat Talon planes; somewhere within that circle he needed a staging base.

By February, Cleveland had moved to Constanta, Romania, and set up the joint special operations task force. His staff chose the name Task Force Viking to reflect 10th Group's European roots. As the clock ticked down toward war, the 4th Infantry Division and its state-of-the-art digitized tanks bobbed offshore in the Mediterranean, waiting for a vote in the Turkish parliament. Policymakers in Washington were still banking on a yes vote. But even if approval finally came, Cleveland knew the poor condition of the road that spanned the length of Turkey, and that the tanks and armored vehicles could not traverse it in time.

In the end, the parliament voted no. Even permission for troops to

overfly Turkey—something Cleveland had believed would be granted—
began to look doubtful. Every day for five days, the men piled into their
planes in Romania, only to be told that Turkey still had not granted
overflight rights. Cleveland had managed by various stratagems to infiltrate an advance force into northern Iraq, but he had to get the main
body there, and soon.

The task force staff cobbled together a circuitous route that would
take two days and two intermediate stops in countries that requested
that their roles remain secret. When the new flight plan was posted at
the operations center in Romania, one of Cleveland's noncommissioned
officers commented: "Damn, that's an ugly baby." The name stuck.

When the ground war in the south kicked off a day early, Cleveland
could wait no longer to implement Operation Ugly Baby. He collected
280 operators and some other task force members and they boarded six
Combat Talons for the long and cumbersome flight around Turkey. On
the final leg of the flight, they entered Iraqi airspace, which was still
guarded by one of the densest air defense networks in the world. The
Iraqi regime loosed every antiaircraft battery in its arsenal upon them.
The Combat Talon pilots, flying with nods and no running lights,
bobbed, weaved, and banked; threw out chaff; and activated electronic
countermeasures, all in a desperate bid to avoid ground fire. The men in
the hold were tossed around like rag dolls. Up they went, then down—
their packs crashing down on them. A few men who had not fastened
their nylon harnesses to the floor were thrown clear out of their webbed
seats.

Despite the pilots' acrobatics, three of the planes were hit, one of
them so badly that it could not go on. Fuel streamed down its fuselage,
the windshield was shattered, and bullets had punctured one engine.
The pilots had no choice but to request permission to make an emergency landing in Turkey. Turkey relented and allowed the plane to land.
The other planes continued on their flight path to Bashur airfield in
northern Iraq, just outside Irbil. They had completed the longest infiltration by Combat Talons into enemy territory in special operations history: fifteen hours total flight time, four and a half at low level over Iraq.

The next day, March 23, Turkey granted overflight rights, and the rest of the task force flew directly from Romania into northern Iraq.

Cleveland had succeeded in getting his men into Iraq, but that was only the first hurdle. His 5,200-man task force had to take on thirteen divisions of the Iraqi army—more than 100,000 soldiers—along a 350-kilometer front. The Special Forces had never before attempted anything like this by themselves. It was a testament to both CENTCOM commander Gen. Tommy Franks' willingness to entrust missions to special operations forces, and the fact that the general was pretty much out of options. The 4th Infantry Division had turned around in the Mediterranean and was steaming toward Kuwait, but it would be weeks before the unit landed, unloaded, and drove into Iraq.

At a minimum, Cleveland's task force had to pin down the Iraqi forces in the northern half of the country to prevent them from attacking the U.S. forces to the south or going to Baghdad's defense. If possible, the task force would overrun and destroy the Iraqi forces and secure the country's third- and fourth-largest cities—Mosul and Kirkuk—and its second-largest oilfields. The thirteen divisions included two Republican Guard divisions, two mechanized divisions, one armored division, eight infantry divisions, plus the Fedayeen Saddam militia. On the face of it, the odds were ludicrous—but Cleveland was undaunted. The task force would aim to seize every inch of territory that it could. His staff came up with a plucky motto for Task Force Viking: Concede Nothing.

Cleveland had no tanks or armored divisions of his own, and air support would be limited. The bulk of the bombers would be aiding the ground assault moving from Kuwait toward Baghdad and the Scud hunters in the west. Because Turkey had opted out, no fighter jets would be available from the bases there. The task force did include special operations airmen and a few of their fearsome AC–130 Spectre gunships, as well as intelligence, signals, and support staff. For the fight on the ground, Cleveland had three Special Forces battalions—about fifty ODAs—and the valiant but lightly armed Kurdish militias. It would be the mother of all unconventional warfare campaigns.

The task force was small for the job but large for a colonel. A general would normally command a force of the size that the sandy-haired colonel was leading. In another historic first, a Special Forces colonel was given tactical control of conventional brigades—a precedent that would surely reverberate through the halls of the infantry schools. In Vietnam, Special Forces had occasionally taken command of smaller battalion-size elements of regular army troops. Cleveland would direct the 173rd Airborne Brigade and the 26th Marine Expeditionary Unit and the two colonels who commanded them once they all arrived in the country. Those units were to help secure the oilfields, Kirkuk, and Mosul. Cleveland jokingly called Task Force Viking a "kluge," which sent his staff members scrambling for a dictionary. The third one they consulted defined it as a cobbled-together collection of unrelated objects, but the staff still wasn't sure if it was a good thing or a bad thing.

Cleveland divided the territory and put each half under the command of his two subordinates, 10th Group's 2nd and 3rd battalion commanders, Lt. Col. Bob Waltemeyer and Lt. Col. Ken Tovo. The battalion and company commanders would need maximum autonomy and agility in this dispersed battlefield, and, in any case, it was Cleveland's style to give subordinates room to operate. He was a West Point grad and the son of an NCO, and he knew the value of both perspectives. Moreover, he trusted these two men implicitly.

An outsider probably would not realize how close the three were, given the Special Forces' penchant for understatement and reticence. Cleveland was particularly low key, except when it came to the Red Sox. Waltemeyer was volatile, quick and sharp, and stood out in a crowd with his smooth-shaven head. Tovo, with his Italian dark-eyed and dark-haired looks, could pass for a Kurd at a distance after he grew a mustache.

"I like to think they know what makes me tick," Cleveland said. Since 1997, the two men had served as his company commanders, his executive officer, and under him in the Balkans. There, Tovo had learned how to interpret the tone of Cleveland's voice and even his silences. In wartime, such intuition can make all the difference when communications are long-distance, via written sitreps (situation reports) or nighttime radio calls.

The meteoric, incisive Waltemeyer and silken-mannered Tovo were considered two of the brightest lights in the SF community. Tovo and Waltemeyer had met as lieutenants, gone through the Q course together seventeen years earlier, and served in 10th Group's forward-based battalion in Germany. Their children were playmates and their families celebrated holidays together. The two men argued like brothers and stuck together like brothers.

Tovo's task was to capture the southern half of the sector centered on oil-rich Kirkuk with the help of the militia of the Patriotic Union of Kurdistan (PUK), while Waltemeyer was to capture the northern half around Mosul to the Turkish border with the Kurdish Democratic Party (KDP) militia. The Iraqi divisions were arrayed around those cities and along the "green line," a diagonal north-south line through northeastern Iraq that marked the boundary of the autonomous Kurdish region. Task Force Viking would attack from the Kurdish zone using any ruses, feints, deception, and night movements that could turn their weaknesses into advantages.

While preparing at Fort Carson, Waltemeyer's men had calculated how many tanks and artillery pieces each ODA would have to destroy with the limited munitions they could carry. The ratios alarmed them, so Waltemeyer had them focus instead on variables they could control. He led them on a twenty-six-mile road march followed by a three-day combat skills test near Pike's Peak, and those who performed best won the choice assignments in the war.

At the behest of his sergeant major, Waltemeyer had returned to Fort Carson from Central Asia, where he had been leading a training program to help Georgia deal with the Chechen rebels who had infiltrated the Pankisi Gorge. His own inclination had been for him to just show up in Iraq and improvise—which was what they would have to do, anyway.

"Not every situation has to be mastered with technology," Waltemeyer advised the men in his battalion. A solid understanding of the people, terrain, and the politics was the best preparation for adaptation. He told them of his earlier 1991 tour in Iraq when he was a young captain leading an ODA in Operation Provide Comfort. The operation was launched to help the Kurds after Saddam Hussein destroyed 400,000 homes and the people had fled freezing into the mountains. Waltemeyer's team had searched long and hard for the Kurdish refugee camp it was assigned to find, finally locating it wedged high in the 14,000-foot mountains, to escape both Iraqi and Turkish forces. The tribal leader had come forward and asked, "What message do you bring us from Haji Bush?" The twenty-something Special Forces captain had acted as the senior diplomat in that wilderness, enunciating U.S. policy and defusing his piece of a tense international standoff.

However daunting the military challenge facing the Special Forces in northern Iraq, the outcome once again hinged on how well they managed the politics. Juggling the myriad competing interests would require major feats of *realpolitik*. The Kurd-Turk-Iraqi triangle contained some of the most heated and strongly held antipathies on earth. The Special Forces would have to lead the Kurds against the Iraqi army while restraining their secessionist impulses, because any move toward Kurdish independence would prompt Turkey to invade northern Iraq.

The area bordering Iran also included a stew of obscure and sinister factions. One of them, a relatively new Islamic extremist group called Ansar al-Islam, was believed to be allied with Al Qaeda. It was occasionally supported by two other fundamentalist Kurdish splinter factions. Additionally, the Badr Corps, an armed band of fundamentalist Iraqi exiles, had infiltrated from Iran, and a group of armed Iranian exiles called the Mujahedeen e Khalq had moved into the region. To anticipate, parry, and neutralize all these factions would take the skills of a Bismarck. Tovo and Waltemeyer, the yin-yang battalion commanders, each sought to rise to the challenge in his own distinctive way.

Time was the critical commodity needed to build a relationship with the Kurdish militias, assess their capabilities, and prepare for combat with them. An advance party of Special Forces had arrived several weeks before the main body of the task force, and a few before that. For their mission, Tovo and his men adopted the native dress of the *shamag* scarves and the ballooning brown pants that were the uniform of the Kurdish *pesh merga* fighters. The soldiers grew mustaches, which afforded them both respect and cover, as facial hair is a sign of manhood in this part of the world: the *pesh merga*, much as the *mujahedeen* in Afghanistan, or the *jundies* of the Arab world, are less inclined to respect the advice or follow the orders of clean-shaven men. Because the Special Forces' early presence was clandestine, they needed to blend in and look as much like Kurds as possible; looking like locals made it less likely that they would be singled out and targeted by their antagonists.

Waltemeyer opted for a different approach in his northern sector. It would not help him deal with the Turkish problem if his men looked like Kurds, so he kept them in army uniforms and regulation hair cuts. He also wanted to make them seem as big, American, and intimidating as possible to the Iraqi divisions. And he wanted to inspire the *pesh merga* to a higher standard of discipline by showing them what the expectations for U.S. soldiers were. "We're the army of the greatest power in the world. This is how we do things," was his way of thinking.

Waltemeyer's first stop was the headquarters of the Kurdish Democratic Party in Salahuddin, and Tovo's was the smaller Patriotic Union of Kurdistan in Sulaimaniya, near the Iranian border. Waltemeyer thought of his "Haji Bush" story as he wound his way up the mountains in a howling snowstorm to the palatial quarters of Masoud Barzani, the KDP leader he would be working with. By way of greeting, Waltemeyer told Barzani he knew of his famous battle at a certain mountain pass and named the camps where he had worked in Provide Comfort.

The next morning Waltemeyer noticed that the Kurds had changed into their brown battle dress, sash, and belt with pistol and knife. They had taken their cue from his combat uniform. The Kurds had been left high and dry in the mid-1990s after the CIA encouraged an uprising and then the United States failed to back them up, but this time, they had decided, the Americans had come to fight.

Waltemeyer told Barzani the ground rules that he had been given. Turkey must not be provoked into coming into the war. To forestall that, the Kurdish forces could not enter Iraq's main cities without his authorization. The first priority was to push Iraqi forces back from the positions where they could lob chemical weapons into Kurdish cities. Despite having been read the riot act, Barzani massed forces and prepared to attack Turkish troops that had come into the border region on the eve of the assault on the Green Line. The Special Forces lieutenant colonel told him that their alliance was in jeopardy. "I will put my men between you and the Turkish forces," he said, forcing the Kurd to back down.

In addition to navigating political shoals, the Special Forces had to solve numerous logistical problems, and transportation was one of the most serious. The operators were forced to borrow or buy whatever vehicles they could from the Kurds. The fleet of white quad-cab Defender pickup trucks they had bought were sitting in Turkey, locked in a warehouse. The few vehicles available were mostly smuggled from Baghdad. The sports utility vehicle that Tovo procured was in such bad shape that one of its wheels fell completely off one day. The entire mission was an exercise in improvisation, as Waltemeyer had predicted, and the soldiers had to solve the problems themselves as no one else was around to help.

The SF devised a system to command and control the Kurdish fighters, so that the units would not mistakenly shoot at each other or wander off to pursue their irredentist designs. To guard against friendly fire accidents, they also needed to be able to identify themselves to whatever aircraft they would have. The ODAs broke down into split teams and paired up with 150 to 1,500 Kurdish militia. Each split team had a radio, and every operator knew how to talk to the pilots. The Special Forces could not predict how many of the estimated 65,000 Kurdish fighters would actually show up to fight. The militias' informality was such that a call would go out and then young and old would arrive, each carrying an AK–47 and a couple magazines of ammunition. They would pile into whatever cars, trucks, or buses were available and head to the front. The Special Forces decided to plan on about half of the "pesh" coming to fight.

The soldiers of 10th Group were as well equipped to grasp the complexities of this human battlefield as anyone in the U.S. military and perhaps the entire government. Many of its senior NCOs had served in northern Iraq during the Kurdish refugee crisis after Desert Storm. Officers like Tovo, who had spent virtually all of his seventeen years in the Special Forces in 10th Group, had a great depth of understanding of the region. They had been prepared to return, just as 5th Group's veterans had been prepared for a sequel to Desert Storm. The wars in the Balkans in the intervening years had greatly added to their experience in managing ethnic tensions, sectarian violence, and shattered communities.

Lieutenant Colonel Tovo was ordered to attack and destroy Ansar al-Islam (AI) before the main assault on the thirteen Iraqi divisions behind the Green Line. The secret mission began with surveillance of the shadowy group, which had at least 700 armed fighters. It controlled about 300 square kilometers called the Halabja salient, a finger of land poking eastward into Iran from Halabja, the city where Hussein had previously bombed the Kurds with mustard gas, sarin, and other chemical weapons.

Information about Ansar al-Islam was still sketchy, but it had been formed sometime around September 2001 with the help of a Palestinian Jordanian named Abu Musab al-Zarqawi. Zarqawi was a somewhat autonomous Al Qaeda associate who received funding from the group, had a network of operatives around Europe, and reportedly had attempted to develop or procure chemical and radiological weapons. Shortly before the war intelligence had indicated that Ansar al-Islam might be harboring senior Al Qaeda members and possibly a chemical weapons facility. The White House decided that the stronghold must be attacked at the outset of the war.

For Tovo, as battlefield commander, the tactical reasons to remove the Ansar al-Islam threat were just as compelling. His Kurdish allies were frequently attacked by the group, and flatly refused to divert their fighters from the AI front to the Green Line until it was neutralized. Tovo needed every body he could to supplement his meager forces. Furthermore, Ansar had already unleashed suicide bombers, and Tovo did not want them creeping up behind them in the middle of the battle on the Green Line.

One of Tovo's teams, ODA 081, was chosen to conduct reconnaissance on the group from an outpost at Gurdy Drozna, on the edge of the Ansar territory. The first time Tovo visited the collection of crude stone bunkers, a greeting from the Ansar militants—a hail of mortars—fell around him as he stood on one of the bunker's roofs. Many of the AI forts sat on bare mountaintops, which afforded them a commanding view of Gurdy Drozna, Halabja, and the surrounding valleys but also made them an easy mark for air strikes. ODA 081 pinpointed these and other entrenched fighting positions and relayed the coordinates of the targets. The Kurdish commanders told the Special Forces that Ansar fighters had also occupied mosques and schools in the region's villages and were using them as bunkers and command posts. The Kurds urged that these be included in the target list, but the Americans refused. They could not add such targets without provocation and without positively identifying military use of such buildings.

At midnight on March 21, waves of Tomahawk missiles were launched from aircraft carriers in the Persian Gulf and flew through the darkness across the length of Iraq toward the targets that ODA 081 had identified. The soldiers stood on the rooftop of the Gurdy Drozna bunker and listened to the strange buzzing of the cruise missiles as they passed a few hundred feet over their heads. A few moments later, the men saw flashes of light and then heard explosions as the missiles slammed into the nearby mountaintops. They were awed by the precise and lethal display of American technology. But the sixty-four missiles arrived in intervals over three hours, and the soldiers watched as Ansar fighters fled in droves by truck. The opening salvo was war by remote control; the next stage would be up close and personal.

Tovo's original plan had been to attack right after the air strikes, but most of his men and equipment were still sitting on the runway in Romania. He was forced to wait until they had the minimum manpower and weaponry to launch the assault. In the coming days, the advance party called in air strikes on Ansar positions and fortified the post at

Gurdy Drozna, by adding sandbags and a tin roof. It was still basically a heap of stones, with enough room for a few men to crawl inside and sleep.

At the Kurdish general headquarters in Halabja, they built a five-by-ten-foot terrain map out of sand that showed the plan of attack. Six color-coded prongs snaked eastward along different ridgelines or valleys. Each prong represented a mixed unit of Special Forces and Kurdish fighters. In the center, the yellow prong marked the main effort, which would attack the heart of Ansar territory and capture the village of Sargat, the AI headquarters. Pink paper cards marked key objectives including Sargat. The green prong, the main supporting effort, ran along the ridge just north of the yellow prong's route. Two prongs, the red and blue, would fight Ansar elements to the south as well as one Kurdish splinter group. One would also drive toward the border town of Biyara. To the north, the orange and black prongs would aim at the other Kurdish splinter group and also cut off Ansar's escape routes there.

Finally Tovo decided they were ready; it was the hardest decision he had to make in the war. Waiting longer would only favor the enemy. They would launch at dawn on March 28. The six available teams had reshuffled missions and divided the weapons they had. The call went out for the *pesh merga* to assemble at several staging areas on the frontlines. The top PUK political leader, Jalal Talabani, had last-minute qualms on March 27. The lieutenant colonel left Halabja and drove two hours to Dukan to see Mam ("Uncle") Jalal. "We're as ready as we're going to be," Tovo advised the Kurd. Then he turned around and drove back to the command post for the final mission brief.

Talabani informed Tovo that the Kurdish splinter group in the north had sent word that it would not fight, having suffered about 100 dead in the March 21 cruise missile strikes. It turned out that the splinter group in the south did not fight either. The four prongs, red, blue, orange, and black, proceeded on the planned routes nonetheless, to attack Ansar outposts and cut off escaping fighters. Tovo and his Charlie Company commander, Major George Thiebes, would monitor the battle from Gurdy Drozna. From there they could watch the initial assault of the main effort, the yellow prong, through binoculars as far as the town of Gulp. After that, the valley turned north and was obscured by mountains. The officers would then be dependent on radio to follow the progress of the yellow prong and the fate of Operation Viking Hammer.

At 1 A.M. on March 28 the captain of ODA 081 lay down on the floor at the Halabja general headquarters to sleep for a couple of hours. He shut his eyes, but they immediately flew open, and he got up again to make sure he had put his radio battery into the charger. Still the captain could not sleep. It had been a memorable night. Lieutenant Colonel Tovo, the company commander, the Kurdish general Kak Mustafa, his lieutenants, and the soldiers had huddled around a big table for a final discussion of the next day's plans. The excitement was palpable. It reminded the captain of a photo Tovo had given them of their OSS forebears, the Jedburghs, and the French resistance gathered in a smoky room on the eve of battle.

In a few hours, the captain would lead his team and several hundred Kurds into the Sargat valley. Until two days ago, he had no idea they would be assigned to carry out the main assault on the yellow prong. The original plan had been for them to conduct the reconnaissance and then move to a southern portion of the Green Line. When the other teams were delayed in arriving, however, ODA 081 was a logical candidate because the men were thoroughly familiar with the Ansar territory. Surprised and pleased, they scrambled to get ready. Three of their sergeants would accompany the ODA on the green prong, and the other six members of 081 would lead the main effort on yellow. They studied their maps and gave the two towns on the yellow prong that they were to capture, Gulp and Sargat, code names beginning with a "Y" for yellow prong: Yahtzee and York.

As he lay in the dark near his teammates, the captain visualized the dirt road to Sargat. It winds through a valley that steadily narrows into a gorge full of caves amid the snowy mountains. From there it was a short dash across the border. What would he and his team find?

From the very first days of surveillance, it had been clear to ODA 081 that it was up against skilled fighters. The Ansar militants had fired mortars at the men whenever they moved. The team had quickly learned to follow the example of its Kurdish allies and scurry from the vehicles into the buildings. Ansar al-Islam was also very well equipped. The accurate aim indicated that the mortar tubes were new and that the AI knew how to use them. They would fire twenty or thirty mortars at a time and were frequently resupplied. The Special Forces did not know how many Ansar fighters remained after the air strikes of the previous week, but they doubted that the group would give up easily. Judging by the fortified positions that the militants had built all over the area, this was not a passing foothold but a place where they intended to stay.

The captain's nervous excitement was understandable; Operation Viking Hammer would be followed closely at high levels of the government, all the way to the White House. It was the captain's first battle. He had just graduated from the Q course, but he was no kid. He was a twenty-nine-year-old college graduate with a degree in chemical engineering which, to his mother's regret, he was not using. The captain had won the confidence of his sergeants simply by respecting their skill and experience. The teams that function most smoothly minimize distinctions of rank in favor of each man pulling his own weight. The captain trusted the men to do their jobs while he did his. His primary responsibility was to advise and assist Sheikh Jafr and the band of Kurds that would provide the mass in the fight. The Kurds liked the friendly and unpretentious American captain, and the PUK leader's son, Baffel Talabani, insisted on coming along as his interpreter.

The firepower would come from the team itself. The captain had no doubt that his team sergeant, who would direct the tactical movements of the other four sergeants, knew what he was doing. The thirty-six-year-old master sergeant was experienced, aggressive, and outspoken, with thirteen years in the Special Forces and seventeen in the military. He'd fought in Desert Storm and Afghanistan, and had served in the special mission units that undertake secret assignments on counterterrorism missions. He had started out in 7th Group under Kevin Higgins, who noticed his talents as a fighter, a self-starter, and a sergeant who had the confidence to deal with embassies and senior foreign officials. The team sergeant's looks also came in handy for this assignment; half Panamanian, he grew a mustache and looked just like a Kurd.

Arriving at 10th Group in the summer of 2002, he was surprised at the youthfulness of the sergeants of ODA 081. He teased them, calling them "the PlayStation 2 generation," and worked them hard, but the sergeants realized that he would be their best friend against great odds in combat. They nicknamed him Grit. The sergeants were young but not inexperienced. Both weapons sergeants were excellent snipers and had brought home combat medals from Kosovo. One medic had been a Ranger, and two sergeants had done long-range reconnaissance in the conventional army, which was good preparation for surveilling the Halabja salient. The men were cross-trained so they could trade off on their heavier weapons—the M2 .50 caliber and M240 machine guns and Mk 19 grenade launcher.

The men roused themselves and strapped on their packs. At 4:30 A.M. they departed Halabja. The commanders drove to the command post at Gurdy Drozna and the ODAs went to their respective staging areas. The Kurdish field marshal, Kak Mustafa, joined Tovo on the bunker's roof to watch the mustering of troops on the plain below them. Tovo, with his olive-toned skin and dazzling smile, might have been Mustafa's tall brother. It was a clear, crisp morning, about forty degrees Fahrenheit. The two men swathed in their *shamags* breathed out frosty air. The flat plain rolled eastward and then abruptly creased into valleys and peaks. The highest line of snow-capped mountains about twelve kilometers away marked the border with Iran. Unlike the sun-baked west and south, northern Iraq was verdant and rugged, with many places for the enemy to hide.

There was something old-fashioned about the sight of Kurds and U.S. soldiers girding for battle in the waning dark. This would be an infantry battle, fought by men on foot, with few high-tech tools and none of the heavy armor that had come to define modern war. It would not even resemble a guerrilla battle because the Kurds attacked frontally, at a run, en masse. Attempts to teach them new tactics like time-phased attacks had not prospered; they had fought this way for generations. The Kurds were lightly armed and wore no helmets or body armor. Many wore tennis shoes, the better to run. Each man had 150 to 200 bullets for his AK–47. The few heavier weapons were a mishmash of Russian machine guns and captured Iraqi artillery.

The U.S. soldiers respected their partners' martial spirit. Young and old, they were fearless fighters who did not quail under fire. *Pesh merga* means "he who faces death." If a man was wounded, he was expected to get back to the rear by himself to seek first aid. The U.S. soldiers manning the first-aid station in the town below the Gurdy Drozna command post were amazed by the first Kurd who arrived later that day. They could not tell what was wrong with him at first—he had been shot in the chest and had walked all the way from the front.

The Special Forces soldiers were much better armed. Each had his M4 automatic rifle and hundreds of rounds of ammunition. Each team or split team also carried 60-mm mortars, a sniper rifle, an M240 light machine gun, an Mk 19 automatic grenade launcher, and an M2 .50-caliber machine gun. They had a pickup truck for the heavier weapons and one for the Kurdish commander.

The starting point for ODA 081 was a crossroads called Dekon. The captain joined the Kurd's senior field commander, Sheikh Jafr, a silver-haired man in his fifties with a bristling mustache. As the light filtered over the snowy mountains hundreds of *pesh merga* arrived in dump trucks, buses, and taxis. Most of them wore the traditional Kurdish baggy tan pants and distinctively tied headscarves, and a few had camouflage jackets or pants. They wore no helmets, so the U.S. troops also did not, to better blend in.

The yellow prong could not launch until the green prong had secured the high ground on the north ridge overlooking the Sargat valley. At 6 A.M., the green prong began its assault, first preparing the way with mortar and artillery fire and then proceeding up the mountain. The hidden Ansar fighting positions and heavy guns still lodged in the mountain crevices would cause havoc for the yellow prong, whose entire route led through the exposed valley floor. The only cover they would have would be what the green prong could provide.

At 7:30 A.M., the yellow prong left Dekon. More than a thousand Kurds walked, rode, and trotted over the open plain toward the Sargat valley. Once they reached Gulp, their first objective, about three hundred Kurds and ODA 091 would split off to enter a valley to the south and then push east to the border. The six soldiers of ODA 081 and about 700 Kurds would continue into the heart of Ansar territory to Sargat. They moved quickly at first, heading east and then south on the road from Dekon. The force was vulnerable to both land mines and mortars on the open road, but it met no resistance.

When the yellow prong reached the valley leading to Sargat, the band turned east onto the dirt road that entered it. The Kurds in front, about 500 meters ahead of the ODA, came under fire from the southern peaks and the advance stalled. Sheik Jafr asked the captain to call in an air strike. He said his men were pinned down and could not go on unless someone took out the guns that were firing on them. Two Navy F/A–18s answered the call and dropped two 500-pound laser-guided munitions (JDAMs). Then the jets wheeled around and strafed the positions.

A cheer went up through the *pesh merga* ranks. Their spirits raised, they charged into the valley at a run—they felt invulnerable. The front half of the force moved forward, while the back half waited for the jammed-up line to uncoil. Suddenly a heavy 12.7-mm DShK machine gun high in the hills opened fire on the men at the rear. The F/A–18s had gone. The team sergeant, "Grit," went to the pickup and lifted the Mk 19 automatic grenade launcher out of the truck bed. He ran with the 70-pound weapon about 200 meters up the hill, under fire, to a position where he could aim back at the DShk. Grit knew it was vital not to lose the momentum that the air strikes had provided. One of the medics grabbed the tripod, the ammunition carriage, and the heavy can of linked 40-mm grenades and followed as fast as he could. They began shooting back. The Kurds assaulted the hill and the weapons sergeant shot at the Ansar gunmen with his sniper rifle. Soon, they had routed their attackers and continued up the valley.

About two kilometers farther, as the soldiers closed in on the town of Gulp, they came under fire again. The team sergeant and the other medic hauled out the Mk 19 and returned fire while the rest of the force assaulted the town. They captured Gulp at 9 A.M.—hours earlier than the captain had expected. The Kurds ran through the streets and searched the rubble left by the previous week's bombing. The mosque was untouched, but, as the Kurds had claimed, it contained sandbagged fighting positions and a command post. The soldiers also found a suicide vest rigged with explosives and a gas mask. During the previous year, many residents had left as the fundamentalist group had imposed draconian Islamic practices and the fighting had escalated. After a brief rest, ODA 091 and several hundred *pesh merga* split off south to head up the adjacent valley. The split team of ODA 081—the captain, the team sergeant, two medics, one weapons sergeant, and one communications sergeant—continued with Sheikh Jafr's Kurds toward Sargat.

The Kurds wanted to charge ahead at a run, but the captain insisted that they clear the road for the vehicles bearing their heavy weapons. They made good time for the next two kilometers, but then started taking fire from two entrenched positions in the mountains on their right. The team brought out its Mk 19 and the M240, and the Kurds followed with their heavy DShK and PKM machine guns. When the Ansar firing subsided, the force continued on again. The team sergeant and a medic stayed behind with the Mk 19 to cover the advance. After shooting about 250 rounds, Grit decided that they should catch up with the rest of the team. He was not surprised that they had to fight their way up the valley and suppress the Ansar positions in the mountains one by one, but he had no idea what was in store next.

Just outside Sargat, the valley widened into a bowl. As Grit and the medic entered it, they came under intense machine-gun fire from the surrounding mountains. The bulk of Ansar fighters had dug in around Sargat to mount its defense. Grit looked around for cover, but the land was as open as a golf course. To the right was a broad field divided by rows of low rock walls barely three feet high. The two men saw their teammates crouched behind the walls farther ahead and dashed for the

Operation Viking Hammer:
Yellow Prong Battle against Ansar al Islam

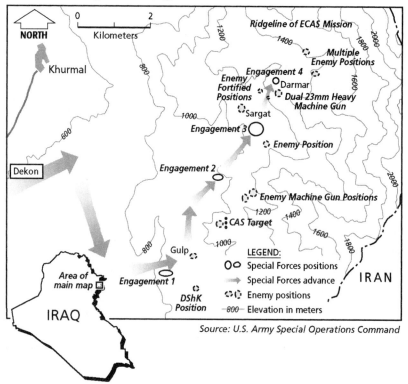

Source: U.S. Army Special Operations Command

nearest one. The soldiers were pinned down. The hidden fighters began lobbing mortars as well, which soon started to land uncomfortably close. The militants knew what they were doing: pin down the prey with machine guns, bracket it with mortars, then adjust fire for the kill. The lethal area for mortars is a 100-meter radius. The team sergeant watched the mortars land closer, no more than twenty-five meters away—they could not survive this for long.

Grit and the twenty-eight-year-old staff sergeant were huddled face to face behind the rock wall. They looked at each other and burst out laughing. It was a death-defying reaction, and the first step toward mobilization.

"Hey man, we gotta go," the team sergeant told him. Grit had been in plenty of fixes before, but this was as hairy as anything he'd seen. He knew they had to move before the next barrage. On the count of three, they dashed to the next wall and hurled themselves behind it. They looked back and saw the next mortar rounds hit the exact spot they had just fled.

The relief was only temporary. The Ansar fighters immediately began adjusting their aim, and within minutes the mortars were kicking up clods of dirt and grass all over them.

"Get the map out," Grit told the medic. "We've got to land some mortars of our own on them." He raised his head to see where the captain was, and a high-velocity bullet immediately cracked above him. He stuck his head up again and spotted the source, a machine gun firing from the mountain on the opposite side of Sargat. "Johnny Cab," he called over the MBITR radio, using the captain's call sign. "We need mortars."

The captain told him the bad news. The Kurds' artillery was behind them in the pickup. He suggested trying to raise green prong on the radio. Grit tried, but it was too far away.

The captain had somehow wound up at the front of the yellow prong assault. He and about forty Kurds had entered the bowl first and drawn a hellish rain of Katusha rockets, RPGs, mortars, and machine guns. The Kurds' DShK, the only heavy gun in front, had jammed, so the captain had run back down the open road to urge the Kurds to bring up their own Katusha artillery. Then he ran back to his rock wall where the Kurdish leader's son, Baffel Talabani, and one of his sergeants waited.

Baffel, a British-raised Kurd about the captain's age, was so impressed by the incredible firefight that he called his cousin, who was part of the green prong, on his Thuraya satellite phone. "We are really in the shit," Baffel told him excitedly. The captain looked at him, wanting to laugh and box his ears at the same time. They had work to do. He needed Baffel to make sure that artillery was brought forward, and fast.

In the middle of the chaos, the company commander radioed from Gurdy Drozna. "Sir, I'll have to call you back," the captain told him. "We're a little busy here right now." At that moment, a DShK let loose with a long burst. The men back at Gurdy Drozna heard the cacophony of fire over the radio and knew the team was in trouble.

Crouching behind the wall the captain noticed grimly that the field they were in was a graveyard. They debated calling for air support. The captain realized he had left his map at the wall behind them, where the other two sergeants lay, so he jumped up again and ran back to get it. The weapons sergeant was lying behind the wall, trying to spot targets with his M21 sniper rifle. He stared, agog, at the captain, who was blithely running back and forth amid the withering fire.

"Geez, captain, I would have brought you the map," he said.

The captain returned to his wall and radioed the team sergeant. They agreed that it was too risky to call in air strikes. Their Kurdish fighters had spread out all over the bowl, and many of them were scaling the back of the mountains to attack the dug-in Ansar positions. Any bombs would surely hit their own men. Besides, the radio was only working intermittently in the deep valley.

The captain knew that they had to mount some kind of counterattack to change the dynamics. Ansar al-Islam had the high ground and the initiative. The group might attempt to overrun them or just play it safe and pick them off one by one.

The captain decided that they had no option but to fight their way through. It would be an infantry battle from start to finish. The weapons sergeant moved forward to the captain's wall to hear the plan. He was to run 200 meters back down the road to their weapons truck, get the M2 .50-caliber gun, and head into the hills.

The weapons sergeant, the communications sergeant, and one of the medics carried the gun and ammunition cans up the mountain to where they could aim into the Ansar al-Islam positions. It was up to them to turn the tide of the battle. The weapons sergeant fired more than 700 rounds as his two teammates spotted targets for him. The Kurds' artillery finally arrived from the rear, and began blasting the Ansar redoubts. The team's second weapons sergeant, who was on the green prong, also came to their aid. From his position on a ridge a kilometer away, he killed several Ansar machine gunners with his sniper rifle.

These combined efforts paid off after three hours of steady fighting. Ansar al-Islam had fought like demons to hold Sargat, but the survivors among them finally withdrew into the caves and mountains beyond.

The captain had asked the Kurds to leave the search of Sargat to the Americans. It was essential to preserve all the evidence. At the outskirts of the town stood the remains of the complex suspected to be the chemical weapons facility. The buildings had been bombed in the previous week's air strikes, but the fence and fortifications around the complex were still intact. Access obviously had been restricted, even though Ansar members were Sargat's only inhabitants. The next day, a sensitive site exploitation team would be brought in to search it. Beside the complex stood brick houses, the nicest in town, where the senior leaders of Ansar al-Islam lived.

The first order of business was to treat the wounded; the medics of 081 set to work on the worst casualties first. One *pesh merga* fighter had an eviscerated stomach wound; another Kurd had been shot twice, once in the jaw and once in the thigh; others had shrapnel wounds. The most seriously wounded were evacuated in one of the trucks.

The captain surveyed the scene. A *pesh merga* truck had just arrived from the rear, carrying a hot lunch of goat kebabs. Sheikh Jafr waved the captain over to partake. It struck him as utterly surreal: the Kurds had not been able to get their artillery to the frontline in less than an hour during a life-or-death battle, but a hot catered meal had shown up right at lunchtime, at I P.M. He shook his head.

It was little short of miraculous that the combined force had not suffered more casualties. The men had been sitting ducks for the shooters as they came through that valley, yet no U.S. soldiers had been wounded. The captain, who had discovered that his back plate was missing from his armored vest, was especially grateful. The moral of the story, he guessed, was to never turn tail.

The Kurds brought the one prisoner they'd captured down from the mountains and handed him over to the Americans. The man did not want to be taken alive, and kept repeating over and over, "God is great, God is great." The papers in his pocket identified him as a Palestinian.

The soldiers and their Kurdish allies ate and rested briefly in the shelter of a cliff at Sargat's edge, and then they set off again to pursue those who were fleeing toward the border. Some Kurds were assigned to stay behind to collect the dead and wounded from the mountains around Sargat. The town itself was deserted; the houses would be searched for evidence later.

The Kurds took the low road into the gorge behind the town while the ODA climbed into the high ground of the mountain pass. The gorge abruptly narrowed into sheer and rocky walls that were honeycombed with dozens of caves. This place, called Diramar, was supposedly off limits to all but senior Ansar members, and Arabs were rumored to stay in these caves. Intelligence sources had said that a radio transmitter was located higher up in the mountain pass. The soldiers now were within shouting distance of Iran.

A hail of gunfire erupted from the caves as the Kurds approached. The *pesh merga* returned fire, and Grit shot high-explosive grenades from his M203 into the caves, but the holed-up militants continued to fire. Grit then unsuccessfully tried to smoke them out with tear-gas grenades. It was time for something bigger. He pulled out a new cave-busting version of the AT–4 antitank missile called a "small D"—which demolished the cave. The men made their way through the gorge, destroying caves, for the better part of an hour. In the middle of it all a Kurd named Wohab, who Sheikh Jafr had assigned as the captain's personal security detail, showed up with cookies and soda pop for the captain. Wohab knew that the captain liked sodas and had figured that it was time for an afternoon break.

The team climbed higher into the pass in search of fleeing fighters and the radio transmitter. The soldiers moved through a cluster of about ten cinderblock huts. They were very near the border. Machine gun fire suddenly ranged in on the team from the steep mountain walls. The men ran back to the closest hut; the heavy-caliber bullets chipped away at the cinderblock. The team radioed for emergency close-air support but cancelled the call when it became apparent that the men had to move. Chunks of the wall fell away and holes opened up—the building was falling apart around them. It was suicidal to call in an air strike and then change position. The team would have to fall back first.

The team sergeant, the medic, and the communications sergeant grabbed the M2 .50-caliber gun and ammunition canisters and started hauling them to a nearby hut to be able to cover the others' retreat. As they ran, rounds plopped into the mud around them, making the same smacking sound as that of bullets hitting flesh. They reached the building and quickly placed the three-foot-long gun on its tripod and threaded the belt of finger-sized bullets into the chamber. The team sergeant cocked the gun and turned it on full automatic, emptying one canister after another as his teammates withdrew. The DShK rounds tore away the flimsy wall shielding them. In just a few minutes Grit shot perhaps 700 rounds, until they had to leave too. As they moved the heavy M2 the tripod slipped, and the scorching hot barrel landed on the medic's hand, searing it. He grabbed the components anyway and ran to rejoin his comrades.

The captain had already called for air support. They were fish in a barrel in the narrow pass; only air strikes could rout their attackers. The minutes ticked by—fifteen, twenty minutes passed before jets were diverted from the Green Line. It seemed like an eternity to the men under fire. The planes arrived and dropped a half-dozen 500-pound JDAMs on positions that the team had been able to identify. Then all went silent.

There was no question of pursuing the Ansar remnants at this hour. It was after five o'clock and getting dark fast. The Kurds were not equipped for night fighting; they had no nods, laser pointers, or aiming devices on their guns. So the men returned to Sargat for the night.

They were exhausted by the day's intense combat. Adrenaline had spurred everyone through the past twelve hours, but now the men gratefully anticipated sleep. When they reached Sargat a hot meal of chicken and pita awaited them. The team bedded down in what had been the house of the Ansar chief. It was largely empty, which did not surprise the team sergeant. They had seen the convoys leaving for Iran after the air strikes the week before.

At dawn the next day, some of the U.S. soldiers and some Kurds returned to the mountains to resume the pursuit. Together they chased Ansar fighters, took out snipers, or fired mortars in running battles all the way to the border. The captain and the team sergeant stayed in Sargat to collect evidence and prepare a preliminary report.

Twenty-four of the Kurdish allies had been wounded or killed, and seventy enemy bodies had been recovered so far. As they searched the enemy corpses, the team members made a startling discovery—almost half the dead bodies were foreigners. The team knew that Ansar al-Islam was a mixture of Kurds and foreigners, but there were many more foreigners in Sargat than expected. On the bodies the soldiers found foreign identity cards, visas, and passports from a wide variety of Middle Eastern countries: Yemen, Sudan, Saudi Arabia, Qatar, Oman, Tunisia, Morocco, and Iran. They also found stubs and receipts of plane tickets in the clothes.

Inside the Ansar houses the team found more passports and tickets. Several of the tickets had been used for travel from Tehran to Doha, Qatar, and back to Tehran. Other documents added to the picture. A book in the Ansar leader's house was autographed by a Mullah Krekar. The inscription wished the Ansar leader continued success in the jihad. Krekar, who lived in Norway, was considered the spiritual leader of Ansar al-Islam. He had been detained on charges of aiding terrorists, but later was released for lack of evidence. The men found a yellow Post-it note with the handwritten name, phone number, and address of a known leader of the Philippine Muslim group Abu Sayyaf, which had been linked to Al Qaeda.

Material found on computer disks suggested some links with the radical Arab groups Hamas and Hezbollah as well as contact with the regime in Baghdad. It was not clear whether Baghdad's intelligence service had been probing Ansar al-Islam or was engaged in some kind of ongoing relationship, but Kurds who had defected from the group earlier had told the PUK that an Iraqi named Abu Wael had been Baghdad's liaison to Ansar.

A sensitive site exploitation team arrived the morning of March 29 and set to work in the suspected chemical facility. The 081 had already unearthed chemical hazard suits, atropine injectors, and manuals written in Arabic on how to make chemical munitions, improvised explosive devices, and mines from mortars. Field tests showed traces of ricin and potassium chloride. The evidence would be thoroughly analyzed in the United States, but it appeared as though there had been at least crude experimentation with chemical materials and bomb-making.

One eerie detail puzzled the medics of 081. Most of the bodies were found carrying an antibiotic commonly used to treat upper respiratory infections. Had something in Sargat made them sick? The captain was concerned when each of his men who went into Sargat also became ill in the following days with chills and symptoms of stomach flu. The men went on to their next battle on the Green Line, but the captain had blood samples drawn just in case the investigation turned up firm evidence of a toxic substance.

It was not the job of ODA 081 to draw conclusions about what it had found; its mission was to capture Sargat and secure any prisoners and evidence. The analysis and official conclusions were the province of the intelligence agencies—but the men had enough training to add up what they had seen and reach their own personal conclusions. They did not know whether Baghdad had been involved, but the central fact seemed indisputable, that this was indeed a major terrorist outpost. The large number of armed Arabs who had been there, the evidence of frequent travel, and signs of linkages to other radical groups all strongly indicated that Sargat was an international terrorist training camp, much like those that Al Qaeda had run in Afghanistan.

Logical conjecture supported this conclusion. The skill and tenacity of the fighters encountered here suggested that they were experienced or at least were trained by professionals. It was reasonable to suppose that Al Qaeda would have searched for an alternative training site and base after the United States forces routed it from Afghanistan in late 2001. This location was ideal, and Ansar al-Islam may have been formed or cultivated precisely to provide a haven for Al Qaeda militants fleeing Afghanistan. While some of those militants had fled into Pakistan, there had been reports of others heading the opposite direction, across Afghanistan into Iran. This camp, right on the Iranian border, was easy to reach from Iran. It provided a 300-square-kilometer enclave with plenty of room for military training. Was it just a coincidence that the Kurds in Halabja had started coming under attack soon after September 2001?

The idea that Al Qaeda, through its associate Zarqawi, had selected this area as its new base of operations struck the team sergeant as far more than plausible. He believed, given the heavy fortifications, ample weaponry, and quality of the fighters, that his team had just invaded the world's largest existing terrorist training camp since the fall of the Taliban in Afghanistan. This was no way station, in his view. It was remote yet in the heart of the region, so radicals could wreak havoc all over the Middle East. It provided a backdoor escape through Iran—a country virtually sealed off to the western world. That is exactly what happened midday on March 28, when a caravan of vehicles congregated in Biyara, the border town south of Sargat. The team on the red prong had spotted senior Al Qaeda operatives in the caravan, and called for air strikes, but no bombers had been available.

The ferocious fighting of Operation Viking Hammer and the details of what had been found at Sargat and Biyara remained virtually unknown to the world at large, but the inner circles of Washington buzzed with news of both as the analysts sifted through the training camp evidence. Abu Musab Zarqawi would emerge as a central figure in the year ahead, and the world had not seen the last of Ansar al-Islam's suicide bombers. Kurdish intelligence sources verified that Zarqawi had been seen not only in Sargat but also in several other villages in the area, including one called Darga-shakhan where many Arabs and Afghans had stayed. As for the battle itself, it was typical of the Special Forces not to ballyhoo the courageous feats in Sargat valley, yet the awarding of three Silver Stars told at least part of the story.

The captain, the team sergeant, and the communications sergeant all received the Silver Star, the army's third-highest combat medal, for their "exceptional gallantry and bravery" in Operation Viking Hammer. The awarding of three Silver Stars for a single battle indicated the extraordinary acts and the intensity of the fighting. Recommendations for multiple awards in the same battle are frequently downgraded to lesser medals as they wend through the bureaucracy—a practice intended to prevent medal inflation. All six men had been nominated by their commanders for the Silver Star because each had repeatedly displayed great courage under fire, but three of them were awarded the next-highest medal, the Bronze Star with valor device. The three other members of 081 on the green prong were also awarded Bronze Stars with valor devices. Yet, none of the men would ever forget March 28, 2003. Sargat would stand as one of the fiercest battles the Special Forces had fought since Vietnam—on foot, under sustained fire from an enemy lodged in the mountains, and with minimal artillery and air support.

On March 29, Lt. Col. Tovo went to Sargat to survey the mop-up operations and then briefed the Kurdish leadership. Operation Viking Hammer had succeeded beyond their wildest expectations. In two days, the yellow, green, orange, black, red, and blue prongs had secured 300 square kilometers of territory and routed Ansar al-Islam. The confirmed enemy toll was 300 dead, from Ansar al-Islam and the northern splinter group, and many more remained uncounted in the caves and mountains. Only twenty-three Kurds had been wounded and three killed, and no Americans had been killed or wounded.

CHAPTER 14

THE GREEN LINE

The only two prerequisite and enduring assets are brains and feet.

—SIR ROBERT THOMPSON

T ASK FORCE VIKING now exerted all its efforts on the Green Line assault. Lieutenant Colonel Tovo sent Charlie Company, which had fought in Operation Viking Hammer, to the southernmost part of the line near Tuz. Bravo Company began to call in air strikes on the ridges at Chamchamal, east of Kirkuk. Alpha Company started its assault along the northern approaches to Kirkuk. The plan was to cut off Kirkuk from three sides, isolate the Iraqi forces, and foment the city's collapse. One ODA planned to mount various subterfuges behind Iraqi lines in the west but never had a chance to execute the plans.

In less than a week, in the face of the air strikes and coordinated onslaught, the Iraqi forces withdrew into Kirkuk. Nine ODAs and thousands of *pesh merga* sent the Iraqis fleeing. Then, on the night of April 9, the day that Baghdad fell, a convoy of SUVs left Kirkuk heading south. ODA 081, watching the approach to Tuz, saw the vehicles but was unable to positively identify what everyone believed—the top military and political leadership was escaping—so the team could not direct the B-52 bomber circling overhead to drop its payload.

Lieutenant Colonel Tovo worked overtime to rein in his Kurdish allies, in particular one general and the rank and file troops who were eager to capture Kirkuk. That city was the tripwire for Turkish involvement, however, because the vast oilfields lay just beyond. The Kurds had an extensive underground network inside the city and desperately wanted to call for an uprising to finish the job. Tovo faced an interesting twist on the Robin Sage scenario of his long-ago Q course: How does one prevent a guerrilla ally's successful insurrection?

On April 10, the top Kurdish leaders, Col. Cleveland, Lt. Col. Tovo, and other task force officers gathered in the middle of PUK territory to discuss how to handle the collapse of the cities and the impending endgame. The original idea had been to surround Kirkuk and wait for U.S. conventional forces to occupy it, thus keeping the Kurds at bay and Turkey placated. As Tovo sat in the meeting, his operations officer brought him updates from the battlefield. Bravo Company reported that it had seized the last ridge east of Kirkuk. A short while later, Alpha Company reported that it had taken the Kani Domlan ridge and that the way was open to Kirkuk. Alpha Company had waged pitched battles to win the ridge over the past three days. The team sergeant of ODA 072, leading a split team, had overrun a much larger Iraqi force and taken out three vehicles, numerous machine guns, and mortar positions, and inflicted heavy casualties.

The meeting was being overtaken by events on the ground. Tovo realized that Kirkuk's fall was imminent. "You'd better get on down there," Cleveland observed. The roads were jammed with Kurds who wanted to visit relatives, former homes, and their principal city, which they had not seen in twenty years. The *pesh merga* set up checkpoints to stop the flood, but the Kurds just streamed through side roads instead. Tovo and his staff moved into the departed governor's office in Kirkuk. He ordered the Special Forces to shave their mustaches, put on their uniforms, and get out to patrol the streets—Alpha Company on one side of the city's river, Bravo on the other. It was now time to make his operators seem as American and visible as possible, to impose order and prevent ethnic violence from erupting. By nightfall, the Kurds, with the help of their local network, had rounded up fifty foreign Arab fighters and turned them over to Tovo. The ODAs shifted seamlessly from their combat roles to the tasks of reconstruction and stabilization. The soldiers knew this so well from their Balkan experience that Tovo had not even rehearsed it. By April 13, they had electricity and water running again, with help from an Iraqi engineer, and were convening town meetings in Kirkuk and Tuz. Supplying basic services went a long way to calming the mood, but the core ethnic tensions remained. Tovo, who had been the company commander in Tuzla, Bosnia, at the start of the American peacekeeping mission there, felt a strange sense of déjà vu. His teams had been in the middle of its thorniest places—Brcko and Srebrenica—and he knew that making peace in such circumstances was far more difficult than making war.

Tovo and his Charlie Company commander also pulled off a final bit of negotiating finesse. They slotted the last piece of the ethnic jigsaw puzzle into place on April 15, when Tovo signed a cease-fire with the Iranian exile group, Mujahedeen e Khalq. MEK fighters occupied a large swath of land south of Tuz, but they had no interest in fighting the U.S. forces—their goal was the overthrow of Tehran. Charlie Company commander George Thiebes had negotiated the deal because his meager forces could not assume the demobilization duties that an outright surrender would require. Tovo also wanted to keep the MEK in place to block both the Badr Corps and his Kurdish allies from moving south into Baghdad, where they would only complicate the capital's politics. The MEK happened to be on the U.S. foreign terrorist list, but Cleveland nonetheless authorized Tovo and Thiebes to proceed. The tactical move worked as planned, and left the ultimate fate of the MEK to be determined later by the political authorities. Cleveland loved the ingenuity of it. A Virginia National Guard lawyer in his task force had come up with legal formulas to permit Special Forces units to execute cease-fire or capitulation agreements because large numbers of Iraqis were expected to surrender. It proved to be an innovative tool for Cleveland's small forces to use in coping with the significantly larger opposing forces on the battlefield.

Although Kirkuk remained miraculously stable for the first week that Tovo's men held it, more manpower was obviously needed. A battalion staff officer led a group of Special Forces to secure a bridge north of Kirkuk so the 173rd Airborne Brigade could come down from the Kurdish autonomous zone to guard the oil fields outside Kirkuk and to help patrol the city. The brigade, based in Italy, had parachuted into the Bashur airfield, along with Maj. Rob Gowan, a public affairs officer for the Special Forces.

Lieutenant Colonel Bob Waltemeyer's 2nd Battalion teams had been fighting since March 30, first to secure the city of Irbil and its airfield from nearby Iraqi troops, and then to march on Mosul. The plan was to move in toward Mosul in a concentric circle and draw a noose around

The Green Line Battle of Task Force Viking

Source: U.S. Army Special Operations Command

the city. Teams would attack from the west, north, and south. The battalion operations officer, an Annapolis native, gave Mosul the code name Baltimore and sent the ODAs to surrounding points along the "beltway." This suited Waltemeyer just fine—he had been born in Baltimore, so he could instantly recognize the location of a team at "Bowie" in relation to "Laurel."

There would be no rout but hard sustained fighting instead. The teams of 2nd Battalion fought seven major battles, some of them lasting for days. The air strikes of the opening days had not dislodged the Iraqis from the northern stretch of the Green Line. The two sides watched each other through binoculars, trading hand gestures and even written messages. In one, the Iraqis said that they were not about to surrender to a bunch of guys in pickup trucks. Mosul was a proud bastion of the regime, the cradle of pan-Arab nationalism, and home to much of the Iraqi officer corps. The area was akin to Northern Virginia or Tampa, Florida, with one of the highest concentrations of retired and active-duty officers anywhere in Iraq.

Waltemeyer was somewhat hamstrung militarily by an agreement that had been reached with Turkey to limit the number of Kurdish fighters to 150 per engagement. It was not always possible to control the Kurds: 9,500 *pesh merga* showed up for one battle. But whenever Waltemeyer came to do a head count, the teams made sure that there were only 150 Kurds in sight. In any case, the Iraqis so outnumbered the combined forces that one of Waltemeyer's men joked that they should mount a *"Gilligan's Island* defense"—paint coconuts to look like extra soldiers' heads and stick them up on the ridges.

The western prong of the attack on Mosul ran into heavy resistance on April 2, midway along the main road from Irbil to Mosul. For the next seven days, ODA 065 and its Kurdish allies fought back and forth across the Great Zab River against two Iraqi brigades. It was a World War II see-saw battle, except that only the Iraqis had tanks. The U.S. forces did have B–52 bombers. At the moment of the planned bomb drop, the massed Kurds would attack at a run, yelling "Ah ah ah ah ah ah!"—echoing the sound of the concussions. These assaults pushed the Iraqis off the high ground, but as soon as the planes left, they surged back.

Finally, after round-the-clock fighting, the U.S. and Kurd forces seized the ridgeline. The team sergeant of 065 called in air strikes, marshaled the Kurds, and led the attack that seized the ridge. The Iraqis retrenched farther west, and for the next three days the two sides pounded each other across a grassy plain. The men, sleepless and exhausted, grew inured to the tank, artillery, and mortar rounds falling around them. Waltemeyer came to the battlefield to assess the situation, and hunkered down with the team behind its small defensive berm. The team sergeant had dark circles under his eyes. The men could not carry on like this, Waltemeyer concluded.

Waltemeyer returned to Irbil and put artillery from the newly arrived 173rd Airborne Brigade together with the Kurds' vintage collection of Russian, Chinese, and Hungarian pieces. Meanwhile, on the front lines, Iraqi trucks were hauling in reinforcements. The Special Forces watched black-clothed Fedayeen force young men into trenches to fight. The team called in air strikes on the departing Fedayeen. At night the men heard machine-gun fire in nearby towns—deserters were being shot.

Two more ODAs and 100 more Kurds arrived to reinforce ODA 065. With their assistance and the artillery support, the weeklong battle was won at last. The U.S. and Kurdish forces had secured twenty-three kilometers of highway, killed 257 Iraqis and captured four, and destroyed two tanks, seven mortars, fifteen bunkers, and thirty-four vehicles. Two Silver Stars were awarded for the battle at Aski Kalak. One of them went to the team sergeant of ODA 065, whose actions were directly credited with: the defeat of three mechanized counterattacks; the destruction of four bunkers, a command post, two tanks, and four mortar positions; the killing of forty enemy soldiers; and the seizing of thirty kilometers of terrain. It was not front-page news, but the Middletown, Connecticut, native had just become another Special Forces quiet hero.

The teams north of Mosul had the toughest terrain to fight in. Villages were notched into the steep mountains, which made it a challenge to capture territory while avoiding civilian casualties. At the town of Ayn Sifni, three ODAs led 1,500 *pesh merga* in an intense battle that captured the town and 240 Iraqi soldiers. Thirty-four were killed and sixty were wounded. The religious leader thanked the teams for preserving the town's historic shrine. Another force composed of two ODAs and 350 *pesh merga* fought for three days in exposed positions to capture the highway leading south into Mosul. Another group of six ODAs and 9,200 *pesh merga* attacked three Iraqi divisions along a forty-kilometer front. Aided by air strikes and artillery, this battle brought the U.S. forces twenty kilometers closer to Mosul.

The battle on the southern approach to Mosul also turned into a dramatic slugfest. Waltemeyer's Alpha Company, 2nd Battalion, and Alpha Company, 3rd Battalion, 3rd Group, which had been attached to the task force for the war, fought an extraordinary battle against two entrenched, mechanized Iraqi brigades at Debecka Pass. A long ridge paralleled the highway from Kirkuk to Mosul, and Debecka Pass was the strategic gap in the ridge that the Special Forces had to cross. With 800 Kurds, they managed to breach the Iraqi trench lines using M2 machine guns, Mk 19 grenade launchers, and the Javelin antitank missiles. The men fought off two armored counterattacks and, during the third one, they called for close air support to drive back the Iraqi tanks.

At this critical point in the battle, Wadji Barzani, a nephew of the top Kurdish Democratic Party (KDP) leader Masoud Barzani, drove up, unannounced, with a caravan of journalists. It was a miserable, cloudy day. Overhead F–14s were circling, hitting targets and trying to help the men crouched behind the ridge who were fighting for their lives. T–55 tanks were massing just a few hundred meters on the other side. These T–55s were exactly the same distance from the ridge as Barzani's caravan, which compounded its inopportune arrival with the decision to park beside a demolished tank. A call for an air strike on the tanks on the opposite side had just been made. A major went over to talk to Barzani, then walked away—unaware of the tragedy about to occur. The pilot, thousands of feet above, dropped the bomb on the wrong cluster of tanks and vehicles. It hit the caravan, killing twelve senior *pesh merga* and wounding others including a journalist. Wadji Barzani had received a severe shrapnel wound—a piece of metal was lodged in his head.

Waltemeyer arrived at the gruesome scene moments later. The medics from the ODAs were treating the wounded Kurds and journalist, even as the battle raged. Waltemeyer arranged Barzani's evacuation to Germany for emergency medical attention, and then he learned that one of the journalists had mistakenly reported that the twelve men who'd been killed were Special Forces soldiers.

Waltemeyer rushed to call his wife in Colorado and reached her as she was leaving for church. She'd already heard the news on the radio, and the wives at Fort Carson had started to call to find out if their husbands were among the fatalities. The report was false, Waltemeyer assured her. Only one SF operator, the major, had been slightly wounded by a piece of shrapnel in the calf. He would be back on duty the next day. Mrs. Waltemeyer hung up with her husband and then made the call to start the battalion's phone tree to give all the families the correct information—military families constantly live with the fear that the phone will ring with bad news.

The battle at Debecka Pass was won despite the friendly fire accident. The teams had just enough Javelin missiles left to destroy the remaining armored vehicles. A staff sergeant became the unofficial ace of 3rd Group by destroying four armored personnel carriers. He and two other Special Forces soldiers were awarded the Silver Star for their exploits—and the stories were retold often to demonstrate that Special Forces and their indigenous allies could outmaneuver and prevail over entrenched armor and artillery.

Alpha Company and 3rd Group's company pushed through the pass; then Alpha continued west to capture two key towns and large amounts of antiaircraft weaponry and FROG–7 missiles. Third group's company turned north on April 10 to capture Makloub Mountain, the pivotal high ground overlooking Mosul. Once the company did, the Special Forces and Kurds would control the northern, western, and southern approaches to the city, and the assault on Mosul could begin.

As these battles were being fought, Waltemeyer had traveled south to attend the strategy meeting of Task Force Viking, Cleveland, Tovo, and the Kurdish leaders on April 10. Waltemeyer listened with growing concern as the reports flowed in about Kirkuk's imminent fall and the rush of Kurds toward the city. The PUK leader, Talabani, and his cohorts broke out drinks to celebrate. Barzani's men, of the rival KDP, cursed and stormed out. Kurds swarming into Kirkuk meant double trouble for Waltemeyer. He had to worry not only about the prospect of Turkish troops rushing into his sector but also about how the KDP Kurdish generals would react if they believed the rival PUK was grabbing Kirkuk to stake its claim. They might well pull their *pesh merga* from the field and rush to Kirkuk, leaving Waltemeyer's ODAs alone to face the Iraqis. He was not about to give up the ground that they had fought so hard to win over the past two weeks. Furious, he left the meeting without another word.

Waltemeyer knew that Cleveland would understand his anger and his need to return north to handle whatever happened next. The lieutenant colonel got on the radio while his sergeant major drove. The Kurdish militia remained in the field, fighting alongside the U.S. soldiers. With Kirkuk crumbling, Mosul's collapse might not be far behind. Waltemeyer called a meeting of the underground network he'd assembled, the Free Mosul Committee, at the headquarters of a KDP general in Dohuk. When he arrived, he was told that Mosul already was a maelstrom of looting and pillaging. Waltemeyer could not let the city disintegrate into chaos; he quickly made his decision and announced it to the group. "We're going into Mosul tomorrow, with or without you. I thank you in advance for your support."

He warned the Kurdish KDP to keep its word and not inundate the city, despite the fact that the PUK down south had not stayed out of Kirkuk. He told each leader to supply ten members for a militia that would go in the next morning, adding, "Kurds may only go in if they are part of the militia."

The next morning, April 11, before they left Dohuk, one of the tribal representatives announced that the Iraqi commander of the V Corps, which surrounded Mosul, was ready to surrender at a crossroads north of the city. Before Waltemeyer could say anything, the men who'd assembled charged out the door and got into their vehicles. There was nothing for the lieutenant colonel to do but get into his truck and follow as fast as he could. If he made it through this improvisational test, he surely would be the Miles Davis of the Special Forces.

When Waltemeyer arrived at the crossroads it was jammed with vehicles, parked every which way, for at least two miles in each direction. The throng of people looked like a scene from Woodstock. Waltemeyer worked his way through the crowd to find at the center not an Iraqi general but an Arab sheikh, the chief of the Jubari tribe, who was resplendent in a black and gold robe and headdress. Wealthy Arabs from Mosul stood around him, their new Mercedes parked nearby. Waltemeyer tried to listen politely to the Arab sheikh's speech but was distracted by truckloads of Kurds bearing down on him. He held up first one hand, then another, like a policeman, all the while smiling and nodding to the Arabs, who offered to escort him into the city—but the tide of Kurds threatened to engulf them all.

Waltemeyer turned and began to run down the highway, weaving through the mob of bodies and cars. He grabbed four of his soldiers and spread them out in a human roadblock across the asphalt. Standing in the middle, he pulled his gun and pointed it at the oncoming Kurds. "Draw your weapons," he told his sergeants. Traffic screeched to a halt. A soldier pulled one of the Special Forces' white quad-cab trucks into the middle of the road. Waltemeyer climbed onto its hood and stood up, his shaven head glistening like a white globe above the crowd. He thrust out his arms, palms out, in the universal sign for "stop."

At that very moment who should appear but his favorite commander Charlie Cleveland. Cleveland looked up at him, a small smile on his face. "So, how are you doing?" he said.

"I've had better days," the bald-headed battalion commander said, his jaw tight.

"What do you plan to do?" said the sandy-haired colonel.

"In a few minutes we're going into Mosul," replied Waltemeyer.

"Just like that?" asked his boss.

"It's the only thing I can think of to do," he said.

The Americans, numbering fewer than thirty, piled into their half-dozen vehicles. Waltemeyer thought it would be a good idea to identify themselves by flying the U.S. flag on his truck. They drove past roadblocks and looters, following the Arabs in Mercedes, who promptly went home. One lone Arab in a Chevy Caprice insisted that they come drink tea in his neighborhood. En route they were persuaded by others to have tea with an important sheikh. It turned out to be a press event staged by the Kurds. Cleveland sat down next to the robed man while Waltemeyer gritted his teeth, fuming at the delay.

Finally, the men made their way to the government building downtown where Waltemeyer hoped to set up a headquarters. The 100 Kurds he had allowed to precede them were holding back an increasingly angry crowd that was not happy to see the Americans, and was not happy to see the Jubari tribe with them. Waltemeyer entered the governate, a clutch of reporters on his heels. Shots rang out and one of the journalists was hit in the foot. It was too volatile to stay downtown, Waltemeyer decided, so he redirected everyone to the airport, the alternate site he had selected.

Looters were ransacking the airport. The soldiers slipped on shattered glass as they ran inside with their guns to clear out the rampaging mob. Cleveland pulled his white Defender around and parked it next to Waltemeyer's. They were being shot at already. Waltemeyer was annoyed that his medics had to patch up the slightly wounded reporter. Then a Fox news crew arrived seeking shelter, and begged to be let in.

"What are you going to do?" asked Cleveland. It was Waltemeyer's area of operations and he was letting him run it.

"I'm going to set up some commo and call in the other teams," Waltemeyer said.

Whatever he did, Waltemeyer was going to need more than thirty men to bring order to a city of 1.7 million, which increasingly resembled the movie *Escape from New York*. People were toting TVs and refrigerators, and setting buildings on fire. Neighborhood militias had sprouted and were shooting at anyone they thought was a looter. That night Waltemeyer's teams, about 200 soldiers, drove quietly through the Iraqi lines they had been fighting for two long weeks. The men saw tanks, artillery pieces, and armored personnel carriers, but no soldiers. They would, however, see plenty of young men aged eighteen to thirty-five in the streets of Mosul in the coming days, who eyed them with sullen hostility.

Fortunately, Waltemeyer's battalion had rehearsed coming into Mosul and knew the location of the airport. The original plan had been to sign capitulation agreements with Iraqi forces and use them to keep order until the postwar plan emerged. But the army had melted away and the collapse of order in the city had made Plan B imperative. The teams had even studied the neighborhoods and provisionally divided them up.

Mosul was one of those challenges that only a Special Forces soldier can relish. Not many people would choose to enter an unknown place full of people who would just as soon shoot them and look for someone's hand to shake. It takes an unusual mixture of politician and undercover cop, someone for whom being vastly outnumbered is just part of the game. It takes a desire to test oneself in a very particular way, to see if one can accomplish by wiles, guts, and persuasion what cannot be accomplished by force. It is not a job for wild-eyed lunatics, adrenaline junkies, or Rambo wannabes, but for individuals with maturity, experience, and nerves of steel—and, yes, a taste for adventure.

Colonel Cleveland wanted a better look at what was happening, so he went into Mosul that night with one of the teams. Patrolling the streets under a moonless sky, they came to a cramped Arab quarter with narrow streets. Without speaking the men tightened up their ranks. The Defender pickup trucks had .50-caliber machine guns mounted on the back, but shooting their way out of the city would be the very last resort. The Special Forces turned onto a street blocked by a barricade. An old man stood beside it, rifle in hand, guarding his and his neighbors' homes. Flames from burning tires cast eerie, leaping shadows. The soldiers approached, motioning for the man to lower his gun. He did not. They drew their weapons, just in case. Suddenly, a young boy, maybe ten

years old, appeared between the columns of a building next to the barricade. He raised an AK–47 at the Americans, then ducked behind a column. They persuaded the old man to lower his gun. Then the boy
popped out again, still pointing the gun, his finger on the trigger. The
tire smoke obscured the soldiers' view. Their rules of engagement permitted them to shoot, but no one did. Finally, the boy decided to lower
the gun, and the soldiers—fathers all—breathed a sigh of relief.

To pacify Mosul, Waltemeyer's weapon of choice was a public relations campaign. He asked the sheikhs to persuade the neighborhood
militias to disband instead of continuing to shoot at each other. He gave
daily press conferences and taped messages to be broadcast each night
on local television. He announced that he would return to the governate
to establish an office for reconstruction and reconciliation projects. The
26th Marine Expeditionary Unit had begun to fly Marines in from its carrier in the Mediterranean, so Waltemeyer sent a company of Marines
and a Civil Affairs team to the governate as an advance party. Marines
also set up checkpoints on the seven river crossings into Mosul. They
were to tell Iraqis that weapons were not permitted in the city, although
the Marines were not numerous enough to forcibly disarm anyone.

On April 15, as announced, Waltemeyer drove downtown with a split
team from his battalion. He saw people milling in the streets, and some
of them spat on his truck. One of the Special Forces soldiers with the
advance team radioed him to say that there had been "some trouble" at
the governate—that was an understatement. About two thousand people packed the square in front of the governate. One car had been over-
turned, and windshields were broken; a dead body was lying on the
ground. Waltemeyer drove into the compound and the men closed the
gate behind him. Marines were lined up behind the wall and inside the
building with machine guns pointing out of every window. They were
locked and loaded, ready to fire. Waltemeyer pulled around back and
went inside.

"What is going on here?" Waltemeyer asked.

"They didn't like our plan," the Civil Affairs captain replied.

"What plan?" Waltemeyer asked.

Before the captain could explain, a member of the Jubari tribe emerged from one of the rooms and greeted him. Waltemeyer groaned inwardly—he had nicknamed this particular character "Crazy Eyes." "Hey Colonel," he said. Whatever he had been up to could not have been good.

Crazy Eyes had installed himself at the governate the day before, claiming to represent some kind of rump city council. When the Civil Affairs captain arrived, he mistakenly thought it would mollify the crowd to bring the Jubari-led councilmen to the front door. The crowd was incensed and began throwing rocks—it appeared that the Americans were endorsing an unpopular pretender. A full-scale riot was underway.

Waltemeyer had visions of Mogadishu 1991, when the U.S. embassy was overrun. Soldiers had fired at shooters in a crowd of civilians and caused many casualties. The dilemmas had been well portrayed in the movie *Rules of Engagement*. The physical setting in Mosul was eerily similar. The governate was in the dead center of a hostile city, looking out on a wide plaza full of angry and armed people. Waltemeyer appreciated the combat power of Marines—his own father and brother were Marines. He knew their basic rule: If shot at, shoot back. There were no easy answers, and there was provocation aplenty. Shooting would have consequences, but so would *not* shooting if the soldiers came under attack.

Waltemeyer went out back to huddle with the split team he'd brought along. It was his best team, whose members had been serving under him for almost two years; they could say anything to one another. The men gathered around the hood of the truck, the traditional spot for conferences in the field. It was the equivalent of gathering around the planning table at headquarters or the hearth at home.

"We've got two options," Waltemeyer said. "Stay put and hope it calms down, or prepare to move out." The team leader argued against leaving, saying, "That's not how you trained us. We're staying." Waltemeyer thought it over, and decided that they would make a stand—200 young Marines and a handful of soldiers. He was proud of their determination. Leaving would have indelibly stamped the U.S. forces as weak and imperiled any future efforts to assert authority.

The crowd had swelled to perhaps three thousand. Iraqis in the crowd armed with AK–47s began firing into the air, and then the mob surged forward against the wall outside the governate. It would not be hard for three thousand Iraqis to overrun the small force in the building. The Marines took fire, and so they shot back.

Waltemeyer rushed to the front of the building as soon as the shooting erupted. He consulted with the Marine battalion commander, who placed a call to the Marines' ship in the Mediterranean. Minutes later, its Harrier jets screamed overhead, banking sideways and flying right in front of the governate. Windows broke, the jets flew so close. The crowd scattered.

Ten to thirteen Iraqis were killed in the shooting, and many dozens more wounded. It was later disputed whether the Iraqis had only shot into the air, over the heads of those trying to scale the governate's wall, or also shot directly at the Marines. In any case, there was no doubt that the Americans were under attack by an angry mob that contained both armed and unarmed Iraqis. Waltemeyer felt badly that unarmed civilians were among the melee's casualties, but he did not think the Marines had been in the wrong.

That night, the Special Forces saw Iraqis pillaging the ammunition dumps near the airport. An insurgency was building, and the city was about to come unglued. AC–130 gunships circled for hours over the governate, watching through their forward-looking infrared radar as Iraqis moved machine guns onto rooftops opposite the square.

The next day, Colonel Cleveland and the colonel who led the 26th Marine Expeditionary Unit showed up to get a feel for the situation. "You should not stay long," Waltemeyer advised. "It's getting hairy."

Cleveland knew that Waltemeyer was wrestling with the difficult choice between letting chaos fill the vacuum and making a brave attempt to assert authority. There were no other U.S. forces around. Waltemeyer had doggedly sought Iraqis who could help calm things down, and one Iraqi police general had called his men back to work. But the hostility continued to build.

Special Forces snipers moved to the roof of the governate, and the Marines took up positions at the front of the building. Gunfire was heard, but unbeknownst to those at the governate, it had come from policemen responding to a bank robbery in progress a few blocks away; they had fired warning shots into the air. Exactly what happened next is unclear. Those shots may have prompted the Iraqi snipers across the plaza to open fire, in the belief that the U.S. troops were shooting at them. In any event, the Marines opened fire. Waltemeyer heard the volleys, ran to the front of the building, and saw the Marines kneeling at the windows. "Stop!" he ordered.

Four Iraqis were killed and several wounded. That night Waltemeyer pulled everyone out. He had made his stand, but it was clear that the governate could not be the hub for reconstruction efforts as long as armed Iraqis contested the Americans' presence. He would have to work on pacifying the city from the airport.

From the airport, Waltemeyer deployed his ODAs into neighborhoods, where they found living quarters and began to meet people, set up networks, and tried to quell the violence. He redoubled his outreach effort with help from a psyop team that Cleveland dispatched from the task force. Waltemeyer broadcast a call to form a retired officers association dedicated to the rebuilding of Mosul. He had already met quietly with several generals in their homes.

The next day, Waltemeyer walked outside the airport compound and saw a honking, snaking line of traffic clogging the two-lane street to the airport entrance. "What in the world is that?" he asked his executive officer, who was seated on a case of MREs, eating his morning ration out of its brown plastic pouch. "Sir, that is probably your retired Iraqi officer association," he said, and kept on eating. Waltemeyer cursed himself for his bright idea, and rounded up a translator and the psyop Humvee with its speakers. He corralled an Iraqi general at the gate to help him.

He asked the crowd to organize itself according to rank and then asked each group to come at an appointed hour. When they finished, they'd registered one thousand officers in the new association, which would turn out to be a very effective mechanism in a nationalistic city with a long martial tradition.

The 101st Airborne Division, under Lt. Gen. David Petraeus, reached Mosul on April 22. In the coming weeks Petraeus took over the job of stabilizing the complex city—the lynchpin of northern Iraq—to get lamb and lion to lie down together: Arab and Kurd, Sunni and Shi'ite, Turkman, Assyrian, and Azzidi.

Lieutenant Colonel Waltemeyer had faced unenviable situations and tough decisions, including those of April 15–16. Pulling out of Mosul without attempting to make a stand might have resulted in greater anarchy or even a takeover by regime loyalists. His battlefield record was unprecedented in military history: a Special Forces battalion and 26,000 *pesh merga* had captured Iraq's third-largest city, defeated six Iraqi divisions, captured 600 and killed 859 enemy soldiers, and seized 6,000 square kilometers of territory. Two hundred Kurds had died and four of Waltemeyer's men had been wounded. He had proven indeed a master of improvisation—backed up by the ultimate quiet professional, Charlie Cleveland—as had his SF brother Tovo, down south.

Task Force Viking had accomplished its seemingly impossible mission of disrupting and defeating thirteen Iraqi divisions. It had prevented the wholesale movement south not only of the Iraqis, but also of its Kurdish allies, which succeeded in keeping Turkey out of the war. Cleveland had known all along that his men would have limited air support and conventional manpower, and a hard time controlling the cities, but they had managed with the resources they were given. They had joined with the available bombers to break the will of the Iraqi divisions—a much more heavily armed and armored opponent than the Taliban had been. If there was any lingering doubt that the Special Forces, augmented by indigenous allies, could prevail on the battlefield, it was erased by their performance in northern Iraq.

After the end of major combat operations was declared on May 1, 2003, Cleveland departed Iraq, and Waltemeyer stayed to oversee the task force and the search for wanted regime figures. During the nightly radio calls via the DCTS computer, Waltemeyer had a chance to catch up with his fellow Special Forces battalion commanders in Iraq. On a visit to Baghdad, he met the 5th Group commander as they gathered for the nightly DCTS conference. "Is Waltemeyer there?" Chris Conner radioed. "Yeah," came the reply. "Better watch your silver. He'll take all your money," Conner deadpanned. The group commander looked at Waltemeyer quizzically. He had no idea that Conner and Waltemeyer were old friends from staff college. Conner was razzing him with a running joke that dated back two years, when Waltemeyer led the Georgia train-and-equip program and Conner worked on the Pentagon's Joint Staff. The joke was that Waltemeyer would make off with everyone's resources, because he had been a strong proponent of the $64-million project—a large sum for the Special Forces.

The truth was that if anyone in this band of brothers needed something, the others would give him the shirts off their backs. Waltemeyer knew that if Tovo, Conner, or any of them asked for help, he really needed it. It turned out that 5th Group did need help, as Baghdad and central Iraq became a hotbed of unrest over the summer. Waltemeyer loaned some teams to 3rd Battalion, 5th Group, and some of the men were wounded in the brewing insurgency. The Special Forces had been very lucky, given the amount of close combat and battlefield risk they had incurred. Their experience, sound tactics, and superior firepower had kept them alive during the major combat phase of Operation Iraqi Freedom. They would not be so fortunate in the year to come.

CHAPTER 15

COMING HOME

"Why do you like them so much?"
"Because they stand on a wall and say 'Nothing is
going to hurt you tonight. Not on my watch.'"

—FROM A FEW GOOD MEN

THE ARMY BUREAUCRACY churns on like a juggernaut even during wartime. One day in late April 2003, an urgent radio call arrived at the Special Forces' camp in the bombed-out air defense base outside Nasiriya. It was for Randy; Conner's staff in Kuwait had received a message that he had orders to report to the Special Warfare Center and School at Fort Bragg on July 1. It did not matter that his company was still fighting a war with a half-dozen teams in the field and hundreds of the Iraqi militia they had trained. He had to leave immediately, uproot fourteen years of life spent at Fort Campbell, and move to Fort Bragg, North Carolina, in time to report for duty at the schoolhouse.

It was the moment Randy had been dreading—the end of his life as a gunslinger. His new job would be to write doctrine and train future warriors. His title, Chief of the Advanced Skills Branch in the Training and Doctrine Division, sounded impressive. It was a perfect transition. Randy had a wealth of knowledge to share and a passionate commitment to the Special Forces. The operators had their own title for guys like him. Henceforth, he would be a F.A.G., a former action guy.

Randy packed his gear and jumped on the next convoy heading south to Kuwait. He bequeathed his "Rawhide" Humvee to Killer and wished Burns and the rest of Charlie Company the best in their last weeks of war. While waiting at Ali al Salem base for a flight back to the United States, he got word that the Civil Affairs unit attached to the company had also returned to Kuwait, and that there had been an accident along the way. While disposing of some grenades in southern Iraq, Randy's old comrade, Warren Foster, had blown up his hand when one of the grenades detonated. Eric Anderson, the medic in his team, had wrapped his hand and dangling fingers in ice and worked on him all the way back to Ali al Salem. Eric, like Warren, was a former Special Forces operator. He was able to perform battlefield surgery, but they were close enough to real surgeons that he wanted to get his friend there. Parts of two fingers were gone.

Big, blond Eric was a formidable marksman and fighter who had served on many direct-action teams, but when he assumed his role of medic he had the compassionate, caring bedside manner of the best physicians. He knew that Warren would be devastated by the injury, but not in the way that most men would be. Warren was such a professional, meticulous soldier that he would berate himself for the injury and fear that his comrades would think him careless. He would worry about the grief it would cause his wife. But, with physical therapy, Warren could regain full use of his hand and become as adept with his rifle as old Steve Rainey, the sharpshooter of Najaf, who had been nominated for a Silver Star for his close-quarter combat despite a similar injury.

Randy was sitting by his side when Warren woke up from surgery. Randy grasped the arm of his old buddy from Desert Storm as he opened his eyes. Warren was deeply chagrined, as predicted, and somehow didn't realize that his brains and skills had long ago assured his reputation among his peers. Still, the injury had been a traumatic blow—the once perennially youthful man looked worn and haggard. Despite Eric's expert emergency care, he was going to require months of therapy. What better friend to console him than Rawhide, who had been exploded and shot at and broken up more than any human being he knew? And Randy had bounced back every time. Randy drew the curtain around his bed and opened a little bottle containing Scotch, illegal in Kuwait, that he'd smuggled into the base hospital, and they drank to Warren's health.

Warren was back home at Fort Bragg by the time Randy moved there. Later that summer, Warren won promotion from captain to major. By the following February he would be back in Iraq, and leading a detachment of twenty men. They would survive numerous ambushes and explosions and help to rebuild schools, clinics, and local governments in two northern provinces.

Five wars had left their mark on Randy. The warrior life was the only life that had ever felt right to him, and he would miss it deeply. It had given him a fistful of medals, but it had also taken its toll in many ways. No one goes through war unscathed, and those who have been in combat carry the marks of it forever. The internal scars were the worst, though most men kept those hidden.

Afghanistan had not been a source of mental anguish to Randy because the memory of the Americans killed on September 11 had fueled the cause. Randy also understood the code of that warlord culture, which is governed by guns but also by certain rules. He had spent his SF career in that world. It was the killing in Kosovo, which was not fighting but slaughter, the veneer of civilization stripped away to reveal a savage order, that haunted him. "It sank into my soul," Randy said.

He could live with the scarred face, the mangled ankle, the inevitable arthritis and scar tissue that would eventually cripple him. His blood did not get enough oxygen from his lungs, a result of the overpressure of so many explosions. His hearing was bad. He, Warren, and the other teammates who had lived in the oil- and smoke-filled aftermath of Desert Storm in Kuwait had all noticed a steady memory loss. The mysterious Gulf War syndrome had never been definitively diagnosed, but at least it had finally been acknowledged as real. According to one theory, it was caused by radiation from the depleted uranium shells fired by tanks. One day when they were driving somewhere, Randy's wife recalled some special occasions they had spent with the families of fellow teammates in the 1990s, but Randy looked at her blankly. He could not remember the occasions that had meant so much to both of them. It made his wife cry.

Operation Iraqi Freedom was also Michael T. Swift's last war. He chose retirement after twenty years of military service, fifteen of them wearing the green beret. The excitement of the next twenty years would pale in comparison to the last twenty, but he wanted to be with his wife and children and both sets of parents. Over the last decade, the Special Forces' op tempo had increased by about 200 percent, and 5th Group had been sent abroad more than any group. Michael T. was going to finish college, alongside his son, and then decide on a new career. Jimmy Newman was retiring too, after twenty-two years. The two friends had spent their free moments in Iraq talking about what the future held in store for them, and both put in their retirement papers as soon as they returned to Fort Campbell that June.

On July 16, 2003, Jimmy came by the teamroom and told Michael T. that his retirement had come through. He was excited about a job offer that he had already received. Most of all, he was happy to be back with his German-born wife on their country spread, looking after their five children and their first grandchild. Early that Saturday morning, July 19, Jimmy drove to the local store and bait shop to have coffee with some Green Beret pals, as he often did. Then he bought milk for the baby and headed home. At 7:15 A.M., his 1990 Nissan pickup ran off the road and crashed into a house, killing him. The police report said he lost control on the curve, but no one would ever know what had caused the crash.

Jimmy's fellow soldiers and the community were stunned by this tragic twist of fate. Fifth Group had made it through Operation Iraqi Freedom without any deaths as of July 2003. Jimmy Newman had survived four wars—Desert Storm, Somalia, Afghanistan, and Iraq—and dozens of hazardous deployments, and then was suddenly taken off this earth just as he was about to embark on a new chapter of a life he lived to its fullest every day. He was only forty years old.

Because Jimmy Newman did not die in a duty-related accident, his untimely death is not marked by a tree in 5th Group's memorial grove. But 5th Group would not forget one of its most skilled and charismatic warriors. At his funeral, his widow was presented with the Bronze Star with a V device for valor and the Legion of Merit for Jimmy's actions in Operation Iraqi Freedom, and he was posthumously promoted to the rank of chief warrant officer 3. Although many of his daring missions would remain a secret, he was renowned as one of the most multi-talented soldiers in the brotherhood—and a master storyteller as only a Cajun can be. Jimmy had put together pictures of Iraq for a talk at the local high school, and he'd hoped to write a book about the humorous events of his career.

Chief Newman epitomized the institution. If the heart and soul of the Special Forces is the ODA, its lifeblood is the chiefs and the team sergeants. Jimmy Newman was a natural mentor whose charm and tremendous sense of humor drew people in like a magnet. His widow, five children, and grandchild lost a doting husband, father, grandfather, and principal breadwinner, and would not receive the financial benefits paid for those who die in combat. The family would grieve amid difficult times.

The coming year in Iraq would see more deaths. The great majority of casualties were among the conventional military, but the Special Forces also lost men in the postwar violence. The bitterest foes of the coalition occupation were the ousted Sunnis, although a militia led by radical Shi'ite cleric Moqtada al-Sadr also launched running guerrilla attacks. Two soldiers from 5th Group's 3rd Battalion were the first SF soldiers killed in Iraq, on September 12, 2003. During a night raid in Ramadi, the heart of the insurgency that raged in the Sunni Triangle of central Iraq, Master Sergeant Kevin Morehead, a friend of Tom Rosenbarger, and one of his teammates were killed. Seven others were wounded in the two-team raid.

In January 2004, a close friend and former teammate of "Grit," the 10th Group master sergeant of Operation Viking Hammer, died of his injuries two days after an improvised explosive device was detonated near his vehicle in Samarra. Master Sergeant Kelly Hornbeck had written an eloquent letter to his parents, who released it to their Texas television station to share their son's devotion to his unit, his faith, and his country.

Chris Conner led 5th Group's 2nd Battalion back to Iraq to pick up the counterinsurgency as well as the lagging effort to create a new Iraqi army. On April 11, 2004, during the most ferocious month of the entire occupation and war, near the most ferocious place in Iraq—Fallujah— Jonathan Burns lost his sergeant major, forty-eight-year-old Mike Stack, who had taken Jim Kilcoyne's place as Charlie Company's senior NCO when Killer moved up to the battalion staff. Seven other men in the company were wounded in an ambush at dusk. The men were terse and stoic. As is common in tough times, the small band of brothers drew together to share its grief in private and nurse the injured back to health.

In all, between the September 11, 2001, attacks and June 2004, twenty-three Special Forces soldiers were killed in action and several dozen wounded. Sixteen died in Afghanistan, the last two in June 2004 when their vehicle drove over a land mine—the same hidden and indiscriminate menace that had felled Sgt. Bobby Deeks in Somalia eleven years earlier. In addition to the war's physical toll of death, injury, and illness was the emotional toll of divorce or separation. In one special operations Civil Affairs unit alone there were three divorces. The men had all sought to resume their personal lives after months away from wives and children. The cumulative effect of being gone for six months or more of each of the past fifteen years was hard on the most resilient families.

Even ironclad marriages with stalwart wives did not always last, and sometimes even the homecomings were disruptive to families that had learned to cope with the absences. However much they might want to, the returning soldiers could not fix bygone problems, dry tears shed months before, or participate in the triumphs large and small that had occurred while they were gone.

The steadily increasing "operational tempo," beyond the already peripatetic routine, left little time for families. The wives who bore up were strong, independent types, but it was all the family members—not just the soldier—who, in effect, devoted their lives to the service. The families of those who were killed, maimed, and damaged paid a permanent price. The great majority of the Special Forces soldiers weather the hardships and stay in the military for twenty years or more. After all, they are volunteers three times over: they volunteer for the army, they volunteer for airborne school, and they voluntarily try out for the Special Forces. For those selected, it becomes a way of life, a calling, rather than a job or even a profession. The men value membership in this elite club and the caliber of the individuals they have the privilege of serving alongside. And, like all those in military service, they make a pledge that very few jobs require: to lay down one's life for others.

The strain on families was a key factor in the decision of those who did choose retirement. Some were lured away by private-sector jobs. After the cold war, the steep reductions in the funds and personnel of the military and other government agencies led to outsourcing and ever more reliance on contractors. Many operators shunned those jobs, however, although they paid six-figure salaries, because the jobs took the men away from home just as often. Some SF retirees missed the brotherhood and came back. The attrition of senior sergeants, especially of team sergeants and chief warrant officers, could seriously damage the Special Forces, because these men, with ten to twenty years' experience in the field, provided practical experience and advice for the young captains to rely upon, and led and mentored the younger sergeants.

There were not only sorrows but also great joys awaiting the soldiers who came home. Two of the happiest men in 5th Group were Master Sgt. Alan Johnson and Major Jonathan Burns, who came home to their first babies. Alan Johnson's son waited until his father arrived to enter the world. In fact, there were so many new babies resulting from that precious honeymoon period between Afghanistan and Iraq that Colonel Conner had arranged a priority "new dads" flight from Kuwait for the fathers in 2nd Battalion. No one had to tell the operators to make the most of their brief respite; they knew they would soon be returning to Iraq.

After they left, Master Sergeant Steve Rainey and the captain of ODA 544 kept close tabs on the gathering Shi'ia storm in Iraq. They avidly read newspaper stories about the drama involving Abdul Munin, their G-chief in Najaf, who had led the only spontaneous uprising in the war and subsequently become the interim mayor. He was arrested by the U.S. forces who took over Najaf after ODA 544 left, and was accused of kidnapping three young Iraqis and embezzling money from the bank. Rainey and the captain pored over the details and wondered, Had he really done those things? Was he being falsely accused?

The team had lived with Abu Hattar, as they called him, for more than a month. They had watched him stand in front of a hail of bullets on his peg leg and not flinch. They believed that he wanted the best for his country: a secular and democratic state where all religious and ethnic groups could coexist. He and the cleric Khoei had shared that vision, but now one was dead and the other imprisoned. Rainey and the captain would not second-guess the troops who had replaced them, but they had a difficult time reconciling what they were reading with their own direct experience. Steve Rainey was not naïve or a stranger to the Arab world. He was a downright cynic, in fact, but he thought Abu Hattar was about as good as they come in a part of the world where democracy and probity are not widespread. Rainey had never witnessed the man commit an illegal or unethical act in all the days they had spent together. The team's own successes in Najaf had been accomplished with the help of Abu Hattar. They agonized over his fate but had no way to know the truth. Like the savage killing of Khoei, such things weighed heavily on the men of ODA 544. They had been at the epicenter of the Shi'ites' liberation after decades of persecution. Their SITREPS and analyses of the awakening Shi'ite majority had been read at the highest levels of the U.S. government. It was the first solid reporting on the ground about Shi'ism, the most important determinant of Iraq's political future, in what was bound to be a turbulent time. The vision of a secular Iraq that was embraced by Abu Hattar and Khoei did not sit well with many clerics. The team knew that Sadr's men had killed Khoei, and it was possible that Abu Hattar had been railroaded.

Another moderate cleric was killed in a car bombing in the fall, further widening the gulf between moderates and radicals in the Shi'ite religious community. The hothead fundamentalists, agitators from Iran, and the grand ayatolloh hidden in his gold mosque in Najaf were all locked in an epic fight for the soul of the Shi'a. With three moderates vanquished, the radicals were on the rise. ODA 544 had been recognized for its keen work at a critical time, but the team never felt that it had done enough.

There were no parades or "welcome home" banners to greet the Special Forces who came back to Fort Campbell. They are so security conscious that they would've cringed at any public display, so, with little fanfare, they took their home leave. The young daughters of Chief Warrant Officer 2 John Pace were delighted to have their father back, and he took up his job as chief playmate with customary verve. He had missed his girls, who had mailed him finger-painted letters which he had taped to the side of his truck in the desert.

Pace, Andy Brittenham, Jim Gavrilis, and the rest of 1st Battalion returned to Iraq in the fall of 2003. As the battalion's operations officer, Major Gavrilis helped design and launch a comprehensive counterinsurgency that began to yield results over the winter. Meanwhile, back

home, the chief warrant officer of ODA 553 continued the long and
painful rehabilitation of his neck vertebrae that he would have to get
through before he could return to the battlefield. The captain of ODA
551 finally got his deck rebuilt.

Second Battalion was slated to return next. Master Sergeant Tom
Rosenbarger, the ultimate team daddy, led his team through the intensive SFAUC urban combat course to prepare for the shooting gallery
that Iraq had become. If a Special Forces team sergeant like Morehead
could be gunned down, Rosenbarger thought, they were in for some
serious firefights. He drove his men through five days of nonstop target practice and drills in close-quarters shooting houses. Dirty,
exhausted, and ready, the soldiers cleaned their guns in gasoline in a
big red aluminum gun bath in a corner of the team room, while swig-
ging Friday afternoon beers from their mini-fridge. The cool-headed
Tony Goble stopped by to rib his former teammate Rosenbarger. Their
decade-long friendship only fueled the competition between their
teams, which helped push the men to their limits. Goble and Rosenbarger were determined to make sure all their men made it home
again alive. They were headed to the hottest spots, Baghdad's Shi'ite
quarter and Fallujah, respectively, and would play pivotal roles in tracking insurgents down.

Conner threw a belated welcome-home barbecue for 2nd Battalion.
He ordered an enormous pig from the Ribb Doctor in Clarksville, and
the retired veterans of the Special Forces Association threw open their
club house (called the "safe house"), with its rolling lawn, for the party.
There was no trace of the soldier, much less the commando; those
things stayed at work. It might have been a cookout in Anywhere,
U.S.A., with dads, moms, kids and babies, and lots of games—face paint-
ing, air houses, a balloon artist, karaoke, races, music, and raffles. The
roast pig vanished and the beer truck ran dry. The hosts, the Vietnam
veterans, stayed long after things began to wind down, listening to the
newcomers' war stories and retelling their own. The elders were an
ingrown bunch, closely bound by their searing losses in Vietnam—
which had earned them the highest proportion of Purple Hearts and

Medals of Honor of any military unit there—and by the pariah treatment they received for fighting an unpopular war. Now the gulf was being bridged, as a new generation of Special Forces soldiers learned what it was like to fight and die.

To their collection of Silver and Bronze Stars from Afghanistan, the Special Forces added another few dozen from Iraq. Most satisfying of all for the senior NCOs who were retiring or nearing the end of their frontline duty was the fact that they had raised a new crop of valiant, expert soldiers like Chiefs Pace and Goble and many more. Randy, Alan, Michael T., Killer, Steve, Andy, and Tom could all be certain that the brotherhood would not lack those who could make that split-second judgment of whether a man was friend or foe, whether he should be shot or spoken to, or whether some unorthodox approach might best serve the long-term goals.

In battalion commanders like Chris Conner, Chris Haas, Bob Waltemeyer, and Ken Tovo the Special Forces had gained a whole class of stellar, rising officers who had both frontline combat experience and the intellectual firepower to lead the organization through its next decade. Thanks to the reforms of the 1980s, they had risen as Special Forces officers rather than shuttling to and from conventional army assignments. They knew the individuals who served under them, and they knew how to let those remarkable ODAs do their thing. If these officers' advice was heeded, the Special Forces would never be misused again, mistaken for an infantry squad, or sent to do tactical reconnaissance. With their leadership, the rest of the armed forces would understand how best to use Special Forces.

On their own, a few ODAs could raise, train, and lead a foreign allied force, or build a network in a country to uncover vital information or suspects. A single ODA could be sent to a hotspot to assess and propose a solution and then execute it, all the while hewing to the strategic policy goals and U.S., foreign, and international legal norms. A senior sergeant could provide a sound analysis of a foreign country's geopolitical

Coming Home

and military situation. This was what each one of them, by dint of their experience and cultural immersion, was prepared to do any day of the year. It was that ability to operate on the plane of strategy and policy that distinguished the Special Forces from the rest.

Lieutenant Colonels Tovo and Waltemeyer moved from 10th Group to assignments at the Special Operations Command and in the Pentagon, but they left behind a generation of combat-tested veterans. Both the 10th and 3rd Group had combat experience that would give their groups both legends and lore to draw upon. Soldiers of both groups had been awarded Silver Stars for their actions at Sargat Valley, Aski Kalak, and Debecka Pass. Tenth Group returned to Iraq for Operation Iraqi Freedom II to work in the north, while 3rd Group continued to provide the bulk of ODAs, along with 19th Group, for Afghanistan, where the job of hunting Al Qaeda and stabilizing the new government continued. Tovo was promoted to colonel and slated to become a group commander following a year at the Army War College. He resumed his passion of coaching wrestling for his sons' teams in his spare time—and his wife was very glad he had shaved off his Kurdish mustache.

Colonel Charlie Cleveland turned over command of 10th Group and packed up to move to Fort Bragg. He sat under a shade tree in Colorado as the movers hauled furniture out of his house, while a Special Forces historian interviewed him about the exploits of Task Force Viking. With typical modesty, he gave all the credit to the men under him, although he had been that rare group commander to lead his men in the field in combat, as the 5th Group commander had in Afghanistan. At Fort Bragg, Cleveland assumed the post of chief of staff of the Army Special Operations Command. His comrades from 7th Group, now-retired legendary colonels like Kevin Higgins, Roy Trumble, and David McCracken, hoped that their friend, one of the best and brightest of their class, would make that final hurdle and win his general's star.

At the U.S. Army John F. Kennedy Special Warfare Center and School, Randy Wurst never got used to flying a desk. He drove his black Ranger pickup every day to the low white building across the street from the red brick Special Forces museum on Ardennes Street. He walked through the Hall of Heroes to get to his office, past the portraits of the Medal of Honor winners from Vietnam and Somalia. The country's highest military honor had been bestowed on the men for their actions there, even though the military had been withdrawn from both countries without prevailing. Did that mean their lives had been lost in vain?

Across the street, outside the museum, stood an artillery piece and photos of firebases in Vietnam. The bases' star-shaped design had been the product of much trial and error. The counterinsurgency and unconventional warfare doctrine, the sniper and explosives manuals, all had been written based on the experiences in that jungle. Similarly, the urban combat training course that the Special Forces all went through was a direct result of Somalia. These were all foundations for the war they were fighting now.

"Rawhide" was now Randy; his spurs were hung up. But he found, to his delight, that his office and the schoolhouse were filled with senior chief warrant officers and veteran master sergeants. Many had served in crisis-response units and some had become special ops pilots. They had fought in the same wars as he had and been chosen for secret missions. Many of their best stories they could tell only to each other. Randy also role-played in some training courses, this time on the delivering and not the grueling receiving end of the challenges. To write a new manual, he went to a special shooting school that he'd never attended. It was great fun, and it would help the next generation of warriors. Randy was a F.A.G., there was no getting around that. But he was still surrounded by eagles.

CHAPTER 16

THE FUTURE OF THE SPECIAL FORCES

For to win one hundred victories in one hundred battles is not the acme of skill. To subdue the enemy without fighting is the acme of skill.

—SUN TZU

THE SPECIAL FORCES' performance in the Afghanistan and Iraq wars was the culmination of a slow rebuilding process that began after the U.S. Army had reached its post-Vietnam nadir. The master sergeants and officers who cut their teeth fifteen years earlier in Panama, El Salvador, and Desert Storm were a new breed. They led troops in the field, in the most intensive combat since the Vietnam war, with audacity and great success. The icon of the Special Forces' regenerated fighting prowess will always be Afghanistan, where fewer than 100 soldiers took down the Taliban regime in less than a month.

The Special Forces achievements in Iraq are less well known but equally impressive. The 10th Special Forces Group led a division's worth of Kurdish surrogate forces and secured northern Iraq against thirteen divisions, and also destroyed key Ansar al-Islam terrorist bases. In the south, 5th Group raised other allies inside Iraq who helped capture the cities, and in the west it secured the western desert with the aid of its allies in the sky. Later, the Special Forces provided valuable intelligence that led to the arrest of nearly half of the wanted men depicted in the "deck of cards" and to the location of prisoner of war Private First Class Jessica Lynch.

This generation of Special Forces soldiers has seen more combat than any other since the Vietnam era. Major Paul Syverson, for example, who was killed in Iraq in early June 2004 on his third deployment of the war, had been wounded in Afghanistan in November 2001, and was one of the first to be awarded the Purple Heart during that war. The battlefield accomplishments from 2001 to 2003 were made possible by the skill and experience accrued over the previous decade, in countries poised between peace and all-out war. As Somalia descended into war in the early 1990s, Special Forces ODAs tapped into the clan network to serve as an early-warning system for the international humanitarian effort. As Bosnia and Kosovo struggled out of their ethnic convulsions, ODAs moved into communities to map their many fissures and help knit the societies back together. Special Forces worked to stabilize Haiti in the mid-1990s, to track Abu Sayyaf in the Philippines after September 11, to train the Georgian army in the Caucasus, to help Colombia fight narco-guerrillas, and to provide training and advice to many other countries. They will likely remain in Afghanistan and Iraq for years to come.

The successes were not unalloyed; mistakes were made as well. In Afghanistan, where the Special Forces were in charge of the theater for the first several months, there were errors that caused deaths of American soldiers, Afghan fighters, and innocent civilians. Close air support helped win the war, but it also caused unintended fatalities. Wrong coordinates provided to pilots and faulty delivery by pilots caused the majority of deaths suffered by the Special Forces in the major combat phase of that war. Procedures for calling in air strikes then were changed to minimize errors in future wars.

There also were mistaken attacks on civilians or friendly Afghan militias due to bad intelligence, some of it provided by rival militias. The worst such case was in the Special Forces assault on Hazar Qadam in Oruzgan in January 2002, where sixteen Afghans were killed. At the last moment, the Afghans had agreed to "switch sides" in the conflict—a culturally accepted practice in Afghanistan. Sadly, the new agreement was not effectively relayed before the raid was conducted as originally planned. A subsequent inquiry found that the Afghans were not hostile forces, but it did not find fault with or recommend any disciplinary action for the soldiers. Compensation was paid to the victims' families.

In Iraq, the major points of controversy involved decisions made by the senior U.S. civilian leadership and top military commanders. The decision to go to war at all was widely debated in 2003 and 2004, after weapons of mass destruction (WMD) were not found, and the intelligence process was severely criticized. Some believed that the war in Iraq shifted the focus and resources away from Afghanistan to the detriment of the global pursuit of Al Qaeda and its allies. Others embraced the argument that Iraq, regardless of WMD issues, was a threat worth going to war over. Another significant issue was abuse of prisoners held by the United States at Abu Ghraib prison in Iraq and at other sites around the world. International outrage in the Muslim world and stories and photographs of unacceptable treatment of prisoners of war and detained civilians dominated the headlines. Many administrative and high-ranking military personnel were cognizant of approval for using "stress conditions" on prisoners. Congress and the military opened investigations into the allegations, and initial changes in policy were made by the administration.

Two monumental errors in the post-combat phase contributed heavily to the postwar turbulence: the decision not to pay the Iraqi military's pensions, which effectively dissolved the scattered force, and the decision to "de-Ba'athify" the country by barring Ba'athists from administrative jobs in the hospitals and other services. Both decisions, made by senior officials, proved to be disastrous. Not only were the best and brightest bureaucrats and technicians banned from putting the country back together, the entire army of trained fighters lost the means to support its soldiers' families. The decisions also denied the Sunni minority—which had filled many of the administrative positions—a stake in the post-Saddam new order. Resistance and armed insurrection forced a reversal of the decisions, but only after much ill will had been created.

These errors were obvious to the Special Forces, which had been involved in transitions to peace in Grenada, Panama, Haiti, and the Balkans. "You don't take the Iraqi army and disband it after you've kicked its rear end," one senior officer said. "You do not wipe out the political infrastructure of a nation and create an insurgency to come right back at you." As soon as the Special Forces had captured cities in the west, south, and north, the majors and captains on the ground had immediately begun organizing Iraqi officers who had surrendered and civilian administrators to assist in security and reconstruction tasks. This was standard procedure for the Special Forces—and a practical necessity given their small numbers.

When these initial stabilization efforts of the SF were superseded by the subsequent political decisions to raze the Saddam-era institutions and start afresh, there were far too few coalition troops in Iraq to perform the security and reconstruction tasks. Chaos, insurgency, and insecurity ensued, and the population grew disenchanted. A popular fallacy has taken hold that the majority of Iraqi people did not welcome the Americans as liberators, when, in fact, Iraqis cheered the troops and thronged the streets all over Iraq. Only when the post-combat phase was mishandled did Iraqi gratitude begin to evaporate.

The larger lesson is that war is not a purely military endeavor: an army and regime can be destroyed but success still might remain elusive. Unless all phases of a conflict—pre-combat, combat, and post-combat—are planned and seamlessly coordinated, a military victory can be jeopardized. This seems obvious but it has been a chronic oversight. In Panama in 1989, a post-combat stabilization operation was thrown together overnight, just in time to succeed. Special Forces Psychological Operations and Civil Affairs soldiers fanned out into the country's provinces and worked for a year with local officials as Panama's military was converted into a police force. After one year, when elected officials were firmly in charge of the police, the Special Forces withdrew.

The inherently political nature of war is even more pronounced in an unconventional conflict, where the adversary is not a state or an army but rather a small irregular force that is hard to detect yet capable of causing major political and psychological impact. It is a fundamentally different type of war—far more a political war, an intelligence war, a psychological war—than a military war. This phenomenon has been recognized and written about since the breakup of the Soviet Union, under rubrics such as fourth-generation warfare, low-intensity or gray-area conflict, and asymmetric warfare. In this type of warfare, the smaller and conventionally weaker adversary turns its attributes into advantages and uses methods that strike at the weakness of the larger and militarily stronger rival.

Many in the military recognize that a great deal more attention must be paid to such threats, and more progress must be made toward forming a comprehensive strategy to deal with them. The strategy, doctrine, and future shape of the Special Forces are a subset of this larger issue and should flow from a national threat assessment and strategy. Understanding the threat—not just the specific threat of Al Qaeda but the general type of threat that it represents—is a prerequisite for developing an adequate response. Ample insights exist in the literature, history, and practice of insurgency. Communists, particularly Maoists, understood deeply the concept that war involves the entire population and is as much a political, psychological, economic, and social phenomenon as a military one.

A comprehensive understanding of today's threats could be gained by placing Islamic extremists in historical context. The latest in a long line of groups seeking radical change, they aim at the destruction of regimes and the creation of a new order. In a similarly ambitious vision, communists sought to demolish the existing order and supplant it with a different socioeconomic system. Other radicals' goals have been more limited; for example, the Irish Republican Army sought to separate Ireland from the United Kingdom, and the Tamil Tigers sought to win a portion of Sri Lanka. Leaving aside the specific content of differing goals, the common features emerge: the antagonists hide in the population, aim at affecting human perception, and target noncombatants as a way of achieving that psychological impact. These are tactics that can be adopted by any entity, as Iraq did shortly after the start of Operation Iraqi Freedom.

As a result of Iraq's postwar turbulence, the words insurgency and counterinsurgency have re-entered the lexicon as useful descriptions of this kind of warfare. Whether driven by religious, sectarian, nationalist, or ideological goals, the combatants in this type of warfare use stealth, deception, and denial as principal tactics—which are effective and difficult to counter. Throughout history, groups other than Islamic fundamentalists have waged such attacks. Terrorism is a term for a specific subset of tactics—lethal methods directed at civilian targets. Some would argue that one man's terrorist is another man's freedom fighter, but the tactics-based definition is unambiguous. Adopting some of the norms of unconventional warfare does not require embracing terrorism, and, in fact, eschewing attacks on civilians is a lodestar for any counterinsurgent or counterterrorist strategy that seeks to claim the moral high ground and to win the population's support—elements that are vital to ultimate success.

One of the senior Special Forces officers who has devoted the most time to thinking about the fundamental questions of the threat, the strategy, the proper role for the Special Forces, and the tools they require is Major General Geoffrey Lambert. These issues formally were his bailiwick when he served as commandant of the U.S. Army John F. Kennedy Special Warfare Center and School, from June 2003 to June 2004, when he retired after thirty-three years of military service. He had been wrestling with the issues for many years, as commanding general of the U.S. Army Special Forces Command (September 2001 to June 2003) and before that as chief of operations, plans, strategy, and requirements at the Special Operations Command in Tampa (the parent command for all the services' special operations forces). General Lambert's brainstorming was not limited to his own staff. He organized seminars with historians, academics, writers, digital gurus, human rights experts, entrepreneurs, retired generals, and others with divergent perspectives. His favorite location for these gatherings was Cody, Wyoming, where the cowboy atmosphere and a community of retired special operators provided a congenial setting.

The starting point for Gen. Lambert's prescription is that asymmetric warfare is here to stay, and therefore should become a permanent part of the military's structure and doctrine. "A wise opponent will fight us asymmetrically because we are so strong conventionally," Lambert said in a January 2004 interview in Cody. That does not mean that he recommends a wholesale shift in the armed forces' orientation, however. "To change everything in the Department of Defense to just fight asymmetric threats would be a terrible mistake," he said, noting the deterrent function of conventional strength as well as the continuing existence of conventional foes or potential foes.

Rather, the gap that currently exists within the military establishment should be filled. In the same way that the Navy is responsible for protecting sea lanes and the Strategic Command the skies, Lambert proposes formally designating the Special Forces as responsible for asymmetric threats. The Special Forces would have the permanent assignment to watch the hundred-plus terrorist groups and insurgencies around the world; to learn everything about them—the interactions among them, the newly emerging groups, and the constantly evolving asymmetric tactics. When a threat to U.S. interests appeared, it would be the job of the Special Forces to raise the flag and propose a course of action to the national leadership, the Special Operations Command, and the combatant commanders responsible for geographic regions. Such a permanent assignment just might, Lambert believes, keep the next Al Qaeda from catching the U.S. government flat-footed.

The military's emphasis has changed from counterinsurgency in the 1960s, to major European combat operations in the 1970s and 1980s, to multiple theater-level wars in the 1990s, to counterterrorism today. It is logical that the military should move from crisis to crisis and change its orientation to meet current demand, but it is in the best interests of the nation that the U.S. Army Special Forces remain dedicated to the unconventional, asymmetric threats.

Another step would be to expand the current national strategy to a more comprehensive and nuanced one. Perhaps naturally, after the September 11 attacks the government focused on hunting down the perpetrators. The focus on global manhunts for terrorist masterminds has dominated ever since, although it is a partial approach that does not address the essence of the terrorist phenomenon, the entire network, or the way it operates, grows, and changes. Continued reliance on manhunts as the primary response fundamentally misunderstands what the United States is up against. Individuals are fungible; there is already ample indication that other terrorist leaders have taken Osama bin Laden's place as the operational masterminds of recent attacks around the world. Manhunts for known terrorist leaders are an essential piece of a strategy but are not a complete strategy.

The current emphasis on preemption as the primary strategy should be broadened, in the view of General Lambert and others, to include prevention. "Preemption, in my opinion, means that we have failed by allowing a threat to develop," Lambert said. The doctrine of preemption has created concern among some that the United States will frequently and cavalierly strike at any target it deems a threat, a perception that does not serve the nation well internationally. Of course, if a threat develops despite preventive measures and an attack against the United States is imminent, the government may well have no other recourse but to wage preemptive war.

A robust prevention policy can reduce the chance that preemption will be required. In the case of Afghanistan, before September 11 the United States made few attempts to address the Taliban problem, other than a cruise missile strike after the 1998 embassy bombings. An aggressive program of prevention, as opposed to preemption, could have entailed a wide range of measures by non-military as well as military actors, including diplomacy, economic and financial incentives or sanctions, influence and psychological operations, allied efforts with other governments, and Special Forces working covertly with the CIA to destabilize the Taliban. Such holistic and aggressive measures might have been effective in preventing the September 11 attacks.

Special operations forces—the umbrella term for all the services' commando forces—would play two types of roles in such a broadened prevention-based strategy, roles which can be characterized as direct and indirect approaches. The direct approach is principally associated with preemption—the last-resort alternative to remove a critical threat that has either gone undetected or proven impervious to other methods. Its primary method is the raid: discrete, unilateral actions to remove a specific, localized threat, or to capture or kill a leadership figure.

The indirect approach is aimed at preventing or mitigating threats by working with local allies and using a variety of tools under the umbrella term of unconventional warfare. Unlike the raid, which is a discrete tactical operation, unconventional warfare is a series of ongoing activities that aim to deal with the entire phenomenon of the threat: the leadership, the base, the environment sustaining it, and the motivation behind it. The hallmark of unconventional warfare is that it is carried out in concert with local allies, whether to advise nations on handling a threat, to build forces to eliminate the threat, or to use combat advisers and surrogate warfare when necessary. "It is best if we can win via the people who have the long-term problem," Lambert said.

Much has been made of a division in the special operations community between the raiders and the unconventional warriors, but farsighted members realize that both capabilities are needed. "My dream is that the national leadership can use indirect and direct capabilities in perfect harmony to win the war on terror," Lambert said.

It is not difficult to discern a natural division of labor. The selection and training of some special operations forces are focused solely on the raiding or direct-action types of missions. These SOF include the Navy SEALs, Rangers, and Delta Force (formally known as Special Forces Operational Detachment-Delta or SFOD-D), supported by special aviators. The U.S. Army Special Forces, while they are trained and able to conduct raids, are focused on a much broader array of tasks in the unconventional warfare spectrum. They have the language skills and cultural training. If the need to conduct raids arises in the course of their mission they are perfectly able to carry them out. But if a mission, such as the capture of a high-value target, requires the most sophisticated raiding skills, then those who train exclusively for those eventualities are the logical force of choice.

A national strategy that is broadened to rely more on preventive and indirect approaches will have the added benefit of being more politically palatable and practically feasible than one that is primarily unilateral and preemptive. Having foreign countries' governments and militaries as partners or having the support of local forces will assuage concerns about the projection of U.S. power and diminish the risk of a backlash over heavy-handed tactics. Enlisting foreign forces whenever possible also reduces the number of U.S. troops needed and, therefore, the cost to U.S. taxpayers. Finally, it is an inherently collaborative approach that reduces turf battles within the U.S. government. While, in some cases, the Special Forces may be the sole U.S. entity on the ground, in many cases the indirect approach would include various U.S. agencies, diplomats, aid workers, non-governmental or multilateral institutions, and multinational coalitions. Most of the so-called influence operations are joint or combined and are entirely overt, as in medical or engineering exercises, training exercises, and allied exercises.

For the Special Forces to carry out this role of being the country's permanent watcher of insurgents, terrorists, and asymmetric tactics and the conductor of unconventional warfare, Lambert proposes building the Special Forces Command at Fort Bragg into a state of the art unconventional warfare center outfitted with command and control, communications, computing, and intelligence equipment on a par with the rest of the special operations community. He would invest in two areas: people and intelligence. The human investment would go to improved language training and expanded overseas educational opportunities. Lambert also urges finding some means to include women and foreign nationals in or alongside ODAs, to better reach parts of the target populations. The Special Forces' ability to understand and operate within foreign cultures is their stock in trade, so innovative measures to enhance it are of utmost importance.

Lambert would also add two or three more active-duty battalions and build a few small technically specialized units to enhance SF's effectiveness. He also urges giving the Special Forces access to the full store of intelligence that the U.S. government possesses. There is a perennial tension between the demands of compartmentalization to prevent leaks and the sharing of information that will help ensure mission success.

For years, the investment in the special operations community has tilted toward providing intelligence, equipment, and platforms for direct-action missions. For the preventive, indirect approach to be effective and to balance the preemptive strike approach concomitant investment is required. That is not to say that investment in the direct-action capability is misplaced. Successfully executing raids in remote, hostile territory is an extremely difficult proposition requiring enormous amounts of technology, intelligence, and training to guarantee security, speed, and surprise. Both direct and indirect capabilities must have adequate funding if the special operations forces are to be the primary military tool for addressing asymmetric threats.

The special operations budget is a tiny fraction of overall military spending, and much of the technology developed eventually benefits the rest of the armed forces, as has been the case with night-vision goggles, the M–4 rifle, lighter-weight body armor, and the new MICH helmets. The robots, smaller UAVs, and nanotechnology now under development also one day will become standard soldier tools.

The community's adage that humans are more important than hardware is especially true of the army Special Forces. Their key attribute is honed human instinct. After enough time in the hinterlands, Special Forces soldiers develop a sixth sense for the foes and friends out there, becoming what Lambert called "cross-cultural warriors." "By simply living outside of the firebases and working with local forces, we acquire considerable information of great value," he says. "We are good at this because of our combination of high tech, low tech, muscle, and the fact that we live in Third World countries as a way of life."

Using all these tools enables the operators to penetrate the adversaries' deception and denial tactics and to work up the chain from the low-level operatives to the leaders. This set of capabilities is unmatched in the U.S. military. The Special Forces soldier is an experienced intelligence collector who can assess and act on the information to accomplish his mission. Such quick reaction times are the holy grail of the special operations community—technocrats refer to it as closing the sensor to shooter loop. The only way that a nimble and elusive adversary can be defeated is if elite soldiers are able to exercise initiative and creativity. "The Special Forces soldier today is audacious, brave, and better than ever, and works best when totally unfettered," Lambert said.

Unfettered and innovative does not mean lawless. The prescription is not to forsake the rule of law, but to give a select group of rigorously trained, experienced, and mature soldiers the freedom to operate within the law. One of General Lambert's predecessors (and an equestrian), Maj. Gen. Sid Shachnow said of the Special Forces soldier: "He's like a thoroughbred. You don't get maximum performance unless you let him have his head." The point of creating such forces is to have a trustworthy, discerning scholar-soldier who can detect something amiss within minutes of entering a village and react appropriately. They are at greater risk of being straitjacketed by conventional-minded commanders, fearful bureaucrats, and technology that fosters micromanagement than of becoming rogue agents running rampant. Senior noncommissioned officers leave in frustration because they are not granted the latitude which they are capable of exercising to great effect. Special Forces soldiers, like all other soldiers, are bound by the strict codes of the military, but they also understand the value of the moral high ground and the utter uselessness of abuses that create enemies, alienate populations, and yield bad intelligence.

The U.S. public rightly seeks assurances and checks and balances to ensure that American values and laws are protected in the prosecution of any conflict. Given the country's traditions of openness and unease with secrecy and unconventional war, public debate over the proper balance is another sign that the checks in the society are working.

There are also institutional checks and oversight provisions. Military operations carried out under Title 10 legislation must be authorized by either the president or the secretary of defense with presidential approval, and are vetted in the interagency process of the National Security Council. The Pentagon's general counsel exhaustively reviews proposed actions, as do the judge advocates at each level of the military command involved. Every soldier is subject to the Uniform Code of Military Justice. Congress frequently attaches further reporting conditions or checks in legislation that provides funding.

While clandestine activities are kept secret in the run-up to their execution, they are not denied if they are discovered or once they are executed. All of these checks pertain to clandestine as well as overt military operations. Covert operations, in which the U.S. authorship is not acknowledged and is designed to be plausibly denied, are conducted with the oversight of the congressional intelligence committees. Title 50, the law that governs covert action, permits the president to specify in a finding which entity will carry out a specific action. Traditionally, it has been the CIA, which has an elaborate infrastructure for creating deep cover for individuals who carry out the missions.

The National Commission on Terrorist Attacks Upon the United States recommended in its final report that "lead responsibility for directing and executing paramilitary operations, whether clandestine or covert, should shift to the Defense Department." The commission cited several practical reasons for reaching this conclusion, among them the fact that the CIA's capability has not been particularly robust and that it has relied on proxies organized by CIA operatives "without the requisite military training. The results were unsatisfactory." The commission logically concluded that, rather than build a redundant capability in the CIA, the responsibility and legal authority for all such operations should be concentrated in the Special Operations Command. It noted that the two entities have fruitfully collaborated in joint missions and recommended that each concentrate on its comparative advantages, which can be described broadly as intelligence collection for the agency and operations for the military. The commission recommends that the CIA's experts "be integrated into the military's training, exercises, and planning," while also holding up the agility of CIA operations as a model for the reputedly cumbersome military bureaucracy to emulate.

Many Americans remain ambivalent about covert operations after past scandals such as the assassination plots of the 1960s and misbegotten ventures like Iran-Contra, but current law does provide for the use of covert operations as one tool in the national security arsenal. The legislation represents an effort to balance the requirements of secrecy versus accountability, agility versus deliberation. It is possible that laws, regulations, and executive orders adopted in the cold war may need revision to meet the threats of the current era. The matter deserves a full and serious debate. In any event, it is vital to reach a consensus about what measures are both legal and effective.

A pessimist might conclude that the United States' political landscape is so riven by partisan bitterness, cynicism, and allegations of bad faith that a united, sustained, and coherent defense of the country and its interests is unlikely. But the attacks of September 11 gave Americans a visceral appreciation of the nature of the threat, and Americans retain a bedrock patriotism that is part of the national identity. The present moment offers opportunities to resolve fundamental national security issues and produce a new, comprehensive charter for the nation's special operations forces.

ACKNOWLEDGMENTS

In this publicity-hungry culture, it is hard to imagine a group of people that does not want their laudable exploits told—or invented, if they do not exist. Most of the men written about in this book will suffer because of it. Either their own modesty will be offended or their peers will excoriate them for grandstanding and breaking their closed society's code of silence.

The Department of the Army and the U.S. Army Special Forces Command granted permission for the project and access to the soldiers, who then agreed to give interviews so that I could write this book. None are named herein except by consent. But even though the project was approved from on high, the fears of negative repercussions linger as the subjects anxiously await publication of this book. I thank each and every one of them, including those who remain unnamed, and their families, for their forbearance and their service to our country.

At bottom, this is a journalist's book about a group of men and their brotherhood. Having spent many years taking an ant's eye view of the world at the ground level of events, I am a confirmed empiricist who believes that is where truth is revealed. That is what led me to become a reporter and to seek out obscure conflicts in remote corners of the world. Readers will reach their own judgments about these soldiers, their institution, and the uses to which they have been put. For my part, I began this journey because I believed that unconventional war and the capabilities of the Special Forces were important topics, but along the way my idealism was renewed by the values and commitment of many of the individuals I met.

Dozens of people are midwives to a book, and some of mine may be inadvertently overlooked in this list. I offer apologies in advance and the caveat that any errors made despite the extensive efforts to educate me are solely my responsibility. Major General Geoffrey Lambert, *U.S. News* Editor Brian Duffy, Flip Brophy of Sterling Lord Literistic, Public-Affairs' publisher Peter Osnos, and my gifted editor Clive Priddle were the proximate enablers of this endeavor and are thanked from the bottom of my heart.

All the soldiers who contributed to this book were patient and generous with their time, including: Randall Wurst, Chris Conner, Charles Cleveland, James Gavrilis, Alan Johnson, David Baratto, Jonathan Burns, Ray Brady, Andy Brittenham, Peter Dillon, Matt Erlacher, Warren Foster, Simon Gardner, Tony Goble, Christopher Haas, Kevin Higgins, James Kilcoyne, Jason Latteri, Lee Linville, Andy Lohman, Tony Martin, David McCracken, Thomas O'Connell, Paul Ott, John Pace, Steve Rainey, Thomas Rosenbarger, Jeffrey Smith, Michael Swift, Kenneth Tovo, Roy Trumble, Robert Waltemeyer, David Wilderman, and many others.

A host of Public Affairs officers bore up under my repeated inquiries and requests, including Kathleen Devine, Rob Gowan, Tim Nye, Kevin Walston, Jim Whatley, Kevin Aandahl, Scott Malcom, Ben Abel, and Hans Bush. USASOC historian Kenn Finlayson graciously provided his perspective, advice, and access to archival material with help from his staff. Other assistance was provided by Jimmy Dean and Steve Stone of the Special Forces Association, SLL's Cia Glover, Gene Taft, Melanie Peirson Johnstone, Martha Deery, and the rest of the PublicAffairs team, and the crack library staff of *U.S. News & World Report*. General Jack Keane supported my wish to cover special operations forces.

Moral support came from my family and friends including Michael Barone, Carolina Garcia Aguilera, Ed Pound, and many others, as well as from coaches over the years who demonstrated how hard it is to write and encouraged me nonetheless: Mark Kramer, Bob Shacochis, Dan Wakefield, John Walcott, and Bill Hyland.

Donations may be made to a scholarship fund managed by the Special Operations Warrior Foundation for the children of all special operations forces killed in combat, and to the Special Forces Association fund established for the five children and grandchild of James Newman, who died after returning from Operation Iraqi Freedom. The respective addresses are:

The Special Operations Warrior Foundation
P.O. Box 14385
Tampa, FL 33690
www.specialops.org

Chapter 38 Special Forces Association Family Assistance Fund
c/o James Newman Family
P.O. Box 223
Fort Campbell, KY 42223-0223

INDEX